"*The Triumph of Life* is exhilarating. A culmination of a lifetime of theological reflection from the visionary thinker Rabbi Irving Greenberg, it offers us a stunning portrait of the Jewish tradition as a grand drama in which God and the Jewish people dream together of a perfect world and work painstakingly to bring it about. Read this book and you will never see the Jewish tradition the same way again." — **Rabbi Shai Held**, president and dean at Hadar and author of *The Heart of Torah*

"*The Triumph of Life* urges voluntary continuation of the original Jewish commitment to covenantal obligation, based on the understanding that what *appears* to be God's gradual withdrawal from intervention in human affairs actually represents a hidden but deeper, more intimate, and mature level of connection with the Divine, grounded on recognition of the importance of human agency in realizing life on all levels as the supreme value. Such enhancement of human responsibility demands development of an equitable ethic of power that allows for pluralism and corrects radicalized interpretations of tradition in light of the evolution of human understanding. Greenberg's culmination of nearly a lifetime of effort is a must-read for all those who grapple with the ability of traditional views of religion to survive today's open society and the challenges of relativism raised by life in a postmodern age." — **Tamar Ross**, professor emerita, Department of Jewish Philosophy, Bar-Ilan University

"*The Triumph of Life* is a brilliant, complex, sophisticated, and accessible guide to becoming a better person and a more effective force in bringing society to a brighter future." — **Rabbi Asher Lopatin**, former president of Yeshivat Chovevei Torah

"*The Triumph of Life* is a visionary, profound, and highly original study of major significance." — **Steven T. Katz**, Alvin J. and Shirley Slater Chair in Jewish Holocaust Studies, Boston University

"Rabbi Irving Greenberg is a sage for our time. I highly recommend his inspiring book, *The Triumph of Life*. His perceptive elucidation of the ways the Divine-human partnership unfolds in Jewish covenantal life offers a capacious vision of Judaism that also transcends the particularities of Jewish life, speaking profoundly to all those seeking wisdom for the healing of our broken world. We Christians have much to learn from him, both to deepen our understanding of Jewish traditions and to reanimate our commitment to participate in the common call to engage in world repair." —**Mary C. Boys**, Skinner and McAlpin Professor of Practical Theology, Union Theological Seminary, New York City

"Rabbi Greenberg's hopeful vision of the meaning of Judaism is an inspiring, uplifting, energizing manifesto that also impels me to be a more faithful Christian. *The Triumph of Life* affirms our calling to actively partner with God in covenant for the healing of the world as we anticipate that day when all people will be treated with the dignity implied by our creation as the image of God." —**J. Richard Middleton**, professor of biblical worldview and exegesis, Northeastern Seminary at Roberts Wesleyan University

"One of the boldest and most creative theological voices on the American Jewish scene has finally provided us with the major comprehensive statement of his theological vision and program for which we have long been waiting—and it is worth the long wait. With its combination of maturity and freshness, *The Triumph of Life* reminds one of such late-in-life masterpieces as Verdi's *Falstaff* or Monet's *Water Lilies* murals. Dazzling in its breadth and sweep, it skillfully integrates macroscopic views of Judaism and Jewish history with precise, often microscopic, details of that religion and history—thereby not only concretizing Rabbi Greenberg's innovative vision but endowing those details with new meaning and significance." —**Lawrence Kaplan**, translator of *Halakhic Man* and associate professor of Jewish studies at McGill University

THE
TRIUMPH
OF LIFE

University of Nebraska Press : Lincoln

THE
TRIUMPH
OF LIFE

A Narrative Theology of Judaism

Rabbi Irving Greenberg

The Jewish Publication Society : Philadelphia

All rights reserved. Published by the University of
Nebraska Press as a Jewish Publication Society book.
Manufactured in the United States of America.

Library of Congress Cataloging-in-Publication Data

Names: Greenberg, Irving, 1933- author.
Title: The triumph of life: a narrative theology of
Judaism / Irving Greenberg.
Description: Philadelphia: Jewish Publication Society;
Lincoln: University of Nebraska Press, [2024] | Includes
bibliographical references and index.
Identifiers: LCCN 2023055303
ISBN 9780827615212 (paperback)
ISBN 9780827619227 (epub)
ISBN 9780827619234 (pdf)
Subjects: LCSH: God (Judaism)--Righteousness. |
Humanity. | Rabbinical literature--History and
criticism. | Bible. Old Testament--Criticism,
interpretation, etc. | BISAC: RELIGION / Judaism /
Theology | RELIGION / Ethics
Classification: LCC BM610 .G75 2024 |
DDC 296.3/114--dc23/eng/20240109
LC record available at https://lccn.loc.gov/2023055303

Set in Merope (Charles Ellertson) by A. Shahan.

This book is dedicated to
Harold Grinspoon
philanthropic genius
peerless friend
who loves the Jewish people

Teach us how to make our
days count, so that we
bring a wise heart to living.
— Psalms 90:12

Contents

Acknowledgments

I begin with thanks to those whose hard work directly enabled this book. Bonny V. Fetterman, the initial primary editor, repeatedly and sensitively cut and reshaped the text to make this book readable and clear. At the suggestion of my treasured agent, Deborah Harris, Claire Wachtel gave this manuscript a second edit to make it more reader friendly. Elisheva Urbas, editorial director of the Hadar Institute, then took on the task of tightening the manuscript to a reasonable reading length, while preserving the core ideas and readability, all with intelligence, skill, respect for the ideas, and great editorial judgment, not to mention good spirit. Mikhael Reuven Kesher, along with Jeremy Tabick, formatted and copyedited manuscript chapters, researched references and citations, and managed the valuable, complicated process of responding to editorial queries from The Jewish Publication Society (JPS). Joy Weinberg, managing editor of JPS, provided a skillful, detailed, and helpful editorial and production review. Barry Schwartz, then JPS director, chose this book for publication; both he and Elias Sacks, the current JPS director, provided generous and insightful editorial reviews.

Along the way, my daughter Judith Greenberg Weil offered editing and guidance that enabled me to complete several important chapters. Steven Bayme, Steven T. Katz, and Blu Greenberg each gave me the benefit of their close readings of various sections. Darren Kleinberg made valuable suggestions. He so believed in the book that he encouraged me to create the J. J. Greenberg Institute for the Advancement of Jewish Life to help finish and disseminate it. I thank him for that wonderful service.

Susan Carloss-Lawrence, Ellen Muss, Meira Rosenberg, and, above all, Tanya Zauderer typed up my difficult handwriting. Tanya patiently and accurately retyped endless revisions. Gabriel and Nina Kretzmer Seed, Shalhevet Schwartz, and Mikhael Reuven Kesher filled out the endnotes.

I am grateful as well to JPS's publishing partner, the University of Nebraska Press, for producing this volume. In particular, I thank project editor Haley Mendlik and copy editor Amy Pattullo for their fine, meticulous work.

This book expresses the sum of a lifetime of thinking, and so I want to take this opportunity to also express my deep gratitude to those who enriched my religious life and shaped my thinking.

My mother taught me—by many actions and few words—that God is ever present, to be turned to as a source of strength no matter what happens in life. My father infused his love and delight in learning even as he communicated to me that a religious life involves doing justice and opposing the mistreatment of people. Most of all, he instilled the lesson that Torah must be applied to make life better for human beings.

While in college, I studied at a refugee yeshiva, Bais Yosef Novardok, whose student body included many survivors of both Nazi concentration camps and Siberian labor camps. The yeshiva taught that the Torah's goal was to make a person into a mensch. It gave me life-changing religious experiences and spirituality, as well as character-building disciplines.

Then my wife Blu came into my life. Her love, her extraordinary humanity and embrace of life, her unquenchable desire to do good to others, her delight in tradition and insistence that it can be improved, became the rock of my existence. Then came our children, Moshe, David, Deborah, Jonathan (J.J., z"l), and Judith, whose love and personal example have sustained me through every turn and trial in life.

In Boston, during my graduate studies, Rabbi Joseph B. Soloveitchik taught me that the halakhic tradition is a system by which to live humanly. His understanding of Judaism as the worldview of a world religion shaped my thinking for life.

In my first academic post, at Yeshiva University, I connected spiritually and intellectually to David Hartman. Over a lifetime, he challenged me to follow the development of my thought with integrity, and not be afraid to push the boundaries of Orthodoxy, as he was doing. Two close friends, Zev (Willy) Frank and Josh Shmidman, became religious influences and role models for me. Sadly, both died too soon.

Since 1961–62, when as a visiting Fulbright lecturer in American intellectual history at Tel Aviv University I intensely encountered the living history of the Holocaust, I have continued to study and struggle with the Holocaust. Many survivors instructed me, including those who lived in my community in Riverdale, and especially Elie Wiesel. Jacob Birnbaum, the visionary founder of the Student Struggle for Soviet Jewry, helped me translate compassion for the living and solidarity with the oppressed into action. When I became the rabbi of Riverdale Jewish Center and tried to create a community that could reflect all these values, the congregants' sustaining responses — including the creation of SAR Academy, an open day school in this spirit — confirmed my path.

In 1974–75 I spent another year living in Israel and studying at Yad Vashem. This immersion pushed me to an ever-greater focus on the supremacy of life in Judaism, and on the classic dialectic of Jewish history of responding to destruction with a counterthrust of rebuilding and redemption. While building CLAL, the National Jewish Center for Learning and Leadership, I began exploring this new narrative of life with faculty and fellows. I am grateful to Steve Greenberg, David Nelson, David Elcott, Reuven Kimelman, David Kraemer, Irwin Kula, Brad Hirschfield, Rachel Sabath Beit-Halachmi, Diane Cohler-Esses, Shira Milgrom, Jen Krause, Benay Lappe, and Janet Kirchheimer for their feedback and insights. CLAL's lay leadership also sustained me. I have treasured the understanding and kindred spirit of the chairpersons and their spouses, Ben and Magda Leuchter, Lee and Rona Javitch,

Neil and Sharon Norry, Irvin and Sharna Frank, Bob and Robyn Loup, Herschel and Goldene Blumberg, Shoshana Cardin, Radine and Bill Spier, Aaron and Marge Ziegelman, and others. The students are too numerous to mention, but all inspired and validated me on what was often an uncharted path.

The most important development of this narrative of the triumph of life occurred through my teaching at the Wexner Heritage Program. I am grateful to Les and Abigail Wexner and Herb Friedman for creating this remarkable program. I am forever indebted to Nathan Laufer, then president of the Wexner Heritage Foundation, who suggested I teach a course on this theme. Thereafter, the teaching was sustained by Jay Moses, director of the Heritage Program; Larry Moses, president of the Wexner Foundation; and his successor, Elka Abrahamson. Jay, Elka, and Ben Berger then turned the course into a video to serve as a permanent curricular resource. The responses of Wexner Heritage students — including taking responsibility for Jewish life, having children, building communities — shaped and reshaped my thinking.

Years later, I was able to teach and reexplore my theology with outstanding rabbinic students at Yeshivat Chovevei Torah. For this opportunity I thank Dov Linzer, Asher Lopatin, and Avi Weiss.

In the 1990s I moved to the Jewish Life Network (JLN) / Steinhardt Foundation to work on innovative philanthropic programs of unprecedented scale and daring, including Taglit-Birthright Israel and Makor, thanks to Michael and Judy Steinhardt's vision and financial backing. I worked and rethought the narrative with an outstanding staff, including David Gedzelman, Josh Elkin, Felicia Herman, Naava Frank, Susan Weinblatt, and J. J. Greenberg, our son of blessed memory, who was JLN's executive director. What a blessing it was to be able to work with J.J. every day, and often long into the night, as his dedication to the Jewish community and future knew no limits. For this opportunity I am forever grateful to Michael Steinhardt.

In 2020 the leadership of Hadar Institute welcomed me as Senior Scholar, supporting the completion of the writing and dissemination of my ideas on many platforms. Their partnership has been a blessing for me. The partners of the J. J. Greenberg Institute, in turn, underwrote this work. I thank the Founding Partners: the Aviv Foundation (Steve and Chani Laufer), Paula and Jerry Gottesman, my children Abbie Gottesman and Moshe Greenberg, Harold Grinspoon and Diane Troderman, and the Micah Foundation (Jeremy and Ann Pava). I additionally thank the Pillar Partners: Sender Cohen, Phil Darivoff, the Sharna and Irvin Frank Foundation, the Genesis Philanthropy Group (Ilia Salita), the Genesis Prize Foundation (Stan Polovets), Michael Jesselson, Lynn and Jules Kroll, Fran and Bobby Lent, the Maimonides Fund (Mark Charendoff), Alan and Elisa Pines, Julie and Marc Platt, and Aryeh and Raquel Rubin. Finally, I thank the Sustaining Partners: Lou Bravmann, the Gewurz Family Foundation (Ilan Gewurz), Peter Joseph and Elizabeth Scheuer, Thomas and Elissa Katz, Joe Kanfer, David and Sally Lowenfeld, and Lizzie and Josh Scheinfeld. I am deeply grateful to all of them for their understanding and support.

At JLN, we established wonderful philanthropic partnerships. I particularly connected with Lynn and Charles Schusterman and Sandy Cardin, Charles Bronfman and Jeff Solomon, Edgar Bronfman, Al and Roseanne Levitt, and Bobby and Fran Lent.

A deep connection was made with Harold Grinspoon and his wife, Diane Troderman. The Grinspoon Foundation underwrote day schools, camps, Israel travel, and teen service and philanthropy for their local community, just as I was urging the national community to do. Harold started out in poverty, graduated to driving an ice cream truck, went on to fix old homes with his own labor, and eventually became one of America's largest owners of rental apartments. I loved the fact that he never lost his working-class roots. He felt comfortable supporting nonglamorous, meat-and-potatoes philanthropy such as the Legacy Project, which signed up people to leave money in their wills to Jewish causes; and the Grinspoon Philanthropic Institute, which helped institutions, mostly camps, build their boards and fundraising capacities.

Harold turned out to be my fantasy of a historic Jewish philanthropist—in real life. A philanthropic genius, he has kept on innovating projects into his nineties. The most remarkable is PJ Library—parents reading Jewish books to their children at bedtime. Using matching grants, he became the largest Jewish children's book distributor in the world, with a system that mails 250,000 copies monthly to families in the United States and to additional families in thirty countries internationally. In Israel, the project, called Sifriyat Pijama, reaches 400,000 Jewish children. A parallel program, Maktabat al-Fanoos (Lantern Library), reaches 190,000 Arab children.

Harold became a friend for life. He has taught his friends how to stay physically vital as they age. To this day he walks, bikes, climbs mountains, and does yoga, Pilates, and whitewater rafting; reshapes and refurbishes homes, conducts business deals, and travels widely; practices continuous culture consumption, explores religious experiences; collects and creates art and sculpture, and more. In all these areas, he pulls in his friends to live intensely along with him. When my partnership with Michael Steinhardt and Jewish Life Network ended, he and Diane also prodded me to go forward, insisting I had an unfinished task as a Jewish thinker. How does one measure the gratitude due for such friendship?

Introduction

All Jews alive today are essentially Jews-by-choice. Very few Jews live in lands of oppression or where social pressure forces them to stay in their own communities. On the contrary, diaspora Jews are typically successful and prosperous; their lifestyles vary little from many of those around them, who in turn see them as part of the general culture and society. Any person who opts to be identified as a Jew, regardless of the level of commitment to Jewish life, is *choosing* to be a Jew.

The choice to be a Jew is an act of faith and courage. Philosopher Emil Fackenheim wrote that, after the Holocaust, every Jewish parent expresses more heroism than the greatest biblical patriarch, Abraham. He bound his son to the altar, putting Isaac's life at risk out of faithfulness to God and his covenantal commitment. The Nazis hunted even the grandchildren of Jews. Unlike for Isaac, for 1.5 million children, there was no substitute ram to save their lives. So in our time, Jewish parents knowingly put their children at risk, binding them for life. Every choosing Jew, including every convert, is committing to share Jewish fate. Most active Jews would testify that the substance of commitment is a rich and fulfilling life, embedded in family and community and connected to a higher purpose; but even so, they recognize that Jewish fate has often involved pain, suffering, and death.

In many ways, this book is driven by the impact of the Holocaust on me personally. For many years I was a fulfilled modern Orthodox Jew: in love with Jewish life and observance, and confident that God was in Heaven and all was right with the world. That was upended in 1961, when as a visiting Fulbright scholar at Tel Aviv University, I began immersing myself in the evidence and accounts of the destruction of six million Jews. I was shattered. I could not comprehend how such a cruel and catastrophic fate could have been inflicted on Jewry without any visible Divine intervention to stop it. This was an all-out assault on the Jewish body and on the religion that taught the sacredness and infinite value of life. If the world was ultimately to live by a moral order, how could God not have intervened?

Since then, over the last sixty years, I have sought to understand whether religion—especially my religion—had lost all credibility. Was my former belief—that Judaism offered an ethical vision of a repaired world—an illusion that had to be rejected if Jews were to survive in a harsh real world?

My loving wife and family saved me from nihilism and despair by showing me the incredible tenacity and unspent power of embracing life. The emergent State of Israel suggested to me that the Divine was still operating in the world, and testified to the human capacity to take power for reestablishing life and reasserting its value. From studying European society, I came to believe that the Holocaust happened both because of the powerlessness of the victims and the local populations' failure to use their powers to stop the slaughter. I concluded that all forms of power have to be taken and employed to rebuild the world. All channels of development have to be redirected toward restoring life and its values.

This raised the challenge of developing an ethic of power that would keep its exercise on the side of life. In this book, I share the record of my response to that challenge.

A Book for People Working to Perfect the World

This book is written, first and foremost, to unpack and illuminate the meaning and the heroism of being Jewish, for all who consider themselves Jewish, and for those who appreciate, uphold, support, or love them.

I hope it will appeal to non-Jewish readers as well, especially to Christians, partners in the struggle to overcome millennia of hostility and delegitimation. People of all religions must work together to repair the world politically, economically, and culturally, and turn the Earth into the paradise all humans deserve. Readers committed to social justice in its various forms will find in these pages a rationale for universal human dignity and an agenda to realize this vision. I hope all who want to change the world will draw inspiration from the Jewish agenda for world repair.

Judaism teaches that our material world is worthy of commitment and repair—and also that the Divine realm, though neither visible nor measurable, is real and ever present. By living life to its depths, humans can encounter the Divine dimension of existence and experience the Divine Presence in everyday "secular" reality. I hope that all those who seek to live life to its depths will also find this book helpful in that search.

A Narrative Theology

Judaism's teaching of One God, beyond human manipulation and control, helped lead the world to monotheism. It challenges human claims of absolutism in religions and cultures, as well as in the exercise of human power. No less impactful has been Jewish messianism, the idea that this planet is intended to become a Garden of Eden in which all human beings will be treated with the dignity, equality, and respect due to them. This aspiration (in its various forms) injected a restlessness into the bloodstream of humanity—a rejection of the status quo, so full of inequality and injustice.

Judaism offers no quick fix for our planet. Humans, as God's partners, must take on the enormous effort of *tikkun olam*, repairing the world. Against the belief that the world deteriorates over time, or that the human condition is cyclical or even fixed, in the past millennium the Jewish vision that you and I can change the world has become increasingly influential. Expressed in secular terms, this messianic vision of humans taking power and improving the human condition drives the complex of values we call modernity, which has in turn become the dominant culture for more than two billion people on the globe, and growing.

Modern civilization has achieved tremendous improvements in material well-being for billions of people. This accomplishment, however, has become detached from the classic Jewish values of partnership, respect for Creation, acceptance of limits, and accountability to a Higher Power. This disjunction has generated new crises: climate change, species destruction, and the misuse of power to inflict oppression, racism, and even genocide.

The method of world repair that Judaism offers us is covenant: partnership between God and human beings. If Judaism's vision is utopian, universal, egalitarian, sweepingly transformational, its covenantal method of *tikkun* is realistic, particularist, personal, conservative, incremental—neither overreaching by glorifying the ideals and imposing them, nor demeaning those who do not live up to the vision. The covenant process is the key to keeping vision intertwined with reality and operating within healthy limits. Rather than simply reinforcing the ideals, covenantal values and methods are complementary, checking potential excesses and keeping respect for human beings paramount.

About This Book

This book explores Judaism's vision of a perfected world. It asks whether and how the process of *tikkun* can itself be repaired through the classic Judaic models of covenant. Finally, it examines modern history through this theological lens, and considers how the commitment to *tikkun olam* can lead us to the triumph of life.

Part 1 offers Judaism's vision of a world created out of love, to be filled with life. Chapters 1 and 2 describe the rhythms injected by the Creator into the world: a movement from chaos to order, from nonlife to life, and from lesser to greater quality of life. The great principle underlying the ethic of the Torah is that every human being—regardless of gender, race, skin color, nationality, or religion—is created in the image of God, and endowed accordingly with three fundamental dignities: infinite value, equality, and uniqueness. Each shares remarkable, God-like capacities—consciousness, capacity for love, the ability to create and harness power, free will. Judaism seeks to persuade humans to develop and use these capacities for world repair.

In chapters 3, 4, and 5, I describe the Bible's utopian vision that humans will use these capabilities to overcome poverty, hunger, oppression, war, even sickness, and thus roll back the realm of death. Upholding life, I argue, is the core of Jewish teaching, in the Bible and in Judaism's subsequent orientation to both daily and ritual behaviors.

Part 2 argues that the method of *tikkun olam* is covenant: a partnership between God and humans and between the generations. Chapter 6 looks at the covenantal method's orientation, in contrast to competing movements for perfecting the world. In most cases over the past two centuries, radical elements in these other world-repair movements led them to a tyrannical totalitarianism that generated oppression on a vastly more destructive scale than the evil status quos they had sought to overcome. The covenantal process, in contrast, starts with one fundamental commitment: no coercion. In the absence of using force to impose the good, the process of *tikkun* inevitably involves compromise and incremental steps cut to human capacity and scale.

Chapters 7 and 8 explore the roles of love and relationship in the covenantal method. Rather than let the *tikkun* be propelled by anger or resentment at the status quo, this method seeks to harness the power of love—for fellow humans, for God, for the goal. Covenantal partnership leads to a sweet spot on the spectrum of human responsibility—avoiding both the Scylla of a view in which humans are alone in an often hostile or indifferent world, and the Charybdis of a reality in which God fully controls disempowered humanity, who wish (rather than act) for improvement or focus on winning divine favor rather than on joining with fellow humans to repair the world. In covenant, people feel the Divine Partner's love and yet they know they, too, must exert all-out effort, in a process built to be within human capacity.

Chapter 9 looks at covenantal time. As human capacity and culture have grown, in step with one another, the covenant has been recalibrated accordingly. The close of the biblical period, when heavenly revelation and the prophetic messages ended, was in fact a stage of renewed covenant in which God became more hidden but actually more present. The Divine Presence had to be discerned, uncovered, and embraced, as if the Israelites stood at Sinai again at a more mature level. Henceforth, their future Exoduses would have to be initiated by their actions, and their future Revelations discerned by their minds, through study. Now humans were called to a higher level of partnership. Human behavior now had greater impact; wise judgment and responsible policies, not simply repentance and Divine favor, would now lead to favorable historical outcomes.

This second stage of the covenant, Rabbinic Judaism, sustained the people of Israel through almost two millennia of challenging history. It gave Jews strength to endure persecution and frequent violent expulsion, and to emerge with their spirit and sense of mission unbroken. It fostered a profound, unbreakable connection to God, as well as a sense of community and a culture that treasured learning and literacy. Notwithstanding all these accomplishments, however, modernity brought us to the end of this second, Rabbinic stage of history.

I argue that the development of modern civilization is humanity's response to a further Divine initiative. In the third stage of covenant, God again self-limited, now to the point of becoming totally hidden in natural laws and material processes. Today, God makes more miracles than ever, but only through human agency—our unlocking the miraculous powers in physical and biological matter that only we can exercise by understanding and utilizing nature's laws. This stage also requires us to arrive at a fully mature relationship with God. Rather than relate to the Divine out of fear, incapacity, or childlike dependency, we are to seek God out of our capacity and free will, and relate to God out of love and a sense of common cause.

Part 3 looks at this new stage's effect on Judaism and the world, and examines where we are headed. Chapter 10 explores modern culture's invitation to humans to take power and improve life through secular activity, in response to the Divine call for partnership. The dawn of modern civilization brought major advances in overcoming afflictions that had plagued humanity for millennia and in realizing the image of God in all human beings. It also made most Jews an offer they could not refuse: full citizenship, and an end to marginality and discrimination. Sadly, however, most religious authorities viewed those expanded opportunities negatively, often seeing them as human encroachments on divine prerogatives. As a result, a disproportionate number of modernity's leaders became detached from religion, or accepted that shedding God or religion was an important part of human liberation and world repair.

The naive engagement with material and cultural modernity came to an end with the world wars of the twentieth century and the catastrophic event of the Holocaust. Popular government, it turned out, could be channeled into totalitarianism, and modernity's amassed political, technological, and military power could be utilized for death and destruction — starting with the Jews'. Chapter 11 describes this process. By inventing realms totally devoted to death and the degradation of life, the Nazis turned the genocide of the Jews into a total assault of death on life — all in the name of utopia and world perfection, ideals by which modernity had inspired billions of people, myself included.

How can we understand our relationship with a God who allowed that catastrophe? Chapter 12 looks at my own and other people's evolving struggles with this question. I myself have come to understand the process of covenant anew. In the Shoah, God was neither absent nor indifferent. The event occurred in an age when God had already self-limited to become totally hidden and totally present. In the face of this contraction, meant to call humanity to the highest level of partnership, the Nazis used their freedom for an all-out attack on the Jews. The Jews had no power to stop the onslaught, but the Allies and the Jews' neighbors failed to use their power to stop the Holocaust. Thus I came to realize that the formulation of a covenantal obligation to take and hold power in ethical ways is a prerequisite for world repair.

These insights call for a reorientation of all religions, including Judaism, regarding the dynamic relationship between God and humanity. With God so deeply hidden, religion must also enter into secular realms in order to uncover the Divine Presence there too. Religion must help restructure society and culture to make God manifest in the achievement of full human dignity and justice for all. Worldwide pluralism is the imperative; partnerships between religions and between religious and secular redemptive movements are fundamental to overcoming the status quo and achieving world repair.

Throughout chapters 13 and 14, I outline the new iteration of Judaism being born, and the emerging new holy secularism, in which every life activity will be maximally oriented to quantity and quality of life. There, in all daily behaviors, the world will be turned toward life, and the immanent Divine Presence will be uncovered. This Third Era, Lay Judaism, is named after the leadership—broadened beyond past models to include every gender and class, every nationality and professional calling.

Arising from the deathbed of the Shoah, secular and religious Jews alike took on power and responsibility for life, especially through creating the State of Israel. Chapter 13 examines the decisions involved in its establishment, its redemptive accomplishments, and its ongoing work to support the guardrail principles that keep power harnessed to covenantal ethics.

Chapter 14 depicts some of the new value-bearing, "secular" institutions that can join inherited historic institutions in advancing Jewish life and a better world. This goal is so vast, it cannot be realized without the alliance of all people of good will in every religion and secular way of life. Here, I try to offer a new paradigm of the sacred for a new millennium. While I apply these understandings primarily to Judaism and Jewish institutions, I hope that readers from other religions and movements will formulate their own applications for their communities.

Finally, the table "The Three Great Eras of Jewish History" at the book's close offers a schematic view of this narrative, depicting the historical events and theological shifts in relation to each other.

Our age began with the overwhelming destruction of the Holocaust and the unprecedented redemption of Israel's establishment. To meet the challenge and the opportunity of the coming millennium—to move the world forward covenantally—we need to gear up our courage and wisdom, as the Rabbis did. They understood that God's higher self-limitation was not abandonment, nor the dissipation of an illusion, but a call for humans to take more responsibility in partnership for *tikkun olam*. They infused this vision into every moment of life, filled every human action with life affirmation, and stepped up the pace of repair toward the final goal of universal redemption. We in turn must avoid the arrogance of thinking that we are the masters of the universe with no accountability to a Higher Power. Nor must we allow the bewildering pace of change to cause us to cower and cling to inherited ways. We must take the baton from the generations before us, hold precious their inheritance, and fill every moment and place on earth with dignity and justice for all. So, too, we must trust in the generations to come: what we do not complete, they will take on and do.

I close this introduction with prayers and blessings for you, the reader of this book. May you be inspired by these chapters to go beyond my understanding. May you reach beyond my imagining, touch more human beings, and reach higher levels of dignity, justice, and equality. If I will have opened a few doors, inspired you to work toward higher standards or future realizations of the noble visions of Judaism, then I am content. I am full of gratitude to you and to all those who will move humanity forward toward the day when, as the prophet Isaiah proclaims (11:9), "they will do no evil or acts of destruction anywhere on My holy mount, for the world will be full of knowledge of the Loving God—as deeply as the waters cover the sea."[1]

PART 1

A Vision of Life in
a Redeemed World

Creation and the Dignity of Life

In the beginning, Judaism starts with Creation. Genesis's narrative of Creation stresses that important processes in the universe started long before humanity, or even life, appeared on the scene. We need to study and understand these natural phenomena, which not only shape and affect our existence but are keys to the meaning and purpose of our lives.

The first chapter of the first book of the Torah starts the story as far back as one can go—to the first moment of existence. This universe is not the outcome of a random physical process, devoid of value and blind to purpose. The world is a creation. Despite the astonishing variety of often conflicting phenomena, there is a fashioned order. There is an underlying unity to the universe: natural laws that govern the operation of forces in the cosmos and the behavior of the particles that make up all existence.

The interpretive key of Creation changes the understanding of the very nature of existence. Creation implies the presence of a Creator. The vastness of the universe implies the infinitude of what we came to call God. The Israelites came to see that there is one universal Presence, Force, and Person—the One God who shapes and sustains Creation. At first, because human understanding is shaped by the filters of local culture, they imagined God as visible, in their midst, speaking, meeting, thundering. They came to understand that God is omnipresent yet invisible, not detectable on the surface of material reality or measurable by physical means.

Then how does one know God? By intuition, by inner experience, by encounter, through emotions, meditation, and imaginative insight. Interior experiences give messages, just as a pressing of the flesh does or stumbling into a hard rock. The spiritual is as real as the physical.

As the relationship with God deepens, believers come to see that this world and the quantifiable surface phenomena are real—yet limited. This mortal life is a thin layer, floating on a sea of spirit and unplumbed depths. One can live on the surface, but this is to experience but a fraction of existence. The religious spirit delights in the variety of daily life and the wonders of Creation, but comes to embrace its many levels of reality. To come to know God is to experience these layers simultaneously—just as in an awakened soul, past and future interpenetrate the present. The spiritual is met in the physical. The presence of God is encountered when one dives deeply into life.

Similarly, the interpretive key of Creation opens our eyes to see the richly shaped, wonderfully wrought world created by God. We are guided to see the art, the subtle patterns and amazing interactions going on everywhere. The planet is to be seen not as a random piece of bric-a-brac or even as a delightfully reshaped piece of driftwood. The key of Creation teaches us to look for the intended effects, the built-in rhythms, the inlaid feasts for the eyes—and savor them. The religious soul grasps that humanity has been given this gift. This insight evokes the instinct "to work it and guard it" (Gen. 2:15). Touched by its beauty, ravished by its melody, one exclaims: "The Earth is the Lord's" (Ps. 24:1). The last thing humans want to do is to deface this scene or to run down the operability of its mechanisms. To degrade is an act of barbarism. Pollution constitutes wanton destruction of a created beauty. The fact that Creation has been carried out over billions of years makes abusing it for the sake of one particular generation all the more outrageous: a desecration of the sacred.

All this is true because there is a Creator—a universal Presence, a Force and Will who brings this and many other possible forms of universe into being, and sustains them.

Humans call this Creator God, and many other names. In the Torah's first chapter, that Power is called Elohim, bespeaking an unlimited, impersonal Force, with infinite expression and boundless energy. The Creator supplies the underlying permanence in the components of reality. God has built characteristic rhythms into natural phenomena, such as growth and limits, and dynamic interactivity between forces or between creatures and environment. These pulses and flows enable and point to desired outcomes, such as life and growth in all its complexity and capacity.

We now know that these processes have been going on for billions and billions of years. They stretch over vast, infinite distances that we can only approximate and imagine. We humans are the first living forms who can even begin to understand the wondrous intricacy of the cosmic process.

Jewish religion teaches that, although the Creator is not perceptible to our senses, we can detect and connect to the Divine. We can intuit and explore dimensions of reality that elude physical detection and measurement. If we fail to expand our consciousness in this way, our perception of reality is cramped, even stunted. We are limited creatures, enclosed in our skins, captives of our cultural context, able to see only what our receptors and organizing concepts let in. The Creation story attempts to break us out of our "cave"—to enable us to see the world from the Divine perspective.

Obviously, the Torah does not free us of our human limitations. The Creation story itself is expressed in the language of Mesopotamian wisdom and terminology, comprehensible to its initial audience of Israelites living in the Middle East in the late Bronze Age. Still, if we can embrace Genesis's view and stand on the Torah's ladder to look over the universe, we will see three fundamental rhythms—instilled by the Creator—that shape our reality.

The Rhythms of Creation

The cosmos is moving *from chaos*—*tohu vavohu*, a chaotic void (Gen. 1:2) in the Torah's language[1]—*to order*, Shabbat in the Torah's language.[2]

This perception of the world goes against the grain of daily human experience, in which the order we create in our lives is constantly disintegrating. In our creaturely experience, the neat, orderly desk of the morning is overrun and disheveled by day's end, while best-laid plans often go awry. But if we can look through the religious lens for a moment, if we assume the perspective of the Eternal, we soon see the advance of local order through the chaos process in nature.

Today, we have a scientific language that illuminates this pattern. The second law of thermodynamics states that, over time, disorder in a closed body will tend to increase. Orderly systems devolve toward disorder, broken symmetry, and high levels of nonhomogeneous distribution of matter (clumping, etc.) with time. Nevertheless, order can be achieved locally at the cost of disorder somewhere else. The balance between those constants must be just so if the tendency toward chaos is going to be locally constructive rather than completely and violently destructive.

Our universe began with a Big Bang, an instant of explosive, chaotic violence in which nothing material can exist, followed within a trillionth of a trillionth of a second by an exponential expansion. The universe continues this expansion to this day. After the Big Bang, the universe was formed with almost perfect symmetry and homogeneity in the distribution of matter. In our universe, the movement toward disorder and complexity actually builds large-scale structures, such as stars, galaxies, galaxy clusters, super-clusters. The cosmos moves from an era where energy is so intense that it exists in the form of radiation, to an age where the energy cools and comes together as bits of matter. The process goes from vast clumping of matter to emergence of galaxies, to the birth of stars, to the condensation or generation of planets so structured and orderly as to be able to sustain life. We live in a universe so finely tuned, so well balanced that even the tendency toward chaos is incorporated into the creation of the universe, as when an errant meteor smashes into a planet and generates a moon circling around it. This exact balance between order and disorder enables the emergence of life. Thanks to the remarkable expansion of consciousness made possible today by knowledge of physics and geology, we can see in the pattern unfolding over billions of years the emergence of an infrastructure of order that has finally resulted in a planet capable of sustaining life, which developed into sentient life and, eventually, into human life. This insight—the operation of this trend toward "ordered chaos"—is what the Creation story seeks to communicate.

This brings us to the second fundamental rhythm in Creation. The world is moving *from nonlife to life*. In the Genesis account, life is a late arrival. In the six days of Creation activity, there is no life in day one or day two. On day three, vegetation makes its appearance, but the Torah categorizes it as less than full life because it is less mobile and less visibly sentient. Not until day five do the living creatures in the sea swarm and develop; amphibians and birds follow. Still later, the latest arrivals, advanced land animals, appear on the scene. Today, with a scientific lens, we better understand just how late life appears. More than thirteen billion years after ignition of the universe, after eons of no life, one-celled life-forms come into being. Since then, there has been an explosion of life on this planet. Life has grown, radiated into every form and shape, migrated into every area. Despite occasional catastrophic setbacks and planetary die-outs, life has proliferated. Humans have identified living forms in ten million species—and counting.

Again, the human perspective on this rhythm is very different. We experience the cycle as going from life to nonlife. From the moment we are born, we begin to die. The life insurance industry with trillions of assets is predicated on clients seeing life from this perspective. However, from the outlook of the Divine, for whom "a thousand years is like . . . a [brief] watch in the night" (Ps. 90:4), the big picture is the movement *toward life*. The Torah suggests that this very proliferation is one of the best signals of the Divine Presence that "gives life to all" (Neh. 9:6).

Given the fact that death is so powerful that it overcomes all individual living things, how can one account for the growth in quantity of life over the course of a billion years? The answer lies in the fact that God who delights in life and blesses it (Gen. 1:12,21–22,25,28,31) has imbued living things with the vital force of fertility and multiplication (Gen. 1:11–12,20–22,28). God is *melekh ḥafetz ba'ḥayim* — "the Ruler who lusts for life."[3] Life expands thanks to an unseen, hidden power of a magnitude greater than the force of death and decay, continually pumping energy into life and its nurturers. To put it into contemporary scientific language, the infrastructure of reality and the interaction of natural forces, at least in this planetary system, favors life and enables it to grow and develop.[4] This is the rhythm and balance of forces built into the Creation by the Creator.

Life is not only expanding quantitatively, but also *developing qualitatively*. This is the third rhythm in Creation. Life-forms have grown from simple, one- or two-celled organisms to creatures with highly complex, interactive systems. From beings controlled by elementary phototropic or chemical reactions, organisms with more and more consciousness have unfolded. There are now beings capable of exercising reason, of measuring the cosmos and mapping its building blocks. From asexual reproduction, life has moved to sexual selection; from chemical and instinct-governed behavior, life has matured to include emotional reactions and the capacity to love.

The Torah describes this process in its language. Humans, like all life, are planted in the ground of the Divine. Just as plants rooted in alkaline soil evolve to become more alkaline and more absorptive of the nutrients in the ground, life itself absorbs the distinctive Godly energy and evolves to become more and more like its ground, the Divine. Put another way: the qualitative development of life is that it is moving *from being less to more and more like God*. That is why the Bible describes the human being, the most developed form of life thus far, as being in "the image of God" (Gen. 1:27). This means that human life, however finite and limited, nevertheless possesses capacities so striking and powerful that they bring to mind the operations of the unlimited capabilities of the Creator.

God's Capabilities and the Image of God

In the rhythms of Creation we can discern five overarching capacities of God, all of them reflected in human beings made in God's image.

1. God possesses *infinite consciousness*. "God counts the number of stars; gives each one a name. . . . God's consciousness is infinite" (Ps. 147:4–5). The Lord is aware of each and every creature in the world. Humans have only a finite consciousness. Still, Homo sapiens with a frontal cortex has developed an extraordinarily high level of insight and understanding of nature. In my lifetime, human beings decoded the sequence of DNA, the code of life. They did not create this code; that is the work of an Infinite Consciousness operating through the process of evolution, inscribed within Creation by the Creator. Nonetheless, decoding the genome is an extraordinary accomplishment that can be fairly described as the work of a Godlike consciousness.

2. The Lord is omnipotent: that is, God possesses *infinite power*. As the psalm proclaims, "Great is God and overflowing in power" (Ps. 147:5). The human being is not the physically strongest animal in the universe, but thanks to the human mind and creativity, humankind has developed motors that generate a million horsepower. Rocket engines put forth millions of pounds of thrust, capable of overcoming the pull of gravity. Human power is not unlimited—one lightning strike generates more electricity than the human-made hydropower dam of Niagara Falls. Yet also in my lifetime, humans unleashed the power of the forces holding the atom together—yielding enough power to light up whole areas of the Earth (or to destroy them).

3. God possesses *infinite love* and capacity for relationship. "God is good to all [because] God's 'mother love' (*raḥamav*) extends to all God's creatures" (Ps. 145:9). The human is a creature who has developed a Godlike capacity for love—love so boundless as to sacrifice one's life for a loved one; love enough to choose marriage and commit to one spouse for a lifetime.[5] Human love, modeled in the Divine image, is strong enough to endure for endless years, through victory and defeat,

loyalty and betrayal, beauty flowering and fading, joy and depression, unexpected successes, unforeseen disasters and loss.

4. The Divine is pure *freedom*. God self-describes to Moses: "I will be what(ever) I will (to) be" (Exod. 3:14). The Bible teaches that there is no magic that can compel God; no service or gift or bribe that can "guarantee" a Divine behavior. When Moses seeks to know God or the Divine essence in a fixed way, the Lord replies: "I shall extend grace to [whomever] I choose to; I shall have compassion for whom I choose to" (Exod. 33:12–13,19). God is totally free to exercise the Divine will. By contrast, the lowly amoeba's behavior is totally controlled by chemical signals and responses. In the case of human beings, the range of freedom is extended so that (finite) free will can be exercised. Again, human liberty is not equal to Divine freedom but is a limited exercise— that is, in the image of God.

5. Finally, there is *life* itself. God is eternally alive, the source of life and its sustainer. The human quality of life and the human capacity to extend the quantity of life summon up the Divine plenitude of the power of life. Thus, the increase (doubling) of life expectancy in the past two centuries and the breakthroughs in fertility treatments are legitimately deemed Godlike achievements. While some religions oppose some of these activities on the very grounds that humans are using Godlike powers to tamper with Divinely ordained processes, paradoxically, even these objections tacitly confirm that increased human intervention is an exercise of a Godlike capacity.

Revelation and the Human Role in Creation

Judaism concludes that Creation's emergent rhythms grew out of capabilities and interactions built by God into the physical matter and processes of existence. Therefore, these subsequent phenomena are the result of God's will. It follows then that nature itself is full of materials with Divinely instilled qualities, processes, laws of behavior that humans can discover if they study and analyze the world. Thus, just as reading a sacred text can be a source of revelation of the Divine, so can properly analyzing nature. Says the Psalmist, "The Heavens declare the glory of God; the sky proclaims God's handiwork" (Ps. 19:2).

However, for the first time there is a form of life capable of grasping these revelations and using them to make "miracles." How else can we describe sending and detecting sound waves around the globe almost instantaneously? Or turning a liquid hydrocarbon into a source of power, electricity, and propulsion? Judaism interprets that God's love for life, paired with God's consciousness, has foreseen and enabled the extraordinary development of life, quantitatively and qualitatively. This process culminates in human beings, capable of detecting and understanding the cosmic rhythms, grasping the Divinely willed direction and outcome of all existence. With this understanding, humans have the power and choice to join into and amplify these rhythms—or to go against them and even seek to defeat them. This capability is what evokes God's direct approach to humanity in the form of religion.

Religion represents God's revelation to humans of the Creator's love and pleasure at their capabilities. Now that they understand the cosmic directions, God also asks them to choose sides. God wants the forces of order and life to win out. God asks humans to live in such a way that in their actions, they join in on the side of order and against chaos, on the side of life and against nonlife and death, on the side of increasing quality of life and against dumbing it down. The commandments and values governing human behavior, imparted in the Torah of Judaism, are intended to direct human behavior to the side of order against chaos, of life against death. Similarly the mitzvot (commandments) and ethical teachings are designed to move human behaviors and learning toward sustaining or upgrading the quality of life—as against degrading it.[6]

Having studied and lived in the Jewish religion all my life, I try to apply this interpretive key to all of Judaism. But God wants to redeem the whole Earth and all of humanity, not just the Jewish people. As such, I believe that all the other religions of the world should teach humans to work for order over chaos, for increasing quality of life and never degrading it, for life as against death.

Judaism and Jewry have had a disproportionate impact on world civilization, but religion started long before the Jews appeared on the scene. I assume that God was reaching out to the earliest Homo sapiens, and earlier religions deciphered the message as best they could. In the Abrahamic traditions Judaism gets the credit for being the first introducer of the one, creator God to humanity, but all faiths have roles to play and their adherents are also asked to be partners.

As in Judaism, they must articulate their commitment to life and quality of life, and refine and redirect these elements in their own tradition that contradict life or assault human dignity. The Jews' understanding of being a Chosen People only means that they grasped the Divine outreach and experienced God's love and articulated it. This does not rule out God's reaching out in love to other peoples and religious communities to share in this calling. There is a lot of Divine love, and a lot of work left to repair the world—enough for everybody.

This is not the only possible understanding of revelation and religion. These cosmic rhythms have been going on for vast periods without human intervention. Some argue that, unaffected by human action, Divinely willed patterns will win out, so humans should stay out of it and not "interfere," or humans ought to play a role in the cosmic processes by doing what comes naturally and not let culture or religion change the vector of their behavior. A traditional religious variant of this idea that the natural process is God's will is the claim that humans should not interfere with natural cycles such as reproduction, through contraception, abortion, or genetic intervention. Rather, they should leave it to Divine will as expressed in the outcomes. An extreme version of this approach is the view expressed in modern Christian Science and by some medieval Jewish commentators that the practice of medicine is a sin against God, for "I the Lord am your healer" (Exod. 15:26).[7]

The enduring Jewish tradition rejects such simplistic understandings of nature as the will of God. God's grandeur is such that "islands are like a speck of dust" and "all of the Earth's inhabitants [together] are like a [bunch of] grasshoppers" (Isa. 40:15,22). Nevertheless, the

Infinite Power is deeply respectful of finite humans and concerned for them. Now that they have developed such Godlike capacities, the Creator wishes to recruit them to work for the goal of perfecting Creation.

Rabbi Joseph B. Soloveitchik goes a step further and argues that the Godlike capacities are a gift of the Almighty (bestowed, by God, through the Divinely crafted process of natural evolution) to enable humans to join in the cosmic struggle for completion.[8] As we will see, this upgrading and completion is the real purpose of revelation and the ultimate goal of religion.

The Dignity of All Life

To have a truly open encounter with living creatures is to be struck with wonder at their intricacy, remarkable interactions, capacity for growth, surprising strengths, and developmental twists and turns. The proper response is to take them seriously: to feel respect, reverence, even awe. This feeling is compounded by the realization that they are fragile and vulnerable and have limited lifespans. Therefore, they should be handled with care—and valued and appreciated all the more.

As life develops over the eons, becoming more and more capable, it becomes increasingly inestimable. The Torah suggests that Adam, the human being, acts as God's regent in valuing creatures by looking at them and giving each one a name (Gen. 2:19–20). They are not anonymous, indistinguishable background noise. They are distinctive, each one a note adding richness and depth to the symphony of Creation. As life develops, it becomes more "weighty"; in Hebrew the word for honor and dignity is *kavod*, from the root *kaved* (weight or weighty). We express our recognition of this qualitative development of life, as it becomes capable of more remarkable and creative activity, by allowing it greater dignity and importance. We give life's needs greater weight, and most weight of all to human needs. Still, we respect and value every form of existence.

The halakhah (Jewish law) seeks to articulate this value by regulating behavior vis-à-vis nonhuman created things. The base law is the Rabbinic interpretation of the ethical precept *bal tash'ḥit,* "do not destroy."[9] It is forbidden to waste, to use up for no purpose or value, any object—even inorganic matter. The ritual prohibition is code language for the importance, the independent dignity, of all in Creation. All forms of existence—alive, inanimate, organic, inorganic—have weight. None should be used for no purpose, let alone abandoned, degraded, polluted, or made toxic. To waste something for no purpose is to treat it as of no account, no value, not worthy of attention. The mere fact that something exists in nature, that is to say, is created by God,[10] means that it is weighty and should be treated as being of account. The aesthetic power in the world (such as vistas in nature) should not be marred unless this is unavoidable and there is a significant reason for making the change. Implicit in this understanding is that any negative effects of human behavior on nature must be minimized.

Since life in all its forms is a significant step up over matter, inorganic and organic, one must give it greater weight and dignity. Jewish tradition expresses this by applying greater restrictions on the manner of using it. The most striking expression of this step up is the law of *tza'ar ba'alei ḥayim* (not to cause pain to living beings). As long as they are not wasted, animals may be used, as in labor, and so too their products, such as milk and eggs, may be eaten. They may even be killed and used up for human benefit—as for meat or for fat, chemicals, medicines, and leather for clothes and shelter. However, it is forbidden to cause any unnecessary suffering to living things at any time, even in the process of killing them for the sake of human beings.[11] True, the Talmud does not apply this restriction to lower animals, insects, etc.—apparently because the science of the day saw these creatures as not having emotions or experiencing pain, or because they were viewed as predators or antagonists to human beings. Here again, postmodern science's enriched awareness of the profound links between all forms of life—the extent to which important parts of the human genome are inherited from and held in common with "lower" animals—paves the way for applying this law more universally and more rigorously. A religious orientation should take seriously antifur and other animal rights positions, Jain religious restrictions, and the vegan food movement.[12]

The halakhic status of *beriah*, a whole living organism, reflects another intensified expression of reverence for other forms of life. If a nonkosher piece of meat (be it animal, fish, bird, insect) falls into a pot of kosher food and it cannot be removed, then if the percentage present is very low (1 in 60 particles = 1.66 percent or less) the non-kosher fragment is "nullified," treated as if it were not present. The whole contents of the pot may be eaten in order not to waste the large amount of kosher food present. However, if the nonkosher piece is in fact a *whole* organism, even if it is only a very small insect, then it is not nullified.[13] As long as the nonkosher element retains the shape and appearance of a whole organism, alive or dead, it should evoke in us an awe that prevents us from ignoring or dismissing its existence.

The more we see life through a religious lens as sacred, the more we should respect the life quality and consciousness found in other living creatures. Proverbs states that "the *tzadik* [holy, righteous person] knows the soul of his animal" (12:10). The Hebrew verb "to know" is conveying not just intellectual cognition: it is an empathetic, emotional experience of the feelings and specialness of the other.[14] This should be expressed in care and consideration and good treatment of the animal.[15]

The religious perspective recognizes the unity and profound interconnection of all life. Life is on a continuum; the difference between species is a matter of degree rather than of essence. Therefore, humans should feel respect for all forms of life. The closer to humans on the continuum of life, the more intense our experiences of the other should be emotionally—and the more respectful.

In sum, the human being is the most developed and most intense form of life (at least on this planet). As we grow and become more human, we are called to live ever more deeply. This includes widening our embrace of all life. We should come to know emotionally, as well as understand intellectually, this miracle of living things. Life is the most precious of forms in the universe, the most wonderful existence in a wondrous Creation. As life develops, it gains in value and dignity; humans should treat it accordingly. This respectful treatment is not to be extended just because some law tells us to act this way. Rather, our behavior should express our core, instinctive, loving, embracing reaction to life as a marvelous phenomenon. Religious laws and rituals should be seen as trying to awaken and guide such responses.

2 Human Beings in the Image of God

The climax of life's becoming more and more like God is the emergence of Homo sapiens, a creature so Godlike as to be able to understand God's purposes and plan for Creation. Reaching the image-of-God level of life represents a quantum leap in dignity, to which every human being is entitled.

As we will see, by dint of being human—created in the image of God—each of us is born with three fundamental dignities. We are called to recognize and honor these dignities in ourselves and in all human beings. We are further called to strengthen these human capacities, which are finite versions of God's infinite capacities. Thereby we increase our human resemblance to God, in whose image we are created.

The Dignities of the Image of God

In the volume of the Mishnah governing judicial procedures, a passage describing an unusual oath for witnesses in capital cases spells out the enormous value of human life.[1] Reading this passage gives us a window into the three dignities that Judaism sees as intrinsic to every human being.

This complex oath ritual was intended to drive home to potential witnesses the weight of a human life. If they understood its extraordinary value, witnesses would strive for absolute precision, restraint, avoidance of hearsay, and so on. The ritual was so awesome, it was almost intimidating, as if its purpose were to make people reluctant to testify. It reflects the Rabbis' ambivalence about capital punishment, precisely because a human life is so weighty.[2]

First, the oath ritual warns that, unlike in civil cases, a miscarriage of justice resulting in the execution of an innocent person can never be corrected. Then the dimension of the awe that a human life should evoke is driven home by explaining the meaning of the creation-of-Adam story: "And God created Adam [the human] in God's image; in the image of God [*tzelem elohim*] God created the human; man and woman, God created them" (Gen. 1:27). Only when the witnesses understand the preciousness of an image of God will they be fit to testify in a case where their words will decide whether the life of a defendant—an image of God—will be preserved or forfeited.

The First Dignity: Infinite Value

The Mishnah continues: "For this reason, [the Torah tells us that] the human was created uniquely/singly.[3] To teach you that one who destroys one life is considered by Scripture as if he has destroyed a whole world. And one who saves one life is considered by Scripture as if he saved a whole world."[4]

But why should one life be considered equal to all lives in the world? There are now eight billion human beings in the world. Why should one life equal eight billion lives?

Rashi's commentary suggests that the analogy is this: from Adam the whole of humanity descended. Wiping out that one person would have wiped out the whole world that followed. Others suggest that in killing one person, one has "killed" thousands (indeed, an indeterminate number) of future descendants.

I propose a different reading. The Mishnah is trying to communicate the Godlike quality and weight of human life. This is akin to the mathematical term in which one is equal to the whole category—that is, infinity. The Mishnah is stating that any human—by dint of being born a human, an image of God—is of *infinite value*. If you save one times infinite value, you have saved infinite value. If you save eight billion times infinite value, you have saved infinite value. As a Godlike creature, each human being possesses a fraction of the infinite value and dignity of God. A fraction of the Divine infinity is of infinite value—and should be treated accordingly. This is fundamental dignity number one: every human being is of infinite value.

How does one treat someone as being of infinite value? This value means that a human life is priceless, beyond any measure of money. Biblical scholar Moshe Greenberg points out that biblical law, uniquely among its peers, would not accept monetary redemption (blood money) from a murderer—not even for the murder of a person of inferior social status.[5] A human life is so valuable that, in principle, no amount of money is too much to spend to save it.

In 2001 I had a heart bypass operation to remove clogged arteries. Because I was over sixty-five, Medicare—that is, the United States government—paid for the surgery. The bills came to more than $250,000. At the time, my life expectancy was just about ten years. In effect, the United States government was making a statement that the life of Yitz Greenberg was worth saving at a cost of $25,000 a year. Had Medicare not covered my operation, I probably could have scraped the money together myself, but tens of thousands of others in my position could not, and so would have forfeited their lives.

While that is not quite an expression of my life's being of infinite value, still it certainly showed that the culture and legal system of the American people valued my life and that of millions of others very highly. This points toward the future possibility of spending at the rate of infinite value.

Sobering statistics show how far we are from upholding human life's infinite value. In the 1990s, the World Health Organization estimated that the vast majority of the millions of children who died each year from dysentery and diarrheal diseases could have been kept alive by a daily dose of oral rehydration tablets (which supply vital electrolytes) together with clean water. Unfortunately, their own government and the humanitarian resources of the world could not—or did not try to—put together the funds to provide them with the tablets. What was the daily cost of the tablets—the de facto value accorded a child's life in those countries at that time? Twenty-five cents a day.[6] Similarly, until recently, almost a million children died of malaria every year in Africa. This number could be very sharply reduced by providing mosquito netting for children's beds at a cost of eight dollars for a net that would last five years. The Bush administration and private philanthropy committed significant money for this purpose, and the death rate was cut almost in half. Nevertheless, to this day the countries involved—and the world—lack the will to raise and administer the less than half-a-penny per day that it would take to save the other almost half-a-million lives by making mosquito netting universally available. This is a gross violation of these children's dignity, their infinite value. This is a measure of the repair that our world needs, the gulf between humanity as it behaves and as it should behave to honor the intrinsic, God-given dignity of infinite value.

Here is another approach to what it would mean to take seriously the Divine economy in which every human being created in the image of God is of infinite value. What is the value of an image of a human being?—that is, of a work of art created by a classic artist? Multiple Picassos have sold for over $100 million. In 2012 Cezanne's painting *The Card Players* sold for $250 million.[7] Leonardo da Vinci's painting *Salvator Mundi* was bought in 2017 for $450 million. In 1990 the world record for a painting at that time was set when one by Van Gogh— itself literally an image of a man, the *Portrait of Dr. Gachet*—was sold for $82.5 million to a Japanese insurance company. As a publicly held company, the Japanese firm had to report what it did with the painting. It chose to display the portrait for prestige and public relations purposes. But since such a valuable painting could be damaged in public exhibitions, the company built a special room to exhibit it. Aside from safety protections, the temperature and moisture in this room had to be properly tuned. If the room was too hot, the paint could be damaged; if too cold, the frame could harden or crack. If the gallery was too humid, the painting and canvas could rot; if too dry, the paint could flake and fall off. Naturally the company built a setting to the exact specifications needed to protect such a precious artistic image.

Keep this picture in mind next time you go downtown in the dead of winter, in some major city favored with an affluent economy. See a homeless man or woman lying in a cardboard box, chilled by freezing winds and then splashed with mud and slush by a passing car. This human is not being treated as a person of infinite value but as a piece of garbage, ignored like flotsam and jetsam in the sea. This not only violates this individual's dignity as an image of God; it is a measure of the gap between the world as it is and the world as it should be. It is also an important marker of why the Jewish tradition insists that this world must be repaired until its standard operating procedures meet the test of treating human beings—each one an image of God, of infinite worth—with all the dignities and care they are entitled to.

The Second Dignity: Equality

The Mishnah continues by observing that the Adam story is taught in the Torah "for the sake of peace between all creatures, for no human can say to his friend: my father is greater than your father."[8] This rejection of hierarchy represents the second inherent dignity of an image of God: equality. In a society marked by inherited status and inequality, the upper-class person can tell the lower-class person that we are not equal because my parent is greater, nobler, more royal than yours. However, as images of God, every human being is intrinsically equal to every other. Differences of lineage, class, privilege are swept away by the fundamental dignity and entitlement of every image of God. Of course, in the real world inequalities are real—but this is a measure of what is wrong with the world, its divergence from the world we aim to realize.

Similarly, differences in skin shades, hair color, gender, and other physical attributes are of no weight against the dignity of equality, and may not be invoked to justify denial of equality, because they do not affect the status of being in the image of God. God is not white. God is not Black. God is not male. God is not female. God is not blonde. God is not Jewish. God is not gentile. Attempts to rate one skin color or gender as being more in God's image are forms of idolatry: that is, they take a human, finite representation of God and claim that this is what God is *really* like. Representing the infinity of God literally, in some finite form, is the ultimate misrepresentation of God. The Torah rejects idolatry—the divinization of something finite or human—as the most objectionable denial of God.

These dignities must be honored in law, in economics, in politics, in social processes. As an image of God, I am entitled to equal treatment before the law. Any discrimination or unjust treatment I experience contravenes my intrinsic dignity and hence constitutes a sin by the standard of the Divine image. In politics, I am entitled to an equal vote, to equal say in public policy; I am not to be deprived of the vote by differential eligibility requirements or by gerrymandered districts, onerous poll taxes, or unreasonable residency rules. In economics, the Torah's vision of full material equality mirrors the intrinsic dignities of every human. In the present unredeemed state of the world, the Torah's conception of the eventual perfected state in a redeemed world is manifest in the biblical institutions of the *seventh* day of the week, Shabbat; the *seventh* or sabbatical year, *shemitah* (Lev. 25:1–7; Deut. 15:1–18); and by the *yovel* or jubilee (Lev. 25:8–55), which takes place after the forty-ninth year.[9]

Under the *shemitah* system, every seven years existing loans were to be wiped out, reducing inequality and enhancing equality (Deut. 15:1–2). During the sabbatical year, instead of owners sowing, harvesting, and collecting crops in private fields as in normal years, fields were opened wide to the public (including "your male and female hand servants, your hired labor, and the outsiders [the needy] living in your midst," and all animals as well—Lev. 25:4–7). In effect, for one year, the private lands were socialized and its produce belonged to all.

The jubilee law envisioned a society in which—even at a time when the scourge of slavery was permitted—enslaved members had to be freed, in order to restore the primordial human equality among the entire community. During the jubilee, all land and agricultural fields were to be returned to their original family holders. In the initial distribution, all families had received equal fields proportionate to their population (Num. 26, especially verses 50–52, and also Num. 34:35); in an agricultural economy this constituted giving each family equal economic resources and equal opportunity to generate income. The redistribution every fifty years meant that the inevitable growth of inequality—as some farmers flourished while others fell behind or lost their property—was canceled.

It is not clear that these ideal laws were ever honored in actual practice—just as the Bible records that bondservant owners often balked at releasing their slaves in the seventh year (Jer. 34, especially verses 12–18), after the slaves had served the six-year limit set by the Torah (Exod. 20:1–2; compare Deut. 15:12–18). Still, the notion of the intrinsic dignity of equality shapes the civil laws of the Torah as ideals, and, I believe, ought to reshape all societal structures.

At the same time, the Torah recognizes the right to property ownership. This is a compromise with the real world—much as the Torah compromises and allows meat eating despite its ideal of vegetarianism. In my view, it is also because the Torah recognizes that human dignity grows in the soil of the individual choices involved in using and disposing of one's own private resources. People work harder, produce more, and exercise greater creativity out of self-interest, ambition, and the dedication to provide for oneself and one's family. With that concession, the Torah regulates property, taxes it to prevent abuses and destructive inequality, and maintains its vision of a final equality.

The Third Dignity: Uniqueness

The third intrinsic dignity of *tzelem elohim*, the image of God, is that every human being is unique. Thus the Mishnah explains that the Torah's story of the creation of Adam teaches the greatness of the Holy One the Blessed. If a human being stamps a number of coins from one mold, they all exactly resemble each other. But the King of Kings, the Holy One the Blessed, stamped every human being in the mold of the first Adam—and not a single one is identical to any other human being.

The third dignity of every human being testifies to God's creative power. Although all humans are descended from one (couple), we are all unique. Even identical twins are not identical. This is not just a physical work of Divine artistry: a fundamental aspect of each human being's inner character is that each of us is a one-and-only. In another place the Talmud says: Just as their human faces do not resemble one another, so do their consciousness and views differ from each other.[10]

Individual distinctiveness constitutes a central part of every human being's dignity. Lumping people together and assessing them only as part of a group violates their uniqueness—and doubly so, if the group by which they are defined is itself portrayed through stereotypes and skewed lenses. Similarly, human views, values, and responses are not fully predictable. One must pay very close attention to truly do justice to what another individual is saying or requesting or teaching. Every person is irreplaceable. Each person's uniqueness demands a distinctive approach and treatment.

Uniqueness is a challenging counterpart to the other fundamental dignities. The dignity of infinite value reinforces the equality of all humans; the equality of human beings means that *all* are of infinite value; and uniqueness multiplies individual value enormously. However, the variety of human talents and abilities, given free play and scope, almost guarantees that some people will accomplish more, be more or less successful, rise above or fall below others' levels. This is not to mention the impact of different circumstances. The tension between equality and uniqueness means that almost every policy that must be applied universally to achieve equality must also be modified, with exemptions granted continuously, if the egalitarian policy is not to override or violate the dignity of uniqueness.

The dignities of infinite value and equality often can be honored and upheld, or their degradation prevented, by passing laws by which society commits to providing needed support. The quality of uniqueness can also be recognized through legislation (for example, provisions for special education), but is more frequently a product of attitude, of interpersonal relationships, and of conscious efforts to seek out and identify distinctive aspects of our individual natures. Parents are challenged and privileged to detect, nurture, and respond to each child's unique qualities, tastes, and needs. Uniqueness—like value and equality—grows in the confirmation; when loved ones respond affirmatively and confirm an individual's unique behavior or view, that person's sense of being unique expands and deepens. With extra effort, political and economic structures can be redesigned to build in space for uniqueness as well.

Divine Love, the Source of All Dignities

Over the years, after teaching this Mishnah on the intrinsic dignities of an image of God, I have asked students—or they have asked me: What is the source of these values? What makes a human being so special as to be more precious than any amount of money? Is this a gift from God and, if so, why has God given a gift of these particular dimensions?

The Lord could have bestowed different or finite values on humans or elected different people to unequal status. Many religions and cultures have asserted just that—that God bestowed royalty on royal families, or aristocracy on certain classes. At the time when the American Declaration of Independence affirmed that "all men are created equal" and justified this claim as "self-evident," slavery was tolerated and women were not treated as equals.

More recently, increasing numbers of people have rejected a range of hierarchical traditions. This response has leapt over cultural barriers, breached religious walls of status, broken down colonial empires. Some authoritarian regimes have claimed that freedom, minority rights, and equality before the law are peculiarly Western values and are not universally valid; yet even in those countries, grassroots movements arise and claim these rights. What accounts for this? Is some kind of personal mechanism or radar at work?

The same question can be posed as to the dignity of uniqueness. Many cultures place great value on the collective. Individualism is often seen as rebellious or even pathological. Yet here, too, more recent times have witnessed the growth of self-assertion and an intensified search for personal meaning. Is there some internal mechanism that generates uniqueness—and the demand to be entitled to its expression?

Over the years, the most frequent answer from my students has been to point to the soul, which, like a spark from the Divine Soul, is a "piece" of God placed in each person, distinguishing human beings from all other creatures. God is infinite life, infinite value, unlimitedly free and unique, and a fraction of God's Divine value and dignity gets integrated into each and every person. It is like placing a valuable diamond into a ring or necklace; the jewel dramatically increases the value of the jewelry.

The statement that humans are *tzelem elohim* reflects that human dignity is rooted in God—which is to say, it does not originate with society. Whether the state respects or violates human dignity, it is *not* its source. However, I am reluctant to attribute human dignities to a specific object or source, like the soul, that can be given and also taken away. The imagery of soul itself, a discrete spirit separate from the body that is inserted at the beginning of life and removed at the moment of death, is also problematic, as is the notion that the soul is an artifact from the Divine realm, infused into the human shell, rather than an intrinsic part of the human organism. I have always felt that the biblical concept of unity of self, in which the spirit and body are "fused," does greater justice to human nature than the dualist approach that separates body and soul. The conception of a unified self also makes for healthier attitudes toward the body.

In reflecting on this conundrum of the source of dignities, I asked myself a question: What in my life is of infinite value, equal, and unique? I have many precious possessions, but none are of infinite value. Many of my friendships, connections, and accomplishments mean a lot to me—but infinitely valuable? Irreplaceably unique? I don't think so.

Then it became clear to me. My wife . . . my children . . . *the ones I love*—are, by dint of that fact, of infinite value to me. Not only would I give away all my possessions to save them; I would give my life itself for the ones I love. If I love someone, that person becomes, ipso facto, equal to me. All I possess is of no consequence compared to the equal value and dignity of my loved one. The same holds true for uniqueness. The one I love is irreplaceably unique. Even elements that society may perceive as idiosyncratic or funny or inferior are parts—treasured parts—of the uniqueness of the people I love.

My wife often tells the story of her father (whom she loved very much and who loved her) walking home. Their house stood on top of a hill in Seattle. One day when she was a young girl, she stood with two friends on the porch looking down the hill at a man walking up slowly. As he drew closer, her friends began to point and laugh: look at that man with the funny walk coming up the hill. Blu, instead, saw her father with his distinctive gait. She was always excited to see the walk, for it meant that her beloved parent would soon be home. For the first time in her life, it occurred to her that he showed a limp—a deformity in gait—in the eyes of others, rather than simply exhibiting the distinctive cadence of the man she loved.[11]

Not only is love the generator of human infinite value, equality, and uniqueness, it is *the main source evoking those very qualities* internally. When receiving love, feeling the depth of the attachment of my lover, my own sense of being of infinite value expands and becomes more rooted within me. My capacity for uniqueness, my willingness to show it, my delight in expressing it—all blossom within me in the interaction with love. Thus the other's love comes to embrace my totality—beyond all the details, the strengths, the limitations.

To speak of *all* human beings being of infinite value, equal, and unique is another way of saying that God loves every human being. Some modern commentaries have suggested that the biblical word for compassion, *rahamim*, comes from the Hebrew word *rehem* (womb). Perhaps a better translation of the Psalms verse is that "God's womb love [mother love] extends to all God's creatures" (Ps. 145:9). Such a boundless love confers the dignity of infinite value and equality on all human beings and evokes their uniqueness, even if they live in a society that denies their dignity or their humanity. In God's eyes, humans are always in this state of dignity.

Despite this ideal, however, in every human society people are sometimes swayed—brainwashed, as it were, by culture and society—that they have none of these dignities. Therefore, the Torah's account in Genesis, telling people that they are images of God, represents an act of love. At Sinai, God intervened in human history and revealed to humans that they were images of God. In the Exodus, the liberation of the slaves revealed to them that they were not Egyptian property. Rather, they were humans, loved and created by God to seek out a homeland and build a society that honored their dignity.

Revelation and religion exist to communicate this truth to all people. Rabbi Akiva says: "Beloved is the human, who was created in the image of God."[12] Rabbi Akiva confirmed that being an image of God—with its attendant dignities—means that one is in a constant state of being loved. Rabbi Akiva then stresses that this love is raised to a further level. Given that human society does not act on this truth and treat all people as they deserve to be treated, God reveals to people that they are loved and made in the image of God: "Even greater love was shown by God in that the human is informed that he was created in the image of God."[13] In Akiva's teaching, the creation of human life stems from God's love. The act of God's revelation to humans of this status is a further act of Divine love.

Strengthening Human Capacities

As an image of God, every human being is born with godlike capacities for consciousness, relationship and love, power and vitality, and freedom. These gifts can be degraded or developed through human interventions. While hostile individuals and oppressive societies can deny these qualities, discourage their use, and diminish them, these godlike capacities and behaviors can also be helped to develop and expand toward their infinite source. Through growth, education, and help from others, the image of God can become more like God. Humans are commanded to strive to become more godly by the instruction, v'halakhta bidrakhav, "You shall walk in God's ways" (Deut. 28:9).

This is one of the great dialectical moves of Jewish tradition. Humans are called to become more godlike—but not to confuse their growing capacity with a loss of boundaries. They are to become more *like* God— but avoid the self-deceiving conclusion that they are becoming God. As we will see, such self-absolutization leads to idolatry, to behaving like a false god, to a self-deified human—a no-God.

Six times the book of Deuteronomy speaks of walking in God's ways (Deut. 10:12, 11:22, 19:9, 26:17, 28:9, 30:16). In all cases, the context is connected to loving God or becoming a committed covenantal partner to God. In all cases, the instruction to observe Divine commandments closely precedes or follows this call to walk in God's ways. From this link, the Talmud deduces that God wants more from humans than observance of commandments, something more personal, more closely connected to the nature of the Divine. Since walking in God's ways cannot be understood literally—God does not walk; and what are God's ways?—the Rabbis conclude that this commandment calls humans to develop an orientation toward humanity that is like God's, by imitating behaviors defined as the expression of God's being. Psalm 146:7–9 says that God "provides justice for the oppressed; gives food for the hungry; sets the imprisoned free; restores sight to the blind; raises up those who are bowed down [and depressed]; gives love to the righteous; protects the stranger; lifts up the orphan and widow [vulnerable people]; and makes the way of the wicked torturous." We should do the same in all these situations. The Talmud's formulation is *mah hu*—just as God does, *af atah*—so should you. In the process of increasing the quality of life for more people, we upgrade the Godlike capacities of our own lives.

Rabbi Soloveitchik suggests that *imitatio dei*, modeling ourselves on God, is a general moral guide that ought to shape our ethical behavior in areas of life beyond specific commandments—a quantum leap in broadening the mitzvah of walking in God's ways.[14] Rather than restrict imitation of God to the formulation *mah hu, af atah*, which directs us to be compassionate, loving, and gracious, Soloveitchik takes off from the characterization of God as the glorious or dignified Ruler (*melekh hakavod*, Ps. 24:8,10), suggesting that humans are called to affirm their dignity and develop all their capacities: the greatness of humanity is to become more Godlike.[15] Becoming more like God is at once an acknowledgment of being rooted in—and an expression of affinity for—the Deity, as well as a desire to partner and cooperate with the Divine plan. As a result, when parents and society develop a human being's capacities, they are engaging in the highest religious act: creating and refining an image of God. Out of improving a human's mind—or capacity for love, or creative power—an infinitely valuable creature emerges, one who can participate in *tikkun olam*, the shared Divine and human partnership to repair the world.

Human Consciousness

The Infinite Divine Consciousness created the vast universe of reality. Humans, using their developed frontal cortex, became the first living forms to make some sense of the universe. The development of mathematics, logic, the scientific method, and, in recent centuries, the grasp of the truly infinite dimensions of the universe in space and time, have raised such understandings to higher levels. Contemporary physics' understanding of the Big Bang, its ability experimentally to detect radio waves from the post–Big Bang noise as well as ripples in time and space that confirm the inflation of the universe in the first trillionth of a trillionth of a second, all express a profoundly expanded consciousness. With every closer step we take to seeing reality as God sees it (however infinite the gap remains), we can experience miracles and wonders in nature more clearly and thus be dazzled by the Divine. This idea expands upon Maimonides' point that physics and astronomy are fundamentals of Torah: methods of understanding God's ways and connecting to the Divine.[16]

Human Power

Rabbi Soloveitchik particularly points us to the religious significance of the increased human power generated in modern civilization; properly used, it intensifies human dignity. He views these activities as a fulfillment of the Divine mandate to be, or become, human, explaining, "Man is a dignified being and to be human means to live with dignity."[17] For Soloveitchik, dignity is specifically equated with man's capability of "exercising control" over his life and fate: "The brute's existence is an undignified one because it is a helpless existence. . . . Man of old who could not fight disease and succumbed in multitudes . . . with degrading helplessness could not lay claim to dignity. Only the man who builds hospitals, discovers therapeutic techniques and saves lives is blessed with dignity."[18]

Soloveitchik extends this perspective to industrial progress as well. Thus the growth of human power—enabled by human consciousness expanding creatively through science, medicine, and technology—is the fulfillment of a "mandate, entrusted to him by his Maker. . . . It is a manifestation of obedience to rather than rebellion against God."[19]

Of course, it is essential that this increased power be used covenantally—that is, with restraint and on the side of life. Soloveitchik insists, "There is no dignity without responsibility"; control must be tempered by respect for the environment and for life, and by awareness that one is accountable to God. Still, humans can only act responsibly insofar as they develop the power to act and change human fate.[20]

Sadly, the increase in human power has often turned into abuse of power. In the past century we have seen widespread environmental exploitation and numerous oppressive regimes, with the enrichment of certain people connected to the impoverishment of others. In the absence of covenantal commitment to God and power limits, these acts diverge from God's direction—the side of life and quality of life—to the side of death and of degrading life. This thrust must be contained or reversed.

An environmental movement is burgeoning worldwide. People throughout the globe are making serious efforts to achieve true democracy for all. While the outcome is far from settled and victory for life far from assured, I believe that, thus far, more humans have been more fully realized as images of God by this process than have been degraded by it. Religion must assure people that increased human power is not intrinsically erosive of relationship to God; rather, it should enable a more active human role in the partnership. Such an approach would enable the covenantal community to make a greater contribution to achieving *tikkun olam*.[21]

Human Love

Another primary capacity of the Divine is love, expressed as a caring relationship to all of Creation. Nature reflects God's "open hand" that pours forth life in profusion—which in turn provides sustenance for all creatures (Ps. 145:16).[22] The Lord hears the cries of need and, distinctively, responds to those suffering or in need (Ps. 145:19). In Isaiah's vision, human beings who are lowly and oppressed—those whom people tend to shun as being weak or marginal—are in fact the ones to whom God draws closer (Isa. 57:15). In the same way, the Divine senses the pain of people who are exploited—orphans, widows, strangers or outsiders—and responds with love and justice (Deut. 10:17-18). True, this is metaphoric language. Still, the Talmud insists that Divine sympathy and emotional bonding with humans is built into reality.[23] The Lord was driven by desire for the ancestors of the Jewish people (Deut. 7:7-8, 10:15) and for the people Israel, enough to single them out and enter into a covenant to liberate them (Deut. 7:7-8; compare Amos 3:2).[24] The same redeeming love is extended to all peoples—even the enemies of Israel, such as the ancient Philistines and the Arameans (Amos 9:7). Isaiah implies the same when he speaks of Egypt and

Assyria being recognized as covenantal peoples someday, just like Israel (Isa. 19:24–25).

The Divine is steadfast and faithful in love, no matter what (Isa. 54:7–10). This does not mean that God gives Israel free rein. God expects Israel to live ethically and create a just society, and chastises the people when they fall short. The commitment God seeks from Israel, the beloved one, is to live with righteousness and justice, with goodness and compassion. Since this is covenantal love, the marriage is forever. Even when the partner falls short, the love and the covenant are renewed.[25]

The task of parents, of society, of religion is to nurture and develop this Godlike capacity for loving in every individual. Religion can hold up the model of a loving and forgiving God and assure people they are never alone. It can teach *"imo anokhi v'tzarah* I am with him [the human] in trouble" (Ps. 91:15). Such teachings can encourage people to get to know the soul of the other, including when that other is an outsider, or is weak (Exod. 22:20; compare Deut. 10:19).

Historically, religion has often shut off certain people from others. Now it is called to encourage contact and enable friendships and relationships to develop. Such shifts can cultivate a greater, more godlike human capacity to love others and to love a neighbor as one truly loves oneself.

Human Freedom

V'halakhta bidrakhav, to walk in God's ways, can also be seen as a call to humans to appreciate and approximate Divine freedom. Here again, religion can condition people, enslave them to routine, narrow their focus to the group (defined in opposition to others), teach them to be obedient and never think for themselves — or it can enlarge people's capacity for freedom. The covenant itself is based on each person's freedom to either act in accordance with the Divine plan or to act against it. Soloveitchik again points to the centrality of freedom: "The very validity of the covenant rests on the juridic-halakhic principle of free negotiation, mutual assumption of duties, and full *recognition of the equal rights* of both parties concerned with the covenant."[26] The covenant both assumes human freedom and nurtures it. The concept of covenant itself, properly taught, encourages freedom to initiate ways of improving the world and social entrepreneurship, for as a partner the person understands that one cannot simply "leave it to God." Hence, developing an individual's freedom can lead to the expansion of that person's image of God. And not only this: it can facilitate more activity to repair the world—which, in turn, can enable more images of God to blossom.

Human Life

Finally, the most fundamental Divine capacity is life itself. Like God, parents and peers should communicate love of life. They can embrace experience and teach children not to fear growth and change. By affirming life, by upgrading it, by creating the ideal conditions for it, the human becomes a partner in God's Creation. In so doing, the human is imitating God and becoming more Godlike at the same time.

The Jewish religion also seeks to play a major role in developing the human capacity for experiencing life. Blessings that celebrate the taste of food, the beauty in people, and the wonders of nature instill this ultimate spirit and mindfulness.[27] This affirmative religious approach to life teaches that "a person will have to stand [answer] in [the final] judgment, for every [legitimate] pleasure they did not take in this world."[28] Soloveitchik affirms: "Holiness means the holiness of earthly, here-and-now life."[29] In sum, upgrading one's human capabilities to live life deeply represents the highest response to God's call to "choose life" (Deut. 30:19). This is the most religious activity we can undertake. It supports our experience of the fundamental dignities of human beings as images of God, helps make humans into better partners, and increases the presence of God in the world.

3

Tikkun Olam and the Triumph of Life

Just as Divine love is the source of human dignity and the motivation for the religious experience of God's revelation, it also drives the second core Jewish narrative or teaching, classically called redemption (*geulah*). After modern Jewish theological discourse, I call this concept *tikkun olam*, the repair and perfection of the world. A love that bestows infinite value on the other wants the best for the other. The present state of the world and the powers-that-be in it do not do justice to the uniqueness of every human being—and often deny or crush it. Therefore, the Divine wants a perfected world for beloved humanity (and other forms of life) to live in. That is why Judaism carries the banner of messianism—a call for a fundamental transformation of the world for the better.

The original Genesis Creation story shows that God wants this world to be a paradise (see Gen. 1, 2). A perfect world—comparable to Shabbat on the seventh day of Creation—is a world full of life and no death, with all needs provided for, with everything in its right place, with peace between all creatures, and with harmony in nature and society. That is the Divine goal for Creation. To attain this, Judaism champions a process of liberation and improvement for humanity, culminating in the Messianic Age. In that future state—the repaired world—the infinite value, equality, and uniqueness of every person will be honored and upheld in all the material conditions and spiritual interactions of daily life. Out of love, God promises that this final state will be reached. Out of love, God calls on humans to join in the process of world repair. This is why Creation is inextricably linked to redemption in Judaism.

The Jewish teaching that the present condition of the world can and must be changed has been a driving element of Judaism's extraordinary impact on human civilization. The Bible insists that the status quo can — and must — be overcome. The final state of the Earth will be far better (for humans and for all living things) than the present reality. Judaism further insists that this transformation will be achieved in this world of material reality, known by the five human senses. Thus the work of redemption must be done in this life and in this world.

Perfect Creation as Model for the Perfected Future

The opening account of Creation is suffused with the concept of final perfection. In the Middle East, where Judaism was born, a mythic trope told of a primordial age in which the Earth was a paradise, and would be again, recovered in an eventual final climax of history. Scholars call this idea *Urzeit ist Endzeit* — the primordial time is mirrored in the end-time.[1] The ancient Israelites to whom Genesis was revealed probably heard the story with the overtone that Genesis was a portrait of this final state.

The biblical prophets, too, evoke Eden in their portrait of the final redemption. For example, Isaiah's idyllic scene of the final peace is clearly an intertextual reference to the Garden of Eden story in Genesis. The humans' forfeit of the right to live as man and woman in the innocent natural paradise led to our flawed world (Gen. 3:1–13). Now there is enmity between the woman's children and the snake's: the human tries to smash the snake's head and the snake bites the human's heel to poison him (Gen. 3:14–15). But, in Messianic times, the human baby will safely play on the lair of a poisonous snake and a nursling will touch the adder's den (Isa. 11:8). Wolves and leopards will live together with sheep and kid goats, and lions will eat vegetation just as cows do (Isa. 11:6–7). As in Eden, there will be harmony among all species (see Gen. 1:29–30).

Messianism is intrinsically tied to Creation. In the Garden of Eden, all forms of life have all they need to live. None are in conflict with one another. None of the enemies of human life and dignity—poverty, hunger, oppression, war, sickness, death—are present. Therefore, humans and all forms of life reach full realization. This is the kind of world that the God who lusts for life seeks to bring into being, one in which fullness of life and all its dignities are realized.[2] Hence, the world as it exists now must be perfected to meet this standard.

Lest anyone think that working to make the Earth a paradise is a fool's errand, the Hebrew prophets repeatedly report a Divine promise that this goal will be realized.[3] The classical prophets of Israel spell out details of the messianic reality, including the figure of a human redeemer who leads the way. Centuries later, the Rabbis further fleshed out aspects of the world-to-come and confirmed the centrality of the doctrine in Judaism.[4] Thus the Jewish religion enters the existing world with a teaching and a mission. The teaching is about the unseen, sustaining, loving God who is committed to perfecting this world to the point where life is prevalent everywhere and sustained in all its fullness. The mission is for humanity to join with the Creator, who has reached out to us, as partners to make this happen (this is the Covenant, which we will discuss in chapter 6). This alliance will complete the work of Creation.

The goal of this partnership is nothing less than achieving the victory of life over all opposing forces that destroy, degrade, or undermine it. Collectively, all of humanity is called on to work to reduce the agents of counterlife, and to develop life-sustaining resources by repairing what is functioning the wrong way. Collectively, all humans are instructed to recreate their societies so that these collectives uphold life as they fully honor the dignities of all beings and deepen the quality of life for all. The Jews are of course part of humanity, but Judaism also asks this particular people to see themselves as role models and pacesetters for this work.

Tikkun Olam: Surmounting the Obstacles to Life

Anything that causes suffering or human degradation is an obstacle to be surmounted in the work of *tikkun olam*, repairing the world, with the aim of its final perfection.

Hunger and Poverty

If the infinite value of human beings is to be upheld, poverty must be overcome. Up to two billion people worldwide currently live on less than two dollars a day—an amount painfully insufficient to their needs. Lack of food and medicine, inadequate shelter, unclean water, poor or no prenatal care—all of these lead to poorer health and higher death rates. Poverty also leads to child labor and impedes children's access to education.

Starvation kills and hunger leaves people vulnerable to killer diseases. Yet, in our time, all that is lacking is money and proper distribution channels. The Earth now produces enough food to feed the entire world population—but the money needed is not in the hands of the hungry, or the food is not in the right places. Since many other people are well off enough to buy sufficient food, the phenomenon of hunger violates the dignity of equality as well as of infinite value.

The task of eliminating hunger is daunting and complicated. Industrial agriculture provides massive food supplies for a burgeoning world population, but it also generates much suffering for animals, environmental degradation, and other problems. Thus, creators of technology and fertility, innovators of crops and seeds, financiers of land development and food distribution are essential for *tikkun olam*. But they—and political leaders upholding proper regulation of these innovations— must establish the controls and limits equally needed to achieve the goal. Daily work and professional accomplishments become part of the movement to redeem the world, provided they do not act destructively or exploitatively toward nature and humans.

Similarly, in the United States of America, one of the wealthiest societies in all of human history, tens of millions of people cannot afford medical insurance. Without coverage, the person who cannot pay the costs of medical visits postpones treatments and consultations until problems become critical. Thus a lack of financial resources effectively devalues human life. Similarly, in the legal system, people who are poor are more frequently jailed for crimes, more likely victimized by inadequate legal representation, and less able to get legal breaks because they cannot afford adequate legal help.[5]

Putting an end to poverty, with the goal of better approximating humans' infinite value in their daily lives, requires a vast increase in wealth. In this generation, China and India have taken hundreds of millions of people out of poverty. The primary engine for this economic advance has been a quantum leap in industrialization and commerce. However, out of desire to keep these new industries competitive, governments have applied lax standards against pollution. To attract investment, they tolerate lower wages and weak safety standards. As a result, industrial cities in both countries, and elsewhere, suffer from highly polluted air. Many illnesses and deaths can be traced to the poor air quality. But despite pressure for tighter regulation and antipollution measures, these reforms have not occurred, in part because the governments and the population (tacitly, or by continuing to flock to cities for work) feel that it is better to die of smog in Beijing at the age of fifty-five or sixty-five than to die of hunger and illness in a farm village at thirty-five. More affluent developed countries have sufficient resources to allow themselves the "luxury" of redeeming environmental degradation. Similarly, the wealthiest countries of Europe have stronger safety nets and welfare provisions for people who are poor and disadvantaged.

Plainly and simply: manufacturing and wealth translate into human dignity and value — or at least their potential. Riches do not automatically lead to better treatment of people. The American safety net is weaker than the European one even though the U.S. could afford a more robust system of care. Religious and ethical concerns must be voiced to translate resources into care. Still, the need for resources remains fundamental. It will take a much higher level of affluence to universally upgrade the value placed on human life and to galvanize the willingness and ability to do what is necessary to fully uphold life.

Reaching the needed level of general affluence is a staggering challenge. The growth of wealth itself places great strains on resources and on the Earth's capacity to sustain development. The high costs of preventing the negative side effects of industrialization add considerably to the necessary increase in economic resources. This growth will not be accomplished overnight, or in one fell swoop. Nor can full equality be achieved by a redistribution of existing resources and assets. That is why adding wealth is part and parcel of *tikkun olam*. Achieving affluence is a steady process that will take generations to complete.

This realization clarifies another facet of the task. *Tikkun olam* is not just about social justice and help for the poor of the world. It includes other necessary steps that grease the wheels of development, including maximizing financing, increasing productivity, generating businesses that distribute goods more efficiently, and creating millions of jobs that can be pathways out of poverty. Maimonides pointed out that the highest form of *tzedakah* (charity) is to give a loan to start a business or to offer a job that enables a person to become self-sufficient. To those receiving this kind of *tzedakah*, overcoming poverty goes hand in hand with a greater dignity and sense of equality. The manufacturer who generates new jobs that pay a living wage and the banker who facilitates the financing of new industries or wider distribution of goods are engaged in the sacred work of *tikkun olam*. They become true partners in the work of redemption, because increasing wealth is a critical part of achieving *tikkun olam*. Isaiah, understanding this task, brings out God's promise to pour forth prosperity in the coming age like a mighty stream in flood (Isa. 66:12).[6]

Oppression

A world that fully honors the dignity of equality will have to end oppression in all its forms. Racism is an assault on the equality of the image of God. Antisemitism usually offers as its rationale that Jews are evil—and less than human. Sexism is an attack on the female image of God.

These "isms" are not merely sins against God. The entrenched tradition that views women as being inferior—including the strong religious traditions that ascribe them second-class status—has material as well as spiritual consequences. The view that women's lives are worth less than infinite value leads to lower levels of care for them—even from their own families. This results in poorer nutrition, lesser medical treatment, reduced educational investment, and shortened lives for women. At the beginning of the twenty-first century, the economist Amartya Sen described a massive deficit of women in East Asia, from infancy to adulthood. The causes, still operating, range from infanticide to poorer feeding to doctors treating boys' but not girls' illnesses. At every step of the life cycle, women receive the short end of the stick. The final outcome is a deficit on the order of hundreds of millions of women.[7] In armed conflicts from the Balkans to Rwanda, armies have practiced systematic rape of women to terrorize local populations and gain territorial advantage. These tactics rely on the ingrained cultural view that women are secondary and the objects of men's power. Tragically, these powerful social conventions generate behavioral assumptions that strangle the inner dignities of women. This cultural filter blocks the recognition of the female image of God—a recognition that would stop such behavior in its tracks.

All too many systems of oppression, rooted in dehumanization, result in violations of human dignity. Antisemitism over the centuries has led to discrimination, robbery, ghettoization, expulsions, violence against, and murder of Jews, culminating in the Holocaust—genocide and cruelty on a total and unprecedented scale. Racism's effects range from enslavement to permanent Jim Crow conditions, from apartheid regimes to deprivations of educational opportunity, each of which deforms and distorts economic patterns throughout the world. Higher levels of poverty, crime, and social exclusion are found in many Muslim and other immigrant communities in Western countries where they suffer from discrimination. All of these mistreatments violate the inherent dignities of every human being created in the image of God. They must be overcome in the process of *tikkun olam.*

Dictatorships also deprive people of justice, legal protection, and the right to exercise free will in behavior and speech. The elimination of protest and other agents of reform degrades citizens' quality of life. Living conditions decline, at least for some, and there is no redress. Tyrannical regimes, therefore, are incompatible with the intrinsic dignities of human beings. The process of *tikkun olam* must extend into the political arena. The day will come when the rulers imitate God and "give judgment for the poor and needy" (Ps. 82:3), "help the deprived and the lowly escape [from oppression]" (Ps. 82:4), and "uplift the orphan and the widow [that is, the vulnerable]" (Ps. 146:9). Isaiah promises that the messianic ruler will judge with justice so that the earthly poor will also have fair and equal treatment before the law (Isa. 11:4).

War

War is incompatible with the preciousness of human life. Wars are won by destroying infinitely valuable, equal and unique, irreplaceable human lives. Even the winners suffer devastating losses. In this unredeemed world, war may sometimes be necessary, as in a defensive war against an invader who threatens to destroy you; or permitted, where a threat is not imminent but judgment suggests that a preventative war would preclude the eventual victory of evil. Still, in the end state of Paradise, war is simply too great an offense against the value of human life. Isaiah and Micah predict that by the end of days, when the nations learn to walk in God's ways, "nations will receive judgment and correction to settle disputes"; then "they will beat their swords into plowshares and their spears into pruning hooks. Nation will not raise up sword against nation and they shall not learn war anymore" (Isa. 2:3–4; Mic. 4:3). In an age of peace, human life will flourish. Thus the work of conflict resolution, of peacemaking, of creating military and political balances of power that prevent war, of the development of international mechanisms upholding freedom and human rights—all these are part of the process of *tikkun olam*.

Sickness

The fullness of human life and dignity demands the overcoming of disease. Not only do illnesses cut life short, they degrade the quality of life along the way. Cancer shortens lives while causing enormous suffering to patients and families. Alzheimer's disease and other forms of dementia assault the dignity of sufferers, ripping away their memories and uniqueness, erasing the particular life experiences that defined and shaped their distinctive personas. Therefore, repair of the world requires a medical, psychological, scientific, and cultural effort to cure disease and heal mental disorders. Rabbi Joseph B. Soloveitchik points out that creative medicine to develop cures is a form of *imitatio dei*.[8] I would stress that this is the expression of true partnership, a form of *tikkun olam* that literally repairs a flaw in the created fabric of existence. Pursuing medicine and science in this manner is a sacred calling. The human being "is trying to carry out the mandate entrusted to him by his Maker."[9]

Tikkun Olam and the Confrontation with Death

The ultimate logic of messianism and of the thrust to realize the fullness of intrinsic human dignities in the world demands that, if we want to achieve a perfect world that fully upholds life, we must confront death itself. Death is the ultimate contradiction to human dignities. Yesterday this person was full of life—equal and unique, loving, creating, teaching—a being of infinite value to me and all who loved her. Today she is dead. Lost is the infinite value; gone is the equality; the lifeless body before us is helpless, unresponsive. The corpse can neither express uniqueness nor feel it within. That fate is so shattering that Ecclesiastes responds to normal death with the outburst "[life is] vanity of vanities; all is vanity [empty, void]" (Eccles. 12:8). The fact that death appears to be indifferent to the quality of the life only deepens the disillusion with life. "For the same fate [death] happens to the righteous and the wicked, to the good and the pure and the impure ... of all that happens on earth, this is the worst, for there is the same fate [death] for all" (Eccles. 9:2-3). Death is the ultimate violation of humans' infinite value, equality, uniqueness. How can it be present in a perfected world?

This suggests that the ultimate goal of messianic repair of the world should be to overcome death itself. This indeed is the prophets' understanding. "Death shall be swallowed up in eternity [of life]," proclaims Isaiah, "the Lord God shall wipe away the tears from all faces" (Isa. 25:8). Hosea prophesies: "From the grave [Sheol], I [God] shall redeem them; from death I shall release them" (Hos. 13:14). Isaiah explains that as long as death exists, it seems to contradict the presence of a loving, Infinite Source of life who wants life to win out in this world. Even if we have religious experiences, even if we verbally affirm our faith, the shocking fate, the collapse of values in death, is dissonant. As it were, it erodes the foundation of the faith, or, if you will, the solidity of the relationship. Messianism that seeks to perfect the world for life and, thereby, make manifest the presence of God must strive to overcome death itself.

This conversation is different in kind from our exploration of *tikkun olam* so far. Death is a universal inescapable force. Is this quest to overcome it a turn to magical and wishful thinking? There is a deeper question here. Death has been a natural limit on human life. Some have been crushed by the phenomenon or knocked off their balance, but others accept this limit and even use it to make something more out of the time allotted to live. Remember, death also puts a limit to all sorts of evils; the worst tyrants cannot live forever. And what about the natural succession and the fresh possibilities brought on by the arrival of a new generation? To the physician, philosopher, and ethicist Leon Kass, trying to escape death smacks of a rebellion against being human. It hints at a vision that rejects and resents human limitations. It is at risk therefore of turning sinister, or of monomaniacal drive that can descend into reckless chase, stopping at nothing and ending in catastrophe.[10] Seeking so drastic a change in the human condition may foreshadow readiness to reengineer mortals and manipulate them (use them up? throw them away?) for an imagined higher purpose.

We might aim instead for a limited version of defeating death, in the forms of a significant extension of life expectancy and a healthier, more vital body during the later years. Indeed, in the past two centuries, life expectancy in developed countries has increased from the high thirties to the high seventies.[11] A classical precedent for this more modest approach to the war on death is found in Isaiah. In a late chapter the prophet suggests that in the Messianic Age, there will be an end to premature and untimely deaths. Life will be so extended that "a person dying at the age of one hundred will be considered to have died as a youth" (Isa. 65:20). Making those later years more vital and healthy would constitute a major expansion of the realm of life.

Our ultimate prize, however, is actually overcoming death. That is in the Torah's original vision: in the Garden of Eden, there was no death (compare Gen. 2:17; 3:3–5,14–19,22). As we shall see, the biblical Tabernacle and Temple complex, meant to be a microcosm of the past and future Eden, also mimicked that goal. No human corpses and no people who had contact with dead human bodies were allowed to enter the Temple. Thus, the House of God presented as a realm of life, exclusively. So, too, the Creation story is intended to engage humans in the cosmic rhythm of moving from nonlife to life and to inspire them to join the struggle on the side of life.

Most importantly, anyone who has deeply loved another human being to the point where the other was of infinite value, equal and unique, will appreciate how heartbreaking and devastating it is to lose that person to death. And no, there is no consolation; there is no filling of that hole in your life no matter the passage of time and the dulling of the pain. This very human love—which the Song of Songs insists "is [should be] as fierce as death" (8:6)—provides the moral ground and the driving force to seek to overcome death. This love, properly channeled, is not pathologically Promethean; it is life-seeking.

This goal—not only to validate, uplift, and enrich, but also extend this mortal life—is one of the boldest and most visionary steps in Jewish religion. Properly motivated, this is not a rejection of humans' brief life, but a desire for more. The Talmud states that in the creation of new life, humans are partners with God;[12] we need not be any less partners in spirit as we try to extend life or reduce the realm of death. Whether the outcome of such an effort is good or bad depends on our spirit in approaching this task. I propose to keep the awareness that we are partners of God, but we are not God—even as we push the envelope to realize the goal of total victory for life.

In this spirit, even as we strive for the messianic goal, we recognize death in our midst as a natural process and a limit on humans. Humans live dialectically with death. Given the brevity of human existence, we respond by living life with greater urgency and we search for significance. Accepting our mortality maturely, we do not resort to evasion or to dulling our senses to dodge the reality of loss. We resist the constant encroachment of inward death in our lives—as experienced in routine and stagnation—through creativity and constant renewal. Then, as Jewish tradition prescribes, when death comes we respond with tender loving care of the dead, honoring their memory while expressing our solidarity with the living.[13]

Resurrection as the Ultimate Expression of World Repair

In truth, the Torah's dream of perfecting the world goes even beyond the overcoming of death. The ultimate statement of its hope is the teaching of resurrection.[14]

It would be remarkable enough to cure all diseases and to strengthen life to the point of preventing all prospective deaths, and yet the Jewish hope soars beyond such incredible outcomes. To make this world perfect, one would have to annul all deaths retroactively. This is Isaiah's end-time vision: "Your dead shall live; my corpse(s) shall stand up. Awake and sing, you who dwell in the dust [grave]" (Isa. 26:19). Confirming this vision, the Rabbis made resurrection a core teaching of

Judaism and a hallmark of the Messianic Age.[15] In fact, the Rabbis were so successful in instilling the centrality of resurrection to the Messianic Age that the best-known religion to emerge out of Judaism and reach the non-Jewish world—namely, Christianity—made resurrection its central teaching and the proof of the arrival of the Messiah.

The Rabbis were so insistent on the centrality of resurrection that they positioned it in the second opening blessing of the *Shemoneh Esrei* (Eighteen Blessings), itself the central prayer of the Rabbinic liturgy. The blessing *meḥayeh hameitim*, who revives the dead, is said three times a day every day at the peak moment of the service, and said four and five times a day on Shabbat and holidays. The Rabbis of the Mishnah even insisted that one who denies resurrection of the body forfeits the Divine gift of immortality of the soul in the world-to-come.[16] I suspect this was their veto of the idea that immortality is more believable than regaining the life of a desiccating body. They were not willing to follow a religious strategy that proposed immortality, and immortality alone, as the consolation prize for having experienced the disappointment of injustice or innocent suffering during our earthly sojourn.

As it happened, the Sadducees, whose adherents included many in the religious establishment of aristocracy and priests, rejected the doctrine of resurrection. Fundamentalists of the Written Torah, they charged that this teaching of resurrection was not articulated in the Torah; rather, the Rabbis were fabricating new divine revelations in their Oral Torah and illicitly, even heretically, including resurrection as a sacred doctrine. The Rabbis struck back, insisting that resurrection was indeed authentic Divine teaching, and that anyone who affirmed resurrection but denied that it was from the Torah thereby forfeited their portion in the world-to-come.[17] In truth, the Rabbis' prooftexts that resurrection is in the Torah are a bit forced. The doctrine is certainly not spelled out in unmistakable detail. The most persuasive resurrection verse in the Torah is found in Deuteronomy 32:39: "See, now, that I, I am He [the God of the universe] and there is no other Lord with Me. *I will inflict Death and will bring to Life. I have wounded and will heal.* And there is none who can save from My hand [power]." The word sequence and the literary parallelism in the verse imply resurrection—the one who is wounded is the one who is healed; the one who is put to death is the one who will be restored to life. This is hardly a broadly descriptive, unequivocal statement of the concept, but the strained nature of the proof does not matter.[18] To the Rabbis, the main point was to reject any attempt to belittle resurrection's importance by suggesting it was of secondary derivation.

There are two profound religious approaches to life at the heart of the Rabbinic insistence on resurrection's central importance: the experience of human love and then the loss of the beloved person to death. When one's life is tied to another's, intertwined in a love so unlimited, fused by a need so urgent, connected by emotions so deeply felt and shared, the tear in the fabric of one's life is irreparable. Judah warned Joseph that their father Jacob was so linked by love to his youngest son, Benjamin, that his failure to come back was liable to lead Jacob to an agonizing decline and death (Gen. 44:18–30, especially vv. 29–30). A pious person may be tempted to find or give easy consolation for such a loss, saying that the deceased is with God, or in a better world. One can reach for new children, new life, as if that will take the place of the lost one. One can try to resolve the agony by saying that God will make up this loss by granting immortality—with a future reunion of the loved ones in a spiritual realm.

Yet all these resolutions have an element of falsity to them. To accept this consolation, one must block out the full presence, the incarnate person whom I loved. That person in all their uniqueness—physical, emotional, intellectual—that person with all their winning behaviors, all their flaws, all their specific being is the one I loved. There is no equivalent being; there is no substitute experience that can make me whole following this loss. A future spiritual reunion may be sublime, but it will lack the bodily, three-dimensional embrace of the person I loved. This sweaty, odoriferous, sometimes vital, sometimes frail, vulnerable, mortal person is the one I loved and who loved me. The only full correction of the loss would be to restore the actual, embodied, whole person whom I loved. This is the moral basis of the human need for nothing less than resurrection. Out of total love, trust, and at-homeness with a loving God, Judaism drew the strength to assert that when the world is perfected, the original love will be confirmed by the restoration of the loved one.

The second religious view on life enshrined in the idea of resurrection is the affirmation of the body—that frail, limited, vulnerable, mortal incarnation of an infinitely valuable, equal, unique body-soul self. The contrast of the often achy, frequently hungry, energetic but tiring body with the quest to experience far-reaching, unlimited human consciousness modeled by the infinitely sublime God prompts people to recoil from the body. For millennia, devotees of Eastern religion have sought to disengage from the body and its needs and drives through enlightenment, and thus connect to a higher, more perfect existence. Devout Jews, Christians, and Muslims have similarly glorified spiritual perfection, trying to starve the body's needs and hence fend off some degradation of behavior and attain a higher spiritual state. In the body's place, they have glorified a soul more worthy of earning God's love and of being at home with the Lord.

The Judaism of *tikkun olam* will have none of that. God loves us in all our limitations, in all our needs and weaknesses, with all our *shtick* and pettiness. The depth of life—in peak moments that end too swiftly, in profound connections that weaken and strengthen, in joy that comes and goes—is the most precious expression of being. At its best, for a finite moment, it is infinite; it is the affirmation, the celebration, the realization of life.[19]

There is nothing more holy than this life. There is no superior realm to work in. Rather, we finite humans should do our best to live, to love, to spend our lives repairing the world for ourselves and others and those yet to come. God so honors this truth that in the course of the final perfection, God will restore the actual beings we love through their resurrection. This is what the Rabbis affirmed by insisting on the teaching of resurrection.

The Rabbis understood how hard it would be to trust in such a doctrine. They fully recognized the universal power of death and the implausibility of being able to undo it. In the prayer of resurrection that they placed at the center of liturgy, they tacitly admitted the problem of credibility, all the while giving signals that pointed to the legitimacy of this hope. They inserted the phrase *mashiv haruach u'morid hagashem* ("[God] the One who sets the wind in motion and brings down rain") to remind people of resurrection experiences before their eyes, such as lifeless landscape bursting forth into the reborn carpet of green life after seasonal rains. They pointed to the daily miracles of the Divine economy—the provision of food to sustain all living—as the parallel that validates God's capacity to restore life to the lifeless, especially in light of God's abundant compassion or mother love. They referenced the upholding of the falling, healing of the sick, freeing of the imprisoned, as validations of the next leap in the series of wonders: that God would keep faith and perform miracles for those who lie in the dust. They acknowledged that this feat is beyond human capacity, but argued in return that God was incomparable. "Who is like You, the master of powers, of heroic accomplishments? Who can compare to You, a ruler who inflicts death and brings life, and grows redemption in stages?" This gave them the strength to affirm that God is faithful and to be trusted to accomplish the impossible—and to recommend this trust (in subtle, modest form) to all their descendants, those engaged in the covenant of redemption, seeking the total repair of the world.[20]

This is why I believe that Judaism's message of *tikkun olam* is best described as the teaching of *the triumph of life*. There is no metaphor that better captures this vision than resurrection. Stretching belief to the breaking point, not settling for reasonably limited goals, the Jewish religion asks humanity to set its course for a world that is so totally transformed that life wins out over all its enemies—and then goes back and reverses its defeats along the way.

I appreciate the scientific and other rational evidence that make this an unlikely assertion. I am not trying to prove resurrection scientifically—although, for the record, I believe that the covenant in Judaism means that the human partner should be able to make, or participate in, many of the miracles so remarkable as to be considered only doable by God. But my first argument to those who just cannot believe this is as follows: Treat it as a poetic reaching for the stars. That perfected state is how far we would like to go. Then work through the covenantal framework Judaism offers. Let us go step by step along the vector of increasing life, curing illness, preventing death, as far as we can go. The end of death will always be a lodestar far ahead that keeps us from settling for a mediocre outcome or settling down with the status quo along the way.

4

The Biblical Struggle of Life against Death

At the heart of the argument for the centrality of life in Judaism lies the biblical emphasis on the primacy of life. Rabbinic and later formulations, which often add richness and detail, were driven by the biblical vision. Nothing can match that vision in illuminating the end goals that Jewish religion seeks, and our examination of the significance of mitzvot as a way of life must be rooted there.

The biblical revelation starts with Creation, but with a central focus and fascination with its epiphenomenon, life. Throughout the world, there is an unrelenting struggle between life and death, or nonlife, to fill the world. God is on the side of life. In Isaiah's description: "This is the word of God, Creator of the Heavens, who alone is the Lord, who formed the Earth and is its Maker, who established it. It was not created to be a void; it was formed to be settled [filled with life]" (Isa. 45:18). To this end, the Torah sets up for human beings a way of life with direction illuminated by ritual, to channel human behaviors to the side of life. The central rituals that the Torah presents in Leviticus constitute nothing less than a code of life and death—to orient human behaviors toward life.

Temple Rituals: Purity vs. Impurity

The Bible describes the ancient Temple's ritual code of life in terms of purity. Life is pure; death is impure. To be in the direct presence of God, one must be pure. Since humans are an example of the highest form of life, a dead human being, the negation of human life, is the ultimate form of impurity, *avi avot hatum'ah*.[1]

Death, and decay as well, are forms of impurity and are to be banished from the Temple's sacred precincts. When animals are killed as sacrifices in the Temple, this is a case of utilizing the animal's life in the service of life and is not considered impure. By contrast, dead non-kosher animals—or animals that, having died from sickness or natural causes, are not kosher for eating—are sources of impurity, and cannot be brought into the Temple. Sin is the ethical code's counterpart of impurity; it represents an act on the side of death, because it is hurtful to another person or life. And so, whereas mitzvot (good deeds) act on the side of life and bring one closer to the Divine, sinful or evil acts remove one from God's presence.

Jacob Milgrom points out that, according to the Torah, there are three zones in human society.[2] First is the holy, in which the Divine Presence is so present that it is "manifest"; therefore, there is room only for life. The second zone is the impure, in which death or decay is dominant. Finally, the common is a neutral zone, which may border on and encounter the sacred; the impure may not. The Temple as House of God is a zone of pure life; no human death, or even a human touched by death, may enter. Those who have been touched by death and want to enter the Tabernacle or Temple go through an elaborate purification ritual that involves being sprinkled with a solution composed of the blood and ashes of a red heifer mixed with other materials (cedar wood, hyssop, and crimson red) that deepen the red color. The ritual cleanses and purges impurity, using blood (the carrier of life—see Lev. 17:11) as part of the ceremony; it symbolically restores a person from a state of impurity back to the side of life. It goes hand in hand with immersion in a *mikveh*, or living body of water, also a classic rebirth ritual.

The priests associated with the House of God are not only barred from coming into the Tabernacle or Temple in a state of impurity; they are restricted from contact with the dead, period. Except for burying a member of their immediate family, they may not enter a cemetery or a room or house where a corpse is present (Lev 21:1–4).[3] The High Priest—the only person allowed to enter the inner sanctum, the Holy of Holies, just once a year, to stand in the most manifest presence of God—may not make himself impure for any person, no matter how close (Lev. 21:11ff). The absence of decay, or rather the presence of the fullness of life, in the Tabernacle is further represented by the requirement that a priest who does Divine service must be a perfect physical specimen (Lev. 21:17–23). If he has physical defects, he may share in priestly food and gifts, but he cannot offer sacrifices or come near the altar (Lev. 21:23).

Why did the Bible allow sacrifices, the slaughter of animals, which in fact bring death into the House of God? Maimonides states that sacrifices were so universal that the Torah could not abolish them without leaving people feeling unconnected to God. Hence the Torah accepted sacrifices, but directed them into channels connecting to God, instead of to pagan gods and natural forces, including chthonic or death deities. Even the permitted animal sacrifices, however, are all about life, enabling "Israel to enter the sanctuary—the realm of holiness—and receive via the sacrifices the Divine blessing (cf. Exod. 20:21) of life-giving procreation and life-sustaining produce (Lev. 19:26; Exod. 23:10–19; Ezek. 44:30; Prov. 3:9–10)."[4]

Besides bringing sacrifices and purging pollution, the priests' further assignment is to teach the Jewish people how to "distinguish between the impure and the pure" and then act on the side of the pure, that is, of life.[5] The Jewish people in turn will serve as priests to the rest of humanity. The priests' task is to expand the zone of holiness, of life. They do this first by creating and running the microcosm of society inside the Tabernacle and Temple. They also teach people how to increase life and extend its sway in the general society.

The message in this code of Temple behavior is intended for the whole Jewish people. The Israelites are called to reach the level where "all of you will be *a kingdom of priests* and a holy nation" (Exod. 19:5). In the Torah's vision, the whole Earth will ultimately be purified of death and evil behaviors. Isaiah predicts that the day will come when "they will do no evil and no destructive acts in My whole Holy Mountain"

(Isa. 11:9). In the messianic context, this is the whole Earth. At present, however, the Earth is not fully redeemed; therefore, the Torah sets up the Tabernacle and then the Temple as the place of immediate perfection. This is, as it were, a messianic zone, where no physical death, spiritual evil, or unethical acts may enter. As Shabbat is in time, so the Temple is in space: the messianic reality in our midst. The priests—among whom there is no death, sin, physical infirmity, or impurity—act and live now as all the people will act in the redeemed future. Being in this place now, seeing these priestly prototypes of future humans now, gives the common people the experience of the messianic future. This encounter keeps them from accepting the present status quo as final. The vision made manifest undermines the mundane, compromised, sin-filled present, and inspires people to push on toward the final goal. Thus the Tabernacle foreshadows the final triumph of life toward which Judaism is forever striving.[6]

The Torah works with microcosms, inner circles that may be expanded. The Temple is the microcosm for space; Shabbat is the inner circle for time; the Jewish people is the inner circle for humanity. In time the inner circles will expand and include all those in the outer circle. Thus holy space will encompass Jerusalem, then Israel, and eventually the whole world. Shabbat will grow until the whole week is the zone of full life. The holy people will expand until all of humanity are holy people.

The Yom Kippur Ritual

The constant struggle between life and death is similarly expressed in the rituals of the Yom Kippur service in the Temple. As Milgrom writes, the purpose of the Yom Kippur ritual is not merely repentance or forgiveness of sins but rather purgation.[7] The purging agent for the sanctuary is the blood of the red heifer (again, blood representing the force of life), and it purges the pollution inflicted on the inner sanctum by any unremoved ritual impurities and the unrepented ethical sins committed by the people of Israel. On Yom Kippur, Israel's sins are "sent away" symbolically, by dispatching a goat to Azazel (wilderness) (Lev. 16:7–10).[8]

The annual Yom Kippur purgation is a response to the likelihood that some individuals will not fully remove their ritual impurities or correct their ethical misbehaviors. Without purification, the pollution of death remains in society and accumulates.[9] The same holds true even more intensively for sins: these too require sacrifices and removal lest their pollution accumulate and "attack" the Temple, the place of intensive Divine Presence.[10] The more powerful the impurity and the more heinous the sin, the more it "pushes" the Divine Presence away. Uncorrected individual impurities invade the outer space of the sanctuary. Unredressed (unintentional) communal sins penetrate more deeply than any individual's failures; they attack the inner (incense) altar. Both individual and communal categories of persisting pollution include instances when purification did not follow moral failures or contact with death or other sources of impurity. Wanton, unrepented sins, however, invade the most deeply—into the Tabernacle, into the Ark, into the inner sanctum. This is why the Yom Kippur purgation must be done annually, lest the pollution, not removed, become dominant in the holiest precincts. Death and evil are antithetical to God's presence in society—that is the message of the ritual code.

To translate this into another idiom, a society that allows a growing presence of death and an atmosphere of moral decay drives out the life-sustaining presence of God. A society that allows evil and murder to grow, without punishing, purging, and repenting regularly, becomes so deeply polluted, it suffocates the vital force of life. At some point, the build-up of pollution drives out God, "canceling" the sanctity of the Holy Temple. God, who normally "dwells with Israel in the midst of its pollutions" (Lev. 16:16), leaves this toxic environment. God's departure leaves an empty shell, void of sanctity, which is then open to destruction by the likes of the Babylonians and the Romans. This is what the prophet Ezekiel is describing when he envisions the Divine chariot leaving the Holy Temple.[11] The state of being cut off from God further weakens the forces of life and good, and feeds the growing power of death and evil.

Dietary Rituals as Expressions of Life Against Death

The Torah's whole dietary regulation system is coded to turn eating into a choice of life against death. The paradox at the heart of eating is that humans (like all life-forms) cannot live without eating: to eat is a choice of life. But this very act can mean the death of another creature. How can one reconcile this clash and maximize life? This is what the dietary laws set out to do.

The Creation narrative in the first chapter of Genesis sets out the ideal that all living beings, human and animal alike, should be vegetarians (Gen. 1:29–30). In a later chapter, the Torah teaches that God accepts the fact that the current world is not an ideal one and decides not to force immediate perfection. Instead, God commits to enter into covenant with humanity, working with humans to mend the world, step by step, until the final perfection. In the Noahide covenant, made after the Flood, God permits humans to eat meat. Still, there are restrictions on meat eating. This is meant to reiterate the ultimate principle of life not taking life. The first dietary restriction is placed on all of humanity: it is forbidden to eat the blood of the animal used for food. Since "the life of the flesh is in the blood," by not eating the blood, humans acknowledge that life is sacred and really should not be taken.[12] This points to the messianic future, when no life will be taken in order to live (Isa. 11:6–7).

The second set of restrictions upholding the sacredness of life concerns the regulation of slaughter. The throat is to be slit in the place where the major blood vessels will quickly and maximally drain the blood; this prevents eating blood. Simultaneously, cutting the jugular vein cuts off the supply of blood to the brain, thus rendering the animal unconscious with a minimum of pain. The subsequent Rabbinic articulation of shehitah (kosher slaughter) strengthens this emphasis on instant death. The knife blade must be razor sharp, perfectly smooth, without dents or nicks that could tear flesh and cause more pain.[13] The killing must be done in one stroke.

Yet a third restriction on meat eating is expressed in the biblical classification of permitted species. Most animals are *not* permitted. Permitted animals are marked by their chewing the cud (Lev. 11:3, 1:2,10,14); they are ruminants, with multiple stomachs to redigest their *exclusively herbivorous food*. All predatory animals are prohibited. (This is true of birds as well: while no signs are given in the Torah to mark kosher birds, the Rabbis conclude that all predatory birds are nonkosher and all nonkosher birds are predators.)[14] In effect, the Torah is saying that, at least symbolically, you are what you eat. You should not eat animals that live primarily on carrion or by killing other animals.

The upshot is that, while humans in general may eat all animals, Israelites, who are a messianic avant-garde, live by a higher standard. They eat fewer forms of life, having taken dietary steps toward eventual perfection. (As the House of God ran at a still higher standard of life affirmation than did the lay Israelites, even fewer animal species were consumed there—only three domestic herbivores and a few birds.)[15]

The general frame to the laws of kashrut also expresses the Torah's opposition to the killing and eating of other species. The higher the level of life, the more sacred it is—so the more eating of it is restricted. Thus fish, the lowest form of life permitted for eating, is restricted only as to species. (Kosher fish species must have fins and scales, ruling out crustaceans and other relatively plentiful Mediterranean seafoods.)[16] Birds, the next level up, are restricted by species *and* the manner of killing: *shehitah* is required to make bird meat kosher. Land animals, the highest level of life permitted for eating, are restricted by species, method of killing, *and* method of preparation. Animal meat, representing the death of the animal, may not be cooked or eaten together with milk, representing mother's milk, a source of life. The prohibition against cooking a kid in its mother's milk, which the Rabbis understood as applying to any preparation of both meat and milk, expresses the absolute contradiction of a source of life, the mother's milk, being used to uphold death itself, in the form of the slaughtered kid.[17] The Rabbis, in the Talmud and subsequent rulings, later added a further restriction: one must wait up to six hours after eating meat before eating milk foods. This "penalty" is solely inflicted on meat eating. No wait (penalty) is required after eating dairy.[18]

Other ritual eating prohibitions reflect this same polarity of life forces and prolife eating against antilife eating. The bans on eating animals associated with death are more intense or sweeping. The pig is singled out as repugnant, because pigs were offered to chthonic deities in the Near East and to gods of the underworld in both Hittite and later Greek cultures; in Egyptian culture, the pig was sacred to Seth, the force of evil.[19] The carcass of a kosher animal that dies without being ritually slaughtered is also prohibited for food, and causes impurity if eaten. The carcasses of certain land crawlers may not be eaten, either, and cause impurity if merely touched. By contrast, touching dead birds or fish brings no ritual impurity. In the symbology of the Torah, fish and birds were born out of the seas; the Torah says about them, on the fifth day of Creation, "Let the waters bring forth swarms of living creatures and birds that fly above the earth" (Gen. 1:20). Water is the great symbol of life in the Bible. Water still in its native habitat—not yet drawn forth from nature by humans—is the medium of purification. Immersion in the source of life restores to purity. By contrast, dead quadruped animals and the land-swarming reptiles are connected in origin to land or even the underground, the realm of death. Not a single species of reptile is kosher. In Leviticus, the Torah adds an extra injunction that calls for Israelites to be holy, on the side of life, and not join the side of death by using the animals that originated on the land and are by association suffused with death (Lev. 11:43–44).[20]

By not eating and not even touching dead animals except for those exempted through kosher slaughter, the Israelites are devoting themselves to holiness, "the way and nature of its God."[21] Israel separates itself—and its eating regimen—from the nations that act immorally (on the side of death) and worship idols, whose nature and ways are associated with death.

Rituals of Body Impurity That Express the Opposition to Death and Its Worship

The Torah goes on to apply the categories of ritual purity and impurity to other life experiences, to reinforce the message that Israelites should live on the side of life. The first concerns a woman who gives birth. Postpartum, she enters a state of ritual impurity (Lev. 14:16–32). Giving birth carries a paradoxical message. On the one hand, the woman / the parents have created life—the most Godlike act and the most powerful possible participation on the side of life. But in giving birth, she has temporarily weakened her body; short term, she has exhausted her fecundity. The postpartum loss of blood, equated with a weakening of life force, associates giving birth with a temporary loss of life-expanding capacity. Similarly, the menstruating woman is considered ritually impure; the menstrual blood reflects the decay and disintegration of an egg that had the potential to be turned into a living person (Lev. 12:1–3). In each case, to recover from her ritual impurity, the woman must undergo a purification rite, essentially a rebirth ceremony, centrally involving immersion in a *mikveh*.

In addition to refraining from sexual intercourse for a week during menstruation and after birth, the postparturient woman goes through an additional period of ritual impurity during which she cannot enter the Tabernacle: thirty-three days for a boy child (Lev. 12:3–4), and twice that long in the case of a baby girl (Lev. 12:5).[22] This distinction reflects her paradoxical relation to life.[23] She has made a climactic contribution to life—but is temporarily exhausted and weakened in life-giving capacity. She acts this out in refraining from sexual intercourse (as during menstruation). For a longer period, she does not enter the sanctuary, the realm of life rampant. As a baby girl may be able in the future to give birth, to produce life, in a way that a boy cannot, the impurity following a baby girl's birth is more intense and total than that of a baby boy.[24] A male's emission of sperm, too, leaves him in a state of impurity vis-à-vis the sanctuary, although it lasts only for a day (Lev. 15:16–18).[25] The pattern suggests that the weakening and loss of life in sperm ejaculation is ritualized for the same reasons but to a lesser degree, because it represents less enervation and is more quickly renewed than the loss of a single egg.

Tzara'at, a set of scale diseases marked by a wasting away of the body, especially in the peeling off of layers of skin, evoking associations with the disintegration of a corpse and the onset of death, are likewise associated with death and decay in the Torah. After the condition is checked or cured, these patients, too, must undergo purification rites. The key elements in purging the person from the power of death and restoring him to life are the usual icons of life force—live waters, crimson thread and red cedar (symbols of blood), and the blood of a sacrificial bird.[26] Those who have recovered bathe, immerse during and after the seven-day period, and bring a sacrifice (Lev. 14:1–9). Blood from the animal and oil from the accompanying libation are put on the patients. The sacrifice both reconnects recovered patients to the God of life and gives them assurance of a renewed flow of energy and vitality from God.[27] As Milgrom summarizes it: "The entire purification process is . . . a ritual, a rite of passage, marking the transition from death to life." In the end, the person "has passed from impurity to holiness, from death to life, is reinstated with his family and is reconciled with his God."[28]

These and similar parallel purification rites share two effects. First, they refute the idea of demonic forces: the Torah ritual teaches that these discharges are natural flows, part of the body's functioning in a natural world that God has established. Second, they underscore that God is (re)connected to these individuals, and has reinforced their ability to live vitally. In sum, these rites reinforce the overall message: to live on the side of life is what living as a Jew is about. This life is the realm of the holy.

The Torah radically opposes praying to the dead, divination, or seeking help from the dead or from gods of the underworld. Only God is

God; there are no independent, other gods who are demonic, malev-olent, and capable of spreading death. The Israelites should work and associate only with forces and creatures associated with life and reject and separate from forces and creatures associated with death. Still, death is a natural force, part of God's Creation. And so, when death occurs—when there is contact with a corpse—a purification rite is needed. Contact with death and the dead may weaken a human's hold on life, so the Torah provides a ceremony to reinvigorate the sense of life and vitality, rejoining the impure person with God on the side of life; however, there are no forces of death that one might be tempted to mollify or serve.[29]

The Holiness Code: Living in the Fullness of Life

The section of Leviticus known as the Holiness Code, beginning with chapter 19, brilliantly elevates and expands the life-death (or purity-impurity) binary to include the realm of ethical behavior.[30] In every choice of good, there is a choice of life; in every choice of evil, there is a choice of death. In Maimonides' words: "The Almighty says 'See, I have set before thee this day life and good, and death and evil' (Deut. 30:15), showing that 'life' and 'good' / 'death' and 'evil' [each duo] are identical."[31] The Torah completes this juxtaposition with the instruc-tion, "Choose life."

Leviticus 19 reiterates the key to the code: Israel—and all covenantal partners—are to imitate God.[32] They are to try to become more like God by becoming more holy: "Be holy, for I the Lord your God am holy" (Lev. 19:2). The biblical text defines holiness as being in the (manifest) presence of God. As the impure is excluded from sacred precincts, this manifest sacred location is always one of pure life. This is in accor-dance with God's nature, which is life raised to its infinite power. It follows that a more holy life is more like God, which is to say, it is *a fuller life*—more completely, more totally, more intensely alive than conventional life. Daily life, the realm of the common, is called *ḥol* in the Torah.[33] Untreated, or misdirected, *ḥol* deteriorates into the level of death. The goal of covenantal living is to raise conventional living to the level of holiness—that is, of intensified life. The holy sector of existence is the antipode to the zone of death.

Leviticus 19 broadens the ritual code in two ways. The fullness of life—closeness to God—is expressed not only in being in the Temple, or through liturgical acts of connecting to God, but in good acts: in treating the Other with justice and full respect. As the Psalmist later says: "Who will ascend God's mountain? . . . One with clean hands and a pure heart" (Ps. 24:3–4). Holiness, and a holistic life, are also expressed in and nurtured by the ritual acts of life. Chapter 19 gives us a set of ritual and ethical commandments, intermixed almost indiscriminately, in which both ritual and ethical actions are focused on the same outcome: the fullness of life. The command to revere parents, who give us the ultimate gift of life, shares a verse with the reminder to keep God's Sabbaths, days of living life to the fullest. Rejection of idolatry is presented alongside the care of fellow human beings, expressed by leaving the corners of one's field for gleaning by the poor and the outsider. Ethical behaviors—not robbing or stealing (v. 11, 13), not lying (v. 11), not swearing falsely (v. 11), not exploiting workers or delaying paying wages (v. 13), not abusing people with disabilities (v. 14), giving fair and equal justice (v. 16), not spreading false or malicious gossip (v. 16), not standing by when someone is being mistreated (v. 16), not being vengeful (v. 17)—all express our fullness of living, in which we do not begrudge or diminish others. These behaviors enable others to live a fuller life as well. They connect us to God, who asks us to live ethically, who loves other human beings, and who asks us to treat them well too. In sum: "Love your fellow as yourself. I am the Lord" (v. 18). People who follow these instructions show that they recognize the presence of the Divine undergirding and linking all of existence. These acts show how people walk with God, and how to behave with a strong consciousness of being in God's presence.

The Holiness Code concludes its interweaving of the code of life and death with the ethical realm by stressing that failure to clean up unethical behavior will lead to a state of impurity for the whole land. The land—which cannot move away from its inhabitants—will cast them out (Lev. 18:27–28, 20:22–23).[34] In the Messianic Age, Isaiah (11:9) reminds us, the ethical, purifying process will spread to the whole Earth. "They shall do no evil and no destructive acts in all of My holy mountain [the Earth], for the land will be full of the knowledge of God."

5

The Commandments and the Supremacy of Life

The Torah's commitment to the eventual complete triumph of
life is lived out now in the individual's lifetime, acting out the
fullness of life both in quantity and in quality. I offer this as
the interpretive principle of all of Judaism. Every commandment, every tradition, every ethical principle and ritual concept
is intended to uphold life and to fight against death. In recognizing the intrinsic dignities of human beings, and in choosing
to elevate life over death, we partner with God to incrementally
move the whole world toward its final redeemed state.

The "Great Principle" as the Root of Mitzvot

The Jerusalem Talmud tells us of a Rabbinic disagreement over
what is the *klal gadol ba-Torah*, the great principle of the Torah.[1]
A "great principle," the commentators explain, when understood
and internalized, leads one's natural behavior to fulfill the majority of positive commandments (requirements to act in a certain
way) and to not violate the negative commandments (prohibitions
on behaviors).[2] Rabbi Akiva states that the great principle of the
Torah is "love your neighbor as yourself" (Lev. 19:18).[3] Loving
your neighbor, he suggests, is not just a specific act; the emotion generates an attitude that leads to many other prescribed
behaviors. For example, when you love your neighbor as yourself,
and your neighbor is hungry, you will use your own money for
the mitzvah of *tzedakah*, and feed your neighbor.[4] You will not
violate the prohibition against degrading speech by spreading
evil tales about them, even if the reports are true.[5] Maimonides
writes that all the Rabbinically defined acts of loving-kindness—

feeding the hungry, visiting the sick, marrying off the bride, comforting the mourners, burying the dead—are, in the end, fulfillments of the commandment, "Love your neighbor as yourself."[6]

However, Akiva's colleague and disputant, Ben Azzai, insists that there is another principle of the Torah even more fundamental than loving one's neighbor as oneself: "The human being is created in the image of God" (Gen. 5:1).[7] This principle undergirds even the command to love your neighbor as yourself. Why should I love myself? Why should an encounter with another human being evoke love? The answer is that when you experience the infinite value of other humans, when you recognize their full equality, when you focus on each one's uniqueness, you will feel love for them. You will want to treat these individuals honorably, seeking their welfare and well-being, rejoicing with them and helping them when needed. The same outcome follows from recognizing one's own self as an image of God.

I take Ben Azzai's principle as the key explanation, along with the commitment to life over death, for all the mitzvot of the Torah. It constitutes a core understanding, one actualized in a variety of positive and negative commandments, and undergirding each and every commandment of the Torah. We are challenged to uncover—and realize—this connection.

The three intrinsic dignities of every image of God—infinite value, equality, uniqueness—add up to giving humans extraordinary standing. Add to these every human being's Godlike capacities and one understands the Psalmist's comment that the human is "only a little less than divine" (Ps. 8:6). If I recognize fellow human beings' infinite value and their equality to me, then I instinctively feel that I cannot take a piece of property or any goods from them by superior force, by trickery, by taking advantage of information that gives me a leg up; instead, I must offer something of equal value in return. So the Torah's commandments "You shall not steal" (Exod. 20:13, seventh of the Ten Commandments) and "You shall not rob" (Lev. 19:11) are nothing more nor less than a recognition of the dignities of the image of God.

Similarly, if I feel the uniqueness and value of another person, I cannot spread slander that degrades this person (Lev. 19:16). I certainly cannot kill this human being (Exod. 20:13—sixth of the Ten Commandments), nor stand idly by when this precious, irreplaceable life is endangered or harmed (Lev. 19:16). If I feel the value and equality of the other, then I feel responsible if I have inflicted damage on the other.[8] I instinctively agree that all our business relationships must be regulated by laws in which we enjoy equal standing, "One set of laws for you and for the stranger living in your midst. . . . One Torah and one law for you and for the outsider who lives with you" (Num. 15:15–16).[9] If I internalize the image of God of every human being, then I cannot bring myself to "torment an outsider" (Exod. 22:20), nor to harm or take advantage of an orphan or a widow (Exod. 22:21), who may be weaker in social status but are equal to me in dignity, and as such must receive help, not affliction. When, due to the haze of negative stereotypes, the other or foreigner is seen as less than human, less than the image of God, people all too often feel free to take advantage. The Torah is revealing and guiding us to appropriate behavior that follows from our encounters with other human beings and our recognition that they are creatures in the image of God, bearing the intrinsic dignities thereof.

And yet, some interpersonal laws in the Torah do not reflect the equality or uniqueness of the other. How is it that slavery is allowed, albeit regulated (Exod. 19:10; 21:1–4,26–27)? How is it that a father can sell his daughter—albeit to someone who will marry her and then treat her as a free wife (Exod. 21:7 11)? The short answer is that we are living in an unredeemed world. In this phase, there are entrenched interests, oppressions, and inequalities. Compromises with negative social conventions are found in Torah laws because the Torah is given to and received by humans inextricably mired in the context of their regnant culture and values. Acting in accordance with ideal standards is not always feasible. Nonetheless, such collaboration carries ethical and social costs. The tradition implicates itself to some extent in the flawed state of reality, in biblical times and still today.

These violations of images of God drive the Torah's goal of *tikkun olam*, repairing the world until it reaches the state where the fullness of human dignities is honored in law, economics, and daily human interactions. As we shall see, the Torah offers a method of perfecting the world—covenant—that operates in the real world at present, even as it seeks to transform society. The key to the integrity of this system is that the covenant keeps functioning. Bearers of the tradition must keep striving for improvement from generation to generation, never yielding more than temporary validity to entrenched violations of human dignity or to pervasive social and economic inequalities.

In the interim, however, I want to suggest that dignities of the image of God are not only a fundamental principle for understanding the Torah's laws. They also provide the vision of the world to be achieved and the guidelines for unfolding the codes along the way; they supply the criteria for deciding where change is needed and how the specific changes should be realized. Particularly when there are major transformations in the general culture, the opportunity is ripe for upgrading covenantal behaviors and moving them closer to the final goals.

Ritual as Reflection of the Core Principle

The core principle that every human being is an image of God (*tzelem elohim*) also motivates the ritual commandments of our annual cycle. Thus the annual holiday of Rosh Hashanah, the monthly celebrations of Rosh Hodesh, the triannual agricultural celebrations of Passover, Shavuot, and Sukkot and, above all, the weekly Shabbat communicate the message of Creation. Creation is the source and the nurturing ground of the image of God; the created world is the setting wherein *tikkun olam* will be realized. Shabbat and the historical aspect of Passover, Shavuot, and Sukkot also teach the once and future Exodus. The associated ritual laws—matzah, bitter herbs, *ḥametz*—dramatize the depth of slavery and the release and greatness of freedom. The Exodus from Egypt was the original liberation. It is confirmation that the future promised universal emancipation is real, a promise to depend on and to work for. The same can be said of the other intermediate redemptions of Jewish history—Hanukkah, Purim, Yom ha-Atzmaut (Israel's Independence Day).[10] They confirm that the Jewish people is alive, and the covenant of liberation is still operational.

Even the fast days and other markers of tragedy in Jewish history—Tisha b'Av and related mourning days for the Temple, the annual remembrances of past great destructions and Yom ha-Shoah's commemoration of the Holocaust—testify to the Divine image. The Jews remember; they have not given in; they have not made peace with the victory of evil.[11] They are spurred by memory of loss to build life more energetically. They are steeled by catastrophe and more determined to achieve redemption. The goal will be reached first in a Jewish society, then in the whole world. The image of God will be fully honored and eventually fully realized.

Other ritual commandments are connected to *tzelem elohim*, too. Kashrut laws, as we have seen, are intended to educate humans to the value of life, more than to command people to worship God. As the Rabbis write: "Do you really think that God the Holy One the Blessed cares whether an animal's death stroke is from the frontal position [as required by kosher slaughter] or from the nape of the neck [which would render the animal not kosher]? Rather, the commandments were given to remove the dross from people."[12] The kashrut code is meant to instill awareness of the awesomeness and dignified nature of all life. In treating fellow human beings, restrictions on behavior are raised to a higher power yet. The life-affirming laws and rituals of family relations, of *niddah* (menstruation) and *mikveh* (immersion), of personal purity and impurity, are fundamentally attempts to shape relationships and guide sexuality itself to meet the standard of recognizing, honoring, pleasuring, and treasuring the image of God of the other.[13] The laws of prayer—and of mezuzah, tallit, and tefillin—are focused on awareness of God and relationship with God's presence, encouraging the individual to feel a deep, sustaining connection with the Divine. This connection implicitly recharges and deepens our consciousness of being in God's image.

Here I would paraphrase the Talmud's observation. Do you really think it is important to God that you offer words of praise, or strap on black leather strips on your head and hands, or affix phrases praising God on your doorposts? Do you think God gets any benefit from these finite, stumbling, inadequate gestures? Do you think—as many did—that God was nurtured by the sacrifices of hecatombs of cows, sheep, and goats, or that rams burned on God's altar pacified Divine anger at human sin? Rather, these commandments were given to purify humans, to help connect them to the infinite Creation, to remind them that they are in a relationship of love with God—precisely the relationship that grew out of their being an image of God.[14]

Increasing the Presence of Life on Earth

The Torah's first commandment is *p'ru urvu*, be fruitful and multiply. This call to increase the presence of life in the world is God's response to the phenomenon of life: God wants more of it.[15] The Creator blesses life and bestows on it the power of replicating and growing—a blessing expressed in the energy, vigor, and vitality of all forms of life (Gen. 1:22,28). When the image of God—that is, the human being—emerges in Creation, this instruction is repeated and the blessing repeated (Gen. 1:28). The blessing is bestowed yet a third time after the massive extinction of human beings during the Flood (Gen. 9:1,7). In this blessing and commandment, we can see how the dual principles of valuing all life and seeing the image of God in human beings come together.

What does it mean that it is a mitzvah to be fruitful and multiply? Why does the Torah treat reproduction not merely as a natural behavior, but as a religious calling? And what kind of commandment or instruction is this, that is given to all of life?

Human life emerges from an evolutionary chain. Had the original primitive life-forms not replicated and developed, the next form of life would never have emerged. The terrific force of reproduction, instituted by the Creator, is continuously culled, shaped, and reshaped under the pressure of death. Life wins this struggle through the survival of the fittest. Had the chain of living been broken at any time, had the life-form not successfully reproduced, the line of succession would have snapped. Along the way, in fact, many forms of life did go extinct. Nevertheless, life radiated and upgraded in so many directions that an abundance of life-forms flowered.

In the life-forms preceding humanity, the power of replication is innate. Genes are programmed for maximum proliferation of life, so that each species can survive an individual's death. The Divine intention is thus instilled, as it were, in nature—a direction established by building these genes and drives into all living things.

Yet with humanity's arrival, life develops the capacity to understand God's plan and to join in its realization. Humans can ramp up—or slow down—the rate of natural increase. Humans can change natural conditions to favor life's multiplication, making previously fatal conditions no longer decisive. Or, tragically, they can make our planet less supportive of life in the future.

Recognizing this human capacity to partner in Creation, the Torah teaches that humans are distinctively commanded to be fruitful and multiply. The instruction implies that humans have the capability of responding positively or negatively to this call: to choose to have children or not. Thanks to the development of human consciousness and the innovations of science, humans have increased capability to enable or disable this process. With assistive reproductive technologies, humans can now bear children in many cases where the emergence of new life would have otherwise been impossible. Humans can assure the survival of babies at risk through genetic intervention and healing operations in the womb. At the same time, contraceptives and safe abortions are available as never before. The life choices available to God's human partner have increased dramatically. Currently, in the developed world, a human being can live a rich and comfortable life without choosing to have children. Yet death comes to all, and so the choice not to have children means that a specific line of life will end. The commandment *p'ru urvu*, then, is a call to humans to choose and act on the side of life. Those who fulfill this mitzvah thereby join in the cosmic movement from little or no life present to the expansion of life's presence in nature.

Joining in on the side of quality of life requires human beings to grow even more in the image of God, to increase their capacity as partners in the Divine plan. As a newborn's consciousness expands, so must the newborn's capacity for love, both self-love and embrace of others. First, the parents—as persons, not only sources of nourishment; then the siblings and other people who approach, treat, deal with, and relate to this new being. In time the child must grow in friendship and ability to relate in deeper and more permanent ways. The individual must develop a passion for life that embraces others and become more capable of love. The embrace of life includes accepting its components of failure, frustration, and loss, while learning to savor its pleasures and depth—a deepening that includes others. A key maturation point comes when love is so deeply felt and reciprocal that it enables a long-term commitment. This renders the lovers more capable of sustaining other lives beyond themselves.

At this point, the dynamism of love leads to consideration of having children. Then powerful, clashing forces come to mind. There is the realization that creating life is a Godlike power beyond any other in its wondrous outcome—that in parenting, I will create a person of infinite value, worth far beyond anything I can create in any other way. There is the counterrealization that I may lack economic resources and physical energy that the child will need. On the one hand, the child's uniqueness will make the interaction an experience like no other on the Earth. The pleasures, the reciprocal love, the joys and rewards are beyond almost any other experience in life. On the other hand, one sees the evidence all around that a child can hurt, can disappoint, can be a source of frustration as no other factor in one's life can. The child's life will be vulnerable and at risk in major and minor ways, so that in becoming a parent, I render myself hostage to all sorts of malevolent factors that can affect me. If I as an individual were to suffer the worst setback—a disease, an accident, a war that ends my life—my pain would stop there; but if as a parent I suffer the ultimate heartbreak, the death of a child, then the unbearable ache starts there and goes on and on. Then there is the consciousness that as a parent, I undertake a lifetime commitment, yet I anticipate that I will not be there for my child's entire lifetime. The knowledge that I will not be able to share the joy, heal the hurt, savor the blessings of my child is one of the most painful aspects of the prospect of my own premature death.

What, then, gives the strength to go ahead? It is a love of life that appreciates its value, whatever the risk and cost. It is a trust in God that assumes a Divine system calibrated to support life, and an appreciation of the order of nature in which life is sustained by strong vital forces. Hence the outcome of my effort is likely to be good. This is especially true if I embrace life, so that I can savor the infinity of every finite moment and not be frightened to face the end or the possible failure of these joys.

Of course, mature love knows that the basic thrust of love is beyond the rational cost/benefit ratio. It is unconditional. To this, Judaism adds yet another attractor force: God, the Infinite Presence, asks me to create another link in the chain of life so that it can go on toward the end goal. The One who will accompany me and sustain me every step of the way (if I allow this to happen) invites me to become part of a larger pattern: to serve in the army of life, to fight for the good, to raise the quality of human life and pass it on to the next level. Out of these deep considerations comes the decision to have children. Damn the torpedoes, full steam ahead. This is how I fulfill the mitzvah of p'ru urvu.

The Talmud asks: What is the minimal fulfillment of the commandment to be fruitful and multiply? The answer is two children.[16] Translating this conclusion, we can say that, if parents have two children, when they die they leave behind no less life in the world than they themselves represented. If you do not cause a deficit in the amount of life found in this world, you have fulfilled the commandment. You have lived your life on the side of life.

The Talmud, nevertheless, says that this achievement is inadequate. The tradition understands Isaiah's declaration that the Earth "was not created to be empty; it was created to be *settled*" (Isa. 45:18) to mean that it was created to be "filled with life."[17] Leaving behind two children constitutes a draw between the forces of life and death. But Judaism is committed to life's triumph. Therefore, a person should have more than two children. The halakhah calls this the Rabbinic mitzvah of *shevet*, literally, to settle the Earth. Universal fulfillment of this mitzvah would eventually fill the Earth with life. Translated: parents who have a third child leave a legacy of increased life. They have lived their lives solidly on the side of life.

The Talmud then comes back once again. Not every child that is born survives; not every child grows up and has children. A family's choice of how many children to have should factor in the ever-present power of death. From this reality, the sages conclude that one should have yet a fourth child. The Talmud makes this point by citing Ecclesiastes 11:6: "In the morning sow your seed; and also in the evening do not put down your hand [stop seeding]. For you do not know which will succeed, this one or that one, or whether both will give equally good [results]."[18] Guaranteeing the survival of life requires repeated effort that can overcome the deficit generated by death. In other words, a fourth child represents the parents' commitment to create and leave behind on the Earth more life than they themselves represent.

Describing *p'ru urvu* simply as a mitzvah does not do justice to what is involved. All other commandments involve some limited effort and finite fulfillment, but having a child is a totally open-ended commitment. Children are most precious, the most infinitely valuable thing we shall ever produce, because they are made by the expenditure of our own infinitely valuable life. Our emotion, our love is expended continuously in nurturing them. All parents are on duty 24/7 for the rest of their lives. The parental commitment is literally boundless. In this way it resembles the life-shaping value we saw with the commandment *v'halakhta bidrakhav*, to imitate God in increasing our own capacities to do good and repair the world.

I had dear, close friends whose beautiful, intelligent, kind, sparkling daughter was invaded by a cancer of the spine that advanced almost up to her neck, leaving her paraplegic and bound to a wheelchair. They took care of her lovingly and endlessly every day for the next ten-plus years. Amazingly, she never lost her hopeful, cheerful approach to life or her warmth to people although, Lord knows, the bystanders and her fellow students in school were not always helpful or considerate. Her mind was unaffected, so she finished college as an honor student. Then the cancer started up again and killed her. Her parents loved, cared, hoped, and cherished her unremittingly to the very end. How they got up to their task every morning, I could never grasp. Yet they never faltered or turned away from God or people.

It is true that parents of children with chronic disease have some of the highest divorce rates. It is true that there are abusive parents, and mothers and fathers who crack under the stress of child rearing. Even the most devoted parents have moments of fear, or weakness, when they need the support of others. Still, the overwhelming majority of parents meet the challenge of unlimited care for years and decades. Thus the commitment to parenting turns out to be like the covenant itself: an unbounded commitment of one's total life. Parenting, like imitating God, is not an obligation to do a finite set of acts. It is giving one's self—in all its infinite value and uniqueness—to the birth and growth of another infinitely valuable, unique life. In the end, I have given my life—that is to say, the time, energy, emotion, wisdom, character that I have—to assure the growth and strength and presence of more life in the world.

There are people who cannot have children due to physical or medical factors, though technological and social changes offer many more people ways to become parents today than in the past. Some people do not find a marriage partner and feel unable to undertake child rearing alone. Does this mitzvah of *p'ru urvu* condemn them or torment them with an instruction impossible for them to accomplish? The answer is no. There are many ways to nurture children. In fact, the tradition treats a person who shaped a child's life or character through nurture or education as equivalent to one who bore or created the child.[19] In this sense, one can be a parent by enabling the quality of another's life, just as one can be a parent by creating a child. People can fulfill this calling by adopting and raising a child or children. One who cannot undertake the responsibilities of adoption can still be a teacher of children. Here, too, the tradition treats a primary teacher as equivalent to a parent, asking us to honor a primary teacher as we would a parent.[20] The ethical penumbra of the mitzvah of *p'ru urvu* as a mandate to support life's flourishing includes all these ways of supporting the next generation.

The Primacy of Saving a Life

One further guideline directs all our religious behaviors to assure these are in the service of life. Judaism's commitment to life can be tested by its approach to those situations where fulfilling a commandment of the Torah can endanger the believer's life. In the most widespread Rabbinic tradition, the total number of commandments in the Torah, positive and negative, is 613.[21] What should one do if keeping any of these observances would endanger a person? The Talmud rules that—with only three exceptions—every single instruction in the Torah should be overruled to save a life.[22] This principle is called *pikuaḥ nefesh* (saving a life). In fact, the Talmud rules that even if there is only a remote possibility that life will be lost, it is a mitzvah to override any of these 610 commandments to save the person's life.[23]

This has been the dominant ruling for more than two thousand years; most people assume that there could be no other way. But there were serious alternative views on this matter, both millennia ago and in later times.

A religion that discovers God and the awesomeness of the Divine can go either of two ways with this insight. One way is to conclude that the Infinite Lord, the Source and Sustainer of all life, the One who has revealed God's Self to humanity, is the All in All. Nothing human, nothing finite, compares to the Eternal; everything human should be subordinated to the Divine. In this conception, the presence of the Infinite God in the world dwarfs, even trivializes, all the significance and weight of finite humanity.

Many religious traditions include some element of this tendency. In the Greek Orthodox tradition, monks who withdraw from daily life and human affairs to devote themselves to meditating on God's Infinite Presence are considered saintly and most devout. In many strands of Hinduism and Buddhism, ego-driven daily reality is regarded as an illusion that one should gladly renounce to attain true wisdom and true being. The infinite, boundless, blissful state of existence negates the meaning and value in the merely human, finite, mortal life. Medieval Judaism, Christianity, and Islam all included teachings that the infinite reward (or pain) of eternity in the world-to-come dwarfs the pleasure or pain of this life, so that one should reduce mortal activity and pleasure seeking to the minimum in order to qualify for the maximum eternal reward. Yet this approach leads easily to valorizing martyrdom. During the Crusades, thousands of Jews chose martyrdom for themselves and their children rather than yield to forced conversion to Christianity. They sacrificed their lives, even in circumstances where Jewish law suggested they could acquiesce to conversion ceremonies they did not intend to honor, and thus save themselves.[24] Maimonides rebuked those who gave their lives unnecessarily rather than live on for a new day when they could live as Jews.[25] Willingness to sacrifice one's life for God and religion is only a step away from choosing death in *jihad* as a fighter and martyr over normal life, a resolution that is the nurturing ground of suicide bombers.

An alternative understanding of religion — of Judaism in particular — is that out of love for humanity and desire to help human beings, God has communicated God's self and presence and revealed a religion to live by. However much Divine worship is esteemed, the end goal

God seeks is not humans serving, honoring, and focusing on God, but rather their entering into covenant to redeem the world, pursuing justice and expressing loving-kindness to fellow humans, the very means to "walk humbly with God" (Mic. 6:8).[26]

This second religious understanding strikes a fine balance. It is a mitzvah to override all the commandments of the Torah (except for three) to save a life (or to prevent loss of a life), because life comes first. Life is the treasure, the blessed object of God, and the goal of religion is to uphold and advance life. Yet even here, there is room to see martyrdom as a form of ultimate witness to faith in God. The commandments are Divinely given. The practices are treasured and taken very seriously because they connect us to God. The choice to live by revelation is the choice to be on the side of life, not death. But sometimes, when the way of life is at stake, when the evil ones seek to suppress the very faith of life, then one can only stand firm. Then one should be willing to jeopardize, even sacrifice one's life to uphold the faith. Since martyrdom is an ultimate sacrifice of the most precious, the infinitely valued, unique life one has, then, in its place, it is rightfully honored. Judaism's covenantal tradition insists, however, that martyrdom is a last resort; it is the religious nuclear option. This sacrificial act should not be resorted to except in a total confrontation situation, when nothing less than the ultimate sacrifice can stop the victory of evil. Short of that, life comes first.

"Saving Life Suspends the Laws of Shabbat"

The showdown for primacy between these two religious values of obedience to God and advancing human life can be dated to a specific moment in Jewish history. According to the book of Maccabees, during the rebellion against the Greek empire that led to the great victory celebrated on Hanukkah, the Pietists, the most devout wing of the Maccabee coalition, hid in the desert to escape the king's decree requiring members of every religion, including Judaism, to "each abandon his own customs,"[27] under which they would have to violate many Torah commandments. Greek soldiers pursued them and "formed a battle line against them on the Sabbath day."[28] The troops offered them amnesty for their surrender — "Come out to us and obey the word of the king and we shall let you live"[29] — but the Pietists rejected the offer. When the soldiers advanced on them, the Pietists "neither replied to them, nor hurled a stone at them, nor blocked the entrance to their hiding places." They refused to fight back, because that would constitute a violation of the Sabbath law, "saying, 'Let us all die in our innocence.'"[30]

By their decision, the Pietists made clear that they chose obedience to God over submission to the king. Rather than yield to religious suppression, they chose martyrdom. However, their refusal to fight back on Shabbat made a further statement: one must die rather than violate a major commandment of the Torah. Thus they upheld the theological conviction that obedience to God, and hence observance of a Divine commandment — even unto death — was the mark of true religion.

This policy, however, was tantamount to suicide: all the Greeks had to do to wipe out the rebels was to attack them on Shabbat. Indeed, the Maccabees, who understood the fatal flaw in the Pietists' policy choice — "If we all do as our brothers have done . . . they will now quickly wipe us off the face of the earth" — concluded: "If any man comes against us in battle on the Sabbath day, we shall fight against him and not die as our brothers did in their hiding places."[31]

The Talmud later makes clear that the Maccabees' decision reflected not just a religious compromise necessary for self-defense, but a principled judgment about the priority of human life over obedience to God's commandments. The Rabbis ask: "How do we know that saving a life suspends the laws of Shabbat?" — that is, that it is permitted to do any or all of the prohibited labors on Shabbat in order to save a life? — and then offers various rationales for overriding the law in order to prevent a death. One argument points to existing traditions to do labor on Shabbat in fulfillment of a ritual, such as circumcision, which is performed on the eighth day of a boy's life even if it occurs on the Sabbath day. If treating one organ is permitted on Shabbat, then treating and saving a whole body should be permitted. Another teaching offers a prudential rationale: "Violate one Shabbat to save him so he will be enabled to observe many, many Sabbath days." Later authorities clarified that it is principle — not prudence — that overrides. Quoting Leviticus (18:5) — "You shall observe My laws and my rules which a human shall do and live" — they generalized a metaprinciple of the Torah: the laws are given so that the human "shall *live by them* — and *not die by them*." If carrying out a law spells death, then the law is suspended to protect the life.[32]

This outlook stems from the Rabbis' understanding that the highest goal of the commandments — the reason God gave them — was not to exercise God's authority, demanding obedience for the sake of obedience. They were given for life — to advance life, to upgrade human life, to enlist humans in the covenant of perfecting the world to fully sustain life. When the operation of the law leads to death — even if it may *only potentially jeopardize* a life — then the law is overridden and suspended, lest it defeat the very cause it was given to advance.[33]

In his legal code, the *Mishneh Torah*, Maimonides strongly affirmed this view. Blasting those who refrained from medical labor necessary to save a life, or even reduce risk to it, on Shabbat, he insisted that "the Shabbat is suspended when it comes to danger to lives, as are all the commandments. . . . When it comes to a sick person whose illness is life threatening, the Shabbat is considered to be like a weekday for any and all things that he needs."[34] Moreover, such work should not be handed off to others, such as gentiles or children, who are not bound by Shabbat laws, but should be "done by great scholars in Israel and by their wise men. It is forbidden to procrastinate when it comes to a person ill with a life threatening disease, as it is written: '[My laws] which a human shall do to live by them — and not die by them.'"[35] His generalization: "Thus you learn that the laws of the Torah are not [God's] vengeance on the world," leading to death rather than life; "rather they are [agents of] mercy [mother love], loving-kindness and peace for the world."[36] He concludes with a harsh attack on those who hold back because they see medical labors as violations of the Shabbat; that is, they are fixated on the letter rather than the life principle animating Jewish law. "And these heretics who say that this [type of labor] constitutes violation of the Sabbath and is prohibited—of them, Scripture says: 'And I have given them laws that were not good and rules by which they could not live'" (Ezek. 20:25). Such "obedience," he insisted, would turn the Torah into a death-dealing rather than life-affirming system.

The Limits of Pikuaḥ Nefesh: When Choosing Death Upholds the Value of Life

But if life is the ultimate principle of the Torah, then why is one commanded to die—if that is what it takes—to avoid violating any of three commandments, three cardinal sins of the Jewish tradition: idolatry, murder, and sexual violation (such as incest)?[37] Because all three of these actions destroy life and the reverence for life. Permitting one to violate them to save his own life would therefore harm, not uphold, the principle that life is uppermost.

The case of murder is the simplest to explain. If a murderer tells me to kill another innocent person in order to save my own life and I refuse and I am killed, my martyrdom strengthens reverence for life. One person has died, but in my death, I give the most powerful witness imaginable that it is worth sacrificing my life to uphold the sanctity of life. Upholding the sacredness of the life of God's image upholds the sacredness of God, Godself. That is why this act of martyrdom is called *kiddush ha-Shem*, sanctification of God's name, the highest form of religious witness. On the other hand, if I yield to the murderer's threat and kill another innocent person to save my own life, while here, too, only one person has died, my act of killing an innocent person weakens respect for life and makes murder more "understandable," even "acceptable." This undercuts the awe and taboo of taking human life.

In the case of sexual violation, such as incest, the Rabbis apparently felt this is so destructive of the abused person that it is equivalent to killing, a "murder of the soul."[38] Permitting the action in order to save a life would thus undercut reverence for life by the same calculation that murder of an innocent weakens the underlying respect for life. Committing incest undercuts the awe at and taboo against such abuse and weakens resistance to such murder of the soul.[39]

The third prohibition, of idolatry, is particularly telling theologically. Because the infinite value of human life grows out of and is sustained by its rootedness in the Infinite Presence of God, idolatry is more than a matter of misplaced devotion.

The Torah was given in the world of pagan religion, in which beneficent as well as malevolent gods and powers inhabited a metadivine realm. There were gods of life and gods of death—including a god called Mot (death). It was prudent to serve, feed—really bribe—the gods; this kind of magic was meant to coerce the gods to do people's will. But the Torah reveals a supreme God—One and Unique—with no competitors or superior forces to contend with. God has set in motion the forces that operate in the universe and their directions as well. Interactions of these forces will lead toward order and life.

There is now one serious force that can join as a partner with God, and work for life—or choose evil and death behaviors, and work against God. This force is the human being. The enormous, Godlike powers of human consciousness, emotion, and freedom have the potential for arrogance and hubris, if allowed to range uncontrolled. The *image* of God may begin to think and act as if that image *is* God.

Idolatry is the sin of taking something finite, human-manufactured, partial, and flawed and absolutizing it—that is, worshiping it as if it were the Infinite God. An idolator projects all value onto this manufactured thing, even at the expense of stripping oneself of all weight and dignity. The deity so created demands total subordination of self, and the idolator supplies it. But the object of idolatrous worship, by definition, cannot sustain the infinite value of human life. In the sacrifices it demands, life is degraded, shrunk, destroyed.

The centrality of life is reflected in the Bible's treatment of idolatry as death: the rival to God and *the* central threat to the moral ecology of human life. The Torah portrays God and idolatry as the either/or, the matter and antimatter, before which humans stand. They must choose on which side to live. God is the Infinite Life, which self-limits out of love to sustain all forms of life. Conversely, idolatry is unlimited death, because it is the finite posing as the Infinite. It can only preserve its comparative greatness by minimizing or degrading all other forms of life.

The Bible makes it clear that there can never be human sacrifice in the House of God. By contrast, idolators in the Bible are associated with worship of underworld and death deities. They turn to magic and sorcery, hoping to escape the limits of the living process instead of trying to work with them and use them for life. They particularly turn to those who consult with ghosts or "make inquiries of the dead" (Deut. 18:10–11). Instead of nurturing a genuine and loving relationship with the God of Life, idolatry seeks to manage and control (through magic) the gods of death (Deut. 18:9–12). In the ultimate statement of turning to death for help—and thus joining up with death—idolators consign their sons and daughters to the side of idolatry and death, which consumes them. An idolatrous demand to sacrifice a child not only takes the most precious element in the parents' life away from them to give to the god; it also demolishes the dignity of the parents' lives. They are nothing and they are left empty and spent after the devastating sacrifice. God of Life detests this (Deut. 18:10) as the ultimate obscenity. Leviticus 18 addresses it directly: "You must keep My laws [of life] and My rules, and you must not do any of these abhorrent things" (v. 26).

The Rabbis felt that if a regime of idolatry ever won out, the infinite value of all humans would soon be forfeited. To surrender to idolatry strengthens the rule of idolatry, bringing closer the day of universal oppression and inevitably damaging the sacredness of life.

This is why the Rabbis ruled that one should defy idolatry and give one's life, if necessary, to reject it. In this case, relinquishing one's life sanctifies God's name and strengthens reverence for life. It is a blow struck for human dignity and infinite value against human authorities, whose absolute claims made them no-Gods, and who would degrade human beings by turning them into disposable artifacts. Martyrdom to stop this is not only heroic; it is at times necessary and unavoidable.

Still, in the end this is the exception that proves the rule. Martyrdom is holy and praiseworthy only if it is the only way to uphold life. Living for God, not dying for God, is the highest calling of religious life.

Judaism thus made clear that all actions on the side of God must be for life and not for death, for good and not for evil. This is how the Rabbis interpreted the verse, "You shall keep My land and My rules which a person shall do and *thereby live*" (Lev. 18:5). This is why every law in the Torah, every tradition is intended to guide people to act on the side of life. This is also the criterion by which to review the current adequacy of these traditions, and the direction in which any can be recalibrated to come closer to the Torah's ideal for life.

PART 2

Covenant as Method
of World Repair

6

The Covenantal Method of Repairing the World

The Divine promise—that if humans do their share, this world will be perfected—is one of the greatest Jewish contributions to world civilization. Even beyond bringing ethical monotheism to the world, it is Judaism's call to transform the status quo that is so liberating and revolutionary for all people. This messianic teaching contributed core insights to both Christianity and Islam, especially the Shiite tradition. The conviction that humans can make the world much better has been a shaping force in modern civilization.

The Jewish tradition's proposed method of world repair, however, offers an equally valuable gift for humanity. Judaism teaches that covenant—a partnership between God and humanity, and between the generations—is the central mechanism to achieve *tikkun olam*. I have come to understand that the covenantal method is critically important to a redemptive outcome.

World Repair without Covenant

The distance between the present and the dreamed-of future is so staggering that only a really extraordinary method could successfully close the gap. All great religions and secular redemption movements have therefore felt a need to offer serious proposals as to method. Some of the most ambitious efforts to perfect the Earth have been undertaken in my lifetime. Many of them turned into evil empires and systems of oppression: fascism, Nazism, communism, Maoism, Khmer Rouge, and others. In these cases, the methods used to attain perfection were the antithesis of the professed goals. In the process, the means defeated the ends.

Examining some of the alternative approaches to mending the world will help us see the ways in which the method of covenantal partnership is more suited to effect the change that our world needs.

Alternative 1: God as the Sole Redeemer

Perhaps the most widespread alternative religious proposal to achieve *tikkun olam* is that God alone will bestow this state of perfection. Given the dimensions of the shortfall, the resistance to change, and the power of evil people to impose their will on others, repair seems too herculean for humans to accomplish. Rather than relinquish the vision of redemption, religions have relied on God to bestow the final perfection miraculously. Alongside teaching the ethics of a good society and the vision of a just and humane world, Christianity, Islam, and Judaism have taught that people should not abandon hope despite the vast chasm between reality and the ideal. Divine power would achieve what humans could not. A loving God would step in and perform miracles. If necessary, the Lord would end the reign of natural laws and forces, and bring a new world into being. In the end, the promise would be fulfilled. In Shiite Islam, as in Judaism, the agent of the ultimate miracle would be a Messiah, a divinely selected and fortified messenger who would defeat the armies of men and the forces of evil. In Christianity, the difficulty of overcoming the powers-that-be was rated so overwhelming that God had to come to achieve the goal in person. As Jesus, whom Christianity teaches is part of the Godhead, God came, and will return to make a "new heaven and a new earth" (Isa. 66:22).

There are two problems with the God-alone teaching. First, *tikkun olam* has not happened. Over the centuries, numerous messianic movements within all three Abrahamic religions have proclaimed the arrival of the final redemption, but all have proven premature; they left the dream unfulfilled. This does not prove that the method is wrong. The final redeemer may come next year, or in the future. In the words of the classic Jewish faith proclamation: "I believe, with complete faith, in the coming of the Messiah. Even if he tarry . . . I still wait expectantly every day that he will come."[1] But the longer the world waits for this miraculous external redemption, the harder it is to maintain confidence in its ultimate arrival.

The second weakness in relying on Divine miracles for redemption is that people do not apply themselves to the task of changing the world. Instead of transforming the facts on the ground, they wait all too patiently for the end to come. Some people feel it is impious for humans to do what God is going to do. When the Zionist movement began, ultra-Orthodox Jews opposed it as a violation of an oath that Jews would not revolt against their fate but would wait for their promised redeemer. This was a catastrophic evasion of responsibility. Only a small number of Jews took on the task to create the future State of Israel, and this stand-pat policy encouraged millions of Jews to stay behind in Europe. The Nazis killed most of them during the Holocaust.

Reliance on miracles leads people to not challenge entrenched interests. They turn for consolation from their deprivations to worship—or to dream of a better spiritual world. As Marx put it cynically, religion can be the opium of the masses. Or, as the Wobblies, an early twentieth-century American labor movement, put it: "There will be pie-in-the-sky in the great bye-and-bye." In the interim, religious hope for the future weakened the unions' efforts to organize for better wages and working conditions. Sadly, the need is so great, the yearning so urgent, and the love of God so potent that to this day, hundreds of millions of people continue to put all their trust in the hope for a miraculous redemption.

Alternative 2: The World-to-Come as the Locus of Redemption

In monotheistic religions, the second widespread approach to achieving a perfect world shifts the focus to the world-to-come—a future state of existence in which the soul, having shed the body, will live in eternity. In essence, this religious conception acknowledges that the world in which we live is a hopeless case. Evil will never be vanquished here; injustice and innocent suffering will always be with us. However, a loving God, who knows that the present condition is wrong, will make up for it. Broadly speaking, in the world-to-come, imagined and articulated in different ways by different faiths and by different schools within each, there will be full justice for all; an end to innocent suffering; no want, deprivation, or illness.

The main accomplishment of this solution is that it upholds a plausible, full, and final perfection in the face of unyielding wrongs in this mortal realm. Billions have learned to bear their suffering in life — thanks to hope and trust in the final recompense. The idea is so compelling that in the medieval period it came to dominate Christianity, Judaism, and Islam. It still is a powerful force in all three religions, in varying degrees.

The problem with this conception is that, like the first alternative, it diverts people from working to improve this world. The essential message is: don't strive for ephemeral achievements in the present world; instead devote all your time to worshiping God.

Sometimes the idea of eternal bliss is used to reduce or dismiss the importance of life on this Earth altogether — life is so short, and eternity so long and blissful, one should not seek out or indulge in pleasures in this life. Various Jewish, Christian, and Muslim sources all proclaim such a notion, that worldly activity is a distraction from concentrating on being worthy of admittance to the future world. Some thinkers, like Maimonides, viewed all bodily pleasures as constituting a threat to the capacity of reason. He called for discipline and moderation, lest worldly desires tempt us to bad behaviors.[2] Lesser thinkers interpreted various Torah restrictions on food and on sexual activity as driven by the intention to reduce physical pleasures. With such reduction, desires would be controllable, and less of an impediment to earning eternal bliss.

The covenantal stream in Judaism counters that the fullness of the human being is in the unified self, body and soul together. The unique experience each person is granted is the flesh-and-blood existence we live out in this world. Moreover, the call to *tikkun olam* is addressed to *us*, to be realized, with God's help, in the *here-and-now*. In Soloveitchik's words: the "goal is not flight to another world that is wholly good, but rather bringing down that eternal [perfect] world into the midst of our world."[3]

Alternative 3: A Different Dimension of
Existence as the Locus of Redemption

In Eastern religions—specifically in Hinduism and Buddhism—there is a very powerful variation on detachment from this world as the key to achieving perfection: the concept of enlightenment. Here, again, at the heart of the concept is the recognition of suffering and injustice in this world along with humanity's unquenchable yearning for wholeness and perfection. These religions start their answer by conceding the incorrigible presence of inescapable evil and pain. However, they argue that this is the outcome of being ensnared in the attractions of this illusory world. The human being is driven by ego to want power, wealth, fame, achievement. But the ego takes these worldly experiences as ultimate. Since there will always be a gap between imagination and reality, even the highest achievers are doomed to unhappiness by unfulfilled desires. Even the most fortunate inheritors of this world's pleasures will be devastated by the shock of death and loss of loved ones. Buddha, after all, was a prince, powerful, balanced by good health, pleasures, and good companions. Then he discovered that there is no ultimate shelter, and all people are destined to suffer—by the uneven distribution of resources and by unavoidable failures of health, of work, of projects undertaken but never achieved—because they are caught up in this world of illusions. The only cure for human pain is to see through the illusions and voluntarily renounce pursuing them. The path of enlightenment leads us to discern the true world from the illusory. Illuminated, we turn from trying to achieve our false goals. When we are not driven by greed, power seeking, or ego gratification, we can choose Buddha's compassionate path and kindness to others, and cease behaviors that harm others and degrade us. The reward of such enlightenment is a growing serenity in this life that will lead to ever higher levels of rebirth. The ultimate reward is to be freed from the round of mortal existence—this wheel of suffering—and to reach nirvana, a perfect state of existence free of all pain, exertions, and details of daily living. This message can give our lives direction, as well as moral improvement, and the capacity to bear the slings and arrows of misfortune.

Nevertheless, serious consequences flow from such an understanding of life. First is the implication that this world is not the real one, and therefore not worth the effort to improve. While this emphasis on enlightenment has given great consolation to billions of people, many of them oppressed and deprived, the deferral of perfection from this world has often been a force for societal passivity, diverting believers from the vigorous social change necessary to perfect this world. By contrast, approaches that emphasize self and body, the importance of this life and human power—all ideas that, in Abrahamic traditions, are shaped by Jewish roots—have generated economic, political, and scientific advances. True, they often were tied to profoundly harmful developments (including colonialism and imperialism), but they transformed material culture and improved living conditions nonetheless.

My second critique of this enlightenment approach is less a criticism and more a bald statement of an alternate orientation toward life. There is no way to prove that this life is illusory—or the alternative, that mortal existence is the deepest, most holistic practice of living. Each approach can point to deep emotional and psychological experiences reported by highly gifted individuals who affirm one vision of existence or the other. When a group of Jewish scholars that I joined met with the Dalai Lama in Dharamsala in 1990, he expressed the feeling that Judaism must be an inferior religion, since it assumes the importance of the material and the worldly, and focuses on daily physical activities. He was mostly unmoved by my arguments that these moments, properly enacted, are suffused with transcendent purpose and depth of living. He only conceded that many of his refugee community had been caught up in work (as an economic necessity and a path for upward mobility) and that he lacked Buddhist values designed to guide or ennoble such activities. The Dalai Lama did not modify his view of Judaism as inferior compared to the more spiritual enlightened state of Tibetan Buddhism until Rabbi Zalman Schachter-Shalomi offered him a mystical approach from the Jewish tradition that also treated the realm of spiritual existence as on a higher plane than it is in normative Judaism.[4]

My own background and orientation predispose me, however, to the covenantal counterstatement: we have only one life, at least as a unified, body-soul self. That life, rooted in God and oriented to perfection, offers experiences of unlimited love, ultimate purpose, and cosmic unity that are fleeting, ephemeral, and fragile, yet infinitely precious and of everlasting significance.

This understanding boils down the choice between these two approaches to a general orientation to life. The covenantal way insists that this world is irreducibly real, albeit finite. It calls for the mortal realm to be improved—transformed—by those who participate in it, *as* they participate in it. This conception stimulates and earns our lifetime efforts by reinforcing them with profound personal experiences and access to another dimension of existence. It incorporates a calling for *tikkun* that has already enabled an extraordinary improvement of the conditions of life for billions.

Alternative 4: Humanity as the Sole Redeemer

Another major alternative to the covenantal approach to *tikkun olam* arises from a radical form of modernity's message that humans must take power to change their fate for the better. Various movements, proliferating in the modern era, proclaim that humans must take total and sole charge of their destiny because all other forces they relied upon in the past were illusory and only hobbled them. In the West, particularly, these movements have often designated God as the illusion, and inherited religions, such as Christianity, as the primary obstacles to achieving major progress.

Secular movements proliferated because dramatic improvement in many areas of life—lifespan, health, social and economic conditions—aroused expectations that change was inevitable and anything was possible. The French Revolution was an early harbinger, although many of its leaders were deists and anticlericals rather than radical secularists. In the nineteenth century the cultural infrastructure was seeded with these ideas; in the twentieth, they flowered.

First came the Bolshevik Revolution, an offshoot of nineteenth-century Marxism. It identified dialectical materialism as the "god" of the process, the laboring classes as the army of liberation, and the Communist party as its avant-garde, supplying leadership. Communists in the Soviet Union declared all-out war on religion as a bastion of the reactionary status quo. They also declared all-out war on entrenched interests, especially the wealthy, whether old aristocrats, capitalists, or *kulaks* (wealthy peasants), deemed resistant to bringing socioeconomic equality to all. To realize the ultimate goals of equality, full concentration of power was demanded and achieved. In due course, a society dragooned by central planning authority emerged. Backed by a uniform message, imposed by state-controlled media that stifled dissent, undergirded by a system of intimidation and terror—secret police, prison camps, and frequent bloodlettings that sought to keep people subservient and incapable of resistance—a movement to achieve a secular paradise instead created the world's largest empire of tyranny, exploitation, and human degradation. Despite all its efforts and focus on improving wealth and dividing it properly, the system performed poorly, giving rise to extended poverty and deprivation. Environmentally destructive decisions, along with the frequent dismissal of public health concerns for the sake of economic advance, only further damaged the public interest.

Nazism also set as its goal the perfection of society. The name of its ruling party says it all: National Socialism—promising the end of poverty and provision for the needs of all Germans. It also promised to end the socioeconomic vulnerability, cycles of inflation, deflation, and depression, that marred the economic advances of modern capitalism. Unlike Marxist socialism—driven by class warfare and threatening the status of the well-to-do—National Socialism promised a holistic society in which the interests of all Germans would be upheld and reconciled. Hitler offered the restoration of a sense of community—a *Gemeinschaft* (community) economy, not one marked by economic competition and excessive individuation, the negative hallmarks of modernity and capitalism.

The promise of perfection was extended through eugenics to improving the "Aryan" master race and winnowing out the defective and the "non-Aryan" (among them, the Jews). While the Nazis did not declare all-out war on Christianity, they sought to domesticate and control it. In its place, the Nazi party bestowed moral and spiritual authority on its incarnation, the Führer. In practice, Hitler became the god—the source of right and wrong, the one who decides who shall live and who shall die. Finally, the Nazis declared that the sine qua non of social perfection was the elimination of the Jews. Initially, this was presented as a process of removing them from the society and economy, thus preventing their alleged exploitation of Aryans. With time, it became clear that removal meant expulsion and the confiscation of their assets. Ultimately, the program became elimination—from Germany and all of conquered Europe—by assault, incarceration, and eventually total obliteration by mass murder. Here again, the society set up for the intended beneficiaries became a centralized tyranny, with enforcement by terror and violence. Similar patterns can be shown for Maoism in China, communism in Vietnam and Southeast Asia, and the Khmer Rouge in Cambodia.

These totalitarian movements have another pattern in common. They came to power in an ongoing process of radicalization and ever more extreme policies. At the same time, the concerted elimination of opposition or independent forces in society removed any moderating influences. The runaway extremism escalated, not checked until either outside forces intervened or an internal counterreaction finally put certain limits on the system—but these breakdowns typically came only after great suffering had been inflicted.

In hindsight, these destructive outcomes were an inescapable result of utopian systems of social perfectionism. Totalitarian revolutionary movements function top down, exercising absolute power that tends to corrupt its users. The removal or neutralization of any transcendent context—God—means that human authorities are totally in charge, accountable to no higher power, and thus able to do whatever they please. I believe that the sense that there is no God sets in motion an unlimited expansion of a human leader's authority to fill the vacuum. The absence of any notion of a higher, limiting norm unleashes an unchecked grandiosity in the powers-that-be. The extraordinary power of the vision of a perfect society energizes its agents to the nth degree. The grandeur of the dream minimizes in the minds of its all-powerful leaders the significance of costs or pain inflicted on the people who stand in the way. This is why liberation movements of the past two centuries have repeatedly brought great evils in their wake and inflicted catastrophic losses on friend and foe alike.

Nevertheless, such movements remain highly seductive, attracting powerful leaders and huge numbers of people. The grand promise that *tikkun olam* can be achieved by purely human action remains the greatest competitor for credibility and loyalty with the covenantal way to redemption.

Fundamental Qualities of the Covenantal Method

The covenantal vision offers a fundamental critique of these approaches. First, in their basic assumptions these movements incorporate a message that contradicts the very values they seek to advance. There is a deep disrespect for human beings in the claim that total change can be accomplished overnight or all at once. By and large, people cannot, or do not voluntarily, change so quickly. Second, noncovenantal movements tend to permit themselves to do evil for the sake of good ends. The way of covenant insists that ends and means cannot be separated.

If unchecked by independent moral authority and norms, revolutionary tactics will undermine the goals.

The covenantal method is built on a set of processes that realistically accept human limitations and needs. This approach is in itself a form of respect for human beings. It supports a commitment to the inalienable dignities of the human being that should not be overruled, not even in the name of a perfected world. Covenantal social change is based on incremental actions combined with built-in checks on the leaders. These partial steps may appear to dilute the focus on the sweeping goals, but they lead to healthier tactics and sounder outcomes along the way.

Three fundamental values guide and shape the steps of the covenantal approach: human freedom, partnership between human beings and God, and incrementalism.

Freedom vs. Coercion

In the Bible, the first articulation of covenant starts with an act of Divine self-limitation. After the Flood, God commits to never again use unlimited power to punish humans for evil acts. Thus the Torah encodes a deeper message. Limits are the key to enabling life. Absolute power should never be used against humans. Even if exercised by God, with the best of intentions — to eradicate evil and restore the world to a state of paradise — it will do more damage than good. Since absolute power will inevitably wreak havoc, the Torah's method of repair is itself limited. The operating procedures of the covenant respect humans and work with them, in all their limitations, to get to a better place.

This act of Divine self-limitation is an act of love designed to make room for the other. When we love another, we want only the best for the person. When our love matures, we no longer condition our love on others being at their best level or fulfilling our expectations. We accept and love them with their flaws and limitations. We still want the best for them, but we cease to pressure them to attain their highest potential. Out of love we move from an attitude of superiority to one of equality. Love equalizes us. I may model a better way, attempt to persuade, maybe even resort to chastising, but I no longer resort to coercing my partner.

This is the first foundation of the covenant.

The Torah says this in the name of (and about) the God of the universe. God says: "Never again will I destroy every living being" (Gen. 8:21). God still wants the world to be *tov me'od*, very good (Gen. 1:31), but God will never again use total, coercive power to punish human beings. The first rule of covenant is therefore to respect human freedom. People should be held accountable for wrongdoing, but overwhelming them for the sake of the right and good is itself wrong. Even intimidating them into doing the right thing is coercive, a violation of their dignity of equality.

The Torah generalizes this principle. God has established a stable, dependable, natural order so humans will live in a world where they feel secure enough to act out of freedom and choice. The natural laws are a signal to humans that Creation is structured to respect their dignity and freedom. "As long as the earth endures, seed time and harvest, cold and heat, summer and winter, day and night shall not cease" (Gen. 8:22). Sinners will not be instantly chastened, or murderers struck with lightning bolts. Nor will there be ever again the mass punishment of humanity witnessed in the Flood. God's pledge to Noah and to renewed humanity is self-restraint: no matter how much God wants the good, God will not force it on people. Rather, God will educate humans as to the good. God will reward and punish—but only to the point where humans can learn or can be incentivized to do good. As One who loves humanity, God wants to enforce and nurture the image of God in human beings so that they will develop their capacities, and voluntarily use them to bring the world to the right place.

This commitment to equality expresses another aspect of covenant. The covenanters—God and humanity, God and Israel—may appear to be quite unequal. The infinity of the Divine dwarfs and trivializes humanity and human effort. As the morning prayer notes: "Are not the mighty like nothing before You, the men of renown as if they had never been, the wise as if they know nothing, and the understanding as if they lack intelligence? For their many works are in vain and the days of their lives like a fleeting breath before You."[5] Nevertheless, the infinite Divine self-limits to enter into the covenant. Within the framework of the covenant, then, the partners are equal.

This explains the classic Jewish tradition of challenging God to live up to the covenant. The patriarch Abraham argues against the destruction of Sodom, saying, "Far be it from You to do such a thing, to bring death on the innocent as well as the guilty. . . . Shall not the Judge of all the earth deal justly?" (Gen. 18:25).[6] Knowing that God is bound to the covenant in which human value and equality are guaranteed can give us an interior sense of value and dignity. We are empowered to exercise judgment, to choose freely, and even to stand up to God for justice, with God's implicit consent.

This Divine loving concession of the right to be free is not a one-time event. Covenant means commitment. The respect of human free will is a permanent Divine undertaking. Like the laws of nature, these are dependable rules, on which you can stake your life.[7]

Likewise, would-be redeemers of society have the right to educate, to persuade, to model—but not to force. Jean-Jacques Rousseau was wrong; humanity cannot be forced to be free. One must respect—and treat accordingly—all the intended addressees of your activity, even your opponents. You have no right to impose your will on the other, even if the cause is noble. The fatal flaw in the grand liberation movements of recent centuries is their employment of coercion, oppression for the sake of freedom. This results in a citizen who is an intimidated, if not totally broken, person who has no sense of security or guaranteed rights. This individual is enslaved, whatever the intentions of the official policy. In democracy and covenant, incrementally progressive laws push and pressure the wielders of inherited hierarchy, but the pressure is calibrated and leaves people free to accept or resist change without risking their lives or fundamental liberties. Thus even those unfairly privileged must be treated as individuals, and though they may lose their unfair advantage, it won't be at expense of their dignity of equality.

Partnership

The second foundation of covenant is that this is a partnership between God and human beings. God is a deeply involved partner, and will be active in the process. But the human is also a partner and must act and take responsibility. God does not want to be a controlling parent whose every word is obeyed, or a tyrannical ruler whom one fears to cross or displease. As much as God wants the human to carry out the Divine plan for *tikkun olam*, God wants the human to mature, and eventually come to do the mission for its own sake and for the sake of the beneficiaries. Out of love, the Divine wants to enable and help humans to grow to their full capacity for right action.

The human being is a partner—not a hired hand who can work fixed hours and go home at five o'clock, leaving others to worry about the global task, or critical deadlines, or unintended consequences. As a partner, I have a serious stake in the outcome, and am responsible for the overall goals, not just for my particular assignment. As a partner, I have authority, but not exclusive control or decision-making power. I must cooperate with others to enlist their help. Any given human partner can make policy and move the project, but must take into account the other partners, their rights, and their say in the matter. Furthermore, every human is a partner with God, but humans are *not* God. As a human, you are not the owner of the world or of humanity. You are not the ultimate power. You are accountable to a higher authority and under judgment; and might does not make right.

Since one joins the covenant in a moment in time, one should see oneself as a partner with generations past as well. Those who brought the covenant to this point have profoundly shaped it and have a stake in it. They made your work possible. In many ways, their achievements (and failures) determine the range of your choices and possibilities.

Therefore, you should be grateful to them and respect them. Their work and decisions should be taken seriously and factored in, even if you are convinced that the covenant must now move on.

Incremental Steps

These two foundational principles lead to a third axiom of the covenantal process. The goal is total transformation, but the next step, the covenantal step, is typically incremental. To win people's assent, the next covenantal action will likely start from where people are, and move forward to a place that people see as within range and reason. Given the rights of the other partners and even of the opposition, the next covenantal step is likely to be the outcome of a compromise. Given the self-restraint that rules out coercion, the enacted policies are not necessarily likely to be the best, but rather the best possible right now.

Idealists may protest. Why should we settle for injustice, for carrying on an inadequate, even if improved, status quo, when our goal is perfection? The answer is implicit in the covenantal process. The partners are human, and so is the setting in which the repair must be made. Forcing a supposedly even better solution on people is an oxymoron, engendering near-term misery, not contentment. Cutting the cloth of policy to the measure of human consent is a legitimate and necessary form of respect for humanity, for the primary purpose of *tikkun* is to improve the lot of humanity not just in the future, but right now as well.

The ideal is often the enemy of the possible. In covenant, the ideal drives us—but out of respect for humanity, it is tempered in application to a sustainable level. True, some injustices may continue; some impaired performances will go on without repair. But the damage avoided by not pushing harder makes up for that cost. The deeper signal in covenant is that life functions, for the most part, within limits and in step-by-step accretions. Incremental change is more likely to be assimilable, and to open up the next step and the one after that. The lesson is that the human way, the way that respects humans even in their limitations, will get there faster and better than a method that prizes the ideal to the point of coercing people or overriding present reality.

As we have seen, the halakhah—the covenantal way of life articulated in law—is built on ideal norms, the norms of choosing life over death and the expectation of the final state of *tikkun olam*. Still, as a guide to living, halakhah often valorizes less than ideal behavior that is nonetheless at a livable level now. For example, slavery directly violates human dignity, freedom, and equality. It is incompatible with the ideal of human dignity as an image of God. God took Israel out of slavery on the very grounds that servitude to humans is incompatible with serving God, explaining that the Israelites "are My servants whom I took out of Egypt; [therefore] they should not be sold into servitude" (Lev. 25:42).

However, the Torah was given in a world where slavery was well established. Given the universal presence of slavery in biblical times, the Torah acted not to abolish it overnight, but to restrict and regulate its practice (Exod. 21:2–6). To start the process of abolition incrementally, the Torah restricted the enslavement of a fellow Hebrew to a maximum term of six years. This was a dramatic conceptual change, to suggest that slavery should never be a lifetime, permanent state. No less important, during the six years of servitude the slave was to be free from labor every seventh day, on Shabbat (Exod. 20:10). In essence the slave was really a free person who was temporarily in servitude. Furthermore, the slave was not to be treated ruthlessly and given servile type of labor (Lev. 25:39). Relatives were called upon to redeem the slave as soon as possible. If all else failed, the slave was to go free in the Jubilee year (Lev. 25:41,54).[8]

Note: these restrictions were primarily for Hebrew slaves. Canaanite slaves were permitted as before—with only a restriction on treating them with what was deemed excessive brutality (Lev. 25:44–46). Only if they were beaten and injured would they be freed (Exod. 21:26–27). This is far from the ideal of full freedom. Still, these incremental repairs started the process of abolition that took millennia.

Even these limits on servitude faced tremendous resistance. The prophet Jeremiah reports that despite a special emancipation of the Hebrew slaves in Babylon—carried out under fear of God's punishment—nevertheless, the owners turned right around and reenslaved their countrymen once the panic subsided (Jer. 34:14–22). Despite resistance, however, the practitioners of the covenantal way continued to try to eliminate slavery in increments. The Talmud continued the process of amelioration, requiring slaveholders to give their slaves food, clothing, and shelter equivalent to those of a free person and actually equivalent to the masters' own.[9] Later the tradition moved to regulate the length of time slaves could be required to work and the tasks they could be assigned, permitting only nonservile tasks, i.e., like those of free labor.[10]

Admittedly, this approach does not always work. In nineteenth-century England, slavery was abolished in stages through a democratic, incremental process of legislation we could call covenantal. In the United States, however, slavery was so entrenched that there was no political force able to overcome it. The Southern states made extension of slavery to new territories their flagship issue, understanding that behind the opposition to extension was the growing illegitimacy of slavery in Northern public opinion. Repeated Northern compromises— usually at slaves' expense, such as the mandatory return of escaped slaves under the Fugitive Slave Act—did not mollify the Southerners. The Civil War that followed wreaked more casualties than any other war in American history, on the way to the abolition amendments to the Constitution. And again, as soon as the rebels regained political power, the Southern states established a Jim Crow society that oppressed, degraded, and impoverished African Americans for another hundred years. Racism and racist attitudes, spread throughout the country, continue to wrack American society to this day.

The truth is that every method of change has its strengths and its costs. Over the centuries, the covenantal, incremental method takes longer, but typically avoids the major ruptures and confrontations that escalate the costs and often result in backlash or breakdown. Nevertheless, there will be neither justice nor adequate resolution of the profound suffering in evils like slavery, exploitation, and environmental destruction if we wait until the masters and profiteers are ready to end their evil ways. That may never happen, or it may come too late.

In lieu of all-out war or totalitarian revolution, the covenantal method requires constantly pressing to close the gap between the ideal and the real. The sweet spot is pushing enough to move the reluctant forward while educating all to accept the rightness of the next step. When enacted as legislation, the law both moves and educates, and allows those holding back to adjust. Compare that to the revolutionary and radical movements, especially in recent centuries, and one realizes Churchill's saying about democracy is also true of covenant: it is the worst approach — except for all the others.

The Incremental as Eternal

The covenantal way prescribes the best possible actions now. How are these compromised actions compatible with the Jewish tradition's teaching that the Torah's instructions are the word of God, and eternally significant?

The Torah aims for a world in which people will live fully in accordance with the Divinely intended outcome, fully respecting the image of God, and repairing the world to uphold this dignity. However, out of love, God configures the revelation so as not to assault or obliterate the human recipient. The goal is to motivate the recipients to come as close to the ideal as is possible for them. Instructions to current action, then, fall somewhere between the current state of society and the ultimate ideal of complete human dignity and freedom.

In the book of Exodus, slaves are not freed totally, but their servitude is restricted to six years, six days a week (Exod. 20:10, 21:2). Despite its dilution of the ultimate principle of the image of God and the right to be free, this instruction is the (doable) will of God at that moment; therefore, this instruction attains the state of being a Divine commandment. In a later time and society, more severe restrictions and even abolition—the true goal—may be possible. In that society, the abolition requirement will be the word of God. Nevertheless, the original commandment remains sacred, because at the time it was the best possible fulfillment of God's will, and because it shaped a more restrictive ethic that paved the way for more complete change in the future. The compromising rule is a legitimate and permanent marker on the way to *tikkun olam*.

This method of transformation and repair—that is, *incremental improvement to the extent possible*—remains the paradigm for abolition of all socioeconomic evils, in all fields. The Talmud states that even if such a law will never be practiced again, it remains a Divine teaching given for the sake of *drosh v'kabel skhar*, meaning: interpret it and gain the reward of being able to apply the method in a wide variety of situations.[11]

People who hold the Torah to be the revealed word of God, by definition perfect and eternal, sometimes struggle to understand this dialectic of the covenantal way. They are tempted, unconsciously, to block out awareness of such morally costly compromises with existing societal norms—even as they are later tempted to deny that we must move beyond the inherited stage of action. Sometimes this inability to grasp the dialectic of the ideal and the real leads people to scorn the biblical norm, instead of recognizing it as the sign of a dynamic, evolving process.

Thus it offends us that the Torah restricted but did not totally abolish a father's right to sell his daughter. The father could only sell her to someone who would marry her; when he married her, she had all the rights of a free wife and was to be treated as such. If the buyer—or his son—did not marry her, then she went free (Exod. 21:7–11). The very fact that these verses are so painful to us today teaches us how far we have come culturally and socially from the past when women were chattels. The truth is that even these partial changes were resisted in their time. Still, the influence of learning and applying the word of God worked its power, and the status of women moved (albeit glacially) toward being recognized fully as images of God.[12]

This observation is not meant to deny the cost of this method. When slavery continued as an institution, countless individuals suffered its degradations. After Sinai, women continued to be second-class and disadvantaged in social standing and personal dignity. Nevertheless, the justification that these commanded steps remain "the word of God" is that the covenantal process does not stop with any one generation's attempted reconciliation of the ideal and the real. The process continues even if the past legislation is enshrined in the Torah. The definition of the best possible at this moment reflects the human condition—this society, at this moment of time. After it has been affected by the covenantal regimen, the society comes to a new place. Social and economic conditions may change for other reasons as well over decades and centuries. Between these two dynamics, a new way of striking a balance between the ideal and the present reality may well emerge. Then the integrity of the covenantal process, and the still-unfulfilled ideal enshrined in the Torah, demand that the next possible (higher) covenantal standard be applied.

The law is not finished as long as the journey to *tikkun olam* is incomplete. The covenantal journey will not be over until the final stage is attained. Each generation lives by the covenantal word of God, takes it forward as far as it can, then passes it on to the next. In a future century, in a different societal setup, improved covenantal behavior may well be possible. That is the role of the Oral Torah, the community, and its religious authorities in every generation: to move instructions to the next level.[13] Each generation takes the past and future members of the covenant as their partners, receiving their starting points and parameters from their predecessors, and expecting the future generation to advance or complete their work.

Klal yisrael—the comprehensive covenantal community of the people Israel—consists of the dead, the living, and future generations: all who have lived the Torah and brought the covenant to its present point, and those who will carry on this communal mission. In the words of Moses, when he renewed the covenant of Sinai and passed it on to the next generation: "I make this covenant . . . not with you alone but both with those who are standing here with us this day before the Lord our God and with those who are not with us here this day" (Deut. 29:13–14). Thus, the covenant is established yet constantly open to the new-comer generation. The covenant is permanent, eternal, yet continuously renewed and changed.

7 Relationship and Choice in the Covenant

Now that we understand the values that define the covenantal method, we can turn to its actual operation in history.

Covenantal Relationship

The covenantal method of repairing the world begins in the relationship between the covenantal partners.

Love

It all starts with love. The Lord brings the vast universe into existence to express Divine love and to have an object for that love.[1] Out of plenitude of love, the boundless God, who completely fills the plenum of existence, self-limits to make room for physical reality. Likewise, the Lord limits Divine power in order to invite humans to join in shaping the world and its unfolding history.

The infinite God, compared to whom all existence is insignificant, nevertheless cares deeply about Creation.[2] Love is the engine that drives the establishment of covenant (Deut. 4:37, 7:7–9). God, out of love, self-limits and enters into covenant with humanity to fill a redeemed world with life (Gen. 9:1,8–17). "God is good to all [because] God's mother love extends to all creatures" (Ps. 145:9).

The same unrestrained flow of love directed at the people Israel, "the least of the nations," led God to single them out and to redeem them from slavery (Deut. 7:7–8). The Torah notes that God envelops "the heavens to their uttermost reaches and the earth and all that is on it," yet there was enough love left in Loving God to "desire madly" (*hashak*) the ancestors and to single out and enter into a special covenant with their children, the children of Israel (Deut. 10:14–15).

The same reciprocal love drove the Israelites to enter into covenant with God. What other emotion could have been strong enough to motivate a conglomeration of beaten-down slaves, afraid of freedom, to leave the green fields of Egypt on the Nile and enter a trackless, forbidding desert? As Jeremiah imparts, "I [will always] remember for you the covenantal love of your youth, your bridal love — when you followed Me in the wilderness, in a land not sown" (Jer. 2:2).

What does God ask in return for saving and guiding Israel but the very same? "Now, Israel, what does the Lord, your Loving God, ask of you? But . . . to love God and to serve the Lord your God with all your heart and soul" (Deut. 10:12). Since God enters into covenant to do good to those whom God loves, the Lord asks Israel to express its love in return by acting "to keep the commandments and laws of Loving God for your own good" (Deut. 10:13). The Rabbis therefore placed a daily renewal of the covenant at the center of the morning prayers. Upon hearing the proclamation of the presence of the Divine Partner, "Hear O Israel, the Lord [is] our God, the Lord is unique," the Israelite responds: "You shall love the Lord your God with all your heart, all your might" (Deut. 6:4–5). That is why, Maimonides writes, after affirming the existence and unity of God, the first commandment is to love the Lord your God.[3] This is why the Rabbis understood the love poetry of the Song of Songs as the most apt metaphor for Israel's relationship with God. What other Divine emotion could have been strong enough to survive Israelite betrayal — lusting after foreign gods, pursuing the promises of prosperity from local gods over fidelity to oaths to serve only God, violating moral codes — actions that enraged God (Hosea, chaps. 1, 2)? Yet, after all that, God responds: "I will speak to her [Israel] tenderly . . . I will marry you forever [covenant]; I will marry you with righteousness and justice, with covenantal love (*ḥesed*) and mother love (*raḥamim*). I will marry you with steadfast love (*emunah*) and you shall know Me as the Loving God" (Hosea 2:16,21–22). This is why the

Rabbis instructed the individual Israelite, who puts on tefillin every weekday to pray, to bind the straps as a marriage ring on the central finger of the hand and declare and recite the very same words to God.[4]

The Divine loves every single human being. This is the unfailing, unretractable source of the dignities of infinite value, equality, and uniqueness, found in every single person. In turn, these dignities supply the ethical norms for interpersonal activities and relationships. Humans are urged to walk in God's ways—that is, to imitate God (Deut. 26:17). One of the most important ways to become more Godlike is to develop the capacity to love, so that I extend love even to others who are not the same as me. "Love the *ger* (outsider, stranger)" (Deut. 10:19). This expansive embrace mirrors the Divine emotion: "God loves the *ger* and gives him or her food and clothing" (Deut. 10:18).

This driving force of love explains why God will never turn away from Israel, and will stay with humanity until the final perfection is achieved. This same undying love has kept Israel clinging to God, even under persecution. This love has withstood isolation, pariah status, and exile for two thousand years.[5] Thus Loving God offered and entered into a covenant with the people, Israel: "I will take you to be My people" (Exod. 6:7). Israel responded in love by joining the covenant and committing to God, thereby embracing the promise that "I will be your God" (Exod. 6:7).[6]

Commitment

As love persists, grows, and matures, it turns this free-flowing emotion into commitment. The lover then takes on the covenant as an obligation, and becomes a partner and spouse. God is not content just to love the world and its creatures. The Divine love seeks the best for the beloved: to establish a world that will sustain all the life in it and fully uphold the dignities each of its living creatures deserves.

But that same love recognizes that such a world cannot simply be bestowed. An imposed paradise is not experienced as a paradise at all; it is taken for granted, as if it were a giveaway, a bribe, a luxury, an accidental condition. Nor can humans be coerced into living the right way. A strong-arm method infantilizes or degrades the "beneficiary" of the pressure to be good.

The only way to get to a sustained perfect state is to undertake a joint process of repairing the world. Its foundation for success is not a potentially transitory passion, no matter how blazing, but a long-term commitment to persistently do whatever is needed. The partner needs the reassurance and trust that the covenanter will be there for as long as it takes.

God voluntarily offers such a covenant to humanity. In so doing, God relinquishes the right to use unlimited force, the power to simply speak and it is done, the ability to get there at God's pace.[7] Out of the wisdom of love, God affirms human dignity by initiating a process suited to human beings. This is the meaning of Divine self-limiting.

The human being also comes to understand that loving God is not enough. This love entails choosing life, cherishing God's creatures, and wanting to treasure and perfect God's Creation. Such love, too, will require a serious, long-term commitment.

The moment of covenanting is like the moment when two lovers decide they want to have children and raise a family. This calls for the more solid basis of marriage: a covenant that reinforces relationship and love. It turns out that, although love is the most powerful, driving emotion in the world, committed love is even stronger. Commitment is a statement of dependability: you can count on me and on this relationship, no matter what. And this is what a covenant is: a partnership composed of, and sustained by, committed love.

This is a paradox, of course. The emotional force of love is what drives me to commit—to assure the beloved that I want this to be a permanent obligation. Yet love is variable. Even in periods of deepest passion, the emotion of love surges and recedes. There are days when I don't feel very loving, and times when I am not very lovable. Many marriages and partnerships fail precisely because love may vary, connections may weaken, attachments may fade away. No matter how powerful love is, the question lurks: How will I feel tomorrow? Will I persist through thick and thin? Will I be there down the road?

My commitment states that I will not vary enough to walk away. How do I know that I will feel this way in a week? In a year? In a lifetime? The answer is, I don't know. But the free will commitment to obligate myself to make it work raises enormously the probability of success and of permanence. Each covenanter's endeavor to try harder and even out the highs and lows through the exercise of will evokes a reciprocal emotional response in the beloved—the thrill of knowing how much the other cares to make a commitment, and the validation that one's self is deserving of the other's permanent love.

Indeed, my partner's dependability releases me to become even more unique, more equal, more magnetic. As long as the emotion is just emotion, there is unspoken pressure. Maybe if I were totally myself, maybe if I explored areas that interest me but are not so meaningful to the other, maybe if they really knew me, I would not be loved. Thus, an internal governor may hold me back from being fully myself. When it becomes emotionally true that I can depend on the other no matter what, I am free to grow, to explore, to become. This likely makes me more interesting, more lovable, in my uniqueness.

Commitment also reassures in another way. In life, inevitable setbacks put stress on all relationships. Almost as inevitably, there are failures in personal behavior: taking for granted, not trying hard enough, being excessively caught up in work, being thrown by small matters, being dazzled or drawn off course by other attractions. Sometimes such experiences may be shattering. But true commitment is resilient, not brittle. Committed partners do not give up easily, but instead offer one another a margin of error to be themselves, to risk failure, to learn from their mistakes and continue to dream mightily. In truth, some of the greatest accomplishments of Jewish covenantal history came after setback and failure: the desert generation's maturing after the Golden Calf disaster; David's reign after Saul's failed kingship; the post-Babylonian restoration; the Rabbinic cultural transformation that won out after the destruction of the Temple and exile; the flowering of Lurianic Kabbalah after the Spanish expulsion; the birth of Hasidism after the pogroms and massacres in seventeenth-century Poland; the creation of the State of Israel after the Holocaust; the exodus of Soviet Jews after decades of repression.

An even more important maturation in going from freestanding love to a committed relationship is undertaking doable, empowering actions to define the relationship. In its initial impact, love may be an "oceanic feeling"—one so all-encompassing, it may operate to the detriment of everything else. Such feelings, in turn, may drive a wedge between the couple or frighten off one or the other, for fear of being inadequate. Consider the challenge: "Show me your unlimited love." No actions can do justice to such a global need.

Entering into covenantal commitment, in contrast, translates herculean tasks into bite-sized, doable projects. Through covenant, "Do you love me?" becomes "Will you remember my birthday? Pay attention to my words, my needs? Respect my opinion? Enjoy my humor?" Through covenant, abstract feeling becomes concrete: "Will you try to feel my pain? Support my dreams? Cook me a meal? Notice my outfit? Pick me up when I am down? Stand by me when I fail?"

When accomplished, these concrete acts deepen our bond and fill us with good feelings. I feel successful, not inadequate. My commitment is not a superhuman task to which I will have to sacrifice everything and will probably fail at in the end, but rather a human responsibility I will gladly exert myself to live up to.

There is a parallel at Sinai. Giving the Torah to the people, the Infinite Unknowable Elohim asked the Israelites to enter into a caring, covenantal relationship with a loving God, and to express this by being kind to each other, looking out for and helping the needy, dealing justly in business relationships, paying assessments in torts, accepting restraints in dealing with people in servitude. These are not easy requests, but they are doable. At Sinai, the Lord translated *tikkun olam* from a cosmic task into a challenge to create a decent society in one small corner of the Earth. The Book of the Covenant explained that direct service of God would require three annual visits to a Tabernacle—not relinquishing all of one's worldly activities and possessions to meditate on God.[8]

There is another maturation message in fusing the emotion of love into an ongoing covenant: love limits itself out of consideration for the other. God leaves some tasks that would be more easily accomplished by Divine power to be done instead by human beings. Thus humans earn their dignity and participate in their own liberation.

In sum, love limits its demands so the beloved can cope with them and even achieve them, one step at a time. The covenantal regimen calls each of us to a mission respectful of our capacities and worthy of our efforts. The subtext is that incremental actions and finite improvements are significant. The art of the possible is an honorable frame for action, one that expresses respect for the status quo, even as it is determined to change it.

The outcome is a kind of alchemy. The expression of an infinite gratitude for liberation is turned into a festive family meal with a taste of unleavened bread or a bite-sized bitter herb at the Passover seder. Thus, the boundless, unknown future and the finished past meet—and blend into a present pregnant with possibilities. An all-encompassing, all-consuming mission turns into a harmonic wave, enriching a thousand daily, nonultimate, very human activities.

The final dimension of the maturation of love is what finally enables and inspires entering into covenant. In the beginning, love is a response to some aspect of the beloved. I fall in love with another human being for her looks, her charm, her mind and wit, her effervescent personality. Maybe her fame, her success, her wealth, her popularity, her usefulness to me attracted me. Perhaps it was her conversation, her kindness and caring, her authenticity, her inner strength and ethical conscience. Maybe it was all of the above. But at some critical point, my love rises above the details and embraces the person, the self, the unique image of God that my soulmate is. That is the moment when my love is no longer fixed on the details. Then I understand that, even if the other's looks, mind, charm, or utility were taken away or lost, I would still want to be with that person for the rest of my life. That is exactly the point of the covenant of marriage. I am so in love that I accept the risks of a life lived with this person. I know that old age will steal the vigor and the looks, that fame and wealth are fleeting, that kindness and caring may be eroded by tragedy or the burden of chronic illness. The twists of life may undermine any one quality of the other—but my love is ready and prepared to handle that. The Talmud describes this phenomenon as the shift from *ahavah hatluyah b'davar*, love that is attached to one thing, as against *ahavah she'eynah tluyah b'davar*, unconditional love that is not fixed on any one factor. Says the Talmud: a conditional love fixed on one aspect of the other— when that factor is gone, then the love passes, too. But unconditional love will never pass away.[9]

When the Divine desire for Israel ripened, when the Israelites rose above gratitude for their Redeemer, or awe at the Divine power, the two joined in a covenant of redemption. God promised to be their God, companion, teacher, partner. The Israelites (and later their descendants) pledged to live a life of covenant for themselves and for the world. There was no way of knowing what failures, burdens, triumphs, or disasters lay ahead. But this is the power of committed love that is not dependent on one factor. Mature, unconditional love undertook a staggering task of immeasurable dimensions. Commitment, the second step of covenant, represents one small step for Israel and humankind, one giant step for redemption.

Community

Community is the third essential component of a covenant. When the goal is world transformation, one individual alone cannot commit to such a covenant. A single person will be dwarfed by the task and likely defeated before starting. If the whole society is unanimously committed to the status quo, and I alone say that it must change, then I am simply out of step, a misfit, even crazy. History is full of cases where individuals could not achieve their visions because they were ahead of their times. To establish covenant, then, I need a community. That is why the Israelites stood together to enter into the *brit* (covenant) at Sinai: "Moses went and repeated to all the people the commands of the Lord and the rules; and all the people answered, with one voice, saying: 'All the things the Lord has commanded we will do'" (Exod. 24:3).

It is not just that the individual needs help to accomplish the task. The community helps validate the person and the project. I am not the odd man out; the community supplies a supportive reference point. Universal agreement that certain ideas are beyond the pale compels individual pioneers to suppress their visions, setting them aside as unworkable or wrongheaded. Yet when I join a covenantal community alongside significant numbers of others cocommitted to the project, this gives me the authority to proceed. When Christianity ruled and often treated Jews as pariahs, when Islam sometimes defined them as second-class subjects, the backing of the Jewish community gave Judaism's leaders the strength to go on testifying that they were God's chosen people.

This sense of community, the antidote to isolation, may well save me from two frequent temptations in personal and communal history: to fall silent, or to turn to extreme acts such as violence or terror. Furthermore, I need a community to pass on the undertaking to my children. Relationships between parents and children can be so fraught that children may well resist taking on a project they heard about only from their parents. It is not a cliché to say that it takes a village to raise children and imbue them with a set of values and a common cause.

Many covenantal ritual moments—prayer, circumcision, marriage, saying Kaddish (the memorial prayer for the dead)—are, ideally or necessarily, performed in a *tzibbur*, a community joined for a sacred purpose. Legally, ten is the minimum number to constitute a minyan, a quorum, a designated cross-section representing the entire people of Israel.[10] In other words, enough others are present that I may get a real sense that this matter is not just my issue, or my family's issue, but one embedded in the larger covenantal community. Therefore, an individual Jew who seeks to join the mission of *tikkun olam* joins the community of Israel.

Rabbi Soloveitchik observes here that it is not enough to bring ten people into a room. Being together in one space does not make a community. A community comprises of a group of people who have come together *for a purpose* and are *united in common cause*. When the people designate a *shaliaḥ tzibbur* (a messenger of the community) to lead them in prayer, they make clear that they have come together to pray. The Israelites shifted from a conglomeration of individual families to a covenantal community when they took on the Torah, thus stating their purpose. The entire Jewish people acting in history and pursuing their mission can be seen as a transgenerational community united in common purpose, *tikkun olam*.

Community sets up an important dialectic in Judaism. Every individual is directly linked to God. One need not go through the community to pray; nor does one require an intermediary to connect to the Lord. Indeed, in Rabbinic tradition, there is no absolution from sin except by individual repentance, regret, and reparation. Still, the individual alone is not enough. The Talmud says that, unlike with an individual's prayers, God never turns back the prayers of a community empty-handed.[11]

Note that God, too, is a member of the covenantal community: "And I [God] shall dwell in their midst" (Exod. 25:8).[12] God, too, rejoices in the community's triumphs and celebrations, and suffers in its defeats and tragedies.[13] Furthermore, the name of God—God's reputation, if you will—rises or falls on the behaviors of the Jewish people.[14] Proper behavior by Jews is called *kiddush ha-Shem* (sanctification of God's name), and improper behavior, *ḥillul ha-Shem* (desecration of God's name). God's membership means that the community can also challenge Divine injustice (or indifference) by the covenant's standards (Gen. 18:28–32). Moreover, community members are in relationship not only with one another, but also with God.[15] Violation of another's dignity and rights is a sin against God.[16] Love and honor for the other are signs of respect for God.

Sometimes, a community member's strength is multiplied by the talents of millions of others. Sometimes, one's convictions are strengthened and deepened by the commitments and understanding of whole generations. Other times, the community may drag a member down in its corruption, or draw people into wrong, even destructive paths by its own recklessness. Regardless, the community sets limits on individual actions. A group may not be able to go as fast as necessary (or as I am able) because of its entrenched interests or the immovability of its conventional wisdom. Even a covenantal community's immediate needs can be in conflict with the overall world vision—which is why a living covenantal community ebbs and surges through the generations, generating renewal movements or even breakaways.

Choice in the Covenantal Process of *Tikkun*

Once love, commitment, and community come together in covenant, the individual is ready to improve the world. Doing so requires us to make choices.

Start Where You Are

The covenantal instruction to each individual in the work of improving the world is to *start where you are*. This points to starting with personal life, where presumably I have the maximum say in decision-making. I need no one else's approval to start living my life covenantally—only the drive to reflect upon my actions.

The covenantal criterion is this: every action in my life will not be done randomly, routinely, or unthinkingly. To live covenantally, I will locate every action in relation to how it will be done when the world reaches perfection, and try to act at this ideal level. If this is not realistic, then I will shape my action to be the closest approximation of the ideal possible now. Starting where I am now, I will give a bit more *tzedakah*. I will eat a little less meat. If, in the present reality, I cannot pay my employees the ideal wages of the future—fair wages, established by mutual consent, that enable workers to support themselves and their families with dignity (today, wages so far above the norm might, in many cases, not be economically viable)—I will at least pay a livable wage and proper overtime rates according to industry standards, and this will constitute meeting covenantal standards.[17] If the industry standards are too low, and hence I may not be able to meet the covenantal requirements, then my religious commitments would dictate that I buck the field's standards and either raise the level successfully or withdraw and go into a business that can meet the minimum covenantal standards.

This reshaping alters any and every action to make it covenantal. Indeed, according to Jewish tradition, the covenantal standard should be applied to *every action in life*. Every biological action, every interpersonal interaction, every work behavior, every creative activity is assessed and imbued with purpose; every life component is maximized (and every death or life-reduction component minimized) toward *tikkun olam*.

Codes of halakhic behavior are our inherited guides to covenantal action in all aspects of life. It is also true that, as social and economic conditions change, the current dominant halakhic practice in various areas does not always meet the standard of closest possible approximation to the ideal. The status of *agunot* women ("chained wives," who cannot obtain a Jewish writ of divorce, called a *get*; see chapter 8) or the attitude to gay people in traditional Judaism are examples of where halakhic norms need ongoing covenantal work.

Jewish religion also adds ritual actions that bring covenantal behaviors into every aspect of life. Some rituals, such as circumcision for male infants and covenant ceremonies for female babies, inculcate the understanding that my family and I are members of the covenantal community. Holiday reenactments, from the joyful recounting of the Exodus on Passover and the acceptance of the Torah on Shavuot to the commemoration of the destruction of the Temple on Tisha b'Av, connect us to moments in the history of covenant; so do contemporary holidays celebrating Israel's statehood (Yom ha-Atzmaut) and commemorating the Holocaust (Yom ha-Shoah). Liturgical traditions, from daily prayer to blessings recited over food, at celebrations, and on encountering remarkable natural experiences all serve to relate the worshiper to God, the covenantal partner. These reminders and psychological frames inculcate values and inspire us to live up to the covenant's demands.

The essence of the covenantal approach is to do the best possible, since in many cases the ideal behavior is not doable right now. Perhaps I am not able to live up to the covenant's full ethical or religious demands. Then the covenantal approach is to start where I am: do the best possible now; seek out help from family and community to do better; work at it and grow until I can reach the fullest measure of covenantal performance.

It is true that in some cases, if the shortfall is egregious enough—especially if it is harming others—doing the next best may not be good enough. At the other extreme, however, falling short should not be compounded by giving up altogether out of the belief that if I am not doing all, then I am not doing anything worthwhile. The covenantal model rejects this passivity. As Anne Frank put it: "How wonderful it is that no one has to wait but can start right now to gradually change [repair] the world."[18] Doing the best possible acknowledges that the world is imperfect and the covenant is not yet realized, but it is still operating. There is room for growth and future improvement, but that change builds on the present.

Start where you are has another meaning. To function covenantally, I have to locate myself accurately, sizing up my abilities, standing, and resources without illusions and evasions. I must also assess my social and societal context: What are its opportunities, problems, limits? As part of the ongoing covenantal community charged with the task of *tikkun olam*, how can I step up according to my particular capacities and scope?

I must stay focused as well, remembering my mission is to deal with the problems and challenges of my own time.[19] I can appreciate those who articulated and fulfilled the covenantal responsibility in times gone by, but rather than sink into nostalgia and get caught up in fighting to restore an imagined golden age that is not restorable—and probably never was golden—I must embrace the fact that I live here and now and so my mission is to make a difference here and now.

Similarly, I must resist the temptation to postpone taking action. I must not tell myself, "Right now, I am building a family, so there is no time to work for community or society," or "I am just a cog in the wheel at my firm, so this isn't the time to rock the boat by pushing for higher standards, but when I become a senior partner or CEO, *then* I will correct the evils I see around me." There are legitimate concerns that may modify the tactics and solutions I undertake. However, if I do nothing now, then I am likely to fall into conventional morality and never act at all. As Hillel says: "Do not say that when I free myself up, then I will study Torah—because you may never free yourself up."[20] By the time you get to be CEO, your accommodations will likely have habituated you to the system and you may well have lost your awareness of what needs to be done. Start, even modestly, and you will get stronger as you go along.

Start where you are also means overcoming one's fear of standing out or being different. To be committed to covenant is to be committed to serving as the avant-garde. I do not rationalize, "Why be a sucker? Everybody else is doing it and benefiting; why should I take a risk?" Rather, I have seen what needs repair; therefore, it is my calling to start the process of *tikkun*. Instead of feeling isolated and alone, I can draw upon being part of the covenantal community. Many past and present members are standing with me in spirit right now.

Starting is often the hardest part of *tikkun*. The entrenched appears unassailable. The obstacles look fearsome. Internal hesitation is at its strongest. So the main point of *start where you are* is the admonition to *start*. Life is fleeting. Wherever I am today is the place to start, since my very next action can always be reframed as a choice of life and an act of *tikkun*. The Torah says: "These words which I command you *today* should be on your heart" (Deut. 6:6). Moses calls out: "You stand before the Lord your God, all of you, *today* . . . to enter into the covenant of the Lord your God, which the Lord your God establishes with you *today*" (Deut. 29:9,11). The covenant is renewed every day. The covenantal life is lived every day. The work of world repair starts *today*.

You Are Not Alone

When you take that first step to change the world, you receive one of the greatest benefits of being part of the covenantal community: a surge of energy and enthusiasm driven by the discovery that *you are not alone*.

First and foremost, you are not alone because the Creator of the Universe who seeks the world's completion, the Sustainer of Life who wants to uphold its full dignity, is your partner in the covenant of redemption. This is one of Judaism's fundamental affirmations.

Given God's cosmic scope, I may think I am too small for Divine attention. But no. God loves each and every unique individual. The Lord is with me — but because God is invisible and without corporeal form, I must go inward, deeper than the surface of existence, to know this. Judaism teaches the doctrine of *hashgaḥah*, Divine Providence. The Lord's consciousness is on every individual life and every human being in particular.[21] And when people feel cut off (as in prison, or lost at sea) (Ps. 107:14,23), or when terror and the plague threaten (Ps. 91:3–11), when we are weak and vulnerable, in slavery, or extreme poverty, or part of an excluded minority (Deut. 10:17–18), then God is even more present. As Isaiah proclaims: "I [God] dwell [especially] with the oppressed and lowly in spirit" (Isa. 57:15). To experience this, I just need to tune in deeply.

The psalms are replete with words of encouragement.[22] When I work to reach the covenantal goal but feel beaten, "when I think that my foot has given way," at this very moment "Your covenantal love, Loving God, sustains me" (Ps. 94:18). The standard image of God's presence has the Lord doing miracles — "a thousand may fall at your left side and ten thousand at your right, but it shall not reach you" (Ps. 91:7). But there is a deeper, less prudential, more loving level of connection for its own sake. God's presence is with me everywhere, sharing the vision and the goal, the pain and the fate. "Though I walk in the valley of the shadow of death, I fear no evil, for You are with me" (Ps. 23:4).[23] When the whole world says: "You are wrong!" the word of God stills the tumult and gives me the strength to go on. It helps me to know that God not only wants but needs me to achieve the goal.

Nor am I alone among my fellow human beings. By joining in the covenantal process, I am linked to my fellow members of the covenant: millions of them, all over the world, working on the side of life. Every other member of the covenant wants me to achieve the same goal— for them and for me. Their range of skills supplements mine. Their energies multiply mine a millionfold.

True, there are only thirteen or fourteen million Jewish participants in the covenant, and there are billions of upholders of the status quo, all too many of whom hold antisemitic beliefs. Often, reflecting on these numbers, I have said to myself: how can fourteen million Jews uphold or transform the whole world? It will never happen. We are going to get a collective hernia! But through Jewish-Christian dialogue I came to realize that many of the world's almost two billion Christians share a version of this covenant of redemption and are likewise trying to lift the world.[24] Moreover, countless individuals in many other religions, along with those in secular redemption movements, are also working on the side of life. I suddenly understood the power and the value of not being alone.

Finally, in yet another extraordinary dimension of the covenantal circle of solidarity, when I join the covenant, all the past generations of the *brit* are with me. My very life and acts are the outcome, the extension, of their work. And their wisdom and guidance come to me in the classic sources of the covenantal canon. Some of the greatest spiritual visionaries of all time, the Hebrew prophets, speak with me and to me. Some of the greatest minds of all time accompany me; the

Rabbis of the Talmud and their teachings are in my possession. The lives of the past generations, the experiences, the lessons learned, the action plans distilled—all are available to enrich my thinking and sustain my hopes. Past generations pursued their lives hoping, or trusting, that one day I, or someone like me, would come along, take up their task, and bring it closer to completion. Knowing this, my mind probes forward to realize that I am not alone in another sense: future generations too will join the covenant and pursue the mission. It is a tremendous relief to recognize the truth of the great covenantal maxim, "It is not your responsibility to complete the work."[25] This is one of the great bonuses of being part of a chain. Others yet unborn will carry on in the future. My responsibility is "not to stand idly by" (see Lev. 19:16). If I am not indifferent, I can trust that the future generations will not be, either.

Choose Life

The primary expression of being in the covenant—and the touchstone of every covenantal act—is to choose life. At the end of the Torah, at the moment when he asks the new generation to take on the covenant, this is how Moses summarizes his instructions: "See I have placed before you this day, life and good, death and evil" (Deut. 30:15). Life and death—these are the two choices facing everybody, all the time. As Maimonides points out, in this verse's framing, all good behaviors constitute a choice to uphold life and all bad or evil behaviors represent a choice to advance death. Then, having spelled out the details—"Love the Lord your God, walk in God's ways, keep the commandments, laws and rules" (Deut. 30:16)—Moses sums it all up: "I have put before you, life and death . . . *choose life*" (Deut. 30:19).

Moses is saying that, since the covenantal goal is to achieve the triumph of life, every life-affirming action is potentially covenantal. Every commandment is a model of how to act on the side of life. In parallel, countless other behaviors can also be shaped and directed to strengthen life. Moses is also acknowledging that God has given humans the dignity of choice. They can exercise their right to act against the covenant and advance death, but he urges Israel to choose life, because the outcome and reward of acting covenantally is more life, "that you and your children will live" (Deut. 30:19).

"Choose life," then, is the guide to living. As we will see, the Torah is striving to implant a general attitude to life. We are called to be open to life, to embrace it, to love living it, to view and experience it as an ever-flowing abundance of fulfillment and pleasure, and to want more of it. Life's unpredictable side should be viewed not as a threat, but as a source of wonder and excitement. True, certain conditions take the joy out of life—unavoidable defeats, losses, and painful setbacks; tense and dangerous situations; depressions so deep they rob us of the will to live; illnesses that disrupt our capacity to relate; obsessions that trap us into compulsive, colorless routines. Bad things happen to good people. But those who choose life understand that the sum is greater than any or all of its parts. They choose life for the good. It is so precious that they are prepared to pay the costs.

"Choose life" also has a deeper meaning. We often think that critical parts of life are involuntary. We act as if, once we are born, the process of living goes on by itself, or maybe within genetic constraints. We tend to underestimate how much of living can be shaped or upgraded by our choices. Babies are born with a certain brain capacity. But if we talk, interact, enrich the environment, stimulate them physically and mentally, bathe them in love and relationship, their synaptic connections multiply. Their emotional capacities are magnified: the quality of life is immensely upgraded. As adults, we have similar choices. We can drift, oblivious to challenges and opportunities. We can slip into routines that deaden emotions, patterns that prescribe unthinking actions, and setups that leave no room for surprises. Or we can decide to stretch our minds, expand our emotional range, learn new tools and methods of understanding that broaden our vision and deepen our life experiences—in short, we can choose to grow. Making such decisions constitutes choosing life. Life grows; death is unchanging.

The covenant not only illuminates a lifepath that might otherwise be cloaked in dimness and mystery; it also lights up every moment of life, asking us to look at the possibilities and identify the choices. Sometimes, we realize, not to decide is to decide—to surrender to the direction of death, not life. If, in preoccupation or inattentiveness, we take a pass on love or on relationship, all it takes for death to win is for us not to choose, or not to exert ourselves to engage in life. The truth is, there is no neutral moment in life. The next word we utter, the next food we eat, the next business decision or medical diagnosis we make or receive can be on the side of life—ours or the other's—or on the side of death—ours or the other's.

In most moments of life, the contrast between life and death is not so stark. In many situations, there is an admixture of elements. For example, without eating, the body will die: to eat is to choose life. But if I choose to eat meat, then I am incorporating the death of another creature into my sustaining nutrition. Since choosing life means minimizing death and maximizing life, I may eat less meat and substitute more plant proteins. Maximizing life may also take the form of eating healthier food so that I strengthen my life. Or it may involve the discipline of not wasting food, or of providing for the less fortunate—that is, the life of another. Kashrut, too, seeks to uphold life, as we saw in chapter 4, and the concept is endlessly expandable. I can choose to eat fish species that are not overfished. I can choose food whose production has not harmed, abused, or exploited people, thus reducing their quality of life. In all aspects of life, these choices can increase the surplus of life over death.

Think of our carbon footprint, which in turn increases or decreases the pollution and disturbances of life on the planet. Here, again, the covenantal way is to increase the life quotient and reduce the death quotient. In everything, from using disposable items to recycling, from shelter to travel, from designing clothing to shopping for computers or smartphones, if we want to consciously increase life, we can make a difference for the whole planet. If we are ready to discipline ourselves in areas of life that we usually treat as throwaways, then the balance of life and death can be turned favorably toward *tikkun*.

We can apply this principle to the choice of lifework or profession. I can seek out a calling like education that enables me to spend my life raising my students' quality of life and their capacities as the images of God. In business or law, I can choose specialties that increase life or improve it for clients and consumers, for workers, for society. I can go into medicine or medical research, contributing to life extension, to defeating deadly diseases, to increasing the quality of life for old and young alike. I can become a police officer and endeavor to reform the police covenantally. (This is particularly crucial, as the culture of policing in America remains infested with racism, such that many people of color fear they are under threat when interacting with law enforcement.) Versions of these same choices can be made in many other roles: firefighters, sanitation workers, social workers, and more.

In the end, the measure of the good life is the value of life added by my efforts and contributions. Every life has a price to be paid in the currency of life itself: the years of life my parents spent to raise me; decades of effort on the part of teachers, rabbis, relatives, and friends to nurture me; the cost of all the food, shelter, clothing, entertainment, and culture I consumed. If I have chosen life, however, there will be more life in the world—created by me, enabled or upgraded by me—than had I not existed. If I have lived and worked in a covenantal community, my contribution is multiplied. If I am productive and caring all my life, if I create again at an advanced age—then I will have lived a good life. I will have left behind a greater life footprint: living proof that I chose life.

8

Humanity in the Covenantal Partnership

How do we approach a goal so vast as the transformation of the world into a paradise, a setting that fully nurtures human life, without dwarfing the individual human role in *tikkun*? How do we adjust the covenantal method to respect the humanity of God's human partners?

Human Scale: Beginning with Microcosms

The answer is: we cannot separate the ends and the means; we cannot achieve positive results for humanity using methods inhospitable to humans. Therefore, despite the huge and daunting scope of the agenda, the project must be done on a *human scale*. All blueprints are to be drawn to this human scale, assuming human agents, institutions, and factors. All programs and policies must allow for human needs, limitations, and weaknesses as respected operating factors.

The watchword in covenantal planning is: think globally but act locally. Human beings operate at their best and sustain their efforts more readily on the local level. Local is human scale.

The pitfalls we saw in surveying alternative schemes for world repair are aggravated by operating at too vast a scale. On the one hand, the sheer size of the problem intimidates and discourages many people from beginning. On the other hand, some would-be repairers turn to extremism, believing that the sacrifice of "mere" individuals is necessary or inconsequential because nothing less will make a dent in the gigantic problem. Here, Kant's famous argument that the universal ethical principle demands that I act toward one individual only as I may treat all people presents a serious moral conundrum. The categorical imperative acts as a check against chauvinism and oppression of the other, but it also inspires revolutionary attempts to change the whole world or an entire society at once in ways that ignore human scale, violate human dignity, and reduce human value. By this means—global to local, or top down—humans run a great risk of overreaching or undercutting the very values they seek to advance. In both scenarios, human beings may be trampled, even destroyed, in the name of repair.

The Torah locates the creation of the Abrahamic covenant in the context of this very issue of scale. After the Flood, God enters into a universal covenant with all of humanity, who set out to rebuild the world. Their first agricultural settlement or city cluster, in the valley of Shinar, enables them to establish large-scale government and hierarchy based on taxes, religion, and culture. But humanity's appetite grows with their success, and the great tower of Babel is conceived (see Gen. 11:1–9). Whether it is a dream of reaching up and storming heaven to bend the Divine to human will, or the glorification of government and human authority to reduce the population to submissive awe, the Torah's point is that large-scale, visionary human projects can unleash a grandiosity of spirit that turns abusive. Heavenly tower-building projects can reduce humans to cogs in the machine.

Divine wisdom understands that concentrations of power must be dispersed, and the scale of *tikkun olam* reduced to a family size. The carriers of the covenant must be a people so linked, so vested in solidarity, that they will never scant the human factor, no matter how lofty or important the project may be. Such a people will go to their particular land. They will work in their own neighborhood and improve the world on a human scale.

Therefore, the Loving God singles out one family, and enters into a covenant of redemption with Abraham and Sarah.[1] The universal covenant made with Noah is thus recreated in the first of particular covenants that will operate locally. This family, in conjunction with all the others, will repair the whole world. The goal is still to increase love, peace, justice, and righteousness in society, and equality and dignity among all the inhabitants of the Earth.[2] However, individuals and groups should embark on this task at a scale they can manage.

To redeem the cosmos, the covenantal strategy starts with a microcosm. Create an ideal *local* environment where the future perfection is realized and made flawless *now*. Then bring other people to it, to experience the power of what is possible. They will be transformed and inspired to go out to the unredeemed sector and raise it up toward the ideal. By tasting perfection now in miniature, they will be empowered to persist in the face of obstacles. They will feel free to overcome the established conventions and reject the argument that it can't be done, because they will know that it has been and can be done.

To save the whole Earth, start with one land or one country. The Jewish people set out to make the Land of Israel a land of holiness where life is sacred and treated accordingly. They sought to create a society that meets the covenantal standards (Lev. 19:33–36). This is the ideal: even while the actual practice (among Jews and non-Jews) is often flawed, ambiguous, and occasionally even abusive, the ideal is before us as a goal for our society, our land, our family.

To redeem a whole country, start with one city. Make it a city of peace (Ps. 122:6–7), where all come to be united in common cause (Ps. 122:3–4).[3] Make it a place where people act ethically (Ps. 125:3) and the needy are provided for (Deut. 14:27–29); where a just government rules (Ps. 122:5); where both citizen and ruler are bound by the same Torah (Deut. 17:18–20), and where both acknowledge the higher authority to which they are accountable (Ps. 122:4).

To make one city into a place of maximum life, start with one neighborhood or one building. Make the building—the Holy Temple—a place where human life is complete and unchecked by death, where the full-time servants before God are in perfect health physically, modeling the future triumph over disease (Lev. 21:17–23).[4] Here the population comes for religious inspiration and to connect to God, but must purify its ethical behavior in order to enter (Ps. 24:3–4).

To redeem the whole week, start with one day, Shabbat. Make it perfect—no work to do, no conflict or war, no poverty or deprivation. Make it a day of family unity and community, of good meals, conversation, and song, of making love and studying texts, of communion with God and with friends. Then extend it out into the workaday week. Use the model to turn the work toward creativity and wholeness. Use the experience to deepen family, friendship, and solidarity during the week. Then expand the circle of redeemed time until it encompasses the whole of time.[5]

Once the model is created, then the redeemed circle must be expanded outward—from building to neighborhood to city to country to globe, from day to week to all the time. What is created on a human scale can be extended, respecting that scale, until the whole planet is perfected.

Human Emotions: From the Particular to the Universal

All people are infinitely valuable; all are equal. How, then, can we choose one location—one country, state, city, or neighborhood—to begin the work of *tikkun olam*? And how might we select one population group, one people, in whom to invest our initial energy and devotion?

Since the human factor must be our guiding principle, and since emotions often make human beings more open to acting beneficently toward those closest to them, the covenantal approach recommends: honor the natural flow of human emotions. To construct your microcosm, start with your own family.

Most people will more readily raise their behavioral standards toward their immediate family. Generally speaking, we are prone to treat kindly and preferentially people who have already extended kindness and help to us. The better I know people, the more familiar and connected they feel to me, the more ready I am to make provisions for their unique needs and capacities, and the more willing I am to hold myself to higher standards in our interactions. Once I begin with my family, I can widen out the circle of concern, wider and wider, until it encompasses everyone.

This approach is not foolproof. Sometimes people do not treat their family rightly. Sometimes family beneficence is only a one-way street. Witness the folk witticism: "Two parents can take care of ten children, but ten children cannot take care of one parent" in need or old age. Still, if relationships are acted out rightly, the family does provide for its own. From family we learn caring and responsibility; there it is modeled and practiced, including on us. When the covenantal process works as it should, one can educate a people to extend family attitudes and care for unknown and unmet others as their own.

"Start with your own family" translates into the Rabbinic principle *kol yisrael arevim zeh lazeh*, every Jew is responsible for every other one.[6] For starters, as a Jew, I have a moral and economic obligation to help members of my family not fall into poverty (Lev. 25:25–28). If relatives have fallen into servitude due to poverty, I have to lend or give them money to get out of it (Lev. 25:35–55). Fulfilling such familial obligations gradually led to the entrenchment of communal policies to support those in financial need. Help for the poor was obligatory—not charity (*caritas*, kindness, compassion) but *tzedakah* (righteousness). The community could tax people to create a *tzedakah* fund.

In the medieval period, when Jews were captured or held for ransom, this translated into the mitzvah of *pidyon shevuyyim*: heroic measures, financial and otherwise, to redeem captives taking priority over all else.[7] These acts of heroism were even performed on behalf of Jews abducted from faraway communities, who were still considered part of the extended family of Jewry.

For many contemporary Jews, acting to rescue our Jewish family has been a primary element of covenantal identity. Early in the twentieth century the Jewish community created the American Jewish Joint Distribution Committee to send staff, money, and special resources to Jews in distress, even in distant communities; as the JDC, it continues this work to this day.[8] From 1948 on, when Israel was established, some American Jews volunteered and helped to create and serve in

Israel's defense forces. They established philanthropic funds to enable immigrant absorption, upgrade education, foster industry, and create jobs and infrastructure. All this was done for people who were only distantly (if at all) related to American Jews: for Jews from Europe sometimes separated from their American cousins for several generations; for Jews from the Middle East—including the Land of Israel—and North Africa, separated from Western Jewry (in many cases) for centuries or a millennium.

In the early 1960s, the activist Jacob Birnbaum told my wife and me about the plight of Soviet Jewry: cut off from other Jews, subjected to oppression, and threatened with cultural extermination. They needed our help, he said. For years thereafter, we would rise early on Sunday mornings and march with our children in demonstrations, calling on Russia to free its Jews and urging America to stand up for their dignity and rights. We persisted even though the demonstrations initially appeared futile. Birnbaum and many others advocated tirelessly. Eventually the U.S. government, then the governments of other countries, were persuaded to act. All this helped lead to a miracle: the redemption of Soviet Jewry.[9]

Later in the 1960s we came in contact with the American Association for Ethiopian Jewry (AAEJ), sparked by a retired social worker, Graenum Berger. AAEJ leaders told us that a Jewish African community, long cut off from world Jewry, lived under terrible conditions compounded by persecution from a Marxist government and their Christian neighbors. They needed our help. To most white American Jews, these "tenth cousins" seemed quite distant. They spoke a language other Jews did not understand; they had a different skin color; they lived in an unfamiliar culture in an impoverished and remote country. Additionally, many voices suggested that the Ethiopian Jewish community was less than a century old, rather than Jews cut off millennia ago from the family and now returning. These gaps between them and the world's other Jewish communities weakened the sense of family. Still, in time the family covenantal responsibility kicked in. The Israeli government and diaspora communities organized and acted to redeem these captives and bring them to the family home in Israel.

This rescue operation occurred in a region plagued by poverty, hunger, and other perils. Human life was cheap. Yet out of covenantal obligation to distant family, millions of dollars were willingly spent for Ethiopian Jews. Major international powers were enlisted; air forces and special transportation were recruited. All this was done to restore the value of the image of God of tens of thousands who were recognized and connected to as family. To this day, the importance of Ethiopian Jews' integration into Israeli society is a matter of consensus among Jewish Israelis. In contrast to the general situation in Africa's poorest countries—where, absent a covenantal process or any sense of family responsibility, the world of hundreds of millions is still not repaired—for Ethiopian Jews, a family connection inspired action. This was an imperfect rescue to be sure (these immigrants, their children, and their grandchildren still face many challenges in Israel today), but a massive and significant one nonetheless.

This is the logic and promise of the covenantal method at its best. If you keep the covenantal process going for millennia and keep widening the circle, expanding its range, eventually you will feel the urge to take responsibility for raising the living standard even of your eighty-second cousin to that due the image of God—infinitely valued, equal, unique. I say "eighty-second cousin" because, according to the projected development of almost eight billion human beings from an original Adam and Eve, understood evolutionarily or biblically, no human being can be farther than an eighty-second cousin from any other. And, ultimately, this is the messianic goal of the covenant: that I experience every human being as a member of my family and an image of God.

That said, the very strength of the human emotional connection that leads to taking responsibility is also a weak point in the covenant's pedagogy. People are prone to stop at the line of family closeness. It is all too easy to turn a universal ethic of responsibility into a tribal code, in which only the related or the insiders get good treatment. This ethic may even be used to justify exploiting outsiders as beyond the family and therefore excluded from the moral code. Criminal gangs operate this way. Inside the group, one's word is sacrosanct; but outside the circle, one may rob, steal, extort, swindle, sell drugs, and run prostitution and human trafficking rings. This paradox is a risk of the covenantal process. Start with your own family and keep widening, and (incrementally) you achieve a universal ethic of *tikkun olam*; start with your own family and stop with your own family, and you have created a mafia morality.

By the ground rules of modern culture, the universal may appear morally superior to the particular, because it covers a broader group and is more equal in treatment of all. Universal redemptive movements have tended to set as their goal equal, identical justice, resource provision, and access for all. In other words, among the dignities of human beings, they have prioritized the dignity of equality over the dignity of uniqueness. This is why the Soviet Marxist-Leninist vision of socioeconomic equality led to the abolition of private property; why those, including Jews, who exhibited loyalties to their own minority cultures were deemed enemies of universal justice and the Soviet Communist paradise in the making. In Mao Zedong's China, too, the family was targeted as a bastion of private, selfish values, and therefore the enemy of the utopia he sought to create. In a less invidious example, Israel's socialist kibbutzim eliminated private property in favor of communally owned land and created children's homes where the young would live together and be socialized to identify with the kibbutz and society instead of the family unit.

In Stalinist Russia in 1932, a fourteen-year-old boy, Pavel Trofimovich Morozov, reported his father to the Soviet secret police for opposing the revolution and undermining collectivization. The father was imprisoned for ten years and later executed. According to the official version, family members murdered the boy in retaliation and in turn were apprehended by the secret police and then executed by firing squad. Pavel was declared a hero of the Soviet Union. Statues of him were placed all over the country. Schools were named for him. His story was introduced into school textbooks and presented as a moral model for emulation by all. But what was the real overriding message in Pavel's glorification? That a claimed ideal justifies oppression, imprisonment, murder, secret police, a captive press. What does it mean when you teach children that in the name of an ideal society one can become a hero by destroying one's own father? The answer is that you have not created a more humane society, but an appallingly inhumane one.[10]

So, too, Mao's attack on the family inflicted pain on the people, set children against parents, wounded social cohesion, and unleashed violence and oppression on millions. Furthermore, the repressed family selfishness turned up — unacknowledged and unadmitted — in the families of the revolutionary leaders themselves. Their children received advantages, privileges, and, later, access to wealth that made a mockery of the ideology of equality. Since the family factor was unacknowledged and unadmitted, such nepotism was usually impossible to check or correct.

The evolution of these movements constitutes strong evidence for the soundness of the covenantal approach. Looking out for those closest to you is not a deterioration from a standard of universal obligation and disinterested equality. Familial connections are so fundamental to human nature that, alongside our obligations to donate to other causes and to help with the general society's problems and emergencies, one can legitimately bend the universal rules of equal obligation to all people to allow for the family's distinctive needs, or for the individual's differentiated urge to help.

Indeed, post-Communist Poland, post-Maoist China, post-revolutionary Vietnam, and post-Marxist liberationist Africa have all made major reductions in world poverty as a result of the extra productivity that comes from working with — and not forcibly against — natural human emotions. Nonetheless, social safety nets and limitations on corruption — essential components of the covenantal ethic — have developed much more slowly in posttotalitarian societies. It is harder to translate a conventional, noncovenantal ethic into relational concern for individuals than it is to expand a covenantal ethic of individuals and relationships to cover everybody.

Of course, not all universal ethics turn into dictatorial, morally deracinating systems; nor do all particularistic, family-rooted ethical codes mature into covenantal ethics. Each approach has strengths, but either approach in its pure, unadulterated, absolute form will almost certainly be humanly invasive and morally degrading. There is no guarantee that any one method will work out—but it is more promising to start with a positive human emotion than to fight or drastically redirect natural human feelings.

Another important aspect of the covenantal wager on human emotions is that people become attached to the familiar, including language, geography, and tradition. They are moved by memories: their own and their people's. The universal and rational, however, tend to wean people from these attachments. Today this phenomenon takes the form of a global culture that bleaches out historical particularity or distinctive memories and rationales. The covenantal approach is predicated on the belief that anchoring universal norms in concrete language, memories, and rituals deepens them and strengthens people's attachments to them. I would argue that this in part accounts for why God has reached out to human beings and set up parallel covenantal communities, rather than staying with one universal Noahide covenant. Diverse covenants allow for distinctive and concrete attachments, differing according to location, culture, and the inner music of the languages. In the end, this approach wins participation through emotional attachments that vary from person to person and group to group. One might add that people's dignity is uplifted when their own family's history and inherited tradition are honored. Here again, the message in the method asserts that respecting human feelings is as important in instilling the values of *tikkun* as pursuing its formal goals. The means confirm the ends and move the world closer to the goal.

Human Pace

The covenantal principle of respect for human nature calls for incremental action. By temperament and preference, most human beings change slowly. They are capable of growing and making significant changes, but if you move them too far too fast, they will resist. For example, the adolescent years are often marked by Sturm und Drang—tension, intrafamily conflicts, social alienation, nonconformity, and rebellion—because the rate of change speeds up during these years. Many teenagers become confused as to who they are, and emotional disturbances—eating disorders, addictions, reckless actions, depression, suicidal behaviors—tend to emerge.

Similarly, rapid social transformation or economic shifts often lead to drastically changed expectations, even revolutionary explosions. Yet the same degree of change spread out over many years is more readily absorbed, and society is kept on an even keel. Where initial reactions to innovation are less extreme, the tools of democracy remain generally available to strengthen that society and change social attitudes over the course of time.

Covenantal success lies in the dialectical techniques that reflect all the sides of human nature. It uses conservative methods—take small steps, bring the past with you, act with deliberate speed—to achieve revolutionary outcomes. Maybe the Torah learned its lesson from the battle with idolatry. Since, as we discussed in chapter 5, idolatry was perceived as the ultimate enemy of God and, consequently, of life, the Torah went all out to abolish idol worship overnight, proclaiming universal destruction of idols and total war against idolators (see Deut. 12:1–3,29–31, 13:2–19). But, as the prophetic record testifies, the full frontal attack basically failed to defeat idolatry.[11] The fact is that the people's beliefs and assumptions about reality confirmed idolatry's claims. The idolatrous conception of gods, including their identity as amoral tyrants whose demands, however cruel, must be satisfied without question, was ubiquitous in the ancient world, and so the Israelites often fell into that mode of worship as well. Individuals like Abraham emancipated themselves from idolatry. But only as the Rabbis raised, step by step, the ethical standards and religious expectations of Divine behavior did the people's cultural assumptions change, and idolatry become truly unacceptable.[12]

The essence of the covenantal approach is the art of the possible. Take a finger where you cannot get a hand; if you can do this five times, you have achieved your goal. In a classic Jewish joke, after the battle of Austerlitz an exultant Napoleon, realizing his army has won him an empire, offers to reward three heroic soldiers with anything they ask. A German and a Pole each ask for the restoration of their fragmented countries, while the Jew limits his request to "one schmaltz herring." When his fellows are contemptuous of the humble request, the Jew responds simply. "I will get a schmaltz herring! We will see what you will get." The covenant may be described as the successful mechanism that repairs the world — one schmaltz herring at a time.

This is not to minimize the costs of an incremental approach. Incremental improvement means that considerable injustice and suffering goes on until the next step is taken, and until the final goal is achieved. Indeed, occasionally a problem is so acute that it demands an immediate, revolutionary solution. The key to the integrity of the system is for each generation to take the next step and the one after it, until all is achieved.

Ultimately, the covenantal act, including the halakhah, must be the best possible *under the circumstances*. When circumstances change, or when people enter into a new society where the social and cultural infrastructure has changed, a *new best possible* is possible.

But people habituated to past norms of behavior may fail to see that the current operation is morally compromised, and therefore dismiss the new opportunity to improve it. An example is the modern situation of the *agunah* — a woman who cannot obtain a Jewish writ of divorce. Over the centuries the halakhic treatment of women in various roles and circumstances evolved, moving somewhat closer to the ideal of treating all people as full and equal images of God. The Rabbis improved on the Torah by adding a *ketubah* (marriage contract), to provide additional legally enforceable rights in marriage and give divorced women financial security, and thus assist women economically in exiting failed marriages. Since husbands had the sole power to issue divorces, the Rabbis moved to reduce the abusive refusal to give one by prescribing cases in which the husband could be coerced into issuing the *get*.[13] Rabbeinu Gershom, "The Light of the Exile," took further steps toward equalization in the eleventh century: his enactments prohibited polygamy and validated a wife's acceptance of the *get* only if it was voluntary.[14] Because a husband could not force a wife to accept it, the balance shifted from his complete control of the *get* process toward his having to address his partner's needs and expectations.

In our own time, however, contemporary halakhah in marriage and divorce has not responded adequately.[15] Jewish decisors could take the next step toward dignity by implementing legal mechanisms such as annulment, mistaken marriage, nullification based on the husband's abuse or abusive behavior in denying a *get*, and *get zikui* (the court acting by issuing a divorce writ when the husband is unable or unwilling to issue a *get*).[16] These steps could free countless women from the suffering of failed marriages, or from extortion by husbands using their one-sided right to hold up the *get*. However, Orthodoxy is so focused on preserving the tradition that halakhists, as a group, have greatly restricted use of these powers. Most have even rejected other courts that used them. And very few are ready to take the next obvious step: to reinterpret the Torah statement, "he [the husband] shall write a writ of divorce" (Deut. 24:1) in ways that would give equal access to this power to wives or to courts acting on their behalf.[17] This is a breakdown of the covenantal process, turning incrementalism into a weakness.

Nonetheless, overall I believe incrementalism's long-term accomplishment is worth the cost. The incremental system of *tikkun* has caused much less suffering than failed revolutionary redemptive movements over the centuries and especially in modern times.

The principle of change at a human pace works best when the practitioners honor the covenantal method's combination of tradition and change. The incremental process protects the sense of continuity, and of identification with a cumulative tradition that exhibits a successful record of gradually repairing the world. The covenantal process has kept Judaism operating and upgrading through three major civilizational stretches of the covenantal journey—ancient, medieval, and modern. Throughout those periods, had the Jews not taken the covenant with them, they would have lost their way. Had they not improved the covenant behaviors incrementally, they might have fallen or been left behind in the march toward *tikkun olam*.

This record suggests another tactical aspect of operating the covenant. It is impossible to strike a perfect balance of continuity and change, between the incremental and the substantial. Therefore, it is helpful to have multiple approaches. Some change 5 percent, some 10; some press for revolution, some for evolution. The positive interaction of these approaches will establish the most effective boundaries and limits, the best defense against overcaution or overextension.

This explains why the Talmud ended up hallowing *maḥloket* (disputation), the process of exploring polarities by arguing for all sides of an issue as the best way to arrive at the true meaning—or range of meanings—of the Torah text. *Maḥloket,* including the practice of recording overruled minority positions alongside majority decisions, was accepted as the best way to arrive at a developed halakhah that could be applied to new and ever-changing conditions. Using the variety and diversity of human minds as a resource, *maḥloket* preserves the range of traditions and also tends to keep change incremental, because the outcomes are the product of give and take. This mode of operation upholds the human factor in the covenant and in the entire process of *tikkun olam*.

Human Models

To make humans partners in the process of repair, the covenantal method must educate people, bringing out their best tendencies, and nurturing these by response and confirmation. Doing this through reward and punishment for good and bad behaviors is inevitably coercive. Instead, the Divine preference for human freedom is to educate through the use of role models: humans who set a faster pace model the process of change and inspire others to follow them. Providing human models — men and women who are the heroes of Jewish tradition — as pacesetters for *tikkun olam* thus expands the covenant's essential promise of respecting human dignity.

This move from coercion to role modeling is articulated in the very initiation of covenant. The Torah tells us that God's "heart was saddened" (Gen. 6:6) that humans used their intelligence and free will to degrade and do evil in the world. The Flood represents an uncontrollable reaction reflecting the deep regret of the perfectionist Deity (Gen. 6:5–7). After the Flood, however, the Divine self-limiting love for humanity kicks in. Without relinquishing the dream of a world made perfect and full of life, the Lord initiates a covenant that binds God to never again overwhelm humankind with coercive punishments — not even for the noblest purpose, *tikkun olam*. The offer of covenant is the moment when Divine love obligates itself to respect human freedom. Henceforth, no matter how humans sin, there will be no punishment or reward so overwhelming as to negate their autonomy. The Divine implicitly moves to a policy of educating and persuading humans to do right and join in the process of *tikkun olam*.

The ultimate logic of this Divine self-limitation is to stop the use of external reward and punishment methods, and to commit to the exclusive use of education, persuasion, and role modeling. However, in the initial, biblical stages of covenant, God still does employ visible reward and punishment methodology. If the Jews obey God, the Deity defeats their enemies. If they don't listen, they are defeated.[18] I suspect this early phase reflects the Torah's recognition of the cultural assumptions of the time. The Torah needed to be able to compete with contemporaneous religious systems and gods that promised direct, visible rewards and punishments.

The turn in Divine methodology is expressed in the tower of Babel story, in which centralized government turns into a power that rebels against God and abuses humans. However, instead of destroying everything, the Divine responds by breaking up the universal language and political units of humankind. The best corrective for absolute power is to fracture and divide it. A covenantal strategy severs coercive unity by promoting diversity.

The same holds true in spiritual matters. As long as there is one universal covenant, the danger of concentration of control, of evil trends going unchecked, is high. So, without canceling Noah's universal covenant, God—who loves and wants to relate to all humans—proceeds to set up a particular covenant with Abraham and his descendants. Abraham agrees to build a model family and community, instructing his descendants after him "to keep the way of the Lord, to do righteousness and justice" (Gen. 18:19). I see this as the first local or group covenant of many to come. This limited, selected group also serves as pacesetters to reach higher, move faster, and work harder toward repair of the world.

The Abrahamic covenant confirms the fundamental Divine turn from coercion to education, thus honoring and enhancing human freedom. Other societies can see that the model works and may be inspired to redirect their energies or reset their standards. The prophet Isaiah articulates this approach when he reports Israel's mission in the world: "I [God] have summoned you in My grace and I have held your hand. I created you and appointed you a covenant people, a light to the nations" (Isa. 42:6). By this logic, other people and other nations can also serve as role models, diversifying the options and touching a variety of chords in other people.[19] Emulation is the least coercive and possibly the most effective way of motivating people.

However, a paradox is inherent in using human models to set standards and the pace of change. One might think that, in order to motivate people to grow, to become more than their current selves, we should hold up a very high-level model, perhaps even a perfect one, so that humans will really have to extend themselves to achieve it. Educationally, however, this is not so. It is essential that the model be like the people to be inspired. If the model is too perfect, the reaction may well be: "I can never be that." Then people back away. They may even regress, discouraged by such an impossible standard. The role model must be different enough to provide an incentive to get better, to try to improve the world, and yet be close enough so that people can say, "Yes, I can do that." So the measure of appropriateness for a model is a ratio, not an absolute, objective standard.

This awareness is at the heart of the distinctive Jewish emphasis on the humanity of role models. You might have thought that a people characterized as "God's treasured people" (Deut. 7:6) would be portrayed as moral paragons. Instead, the Bible describes a flawed, very human people, constantly trying but often failing. The ancient Israelites were a newly liberated band of slaves who struggled to shake off the slave mentality and mostly could not do it. The later Israelites often repent— and backslide. Sometimes they rise to faith and noble self-sacrifice, and sometimes they sell out for promised rewards from idolatrous cults. Isaiah and other classical prophets repeatedly recount how the Israelites break God's heart with their selfishness, or thievery, or recklessness. The deeper lesson is that Jews in the Bible are very human. That is part of the reason that God chose them. Their fallibility makes them a perfect test case. If people with all these human limitations can carry God's covenant, then all the world can do it. If God can keep loving this people, with all their failures, then God can love all of humanity.

Over the long history of persecution, Christians have often misread the prophetic critique to convict the Jews of being terrible people, citing the condemnations of the Jews' own seers. But the deeper truth is quite different. This record should be read with love—including love for humanity. As the Jewish theologian Michael Wyschogrod points out: If the infinite Divine love is bestowed in grace on such a stiff-necked, hard-to-change people, then surely it is extended to all humans, whatever the level of their spirit or the depth of their flaws.[20]

The Jewish tradition's heroes and models are very human beings. They live human lives of love and reflection, striving and failure. They often rise to greatness, but they never escape their human frailty. Those weaknesses make them great role models. They start where all people start. Therefore, they can be emulated. One can walk in their footsteps and stand in their shoes when making judgments.

The patriarch, Abraham, once the world's sole believer in the one God, is a person of immense inner strength. Think of the inner fortitude needed to withstand a vast, uniform consensus that there is no one god, no universal creator and moral judge. When his nephew, Lot, is taken hostage, he organizes his followers and fearlessly attacks four mighty kings who have already defeated an invasion by five other rulers. Out of the same conscience and courage, Abraham challenges God to live up to Divine covenantal standards and not destroy Sodom. He shows the same unbelievable inner fortitude in walking for three days, alone with God, toward a sacrifice of the son of his late years, Isaac, the son of his hope. Yet Abraham is no superhuman knight of faith. Early in his career, when he arrives in Egypt and realizes that Pharaoh has an eye for beautiful women and is likely to kill him in order to take Sarah for himself, he asks his wife to pose as his sister. When Pharaoh takes Sarah to his palace, he says not a word. When Pharaoh lavishes him with gifts—for what services is he receiving or expecting from Sarah?—Abraham shuts his mouth. He is not a fearless exemplar. He is a fearful human being.

Sarah, matriarch of the Jewish people, is a strong woman, loving and devoted to Abraham. She follows him unhesitatingly into being a minority of two. She puts her own body and dignity on the line, covering for him before Pharaoh, in order to save his life when his moral backbone has turned to jelly. She totally identifies with him and with the need for a child to continue the line and fulfill the covenant. When she remains childless, she suggests that Abraham take her servant Hagar to sire a son. But when the maid becomes pregnant, Sarah is very human. She is gripped by a fever of jealousy and a sense of insecurity that she will not be the mother of the covenantal legacy. In her jealousy, she cannot abide Hagar's son Ishmael. When her own son is miraculously born, she drives Hagar and Ishmael out.

The record of the next generations of the covenantal family is also mixed. Isaac's is the epitome of a dysfunctional but maturing family: Isaac himself, the posttraumatic stressed father; his wife Rebecca, unable to talk openly with her husband and instead devising a scheme to deceive him and procure his blessing for her favored son, Jacob; the two brothers' tormented relationship; and, finally, Jacob growing from a trickster into the man who can confront and wrestle with God and humans. The story continues with Jacob, who loves his wife Rachel; loses her, heartbreakingly, in childbirth; and compensates by fixating on their son, Joseph, thus sparking Joseph's brothers' fratricidal jealousy against him — and finally concludes with Joseph's own moments of retribution and reconciliation. All this is going on while the Jewish people is being born. The Torah relates all of it, miracles, warts, and all.

The biblical view is that heroes and role models, however great, are human and flawed. Moses spends more time, face to face, in direct encounter with the Divine Presence than anyone in history (Num. 12:7–8; Deut. 34:10), yet initially, lacking confidence or perhaps enthusiasm, he attempts to extricate himself from his life mission (Exod. 4:1–16). On one occasion he is prepared to confront God in defense of the Israelites — "Erase me from Your book" but don't harm them (Exod. 32:31–35) — yet on another, he is so fed up with the Israelites' constant complaints and petty demands that he boils over in a whining, self-pitying plea, asking God to put him out of his misery and let him go (Num. 11:10–15). The Israelites who left Egypt were the founding generation of the Jewish people, the generation that stood at Sinai and accepted the Torah on behalf of all future generations. Yet the Torah does not spare us one moment of their immaturity, their slave mentality, their damaged psyche, their frequent sinfulness, including worshiping a Golden Calf idol. In the end, they live out their lives in the desert, unable to fight and win a homeland, unfit to enter the land and set up a free society.

Nor does this kind of human portrayal end with Torah itself. King David, who unites the Kingdom of Judah and Israel and whose very name means "Beloved," is chosen by God, anointed by the prophet Samuel, and loved by his men precisely because he is so human, a buddy, a fearless fighter who risks his life along with them. He is direct, outspoken, intense; he holds nothing back. His love of God and religious spirit is so strong that the tradition insists that he wrote the Psalms. Horrifyingly, that same passion and impulsivity lead him to take Bathsheba, another man's wife (2 Sam. 11:2–15). None of his impulses or contradictions are left out of the Bible's portrait.

The Talmud, too, presents a galaxy of people — sages, scholars, visionaries — in all their human complexity. Rabban Yochanan ben Zakkai takes a historic gamble in abandoning Jerusalem and the Temple to destruction to recreate Jewish life at Yavneh.[21] Rabbi Akiva is rescued from the life of an impoverished, illiterate shepherd by the heiress to the richest fortune in Jerusalem.[22] He rises to become the greatest teacher of his generation, followed by tens of thousands of students — and loses them all in the aftermath of the messianic rebellion in which he supported Bar Kochba as the messiah. At the age of eighty he starts over and trains a new generation of scholars, who write the Mishnah; he ultimately dies under excruciating torture by the Romans, yet with his faith intact.[23]

The pattern of finding our role models in all-too-human leaders is particularly striking in contrast to some strands of Christianity, which, when it broke away from Judaism, often set up its heroes as perfect human beings. Jews understood that the chasm between ideal and reality was so great that it would take extraordinary actions from both the Divine and human partners to close the gap. These strands of Christianity, in contrast, responded to this gap by concluding that only God could close it — so God had to become human and lead the way. This Divine perfection was incorporated into portraits of Jesus as perfect and without sin. Both Jesus and his mother were untouched by human sexuality (Matt. 1:18–23). The saints of the Catholic Church were pure, or purified and sanctified on their ascent to sainthood. A deep theological conviction that human fallibility and physical needs are so strong that they must be eradicated in order to achieve higher goals helped lead, in part, to the Catholic tradition of celibacy for priests, who wield sacramental powers.

Jewish tradition also has elements, starting in antiquity, that sought to repaint the founding figures as perfect. In modern times, in the ultra-Orthodox community, this has become the party line. Charges of heresy against those who humanize biblical figures are rife.[24] Still, the dominant effect of the Jewish covenantal approach is to affirm the humanness of the human partner. By entering into covenant with humanity, God has embraced humans in all their weaknesses and flaws. This is an expression of God's love. As the Yom Kippur prayer points out, the Infinite God, who controls cosmic forces and is praised by heavenly, angelic powers, nevertheless desires the service and partnership of mortals. God prefers the praise of humans, however short-lived, burdened by pain and frustration, and flecked with sin. Moreover, this very preference for the worship of mortals constitutes God's glory.[25] Judaism insists that humans, together with God, can achieve the end goal—that finite, limited humans, in covenant, can grow and achieve cosmic outcomes. This affirmation is a distinctive mark of the Jewish covenantal process. It builds on human material; it acknowledges and allows for human weakness; yet it represents—and enables—the triumph of human capacity.

The dependence on human beings' leadership does not blind the system to the likely failures. Indeed, the processes of repentance and renewal, and the presence of second chances, feature prominently in the expositions of the covenantal process. The affirmation of a second life—creating again in old age, starting over after catastrophe—also plays a central role in the process. These are all frequent tropes in the history of the covenant.

Building checks and balances into the system is another way of allowing for human limitations and weaknesses. The biblical prophets were separated from kings' courts and Temple payrolls so that they might serve as independent speakers of truth to those in power.[26] Similarly, the king was denied the right to serve in the Temple, so that channel to God was kept separate from royal authority.[27] The Rabbis sometimes cooperated with the Hasmonean rulers and sometimes clashed with them.[28] There was a constant teaching emphasis that "might does not make right." All authorities were accountable to God, the Divine Partner, "the great, mighty and awesome God, who does not show favoritism or accept bribes" (Deut. 10:17).

Finally, lest allowing for human frailty and limitations lead to compromising ideal standards, the system built in repeated exposure to representations of the ideal. The ever-recurring experience of the Shabbat day itself, reading the prophets' messianic visions on many occasions during the year, the annual rereading of the Creation and Garden of Eden stories—all were meant to reassert the transcending vision of a perfected world toward which human beings, even in their imperfection, should aspire and strive.

9

Covenantal Time

As I pledge the sum total of my life's behaviors to the cause of complete *tikkun olam*, I need to acknowledge in tandem the minute chance that this goal will be achieved in my own lifetime. This shapes the very psychology of the Divine-human partnership.

From Generation to Generation

The joiners of covenant must combine two qualities not always brought together harmoniously. On the one hand, I must feel a strong sense of personal responsibility for improving the world. This generates both a commitment to the work and a real sense of obligation to carry it out; indeed, that personal urgency drives me to enter the *brit* (covenant) in the first place. On the other hand, *brit* requires modesty and a sense of limits. I cannot do it alone. Since I need the help of many other people to get there, I must make room for others' input and modifications. Rabbi Tarfon provides the classic covenantal guidance in *Pirkei Avot* (Ethics of the Fathers): *"Lo alekha ha'melakhah ligmor"*—which properly translated means: "Finishing the job is not the measure of your accomplishment. Do not be put off by the fact that you cannot complete the mission."[1] The next clause reads: *"v'lo atah ben ḥorin lehibatel mimenah,"* "but nevertheless, you must act." You are not at liberty to use the excuse that, since I can't finish, there is no point in starting. This is not about you. The ultimate cause, *tikkun olam*, needs you and many others. Your responsibility is to act now, in this lifetime. Take it as far as you can. Then hand it over to those you have covenanted with to carry it on.

To succeed, this dialectical commitment—combining urgency and limits—must be pursued with a level of intensity that characterizes most successful agents of change, while tempering the impatience typical of revolutionaries. The person who says that the goal must be achieved in my lifetime and under my direction is really saying that no one else can be trusted to follow through and make the world right. This covert arrogance often leads revolutionary leaders to eliminate opposition and centralize all power in their own hands—a problem compounded by the absence of any sense of their own accountability to a higher power like God.

By contrast, the realization that I cannot complete the covenant mission by myself leads to the recognition that I need to enter into a *brit*, not only with God, but with the generations before and after me. True, if the future generations do not carry on and complete the job, then all my efforts will be for naught. But at the same time, I come to realize that all the generations before me also lived in vain unless I take up their mission and carry it on toward completion.

How can I bind future generations that do not yet exist to take responsibility for my covenant? Commentators have tried to solve this problem with the beautiful midrash that all the Jewish souls of all time stood at Sinai and took on the *brit*. Yet this technical fix—acknowledging that one must take on a contract consciously and voluntarily—does not do justice to the issue. For one thing, its conception of the soul, separate from the body, existing in all of time and in attendance at Sinai, is based on a highly questionable understanding of what a soul is. I would argue that soul is emergent in organism, embedded in the embodied self, and not a separate spiritual entity, preexisting and infused into a body in some later time. Furthermore, how would you respond if someone informed you that when the two of you previously met in an incorporeal existence, you assented to a commitment that you must now fulfill with your whole life, in all your actions and relationships? Would you feel bound to honor that contract?

Yet the *tikkun olam* goal does span generations, lifetimes, and millennia. Moses says: "It is not with you alone that I establish this covenant . . . but with whoever is here today standing before the Lord our God and *with whoever is not here with us today*" (Deut. 29:13–14). The individual covenanter enters into a *brit* that is open to all who choose to join it. The covenant is always open for later generations to join.

This process trains people to an extraordinary level of trust and respect for others. It helps you realize that you are not the only one who "gets it." The covenanter is taught: trust that there are countless other people who will want to be on the side of life and good. Start your covenantal activity. Show them that one person or one group can make a difference. Record what happens and pass it on. Give your descendants models and instructions that work. Then trust that other people, even people as yet unborn, will be inspired and want to carry on this work.

Because this approach places the issue of continuity front and center in all policy calculations — because it makes recruiting the following generations a prime focus — covenant focuses naturally on family. As we have seen, the family is a unit of solidarity nurturing beneficent relationships and humane interactions that represent *tikkun*. But, additionally, in covenantal time, the family is the foundation for a better world, because it creates children and brings them into the *brit*.

This is expressed in the mitzvah of bringing one's sons into the covenant of Abraham through circumcision. This ceremony is suffused with messianic overtones — because if parents keep the covenant going, the world will get to the messianic denouement eventually. In our time, covenantal induction ceremonies for daughters make clear that they, too, are equally vital to carrying on the covenant. Such ceremonies express the family's desire to pass on values and goals to the next generation. Tacitly, the ceremonies ask children to step up and take on the mission.

Even in its approach to the family's continuity, the covenantal method shifts the focus beyond biology to education. The Jewish family writ large is a covenantal community that can be joined by nonbiologically related individuals on the basis of shared values and responsibilities. This is why Judaism developed a conversion process that opened Jewry up to all humanity. Conversion is based on the metaphor of being born again, expressed in circumcision and immersion in a *mikveh*. The convert is not joining an organization, but rather becoming a member of a family. The ultimate goal is to widen the mutual help and fair treatment inside the family, to encompass ever more families. Eventually, all of humanity will be included in the covenant circle.

Just as the convert studies and learns about the covenant, so education recruits the next generation to join in the *brit*. From the Rabbis on, Judaism has placed tremendous emphasis on education — that is, persuasion — enriching understanding so that people want to join in. The pedagogical goal was and is to evoke loyalty, not to impose observance. Texts, stories, role models are studied, discussed, and internalized. Past generations and their experiences, instructions, and achievements are explored and appreciated; people identify with them. Predecessors' names are known, and given to children and grandchildren, who instinctively understand they are carrying on their namesakes' work — bringing their ancestors' dreams, now their own, closer to fruition.

Covenant process teaches that no one starts from a blank slate. One's predecessors' efforts establish the place from which the present generation's work begins. The covenantal community is transgenerational. Once each generation grasps this deep link, it experiences its predecessors as part of its community, and in conversation with the present carriers of the *brit*.

A core halakhic method of preserving the memory of past events intensifies this effort. Holidays and rituals such as Pesach not only carry the memories of the Exodus; they feature a *reenactment of the past*. On Shavuot, people stand at Sinai again. On Sukkot, they march around the altar with lulav and etrog as of old. Going through the event ritually is experienced as if it happens in every generation, and it just happened to me. The deeper conclusion is that the past generations' lives did not end with their deaths. They counted on me; they passed the responsibility to me. That is why the mission did not die when they physically passed away. They live on in me and their work goes on.

In the same spirit, everyone who enters into the covenant should know the extraordinary benefit: my life does not end when my life ends. My work will go on—if I have recruited the next generation, and the chain is not broken. In truth, I feel a deep sense of gratitude to the future covenanters, the great grandchildren to the end of time, whom I will never meet. I feel a gratefulness that ripens into love. They share my dreams; they feel my pain; they take over out of respect and connection to me. Once I understand, I really get to love them.

I cannot personally educate the generation that will be born one hundred years from now—but I can teach and inspire the one in my presence. As these Jews become involved and responsible, they will do the same. This is how the chain has grown and expanded and linked generations, for more than three thousand years. The covenant's teachings are inscribed not on stones, which are durable and can last for ages, but on the hearts of people. The hearts of flesh and blood are soft and vulnerable to illness; they are fated to stop. Nevertheless, by linking to the next generation and the next, this feeble flesh has outlasted rock and metal. That is the power of the human connection that has transmitted the Torah and developed it from generation to generation.

In the covenantal mind, I, the living generation, am a link in the chain. The practices I follow were consecrated by the energy and blood of my ancestors. The prayers I say are the same words, the tears I shed are poured into the same texts and blessings chanted by my great, great-great-great-grandparents centuries ago. I feel about this as I do about a family heirloom. I want to pass it on to my children and grandchildren. I am determined not to be the last link or to break the connection.

In recent decades, many have criticized various American Jewish communal organizations for their messages emphasizing Jewish survival. Critics have argued that our purpose is not survival for its own sake; rather, our survival must serve some greater purpose. Yet this dismissal misses the deeper point. People sense that something immensely important is at stake. The "survivalists" may lack or have lost the knowledge of what makes the chain important, but still, they intuit that, as long as the chain goes on, the great possibility of *tikkun olam* goes on. Without knowing its full depth or weight, they sense that this received tradition is too important for them to fail it now. There is this gut feeling that the hopes and efforts of past generations will not end on their watch. This sense of the bond of the generations is why the most devout Jews pray to "our God and God of our ancestors." This is why the most seemingly secular Jewish redemptive activist works, intentionally or not, for the redemption goal for which our ancestors gave their all. However it has been reshaped, dressed in unrecognized garb, revised, and re-envisioned, the goal of redemption is nevertheless a shared dream.

Ongoing Renewal

In the end, covenantal responsibility is not really based on an ancient acceptance. Nor does its authority in my life simply derive from an order from God that I have no choice but to obey. It is rooted in my free will to accept the classic covenant wholeheartedly. Inasmuch as the covenant is inherited, it is not really fully motivating until it is born again in my life. The renewal of the covenant is an indispensable step in keeping the partnership alive and operative.

Once a year, on the holiday of Shavuot, the entire community recreates the primordial magical moment. After hearing the tale of the preparations, the entire congregation stands, and the Ten Commandments are read out loud from the sacred Torah scroll; as it says in Exodus, "all the people see the voices and hear the lightning" (Exod. 20:15), and their hearts sing "Amen" to the promise that "all that Loving God has spoken we will do" (Exod. 19:8).[2] In medieval times, the Simḥat Torah (rejoicing in the Torah) holiday six months later developed as a counterpart celebration of the acceptance of the covenant. Traditionally, each community would parade and dance with all its scrolls (removed from the ark), and all the male participants would be called up to say the blessing over the reading. In recent decades, ever more communities have included women, too, in this process of taking ownership of and celebrating with the Torah.

Weekly, every Shabbat includes a miniature reenactment of Sinai. The Torah is taken out and marched through the congregation to be kissed, honored, embraced.[3] A portion is read, then studied and analyzed. Interpreted through a preacher or teacher's words, its lessons are taken into my heart; its instructions are taken into my life.

The Rabbis wanted to make every action in life an expression of the covenantal commitment. Therefore, they inserted into the daily morning and evening prayer services a covenant acceptance ceremony: the recitation of the Shema and its blessings, which state, "And these words that I command you today shall be on your heart."[4] Says Rashi: "Every day they should be as new—and eagerly pursued by you," adding that "today" reminds us that these words should not be like some ancient ruling, but like a freshly received instruction.[5] Leading up to the Shema, the circumstances that justify entering the covenant are reviewed. One blessing is offered for Creation and God's wonderful world; a second for the great love expressed by God in giving our ancestors and us "laws of life"—that is, the Torah; and a third blessing, following the Shema itself, tells how the Lord liberated us from slavery to freedom, justifying God's right to offer us a partnership and showing God's faithfulness as a partner.[6] In the midst of this recital, the people chant the words: "Hear O Israel, the Lord is the God. The Lord is Unique" (Deut. 6:4). Then, with proper concentration, they respond with this truth embedded in covenant: "You shall love the Lord your God with all your heart, all your soul, all your might" (Deut. 6:5). Finally, they conclude with the instruction: "Teach it (pass it on) to your children" (Deut. 6:7).

Such acceptance moments have been woven into many aspects of the Jewish life cycle and calendar over the centuries. The ancient circumcision ceremony entering a male child into the *brit* is mirrored in modern times with bat and bar mitzvah ceremonies in which maturing children voluntarily affirm their own commitment to the tradition — the very acceptance their parents had imprinted at the primordial level when they were just born.

The Bible records that the Israelite people gathered in Jerusalem every seventh year in the *hakhel* (assembly) ceremony, to hear the ruler read the entire Torah aloud. Rabbi Shai Held argues persuasively that *hakhel* is the Torah's ceremony of reenactment of the revelation at Sinai, when all Israel heard the Ten Commandments and willingly accepted the covenant.[7] This ceremony takes place in the *shemitah* year, in which debts are forgiven and private property restrictions are lifted, restoring greater equality and enhancing the sense of being redeemed to personal dignity and independence. This summons up an association with the Exodus, the liberation of the Hebrew slaves. Thus every seventh year, *hakhel* renews the association between the reenacted entrance into the covenant (Sinai) and the emancipation and grant of freedom (the Exodus). This practice, interrupted when the Israelites went into exile, was partially revived at the Western Wall in the twentieth century.

In the sixteenth century, the Kabbalists expanded the Sinai reenactment on Shavuot with the invention of the *Tikkun Leil Shavuot*, an all-night study session. Text passages taken from every part of Written Torah and Oral Torah were studied, so that people would have at least a précis of the full content of the covenant they were taking on. This custom has grown and spread over the past few centuries. It has enjoyed a remarkable new life among secular or cultural Jews in Israel and America, who thus reclaim their share in the ancient covenant, reshaped and given a new spirit.

The constantly renewed covenantal commitment continues to sustain Jews on their journey toward *tikkun olam*. This journey has lasted from ancient civilization, through the Middle Ages, on through the modern era. At every step of the journey, the covenant's canon has been expanded — from written Scripture to Oral Torah and Talmud;

from legal compilations to aggadic narratives and midrashic homilies; from poetry to philosophy; from manuals of piety to ethical treatises and character formation handbooks; from legal codes to commentaries, and commentaries on those commentaries. In modern times, the canon has been enriched again by literature, by fiction and nonfiction, by academic studies and archaeological findings. In the past generation, a thousand flowers of piety and sacredness have blossomed. In Israel, the twenty-first century has already seen an incredible renaissance of musical expression, from revival of the *piyyutim* (sacred liturgical compositions for various parts of the year) to *Mizraḥi* (Sephardi and Arabic influenced) songs, to syntheses of sacred texts with rock and roll and heavy metal music. All of these, some overtly, some covertly, engage with the tradition and the past record of the Jewish journey, renewing it for new generations.

Maturation in the Covenant

The covenant is not merely renewed in every age and every life, offered again and again in its original form and accepted repeatedly by the people. That in itself would be remarkable, given the tremendous span of time that this transmission has been going on. Even more remarkable, however, built into the covenantal process is the growth of the human partners, and the maturation of their capacity to live the covenant at a higher, more spiritual, more selfless level. This is a deeper process: maturation of the covenant itself.

This maturation reveals another dimension of Divine love. As we have seen, God's love reaches out to humans and confirms them as being of infinite value, equality, and uniqueness. The Lord self-limits, reducing Divine intervention and control, so that humans can grow in these dignities, and enlarge their God-given capacities in order to participate fully in the project of *tikkun olam*. The covenantal method was designed so that humans would grow and emerge from this process fully valuable, equal, and unique. It follows that Divine love would not offer, let alone bestow, covenant just once and forever. The covenant was designed to engage the Israelites at the level of their capacity to become partners with God. As this alliance operates, the human partners grow in capacity—due in no small measure to the effects of covenantal living on their emotional capability and intellectual reach. As they mature, God responds to this growth by self-limiting again, summoning Jews and, in turn, humanity, to a higher level of agency and a purer level of participation in the *brit*.

I have come to see the covenant as unfolding in three stages, each initiated by God through *tzimtzum* (Divine contraction), but reshaped by the response of the people Israel: the biblical era, the Rabbinic era, and the lay era now unfolding (see table, "The Three Great Eras of Jewish History," following chapter 14).

In the first phase of covenant, God reached out to Israel as a parent would to a child. The vision was *tikkun olam*; the method was partnership. Still, at the time the Children of Israel were an enslaved minority on the periphery of Mesopotamian culture. The midrash tells us that, when God called Moses to his life's mission as prophet and leader, the Lord spoke to him in the voice of his father.[8] In other words, rather than terrify and overwhelm Moses with an unmodulated Divine voice, God self-limited in presentation, in a form Moses would find hearable and familiar.

Similarly, as a loving parent God invited Israel to join in the covenantal process at the people's own level of functioning. In this stage, God performed many tasks for God's human partners and dominated many of these "joint" projects. God gave the Israelites detailed directions on how to live, along with promised rewards for living the covenantal way and punishments for failing to do so. Hence, God was very much the controlling partner in the *brit*. So, too, when the Israelites were enslaved and crushed in spirit, God initiated their emancipation by sending Moses—who went reluctantly, at God's prodding (Exod. 3–4). When the slaves feared standing up to Pharaoh, God relentlessly broke the arrogance of the master. A series of escalating plagues, signs, and wonders crumbled their oppressor and freed the slaves from their awe of Pharaoh (Exod. 7–13). At the Reed Sea, when the Children of Israel were paralyzed by fear of the Egyptian army and ready to return to their house of bondage, Moses told them: "(Almighty) God will fight for you; and you just be silent" (Exod. 14:14). God did so, by the miracle of the splitting of the sea, in which the Egyptians were subsequently destroyed. Thus, the Israelites passively received their liberty.

In like paternalistic fashion, God revealed the Torah at Sinai, speaking in a voice from heaven with signs and phenomena that awed the people, who then accepted the covenant (Exod. 19, 24). Thus the pattern was set in the desert for the whole Bible. The Israelites' fate was not so much determined by their actions in the world as by their behavior toward God. When they had faith, showed trust, and obeyed God, their enemies were defeated. When they lacked faith, or turned to foreign gods, they were punished and defeated (see Exod. 17; Num. 13, 14). When the Israelites demonstrated in the episode of the Golden Calf that they were not yet capable of relating to an invisible deity, God gave them a Tabernacle to make the Divine Presence palpable in their midst. God also provided rituals of sacrifice and observance familiar to them from the surrounding culture to help them connect to the Divine in recognizable, acceptable ways. They worshiped the transcendent God safely through a priesthood that mediated between God and them, absorbing the risks of direct contact (see Lev. 9–11; Num. 16–18). Then God oriented the Israelites step by step through their history, sending them prophets to guide their choice of kings, their war or peace policies, their relationships with their neighbors.[9] Alternatively, they sometimes received direction from heaven by asking for an oracle from God in the Tent of Meeting, or by consulting the *urim* and *tummim*—objects used in divination by the High Priest in the Holy Temple.[10]

When the Israelites were faithful to God and the *brit*, God saved them from oppression directly or through liberators sent to them under the terms of the covenant. When they disobeyed or ran after foreign gods and worshiped them, God punished them directly or through oppressors inflicted on them under the terms of the covenant.[11] Throughout this period, the junior partner, Israel, was relatively passive, mostly the object of Divine action and foreign invasions. The covenant was the dominant form of Jewish life, and the degree of the people's faithfulness to it predicted and determined their fate. This was an age of visible miracles (albeit declining in number and salience), and of prophets bearing direct messages from God.[12] Such Divine clarity explains why no two true prophets could disagree with each other. When two prophets clashed and reported contradictory instruction from God, one of them was ipso facto a false prophet (Jer. 28).

In retrospect, the one great religious crisis in the biblical period—the Babylonians' destruction of the First Temple, Solomon's Temple, in 586 BCE—was a moment of religious maturation. God, disgusted at the internal social oppression and exploitation of the poor as well as the whoring after foreign gods, abandoned the sanctuary.[13] The military and political might of the neighboring countries had undoubtedly strengthened the Israelites' tendency to turn to other gods, and in the terms of the time, the power of the country reflected the might of its gods. For this reason, the Israelites were unprepared for the destruction of their House of God. An omnipotent God, they reasoned, would never have allowed God's house to be violated and destroyed. Thus, the destruction raised the fear that God, fed up with the people's constant disloyalty and breaches of covenantal ethics, had rejected the covenant with Israel.

Prior to the destruction, the great prophets had railed against the people's mistreatment of fellow Jews, warning that God wanted the people to do justice and would not be bribed by rituals and worship, but the people mostly ignored and slighted their admonitions. In its aftermath, the Israelites grasped that these prophets had spoken the truth, and that the covenant demanded a higher ethical standard. At the same time, the great prophets brought a stunning message of a Divine love that would punish *but never reject Israel*.[14] The commitment was unbreakable.

Chastened by punishment but inspired by love, a minority of the Israelites living in Babylonia grew to further sophistication and understanding of God's universality. When the minority finally returned to Israel and restored a much-reduced commonwealth, they became more active and engaged in the religion. In retrospect, we can say that they became more rooted in the covenant and more understanding of its values as they internalized its ethics. The Second Commonwealth outlasted the Persian Empire that had enabled them to go back to Israel.

Then the Israelites came under the cultural influence of a spreading Hellenism and the political control of Alexander the Great's Ptolemaic and Seleucid successors. Eventually the Romans succeeded the Hellenistic Empire. Their oppressive control and frequent violations of the sacred Temple led to the Jewish revolt against Rome. After initial victories, however, the Romans relentlessly ground down the Jewish rebellion. In the end, the Second Temple was destroyed, and the remnants of Jewish sovereignty eliminated. The majority of the surviving people went into exile, while a minority remained in the Galilee and Northern Israel and accepted Roman domination.

From the second century BCE on, however, a group of teachers arose in Israel who brought a new understanding of the relationship with God. Initially they had no title, but around the first century CE they started to call themselves Rabbis. They offered a new conception of the human role in the covenant and of Israel's relationship with God. Over the next six centuries, they reached out to Jews everywhere, teaching their Torah, and gradually they won the hearts and minds of the Jewish people. They had started their work before the destruction of the Second Temple, but the crushing of the center of the old religious life, together with the new conditions of dependence and exile, sealed their victory as the religious guides of the Jewish people.

I believe that the schools that gave birth to the Rabbinic movement grew in response to a new covenantal initiative given by God to Israel and the nations. After more than a millennium of covenantal living, the Israelites had come to internalize the covenantal regime of life. Recognizing that they were now capable of living at a higher, more responsible level of religious life, God became less transcendent and more hidden and immanent in Jewish life. In dialing down the Divine voltage, God intended to come *closer* to the people. Rabbinic tradition popularized a new name for God, the *Shekhinah* (Divine Presence), connoting a new understanding of God—more intimate, personal, and present; less dangerous, controlling, and intervening in history. Divine self-limitation was designed to call the Jews to a more active role in the covenant.

This outreach to Israel—inviting the people to undertake a second, higher level of covenantal responsibility—was matched by a Divine initiative to the nations. Even as the biblical religion morphed into Rabbinic Judaism, by God's will, one breakaway from biblical Judaism grew into Christianity. Consistent with the Divine love for all of humanity and desire to partner with human beings, this outreach to the gentiles would engage them at the entry level of covenant, as was initially done with the Children of Israel. This took the form of Christianity's separation and emergence from Judaism. It is no mere coincidence that Christianity materialized and developed at the same time as Judaism entered its second, Rabbinic, phase of the covenant.[15]

As the Rabbis interpreted the Divine signal, the Divine was self-limiting again. In later kabbalistic tradition, this movement came to be called *tzimtzum*, a Divine contraction meant to leave room for something besides God. Henceforth there would no longer be revelation in the form of a Divine voice speaking from heaven.

The Rabbis showed their rigorous understanding of this principle in a talmudic story in which they argued among themselves over the ritual purity of a certain type of stove. After the majority ruled that it was impure, Rabbi Eliezer, in the minority, appealed to heaven, calling forth miracles to prove that he was right. Indeed, a voice from heaven proclaimed: Rabbi Eliezer is right! Unfazed, however, the majority voted again to uphold their judgment, overruling the transcendent voice speaking from heaven by authority of the weight of their majority view. As Rabbi Yehoshua ben Hananiah said, quoting Deuteronomy 30:12, "The Torah is not in the heavens."[16] In other words, determinations of what the Torah was instructing would no longer come directly from a Divine voice. Henceforth, in this new period, Israel would know God's will and directions through discussion and consensus. God was calling on humans to step up and actively discover God's instructions.

The Rabbis taught that because the infinite Divine wisdom was directed at all people and for all time, God's word had multiple levels of meaning. The initial recipients had only heard the surface meaning of Torah; they may not have been equipped to detect or understand the other levels. Perhaps these had been broadcast on a wavelength that the culture of their time could not yet receive.

Now in the new Rabbinic era, *tzimtzum* paved the way for the Jewish people to receive Torah on those hitherto undetected wavelengths. Now wise people who learned Torah used their intelligence and judgment to reanalyze classic sources. They could utilize inherited techniques of literary analysis and traditional interpretation and find new levels of meaning. They could also apply the classic models to new situations.

This inventorying, analysis, and interpretation of past texts and the present situation became the Rabbis' primary preoccupation and remains a core facet of what rabbis do today. Such rabbinic activity is no less a prophetic role — hearing Divine messages and communicating them to the people. In the words of the Talmud: "Since the time of the destruction of the Temple, prophecy was taken from the prophets and given to the wise."[17] The prophetic channel communicating Divine messages was now operating through human analysis and inspiration.

Using their methods, the Rabbis were able to gather new Divine instructions for the drastically changed conditions of life, especially in exile. They stressed that this *Torah she-Be'al Peh* (Oral Torah) was not a new creation, but rather an uncovering of layers of meaning and instruction originally infused — with infinite, Divine wisdom and care — in the *Torah she-Bikhtav* (Written Torah). These layers were intended to guide the people in new conditions of life and to serve as models for new realities.

The Rabbis developed the imagery of God as lover and spouse of

Israel, as compared to the parental imagery that had dominated the biblical language. They even initiated the language of *shutafut*, partnership with God.[18] God had stopped visibly speaking directly to humans, but the Rabbis understood that the covenantal conversation must not stop—the deep connection between God and humanity could not be lost. God's silence, they saw, was not a withdrawal from the dialogue, but was intended to evoke greater human activity. It meant humans should speak to God.[19] This was the driving force for the expansion of prayer, and its installation as the central channel of Divine service. In a world where God was more hidden, people would be more engaged and less mere observers of ritual. Since God would not be encountered in a manifest way—such as experiencing the Divine Presence in the Temple—the prayer service would connect people to God at a new, internal level. The Psalms would illuminate God's presence in nature, while blessings would connect people to God as Creator. All the while, remembrance of the redemption in the Exodus confirmed God's presence in history and God's availability in the life of the congregation. The Rabbis also coined hundreds of blessings that made the hidden Divine Presence manifest. Blessings over food reminded the individual that God had "created the fruit of the ground," "created the fruit of the tree," and that "all came into being by God's word."

There was another consequence of God's *tzimtzum*. A more immanent, more hidden God actually had come closer to human beings. Before, the area of holiness was confined to limited, manifest places like the Temple, where the Divine force had to be shielded and mediated by priests, so that regular individuals would not be harmed by the close encounter with God. Now the home—where kosher food could be prepared, blessings said, and limited purification rites like ritual hand washings conducted—could become the locus of sacred meals before God.

The areas and details of halakhic observance expanded considerably. The Divine was more hidden, but the Divine Presence could be experienced everywhere. This was especially true if you recognized that human beings were the image of God. If you looked more deeply—learning with them, relating to them, or making love with them—and cared more deeply—hosting them in their weariness, visiting them in their sickness, or comforting them in their mourning—then you could meet God, *Shekhinah*, everywhere as never before, and at a deeper level.

God's new self-restraint meant that, just as the age of manifest revelation was over, so was the age of visible miracles. Henceforth there would be only hidden miracles, and humans would have to be active and generate the circumstances where a miracle could swing the outcome. Thus Purim became the model of Divine redemption. Esther's name in Hebrew is associated with hiddenness.[20] The name of God is hidden in the book of Esther. It appears nowhere, unless one interprets the word "king" to refer to God.[21] Had Mordecai and Esther not initiated the reversal of Haman's planned genocide, then God's hidden contribution, keeping King Achashverosh awake, would have made no difference. Had they not won over the king, the miracle of redemption would have never happened. Human actions now accounted for a much larger part of historical outcomes.

The Rabbis applied this calculus to the destruction of the Second Temple. The rebellion against Rome had been driven by the Jews' faith and zeal for God, demanding more respect for the Temple and removal of idolatrous likenesses of the emperor from the sacred precincts. Then why did the Jews lose? By the biblical model of covenant, such a national assertion of fidelity to God and Torah should have evoked Divine miracles and brought them victory. Why hadn't God split the Mediterranean Sea and drowned all the armies of Rome, as God had done so decisively in Egypt?

The Rabbis' answer was that God no longer operated in the biblical way, engendering sweeping reversals of the normal balance of power or of military operations. They did attribute the Second Temple's destruction to Israel's sins. However, unlike in the First Temple, the sins were not against God as much as bad behaviors between people, and poor judgments in interpersonal relationships. A talmudic story portrays this destruction as originating in a fight between two Jews in which one was deeply humiliated. The Rabbis stood by and did not intervene, and the hurt party instigated the Romans against the Jews. Human failures were compounded by destructive policies. A rigid, legalist Rabbi ruled against appeasing the Romans (or eliminating the instigator). The rebels, called zealots, had exhibited reckless behaviors—partaking in internecine warfare, burning Jerusalem's food stores—that precluded a surrender in time to save the city and its people.[22] Whereas in the biblical age, God would have singlehandedly reversed the outcome to reward the covenant people, in this new age, such bad and irresponsible behavior brought defeat. God's interventions were restricted; Divine action would not override human vindictiveness, political blindness, irrational behavior, and civil war. Wisdom and good behavior (as in Purim) would be given extra help to succeed, but destructive and unreasonable behavior—even if done in the name of God—would not be overturned by miraculous action.

The Talmud explains the difference between the historical outcomes in the biblical and Rabbinic ages. "Why was the First Temple destroyed? [as punishment by God, through the Babylonians] for three behaviors which prevailed there—idolatry, sexual immorality, and bloodshed." These are sins that deeply offend God. "But the Second Temple—where they occupied themselves with learning Torah, commandments, and acts of loving-kindness—why was it destroyed? Because groundless hatred (*sinat ḥinam*) prevailed there"—vindictiveness, legalism, sectarian and extremist violence, unjustified hatred, and civil war.[23] By the will of God, the age of greater human activity in the covenant was here: intensified responsibility and accountability for bad behaviors followed.

One might argue that the very terms of the covenant had been altered to the point where it was no longer binding. After all, God no longer gave revelation from heaven, or performed visible miracles, to uphold the covenant and deter the evildoers. Nor did God assure those who were faithful to God and covenant that they would be saved, no matter what. The level of human responsibility, and of its associated risk, had escalated. After such material changes in the terms, why should the original Sinai covenant still be binding?

Making a wordplay in the Torah statement that at Sinai the Israelites "stood under the mountain" (Exod. 19:17), Rav Avdimi bar Hama bar Hasa says that, in retrospect, the original covenant acceptance at Sinai was coerced: "God held the mountain over their head like a barrel and said to them: 'If you accept the Torah, good, but if not you will be buried here.'" Given the level of Divine force they had seen— ten plagues, splitting of the sea, food from heaven, revelation directly from God—how could the Jewish people refuse the offer? Rav Aha bar Ya'akov says: "[If so,] this is a legal out from the Torah's obligation!" To this, another sage, Rava, responds that, though this logic is correct, the Torah and the covenant are still binding, because the Jewish people nonetheless "reaccepted it in the days of Achashverosh; as it is written 'The Jews undertook and upheld' (Esther 9:27)"—that is, without coercion they irrevocably obligated themselves in the covenant they had undertaken already at Sinai.[24]

In responding to Purim, the Jews recognized that God was hidden now, and performing only hidden miracles. They themselves had to magnify their actions to enable the right results. Ratifying the holiday of Purim, they determined to take heightened responsibility for the covenant's outcomes. The Jews thus renewed the Sinaitic covenant on new terms, without visible miracles and guaranteed rewards and punishments. In effect, they connected to the Covenant Partner at a higher level. They committed to serve God more selflessly, out of deeper relationship to God for its own sake. This was not just a renewal but a maturation of the covenant.

This understanding of the maturation of the human role in the covenant is critical to the interpretation of this central mechanism of the Jewish religion. It shows that covenant is not just a one-time event or an immutable legal code revealed at one point in Jewish history, but a dynamic relationship between God and Israel (and between God and humanity). While the love that drives this relationship has proven steadfast and unconditional, strong enough to survive great failures and great shocks in Jewish history, the covenant itself is not "fixed." Sustaining love has enabled the partners to grow together, and to deepen and renew their ongoing relationship.

I believe that the Divine *tzimtzum* evoked and enabled the development of Rabbinic Judaism, which so transformed and yet is so continuous with biblical Judaism. The two are deeply and seamlessly interlinked. Yet Rabbinic Jews expanded the realm of holiness: they drew closer to God in spirit, internalized the values and methods more deeply than their predecessors, and became increasingly active in their roles (compare saying prayers with bringing sacrifices). The result was the miracle of a people and a religion enduring — even flourishing — despite being driven out of their land and independent society. Has any other group survived such an experience, let alone managed to keep the connection to the homeland alive enough to shape a movement that would go back, reconnect, and rebuild? Amazingly, in our day, this new sovereignty feels continuous and linked to the past, despite enormous civilizational transformations between then and now.

Divine *tzimtzum* and the maturation of the covenant supply the interpretive key to the history of Jewish religion, past and future. The interactive maturation in the second stage shows that the original intent of the covenant was pedagogical: that God brought Israel and, by implication, humanity, into a covenantal partnership relationship that would enable them to grow into even greater responsibility for their lives and for the outcomes of history. From the beginning, the goal of covenant has been to nurture human beings to fully become the image of God: to create, take charge of their fate, and participate in their own liberation. Like a loving parent, God seeks to give needed direction, personal inspiration, and just enough help to enable the full development of a moral, responsible human being.

As we will see, the final maturation and full human assumption of responsibility for the covenant is occurring today, in the new era of Jewish history now unfolding.

PART 3

The Covenant
in the Third Era

10 Modernity

At the core of *tzimtzum* is a paradox. The Creator is infinite and beyond finite categories or understanding. For example, the Divine is not visible to human senses. God is so vast as to make this planet—and even more so humanity—less than a point on an infinite line. Nevertheless, this Infinite Power and Infinite Person is deeply connected to and concerned for humanity— perhaps because humans are the only form of life able to relate to God and respond to a Divine call.

As humans have become capable of understanding the pattern of Creation, they have come to see that the Divine restraint, as it were, allows them freedom to live and act in the world. Sin is not punished instantaneously, nor are humans programmed to do good robotically. Nor does God intervene openly and on the spot to awe people into submission. Even the Divine revelation is held in check, so that some fraction of it can be grasped by finite mortals, within the limits of their minds and understanding.

From a human perspective, *tzimtzum* is experienced as a change in religious consciousness. The Rabbis saw the *tzimtzum* of their time as a Divine initiative to reshape the relationship with human- ity. After *tzimtzum*, God is experienced as closer—not so much distant in the heavens but present in the warp and woof of life, at hand in every place, inherent in deeper human relationships. Revelation comes not as a commanding voice from the heav- ens, but as instruction planted within classic text, to be uncov- ered by human interpreters and transmitted to the people. The previous contact points with God no longer provide the same connection—but the channel of prayer and of human communication to God from the heart and the mind is opened wider. Human religious consciousness goes more inward and experiences the Divine as filling Creation, not as manipulating it from without.

The Rabbis present their Torah as the response to that Divine self-limitation. Rabbis represent the mortal partners having matured sufficiently to take on more responsibility to expound the Torah and repair the world. The reduction of visible Divine intervention is designed to evoke a step up in human activity and responsibility in repairing the world. While profoundly continuous with the Bible, Rabbinic Judaism is marked by a much higher degree of human activity. Revelation is now uncovered and discovered by human minds, without external signs from above or beyond. The Divine interventions in history are subtler and more restrained, and human activity determines a greater degree of the outcome.

The Rabbis' paradigm is a reminder that one should not think of the *tzimtzum* as a one-time, total transformation event. It took centuries to arrive at this new understanding, and even longer for the new culture to spread. Then it took hundreds of years more to persuade the bulk of the Jewish people to perform covenantally in accordance with the new human and Divine roles. In the biblical era, too, the recession of visible Divine intervention began in small steps over many centuries.[1] This is as one would expect, given the covenant's underlying pedagogical model. The Lord turns over more responsibility for initiative and discovery to the people as their capacity to handle these tasks expands. Humans typically — and, certainly, en masse — grow incrementally and by steps, not all at once. Only in retrospect are all the little steps recognizable as adding up to a full-scale Divine self-limitation.

A New *Tzimtzum*: The Challenge of Modernity

In the modern age, God is totally hidden. I believe that this extra measure of hiddenness is a sign of another self-limitation, another *tzimtzum*, on God's part. The past narrative of Jewish tradition suggests that the Divine chose this new *tzimtzum* because God wants humans to take power and more responsibility to achieve *tikkun olam*. Understanding that more hidden equals more present and less controlling, we can deduce that a totally hidden God is universally present, and that humans are fully responsible for their future. The Divine message of modernity to humanity would be: "I (the Lord) am contracting in order to call you to a higher level of covenantal activity. It is time for humans to take full responsibility for their fate, by taking power."

In this moment, God becomes totally hidden, not to distance from humanity but to come closer yet again. This means becoming totally immanent, ever present, binding the outcome of God's vision totally to humanity. This movement reflects a judgment that humans are capable of grasping the plan and repairing the world at a much higher level than before. Henceforth, humans will execute the Divine interventions that rise to the level of miracles. God will be present and participating, but miracles will not represent changes of natural law by an "outside" or Divine mind. Rather, they will represent human actions and understandings of God-given nature that trigger remarkable outcomes, using natural phenomena and directing them consciously to needed results and cures. The miracles are inherent in the natural laws that govern the interactions of matter; humans will bring them out.

God's contraction also represents a Divine wish that humans relate to God not out of need for payoffs, nor out of being overawed by infinity, nor out of fear of bad things happening. God wants to be linked to humanity by unconditional love, by relationship and shared vision, by common cause. Since in the previous stage, the more self-centered motives were key props that undergirded religion and religious services, this contraction makes crystal clear that revelation was not really about getting people to worship God. It was intended to give people a vision of perfection, so they could liberate themselves from the given state of affairs and energize themselves to work to repair the world.

In this vision, birth or inherited status is not a life sentence. Nor is human inequality, whether based on class, race, gender, skin color, or sexual orientation, the will of God. Contrary to traditional, inherited expectations, prayer should now be understood as a call for action by the human partner. No secret formula can coerce the Lord to fulfill human dreams, nor are there demonic forces that must be placated. Now humanity must focus on this material existence—this mortal life—and, taking power, ethically, repair the world completely.

This call to empowerment has proven to be modernity's most impactful message. As humans stepped up their capability and their responsibility, they increasingly improved daily life. Modern culture promised to overcome all the enemies of life that were to be defeated in the Messianic Era: poverty, hunger, oppression (every form of injustice and inequality), war, and sickness. Now the causes of these afflictions could be identified, and corrected, so that life would win out. Economic activity (raised to a system in capitalism and socialism), political action (raised to a system in liberal democracy), and social reform set about abolishing deprivation and inequality. Science and medicine, wielding more empirical and disciplined approaches, analyzed the material realm and manipulated it to strengthen the force of life over death. In all fields, activists agreed that being bound by past rules or givens was no longer justifiable. It was not a matter of rejecting past norms and codes. Rather, it was the conviction that a values-free science, operating without dogmatic barriers or sacred cows, could figure out how the world works, and could use this insight to improve human health and life. Art, music, and culture, too, promised to build on the new affluence and new science, by creativity and activity that would supply depth and fullness to life.

The new culture of modernity proceeded to substantially deliver on these promises. Beginning in Western Europe, it often produced a remarkable rise in affluence, material well-being, public health, and day-to-day security. Despite powerful negative side effects of the modernization process—including violence perpetrated against many groups, and wars on an unprecedented, even gigantic scale—this new culture gradually and increasingly delivered an extraordinary extension of life to all in its orbit. Since modernity's onset, human life expectancy has shot up—and more of those years have been healthier, safer, and pleasanter than before. While these blessings have not been distributed equally—even within societies that benefited most, many suffered along the way—still, many more people found better, healthier, more secure lives. Many harsh or brutal inherited religious instructions were softened, upgraded, and humanized. Over the centuries, the pace of improvement has escalated and spread to more people.

Modern life brought values of equality, human dignity, and entitlement to wider and wider circles. Even among those victimized, overlooked, or exploited in this process, many demanded to be let into the emerging culture rather than rejecting it. The combination of material rewards and internalizing or achieving the uplifting ideals proved extraordinarily compelling. An old Yiddish proverb says, "Love is wonderful—but love with noodles is even better." Modernity often delivered love with noodles.

Humanity without a Divine Partner

Tzimtzum is never just an event in Jewish history. Movements by a cosmic Lord—perhaps better understood as signals broadcast from a Divine source—are intended for all humanity. They should manifest in human consciousness and behaviors beyond those of the Jewish people.

In the *tzimtzum* of the modern era, neither prophets nor rabbis took the lead in decoding the prime message. Initially, laypeople in a handful of Western European countries grasped the new message, articulated it, and acted on it. In developing Newton's physics and higher mathematics, in shifting to more empirical and scientific medicines, in fostering liberal and democratic politics, in investing in the Industrial Revolution, a diverse array of people gradually moved to take control of their fate and increase productivity. And within a short time Jews disproportionately joined the front rank of secular "prophets" of the new dispensation in many arenas.

Neither the leadership elements of the emerging modern world nor the majority of the Jews explicitly understood that God was self-limiting, summoning humans to a higher level of partnership for *tikkun olam*. Many interpreted the loss of all the ways and places that the Deity had been manifest in the previous civilization as a sign that there was, in fact, no God at all, or no covenanting Deity. In the first part of the Enlightenment, even those steeped in religion, including many scientists and even Newton himself, grasped a vaster scale for the cosmos and a more rigorous view of natural laws, one without exceptions for miraculous Divine interventions. Many came to believe in a Deist god — not a caring, deeply involved Lord who is in an active partnership with humanity to improve the world.[2] They found deep religious emotion in uncovering the magnificence of God's cosmos, the exquisite order in the laws and mechanisms embodying the operating system of the universe as well as the beauty and symmetry of Creation. But traditional religious life seemed primitive or superstitious.

A more radical current of later secular thinkers was convinced that God's disappearance into a secularly explained natural order proved that there never had been a god. God was explained away as a projection of the primitive human mind, an explanatory hypothesis of a premodern science. Religion was merely an opiate created by priests or ruling classes to persuade people of the sanctity and inalterability of unjust socioeconomic orders.

Secularizers developed moral codes based on reason or alternate authority. Some held that, with no God, humans were ruled only by power and pleasure: "If God is dead, then all is permitted." Others struggled to articulate new ethical models. In this thinking, the idea of covenant as a human-Divine attachment was gone. The corollary to this loss of the sense of partnership became that I, the human being, am fully in charge. I am not a partner in Creation. I am not a partner in a world that — like its Creator — is vaster than I am. On the contrary, no higher authority, no previous commitment, no intrinsic sanctity restrains me from doing what I will. Thus in modernity a self-sufficient or exclusive humanism became a widely available, if not the default, mechanism to understand the world.

Sadly, Western religious authorities did not do much better in grasping the event of *tzimtzum* and its message. By and large, they responded defensively to modernity, seeing the turn away from dependence on God as an attack. When the new science differed from accounts found in sacred writings, many deemed this a sin against God. From the Church's opposition to Copernican astronomy to the conflict between evolution and the Creation story, scientific, human-generated portraits of nature were seen as invading the Divine prerogative to define reality. The new astronomy, geology, and biology were undermining the divinity of Scriptures and dogma. When the new sciences became too strong to strangle in their cribs, many religious authorities closed ranks to exclude the teachings (at least from their own communities) as best they could.

While the modernization processes strengthened forces opposed to the status quo, many Christian churches supported the established order. From the nineteenth century onward, when Orthodox Jews increasingly participated in political processes, particularly across Europe and North America, many allied with the parties of conservatism and reaction out of an overriding need to resist political and cultural change that was undermining religion and God's authority. They ignored strong antisemitic attitudes in the parties of the right in order to collaborate with them in opposing their common enemy, modernity. Many Christian and Jewish religious authorities opposed Marxism and communism largely because these were perceived as godless movements. Ideologically, they expressed this in teaching that God authorizes hierarchies and political authorities, or they criticized liberation movements as seeking to throw off all restraints and necessary order. In short, many religious authorities identified the trend of humans taking power to change human fate with revolt against God.

In practice, these authorities' efforts to stay out of modernity, and their opposition to this new degree of human autonomy, carried the messages that activities that aggrandize human power are ipso facto wrong, and that anyone who considers joining these new fields must choose between modernity and religion. Nor did modernizers, for their part, view religion as a source of salutary criticism and caution. Most, or at least many, were sure that religion would be progressively displaced by reason as modernity won out.[3] In effect, both sides concurred that, for those who chose modernity, religion and religious structures had nothing further to say. This total polarization meant that modernity was effectively absolutized. Whereas this book's view of modernity as reflecting God's *tzimtzum* encourages humans to improve the world—albeit constrained by God's authority and covenantal guidelines in their exercise of modern power—the traditionalists' decision to resist modern culture weakened a potential source of healthy limitation and strengthened the tendency of modern forms of power to grow out of control.

Modernity without Limits

As the new culture's successes grew, its prestige and norms became increasingly axiomatic. In politics, economics, society, and culture, modernity became unchecked, its claims nearly absolute. This had particularly bad consequences. It turned out that many of the processes that generated modernity were beneficent *within limits*. Over a certain range of their operations, they created added value aplenty. However, just as truths taken out of their moment turned into lies or distortions, so, too, modernity's processes, uncontrolled, turned pathological.

In the initial phases of the Industrial Revolution, for example, the productivity dividend increased wealth. Modernization raised the standard of living for many. It rewarded enterprise and set in motion a virtuous cycle of investment, production, and distribution. Over time, along with higher living standards, society saw major improvements in health and life expectancy.[4] However, even in this phase, problems such as exploitative labor or environmental degradation proliferated unchecked. Moreover, governments and people hesitated to impose controls lest they kill the goose laying the golden eggs. Consequently, as these processes grew dominant and were disseminated, they developed serious pathologies in the very operations that had initially led to beneficial outcomes.

During this period, this version of modernization was exported to Eastern Europe, Asia, and Africa. The benefits were mostly siphoned off to Western European imperialist nations (as well as the United States), while the groups subject to it were in some cases more radically exploited, treated as inferior, and pushed off their home grounds. To be sure, not every colony was as totally degraded and extorted as the Belgian Congo, where slavery, abuse, and massacre became standard operating procedures, nor did every country set up a white master class that ended up systematically segregating and devaluing the local majority, as in South Africa.[5] Still, throughout this period the benefits were skimmed off and directed to the imperial powers, and the mistreatment, exploitation, and violence more openly imposed—all justified by the claim that modern culture would "civilize" or improve the lot of people whose race, skin color, or condition made them less than human.

As the Industrial Revolution spread worldwide, the sheer scope of the transformation increasingly turned blessings into mixed blessings or curses. Worldwide standards of nutrition improved, but industrial agriculture overwhelmed local environments and raised and disposed of billions of animals cruelly. Increases in productivity reached planetary proportions, which led to climate change, global warming, species depletion or destruction—to the point of impending environmental disaster. Almost every step of this way increased life for at least some groups—better food; wider distribution of shelter, clothing, and comfort; rising productivity; more efficient and useful technology. Yet, by the twentieth century, catastrophes loomed.

Individualization was one of modernity's great benefits. Cultural and political affirmation of individual freedoms, including the right to choose one's own lifestyle, and exponentially increased channels of expression all fed the growth of individual rights and identities. As these phenomena and values spread, however, the balancing mechanisms of community and family grew weaker. Unchecked, individualization undermined community and social responsibility.[6]

The weakening of the family ethos is an instructive example. In its first stage, the critique of family made important, constructive changes. More women achieved in the workplace and took leadership roles in society. Women who in the past would have been obliged to enter or stay in unsatisfying or destructive marriages now had the option of remaining single or divorcing—thus saving a lot of suffering. Similarly, the growth of individualism enabled some people who might otherwise have forced themselves with great suffering into heterosexual marriages to express themselves more openly and authentically.

However, as individualist values increased to the point of dominance, they had negative fallout. Individualism slipped into an overweening sense of entitlement, or reluctance to delay one's own gratification in order to meet the needs of another. As tolerance for frustration—or readiness to accept costs in gratification—declined, the willingness to engage in relationship and the capacity to sustain it shrank. Loneliness, a decline in marriage, and family instability became more serious social ills. Some forms of individualism turned into narcissism, paralyzing individuals' capacity to see or relate beyond themselves. Thus individualism—one of modernity's blessings—turned out to be a blessing over part of its range, yet negative when it went beyond that point.

Unfortunately, for most modern blessings there is no clear line where a healthy limit can be established: the point at which it becomes negative is not apparent in advance. Moreover, the ideal balance between individual and family or community may vary from person to person.

The deeper problem is that, as modernity spread and succeeded, the countervailing forces—of community and family, partnership and accountability—weakened. When religious groups and other proponents of these values limited their own participation, they yielded the opportunity to criticize or to shape society. When society needed countervailing forces, those upholding them were too weakened to check the growing pathologies. Polarized positions grew stronger, and the pathological side effects of modernity's positive progress intensified. One case may be instructive. In the initial shift from sustenance agriculture and industry to a distributive, exchange economy, the monetization of value and the establishment of financial instruments that enabled larger scale production and commerce were major sources of greater wealth and affluence. Removing barriers to trade and distribution led to more trade between nations — and fewer warlike interactions. Moreover, since money is neutral and its possession may be detached from ancestry and class, the initial effect was often to reduce discrimination and encourage broader access to citizenship.

Over time, however, monetization began to suffuse and affect relationships. Inequality grew between the possessors of wealth and those who lacked it. Efficiency and profit motives became so culturally entrenched that some businesspeople, engineers, bankers, and lawyers cut corners on safety or quality, while profits covered up their cheating. Thus did German firms compete, in the twentieth century, for the business of producing gas chambers and crematoria, all the while knowing these would likely be used for mass murder. The reification of value in money led to a culture of consumerism, in which people spent money constantly in pursuit of being themselves considered of value.

Can humans curb these excesses? Can we set limits that keep these modern patterns operating on the side of life, without undermining freedom or crushing benevolent individualism? The answers are not clear.

Jewish Responses to Modernity

Jews responded to this version of modernity like other people, only more so (as the saying goes). The problems generated in the Jewish adjustment to modernity reflect the deeper problems in modernity's development. They especially illuminate how the Divine *tzimtzum* was understood — or not understood.

In addition to all the benefits bestowed on others, many Jews in Europe and North America were offered the end of persecution and pariah status, plus the blessings of citizenship and, eventually, equal rights. In the nineteenth and twentieth centuries, marginal Jews especially pinned their hopes of an end to Jews' negative cultural and religious standing and unequal rights on revolutionary movements—in economics, politics, arts—which they joined disproportionately, seeking total transformation. In the brave new world, all the old invidious distinctions would disappear. Joining the revolution—working to bring the secular messiah—was frequently accompanied by a conscious distancing from the Jewish people and culture, in order to hasten the glorious end-time for all humanity as one group. This total giving of themselves proved to be a spur for antisemitism among those groups that resented modernization or were displaced by it. As far as they were concerned, those revolutionary "non-Jewish Jews" were still Jews—making trouble.

There are two other reasons why Jews jumped into modernity with both feet. First, civil emancipation in Western Europe finally gave them the rights of citizenship in the countries where they lived. They saw an end to ghettoization and other medieval restrictions, and they recognized the many opportunities opening up. Unlike some other outcast groups that, battered by persecution, labored under the burdens of residual deculturation, damaged families, and wounded self-image, the Jews' social capital was relatively intact—so they could seize the moment. Rabbinic culture deserves much of the credit. It had managed to preserve family and communal solidarity. It upheld high expectations for self and high ratings for education, while nurturing a sense of chosenness, of difference, as a mark of special, not degraded, status.

Jews disproportionately flooded into the pioneering and rewarding institutions of the emerging modern order whenever they were let in. They ended up, in high numbers, in banking and finance, science, medicine, law, civil service, and university life. This process only escalated as the spread of modernity's ideals broke down barriers and opened new fields to unrestricted Jewish entry. Jewish success evoked serious antisemitic responses—especially from those who felt a loss of power, or felt left out under the norms of the emerging system. Hatred of Jews proved to be a virulent pathogen, mutating from medieval forms of anti-Judaism in European Christian culture into "scientific," racial, nationalist, revolutionary versions of antisemitism that persisted and even thrived under new conditions.

Helped by the push of the old culture's decline, the pull of modernity became a dominant force in Jewish life everywhere it penetrated. If one defines God as the source of norms, the arbiter of right and wrong, the ultimate authority who must be satisfied, then Modernity became the de facto god of many Jews. Jewish life, religion, and culture were revamped to meet its criteria. Different groups defined themselves by diverse understandings of what joining modernity actually required of the Jewish people. Specific outcomes reflected the extent to which host countries had modernized, and the degree of Jewish integration in modern society, leavened by the degree to which they were still immersed in their inherited Jewish culture and tradition.

Some Jews left Judaism. Those who interpreted modernity's offer as "give up Jewishness and become one with us" assimilated, abandoning religion or converting to Christianity. Others heard it as "give up Jewishness as part of a drive to abolish all differences, so that a kingdom of universal justice and peace will reign," and joined various revolutionary and socialist movements. Some secular Jews continued to regard themselves as part of the Jewish people, but understood modernizing to mean giving up religion, and living a productive, secular life as an ethnic Jew. One stream of this approach, especially after European emancipation, concluded that modernity authorizes nationalism as an expression of self and communal dignity. Most adherents became citizens of their home countries. Others, especially those feeling that emancipation had failed to solve the problems of antisemitism, became Zionists. They believed Jews should recreate their own national homeland.

Political Zionists like Theodor Herzl came to dominate the Zionist movement. They believed that, if the Jews were to successfully create their own state, they would transcend their identity as rootless cosmopolitans and be accepted in their European home countries as well. Western European Jews called for that state to embody modern values such as bourgeois liberalism and democracy, while Eastern Europeans leaned toward various forms of socialism. Cultural Zionists, steeped in tradition, valued their own national culture and languages, and dreamed of a place where these could blossom. The Zionist dream, in all its varieties, was born in a hunger for modernity.

Jewish Religious Responses to Modernity

Many Jews concluded that modernity did allow room for religious life — but religion would have to meet modern criteria of moral and religious credibility. Reform Judaism emerged as one expression of this view. Appealing to Jews in the most modernized countries, Reform eventually became the largest denomination in Germany and, later, in the United States.

As early Reform saw it, modern culture meant that only rational and moral commandments could evoke respect and obedience. Judaism represented ethical monotheism. Jewish nationalist prayers that expressed longing for restoration to Zion conflicted with citizenship and patriotism, and had to be repudiated. Prayer services had to be dignified and modern, not "Oriental." They were to be modeled on short, proper, Protestant church services, enriched with organ music and sermons. Separatist, particularist, and, typically, nonrational rituals had to go. All laws that "regulated diet, priestly purity, and dress" were dismissed as "entirely foreign to our present mental and spiritual state."[7]

There was a profound partial truth in the early Reform teaching. Rituals and laws do have to persuade and educate those who practice them or they become rote actions, with little impact on the behaviors and lives of the faithful. Reform Jews found the ritual laws tended "rather to obstruct than to further modern spiritual elevation."[8] But part of persuasion is to critique the general culture when it contradicts Jewish tradition. As such, the statement in the 1885 Pittsburgh Platform — the first American manifesto of the Reform rabbinic body—that instructed Reform Jews to "reject all such [Torah rituals and ceremonies] as are not adapted to the views and habits of modern civilization"[9] contained a double error. It gave absolute authority to modern culture as the source of credibility and persuasion. In addition, it gave negative features of modernity—such as materialism and consumerism—normative power without challenging them. This last surrender proved to be the greatest danger, enabling a transfer of loyalty. When Judaism had been reworked so that all its moral claims, as well as ritual practices, were totally congruent with modernity, and modern society opened up socially to Jews, as in America, it was a small step to simply join the general society and become one with it. In and beyond the Reform movement, whenever the affirmation of modernity without critique became normative, Jewish intermarriage and assimilation rates soared.

Much of Reform's abandonment of ritual in the nineteenth and early twentieth centuries was driven by the need of laypeople to integrate and meet the social expectations of the non-Jewish majority. Reform rabbis, for their part, believed they had the authority to ratify these changes, seeing them as unstoppable and, at a different level, as part of the process of refashioning Judaism into a rational, universal, pro-phetic, modern religion. Indeed, some Reform rabbis saw themselves less as accommodationists than as prophets, leading the charge of the Jewish people to the head of the line in a culture that promised fulfill-ment for Jewish prophetic visions. As the Pittsburgh Platform put it: "We recognize in the modern era of universal culture and of heart and intellect, the approaching of the realization of Israel's great Messianic hope for the establishment of the Kingdom of truth, justice, and peace among all men."[10] When Judaism was sufficiently modernized, some Reform rabbis felt, it would be more fit than Christianity to serve as the universal religion of ethical monotheism for all. After all, it was not saddled with such allegedly irrational myths as a god incarnate in human flesh or a virgin birth, nor was it stained with a dogma of universal evil in human nature due to original sin. Ennobling Judaism and restoring its prophetic luster by modernizing it promised to hasten the redemption.

Among more traditionally religiously observant European Jews, two different approaches to modernity emerged. In Eastern Europe, the process of modernization was weaker and more marginal; Jews were still mostly excluded from the wider society, cordoned off by strong walls of antisemitism and social hostility. Hasidic communities with powerful social bonds and intense spiritual currents were still strong. These factors emboldened religious leadership to close ranks and fight modernization tooth and nail. Similar processes occurred in some communities further to the west. In Hungary, Rabbi Moses Sopher, known as the Ḥatam Sofer, so forcefully rejected modernity that he even prohibited some practices that had been permitted, such as vernacular prayers, because they resembled changes favored by Reform. In a similar spirit, Rabbi Akiva Eiger, a towering Torah giant of nineteenth-century Germany, wrote to Napoleon asking him *not* to emancipate the Jews, because modernization led Jews to betray the oath they had taken at Sinai. These Orthodox leaders, precursors of the ultra-Orthodox movement that would later be called *haredim*, saw modernity as highly addictive: in any conversation that admitted the axioms and terms of modernity, premodern ideas and practices would lose. One might say they agreed with the assimilated and revolutionary Jews that modernity was an absolute master, demanding total obedience and an end to any Jewishness. Therefore, they were prepared to renounce all the new messianic possibilities in order to stay faithful to the Torah.

In retrospect, these traditionalist leaders seriously underestimated the extent to which modernity's rewards of dignity, acceptance, affluence, and security would attract the bulk of Jewry. They miscalculated that it was possible to escape from modernity indefinitely. Above all, they completely missed the message of the *tzimtzum* (as well as of the purely secular version of human capacity) that swept the world over the next two centuries. In essence, the *haredi* position meant that its people rejected the call to take power to improve human life. Refusal to join the educational and economic system of modernity had the consequence that the Torah, as they understood it, would not function in what turned out to be the most powerful, most liberating, most creative culture of all time. Furthermore, their religious society could not participate in or profit from the creation of the new economy, or the new science and medicine. In time they learned to reach out for the new social services and health benefits. Indeed, the improvements in public health enabled a population explosion for Jews—especially in Eastern Europe, where the culture of prizing children and family remained strong.

The really catastrophic consequence of denying the legitimacy of humans taking power came out of the *haredi* active theological opposition to Zionism. God, they claimed, had imposed an oath on Israel—not to revolt against the nations, but rather to wait for the Messiah, the Divinely sent miraculous redeemer who would restore Israel. Therefore, religious Jews were a small fraction in the new *Yishuv* (pre-State settlement), and later in the State of Israel. As a result, religious Jews would initially play a smaller role in building the most important new Jewish community in two millennia of Jewish history.

Moreover, millions of religious Jews who refused to take action and assume power by making *aliyah* to the Land of Israel remained in Europe as sitting ducks before the Nazi genocidal onslaught. Of course, millions of secular Jews were also caught in Europe with no place to go. Still, lacking even the meager resources possessed by secular Jews, those furthest from modern culture (and perhaps least connected to their diaspora homes) suffered even higher rates of loss.

In many communities in Western Europe, where a more powerful modernization process quickly came to dominate the host society and culture, total rejection of modernity was not a plausible policy for observant Jews. The foundation of what came to be known as Modern Orthodoxy was the recognition that religiously observant Jews would have to live in the new culture, because they could not escape it. The deeper insight was that the Torah could indeed live, and observance flourish, in a modernized culture. The weakness in the approach, however, was in not grasping the depth of the questions the new culture was posing to Judaism. Forerunners of Modern Orthodoxy like Rabbi Samson Raphael Hirsch thought that bringing out the universal and ethical aspects of Judaism would satisfy the expectations of modernity. This approach, plus adopting the dress, language, respectable social practices, and good citizenship patterns of modern Germans, would enable Judaism to hold its own in the new civilization. On the other hand, when there were clashes between modern and traditional practices or values, Hirsch insisted that the Torah was eternal, and modernity had to be cut to its measure — not vice versa. His two nostrums — higher, better education and a more modern hermeneutic of tradition — worked best for those steeped in tradition and community.[11] Hirsch failed to grasp the cutting edge of historical thinking, and the growing evidence of change and development in all religious traditions. He insisted that Judaism, coming straight from God and heaven, was not culture-bound in its origins, and therefore was not subject to decay as the old host culture passed away — so it need not change.[12]

There was a profound partial truth in Hirsch's insistence that Torah's origin in the Divine placed it beyond criticism and change. The tradition not only contained revelation; it had stood the test of millennia. Why then should it be carved up to fit the Procrustean bed of modern culture, however persuasive or attractive this new culture appeared to be?

Yet two other truths of the classic tradition contradicted Hirsch's authority claim. First, his teaching diminished the covenantal character of Judaism's heritage. He obscured all the ways humans are involved in its composition, from interpreting it to modifying it, integrating circumstances and elements of the host culture along the way. His approach also ignored the ways in which Divine revelations had been shaped to the imperfect capacity of the audience and conditions of their culture, which led to the incorporation of serious moral and other problematic elements absorbed (or read into the Torah) in those earlier cultures.

Second, Hirsch's approach to pure, canonized revelation as providing an untouchable, unchangeable authority additionally overlooked or disregarded past human corrections of some of these flaws, as well as the implicit covenantal assignment to living Jews to update the Torah as partners. This orientation worked only as long as it was not undermined by the challenge of historical research that portrayed Torah as growing in a cultural context, and as having undergone change. Hirsch dismissed history and historical evidence as having no weight against the revealed Torah. He rejected evidence of past changes, or archaeological evidence of errors of historical fact in Scriptures, and opposed teaching or studying such material. Strengthened by the influence of yeshiva and *haredi* culture, which totally denied any human or historical elements in Torah, this approach to history became the dominant Orthodox party line over the next century.

Haredi institutions and teachers, exercising considerable control over the educational access of their students, could get away with this tactic. It was much harder to achieve such exclusion in Modern Orthodoxy, because many adherents went to university and were exposed to alternate approaches and scholarship. Nonetheless, many Modern Orthodox leaders, too, insisted they had no power to substantially reinterpret halakhah. Proclaiming that the Shulḥan Arukh and the authority of earlier generations was sacrosanct meant that the present generation lacked authority to depart from inherited tradition. They did innovate in limited ways: allowing new interactions with gentiles, particularly with secular culture; developing women's Jewish education; going with uncovered heads; shaving; wearing gentile dress. By and large, though, they did not grasp the moral and ethical depth of many issues needing new approaches, let alone enable the halakhic community to extend or modify the halakhah as necessary. At the time, their adjustments met the needs of their own constituents, although Reform Jews found these responses inadequate. But once modernity's expectations grew—for example, as the status of women extended and deepened over time—Modern Orthodoxy came to find itself less capable of grappling meaningfully with such matters.

Focused on becoming citizens of their own countries, many German- and English-speaking Modern Orthodox Jews did not grasp the Zionist model of Jews taking political power by building the Land of Israel. Moreover, seeing the secular, nonobservant culture of most Zionist groups, they associated human assumption of power with rebellion against God, and aligned instead with Agudat Israel, the anti-Zionist Orthodox, whose center of equilibrium was among those totally opposed to modernity and any assumption of political power. Fortunately for Modern Orthodoxy, its Eastern European branch, and its groups on the continent and in America, many did join the Zionist enterprise, thus saving the tradition a role in the transformation of Jewish history by returning to the homeland.

The Modern Orthodox logic for removing the halakhah from the realm of history was the same as that of the ultra-Orthodox. Many Jewish laws were morally problematic in modern culture (halakhic preference for Jews, for example, or gross inequality for women), or culturally problematic (animal sacrifices, or prohibition of intermarriage), or simply difficult to observe when integrated in a modern society (Shabbat and kashrut). Any acknowledgment that humans were involved in generating these laws, or that these laws had undergone development and change in history, would have given irresistible force to a popular argument that what had once been developed by humans could be changed by humans, in accordance with modern standards. Modern Orthodox leaders believed that attributing authorship exclusively to God and denying any development process would preserve the law as authoritative and untouchable. They did not foresee how, as modernity deepened, historical research and historicist thinking would gain intellectual currency—making the claim of the out-of-this-world nature of the Torah increasingly problematic.

Meanwhile, to uphold the unchangeability of the laws, the position emerged that humans in the living generation had no power to change God's decrees, even if they wanted to. The generations had declined. Modern halakhic leadership lacked the authority of its predecessors.

This had a subtler but, in the long run, even more paralyzing effect on Modern Orthodox legal decision-making. First of all, there was a moral coarsening. There is a strong cognitive dissonance between feeling something is morally wrong and considering it untouchable because it is the word of God. This was the case, for example, with laws that totally excluded the children of adultery, making them unmarriage-able, and those that treated women unequally and subjected them to abusive husbands. As Rabbi David Hartman put it: "It is tempting to reduce the dissonance by minimizing the moral issue, or hardening one's heart toward those suffering from the law."[13]

A second effect was more disabling. Removing the human element translated the law into a self-contained system from God—purely a matter of legal precedents and analysis. Therefore, one no longer thought of it as a system that had to work in real situations. Yet a legal system responsible for reality has to make allowances for real factors. Indeed, historically, the halakhic system had included allowances to avoid inflicting excessive economic costs on people—for example, by creating a fictitious sale of ḥametz (leavened) products for Pass-over, since strict enforcement of the Torah's prohibition on benefiting from owning ḥametz during the holiday would impose great losses on certain Jewish businesses. In an effective, real-world legal system, when enforcement of the law leads to injustice and unjustified suffer-ing, judges can turn to the principle of equity to correct the evil. But when modern decisors confronted, for example, the plight of agunot, "chained wives," the chief excuse for inaction was that they lacked the authority—that is, the power—to correct the injustice. Halakhah was functioning as if it were not responsible for the operation of a full soci-ety, making it unworkable and removed from its societal context. Far from responding to the Divine tzimtzum (as the Rabbis in the Talmud had done) by taking more responsibility and power to act on behalf of the covenant and its goals, contemporary halakhists were renouncing their capacity to make halakhah work in real time.

This type of halakhic heavy-handedness was a departure from and a violation of the talmudic foundational principle, "You shall observe My laws and My rules *by which a person shall live*" (Lev. 18:5). As discussed earlier, the Talmud applied this to lifesaving situations: one may violate any of 610 out of the 613 commandments to save a life. The lesson of saving a life on Shabbat, as Maimonides wrote in the *Mishneh Torah*, is that the Torah laws are not "punitive" or "vengeful" decrees (and human welfare be damned!) by a tyrannical God. Rather, the Torah laws are meant to be a source of "compassion, loving-kindness, and peace in the world."[14] One whose rulings turn Torah laws into the enemy of quality of life and livability is guilty of turning the Torah into "no-good decrees and laws by which people cannot live."[15]

This Maimonidean understanding should be applied over a broader framework. In light of its commitment to life, the halakhic system should be functionally livable in any humane society. The psychology of denying human beings the right to exercise power encourages an irresponsible ethic of using power when, in the last resort, it is reluctantly exercised. The net outcome of not accepting responsibility to run a society—shirking, too, the corollary obligation to be reflective on the actual use of the power and to hold all such exercises accountable—is widespread use—and abuse—of power without accountability.

In a classic example of taking responsibility for Torah in the real world, Rabbi Abraham Isaac Kook (known as Rav Kook), later the first Ashkenazi chief rabbi in pre-State Israel, saw that enforcing the Torah's ban on agriculture in the sabbatical year would destroy the fledgling agricultural economy of the Jewish settlements in Palestine. In response, he worked out a fictitious legal sale of the land to a non-Jew not bound to rest from farming in the sabbatical year. In effect, Rav Kook sacrificed the immediate observance of *shemitah*, the sabbatical year, so that the halakhah could guide present reality in a functional way, keeping open the possibility that a future, fully developed agricultural society could practice comprehensive *shemitah*—not to mention other values, such as ecologically sound farming and sharing the wealth. Kook's *heter*, the permission to enact such sales, enabled the economic survival of the nascent farming economy without repudiating the Torah's laws of sabbatical rest for the Land of Israel. He won sufficient support from other halakhic greats to enable Jewish agriculture to flourish in the land throughout the twentieth century.

By the twenty-first century, however, the growth of *haredi* political power and orientation to halakhic decision-making substantially undermined the granting of this sale permission. In the 2007–8 *shemitah* year, for example, some *haredi* authorities rejected the *heter*, creating chaos among the Orthodox public and threatening the agricultural economy with tens of millions of dollars in estimated losses. Using the lever of Orthodox power and claiming to enforce God's will, the traditionalists inflicted a massive wound on the lives, or quality of life, of hundreds of thousands. That is the price of a conception of Torah and halakhah that is not on the side of life, or committed to livability for all.

In the early stage of building the state, religious Zionists such as Rav Kook cooperated with secularists, and played a major role in building a new society, economy, and culture. To accomplish all this, religious Zionists did many things other halakhic leaders forbade. They cooperated with nonobservant Jews. They enabled secularists to create a society that did not observe many ritual laws. Nor was the Zionist enterprise bound by traditional views on women's roles or inherited halakhic modesty standards. In religious kibbutzim and other Zionist settings, women worked alongside men. They actively participated in traditionally male fields and violated traditional segregated norms. Many uncovered their hair. They dressed for the heat with short sleeves, or wore pants to work. They sang freely, and participated in cultural activity as they mingled with men. They voted in elections and took leadership roles. The lack of official sanction and the departure from past norms were overridden by the needs and demands of reality. Ultimately, the unspoken, axiomatic, normative power of modernity created the true sanction for these behaviors. In fact, some religious Zionists openly dismissed traditional rabbinic rulings as being reflective of a Torah of the *galut* (diaspora, exile). Since they had not had to rule for a total society, their legal thinking was not up to the challenge of the new reality in the homeland.

The paradoxical effect of eliding these restrictions was that the religious Zionists built a strong religious culture and society, functioning in real life, suffused with modernity and modern cultural values, and with vital Jewish traditions, memories, and practices. They influenced and anchored the secular Zionists, so that the State of Israel that emerged was, in key respects, deeply Jewish. For a variety of reasons, including respect for religious Zionists and attentiveness to this group's role in Israeli society, the state affirmed aspects of traditional observance and support for Jewish religious life—at least in public institutions.

But the underlying infrastructure of religious law and theological Torah did not keep up, even in the State of Israel. Halakhic decisors failed to apply to the realm of religion and halakhah the modern theological imperative to take power for the sake of life. They did not abolish gender inequality, even though this clashed with democracy. They did not rule to enable the state's provision of public services that were needed even on sacred days. Nor did they deal with the development of industries that require seven-days-a-week operation, an omission with subsequent negative consequences for the economy and the political order.

Twentieth-century modern Orthodox thought leadership was increasingly congruent with *haredi* Orthodox thinking. Rather than develop the halakhic system and bring it up to date, leaders viewed modernity-driven innovations as deviations from recognized, legitimated practices. Consequently, preventing any halakhic change (lest it undermine observance) became the defensive norm.

Thus the halakhah increasingly turned into a code for a private club that allowed itself to live by highly restrictive or high-cost rules by which the whole society could not function. Imposing moral or emotional violations on people in the name of enforcing God's decrees, using the halakhic system to deny women the many public roles they now play in modern society, failing to adequately incorporate the State of Israel into the system, and promulgating stringencies that piled excessive costs on businesses and households, all made the Torah exclusionary and almost nonlivable for many people, while leading the Orthodox to look down on the people they excluded. This, in turn, encouraged the bulk of the Jewish people to turn away from halakhic guidance for daily living.

Modernity and the Survival of Jewry

As Jews' integration and achievements reached such levels that modernity became the dominant force in Jewish life, many Jews left to join world-transforming movements, and many more actively assimilated into the emerging liberal democratic cultural ethos. Still, even the internal life of Jewry was dominated by modernity. Secular Jewish movements grew steadily over time, from Yiddishism and socialism in prewar Eastern Europe, to Zionism and Hebrew in the new *Yishuv*, to progressive politics in many parts of the Diaspora.

Modernizing religious movements also became ever stronger. In America, Reform grew steadily, eventually becoming the largest denomination. In the 1950s, much of American Jewry moved out of immigrant neighborhoods and settled in suburbs, where they expressed their Americanization by joining non-Orthodox synagogues and Jewish Community Centers. American Jews who did express their traditionalism and Jewish ethnic loyalty by associating themselves with Orthodoxy were likely to be less than fully observant, and to join the more "modern," more "American" version of Orthodoxy, more closely associated with the dominant culture that was a source of authority and credibility. In England, where the Jewish population tended to be more traditional, the majority of Jewry maintained Modern Orthodox synagogue affiliation even as they became less observant. Everywhere, modernity's dominance meant that traditionalists had little power to resist the process of its universalization and triumph. As a result, Jews suffered from the unchecked dominance of modern values like other people — only more so.

The absolutization of modern values had three additional negative impacts on Jewry. First, distinctive pathological developments in modern culture tended to turn on the Jews, who were, and are, often seen as modernity's chief beneficiaries. Enemies of liberalism and democracy from the right have often pointed to the extraordinary presence of Jews in modern civilization, blaming them for being agents or the moving force in unwanted developments.

Meanwhile, it became clearer that driving forces of modern culture — especially technology — could also be harnessed in powerful ways for antidemocratic goals. Mass movements arose promising to restore a sense of group or community to those who felt diminished and threatened by their isolation and vulnerability to economic or social setback in a free market economy. These movements turned against "outsiders"; in the case of Nazism, the Jews were identified as the ultimate outsider, and a subversive threat to national unity and welfare.

The concentration of technological access to entire populations, with bureaucratic machinery that could organize and control all sectors, enabled strong movements to unify the nation under one party, one leader, one concentrated source of power and control. Of course, they claimed they would deliver the affluence and improved living standards that were at the heart of modernity's promise. Totalitarianism represented the climax — and breakdown or pathological form — of modernity. In the case of the Soviet Union, Stalin's regime imposed centralized control, using all the technology, bureaucracy, and military power available to create total tyranny. The Soviet state specifically suppressed Jewish culture and religion in the name of a utopianism that promised to heal all of modernity's problems and achieve utopian goals — indeed, the very messianic visions that had so attracted Jews. By the late 1930s, the Communist government shifted to an openly antisemitic policy. Having committed their all to the nation and to the modernization process, the Jews were not in a position to check these pathological developments. Nor did Jews' non-Jewish compatriots defend them as the hegemonic forces in society turned against them.

Self-correcting mechanisms in modernity did generate some resistance to these negative tendencies. In the case of England and the United States, democracy survived. While antisemitism rose in both countries in the first half of the twentieth century, the vibrancy of democracy protected the Jews from the major, systematic persecution seen elsewhere. One reason American Jews identified so strongly with Franklin D. Roosevelt and the New Deal was that they perceived him as having saved America from the kind of reactionary dictatorship and full triumph of antisemitism that reared up elsewhere in the world. Jews themselves, however, never reached enough of a critical mass in any diaspora country to exert decisive influence on the fate of democracy, or to stop totalitarian movements from coming to power.

The second way Jews suffered from this absolutization of modernity and its triumph in their midst was in their failure to develop power through political action. The notable exception was the Zionist movement. Despite its limited following, the Zionist organization built steadily toward a future where Jews would wield their own power. Tragically, their movement was not strong enough at the time to stop the Holocaust, nor did it then have the sovereignty needed—which would not come until the establishment of the State of Israel in 1948— to mitigate the catastrophe by offering asylum to Jews in need. The rest of the Jews, however, were largely committed to the nationalism of the countries they lived in, or to the universal promises of modernity. Early in the twentieth century they made little effort to build Jewish political power in their host countries. Some feared that open articulation of Jewish interests would be perceived as Jews not being good citizens, or as validation of the old claims that Jews were not truly loyal citizens of their respective nations. Thus in the United States, even as late as the 1920s, the Reform movement not only repudiated histori-cal prayers for restoration to Israel, but largely eschewed the modern Zionist movement as well. Many of its influential leaders were then active in the American Council for Judaism, which aggressively rejected Zionism and insisted that Jews had no need for political power in the land of Palestine—or in America.

Identification with the host nation and its culture ran so deep that many Jews were increasingly unable to recognize when their host nation was mutating, and a profound conflict between Jewish inter-est and the nation's direction was at hand. Thus many German Jews treated Hitler's rise as an aberration from true German culture; these individuals identified so deeply as Germans that they could not imag-ine leaving the country. Of course, the shock of Hitler's rise to power in 1933 with an openly vicious anti-Jewish program galvanized many Jews into flight—but even then, many were still sure that Nazism would soon vanish. Only after the violent, brutal pogrom of Kristallnacht was the web of illusion torn away and were the Jews forced to confront the decisive turn Germany had taken. A frantic scramble to leave followed, but by then the scarcity of places of refuge and the closing of Pales-tine to Jewish immigration made flight impossible for many. Nor did the vast majority of American or English Jews wake up to the coming need for Jewish political power, to get the Allied governments to take specific actions to help European Jewry during the Holocaust. To the very end of the Holocaust, American Jews and their communal orga-nizations were generally not prepared to fully admit the clash between national policy and Jewish needs. They did not take political action strong enough to save more of their brethren in Europe.

The third, most elusive, yet powerful way in which Jewry suffered due to the triumph of modern values in its internal life came to a head in the latter half of the twentieth century, when rising affluence and surging economic growth reached unprecedented heights in English-speaking countries. Jews were major leaders and beneficiaries of these developments. These countries had rejected the alternatives to democracy and liberalism, and had fought Nazism. In the course of World War II and its aftermath, xenophobia and racism gradually came to be identified with ultimate evil. Barriers that had impeded social connections between Jews and non-Jews fell rapidly as Jews were admitted into ever more areas of national life. By now, many Jews' identification with modernity's liberalism, humanism, and universalism was complete (or nearly so). As even more barriers fell, the Jews' image as creative cultural leaders made them increasingly socially desirable. Suddenly the distinctions between Jews and non-Jews seemed very minor, even residual.

For many Jews, the culture of modernity had displaced Jewishness as their most salient identification. In the United States particularly, voluntary assimilation grew rapidly. The most powerful expression of this trend was in the sharp rise in interfaith marriage from the sixties on. Most Jews did not perceive it as a flight from Jewish identity. Rather, in some cases, Jewish identity and culture were simply increasingly marginal. Opposition to interfaith marriage appeared to others to be exclusionary, even racist. As ethnic bonds weakened, the idea that Jews had a special responsibility for, or reason to connect more strongly to, fellow Jews seemed reactionary. Many American Jews now felt they had more in common with liberal fellow Americans generally than with Jews in particular.

To put it another way: Most American Jews believed that the promises of classical Judaism's redemptive vision—the overcoming of poverty, hunger, oppression, discrimination, war, and sickness—were on track to be fulfilled by the dominant multicultural, liberal culture, in its universalist reading. Furthermore, the promises of quality of life, freedom, self-expression, and higher fulfillment also appeared more reachable through the general culture, with its opportunities and options. Moreover, many Jews were increasingly concerned that all of humanity deserved to be—and could be—redeemed as well. Since most of these channels of redemption existed outside of the Jewish community, ever more Jews wanted to participate there. In many cases, it was not that these individuals were ashamed of their Jewish identity. They were proud of it. Jewishness was now associated with high achievement and the cultural avant-garde. It was just that Jewish identity and lifestyle appeared less important than participating in all the other exciting, enriching, and ennobling ways of living available in America.

The Holocaust

11

For a theology based on Torah and covenant, the Shoah presents distinctive challenges to our understanding. The Holocaust puts before us with great force the moral risks of modernity, in which growing human power, with all its effect for goodness and life, may nonetheless be harnessed for evil. Simultaneously, its exceptional level of destruction has extraordinarily challenged Jews of its generation, and ours, to ask why God's covenantal partners should have suffered such a catastrophic fate. In its wake, we must ask about the future of modern society, and especially the future of Jews in modern society. That the total devastation was unchecked from above requires that we articulate a credible Jewish conception of the next stage of our partnership with God in the work of covenant.

The Triumph and Tragedy of Modernity

The Nazis revealed how important values and forces generated by modernity, many of them sources of life and blessing, could be channeled beyond their range of validity and beneficence into forces for death and destruction. Growing out of the high culture of modernity, Nazism promised to bring all of modernity's good qualities to climactic fulfillment, while curing modern society's negative effects. The Nazis drafted many beneficent forces unleashed by modernity—from science to the rule of law to the very principle of universality—into the mechanisms of genocidal extermination. Moreover, they assumed control of the very social and political institutions that should have opposed or blocked such a concentration of force for evil. In so doing, they illuminated one of the great pathologies of modernity: the sheer force built up in modern civilization's industrial, commercial, technological, communication, scientific, and military infrastructure generates unprecedented power that can be seized, harnessed to evil goals, and used on a monstrous scale for cruelty and death.

Modern science had enormous power to transform the world for good, but the Nazis hijacked that power for their agenda of racism and murder. New communications technology fortified the arts of propaganda to connect and control the population, and new understandings of economics bolstered the Nazi war-machine economy. Exploiting the achievements of modern medicine and science, the Nazi leaders and the doctors who worked with them developed and implemented a eugenics program, engineering the systematic murder of people with developmental and intellectual disabilities. Moreover, this program served as an experimental and training center for officials who later carried out systematic murder of the Jews.[1] Modern science prided itself on being beholden only to the scientific process, free of religious and clerical controls and untainted by emotions that might distort results or close off areas of research. The irrelevance of such traditions and feelings and other sources of ethical codes paved the way for Nazi doctors who experimented on humans or served as selectors for death. Doctors harnessed the language of therapeutic medicine as a sanitizing vocabulary to legitimate selecting human beings to be killed. The victims were "bacilli" or "virulent pathogens" to be eliminated for the sake of humanity's health.

So, too, the Nazis corralled the concepts of law and bureaucracy in their war against the Jews. Many great achievements of modernity have resulted from proper legislation, broadly applied by an efficient bureaucracy, improving the dignity, security, and health of millions. Moreover, adherence to the rule of law has generally protected citizens from abuse, promising them the security (and inner sense of dignity) of possessing rights and value in society. Yet the Nazis upended these powerful civic tools for their own evil purposes. They unleashed a massive wave of laws and decrees that turned the Jews into legal nonpersons. Laws stripped Jews of citizenship rights, validated murder and sterilization, created concentration camps, and crushed the political opposition. Bureaucrats zealously, dependably, and professionally executed their orders.[2] Bureaucracy was essential to the process of identification and registration of the Jews, as well as in Aryanization—the "legal" sequestration of the Jews' property. Later on, it took enormous administrative efforts to organize the transportation of the Jews to their deaths. Thousands of officials in government and railway organizations were involved in the commissioning and construction of gas chambers, the purchase and distribution of lethal gas, and the transportation of the victims to the killing centers.[3] Germany's cultural conditioning to follow the modern rule of law "legalized" and sanitized these laws and procedures, and in this same spirit, government workers and bureaucrats developed and enforced these regulations, whether or not they themselves held Nazi beliefs.

Another orientation of modernity is its universalism. Modern culture, as observed in the last chapter, sees that which covers all alike as more proper than and morally superior to particularistic moral regimes or exceptional cases. The universal is more objective; it is also more comprehensive and, in principle, equal in its impacts. In many democracies, the equality of all citizens is a sacrosanct legal and philosophical principle; there are no invidious exclusions. The Nazis twisted this modern concept of universal applicability to mean that all Jews must die. In a 1943 speech, Heinrich Himmler, *Reichsführer* of the SS, rebuked supposedly "good Germans"—who supported the murder of Jews in general—because "every one of them has his decent Jew" whom he thinks should be an exception. There would be no exemptions and, his contemptuous tone conveyed, people asking for them were weak. By contrast, SS officers had backbone and conscience—in effect, they were principled enough to carry out the killing in its totality.[4]

In many ways, Nazism had a messianic vision, just as modernity did. Modernity promised to abolish poverty, hunger, oppression, war, and sickness, and in some important respects it began to deliver on those promises. Nazism made many of the same promises—to cure modern society's negative effects, such as depression and economic vulnerability—using many of the same tools, but it made them only to the limited group it considered fully human. The world-embracing nature of National Socialism's vision—creating a harmonious society while using science and eugenics to perfect the human population—was a twisted version of world redemption, an outgrowth of the utopianism unleashed by modernity's outsize ambition and achievements.

Totalizing Nazi Idolatry

As National Socialism set out to "redeem" the world, it installed its leader, its Führer, as the ultimate and sole authority of the movement. With time, Hitler became ever more convinced of his own infallibility, and the German people came to view the Führer's decrees as more authoritative than the prohibitions they had imbibed from education, culture, and their religion before him. Hitler now became the focus for their worship and adoration, someone whose judgment of right and wrong constituted the new code of ethics and at whose word people would live or die—in effect, a god. This is the essence of idolatry: declaring or worshiping a finite human being or a limited human institution or creation as absolute. Thus at the Wannsee Conference, where the Final Solution was planned, not a single attendee expressed a dissent regarding the Führer's goal, even to comment on the enormity of such an endeavor. All the discussion was about tactics.[5]

In its worldview, Nazism was the most ambitious, most totalizing movement. It aimed to be the most powerful redemptive movement of all time. The absolute worship of Hitler matched the totalizing nature of its vision, and the totality of its vision left no room for anything else. The Nazi form of messianism meant believing that starting all over again—destroying existing social and political structures as well as inherited frameworks of meaning—would usher in a new world that could solve all problems. Idolatry of this grandiose worldview justified the acceptance that anything deemed antithetical to Nazism deserved to be destroyed.

This totalizing in the service of the redemption goal played a big part in conceiving and executing the Shoah. For the Nazis, the Jews were representatives of the old frameworks of meaning. They were a threat to Nazi ideology because they represented alternatives. Jews had helped create the dominant frames of meaning in Europe, starting with the Hebrew Bible, and they were highly visible in various modernizing movements. Removing the Jews totally would radically clean the slate of history and culture, thus allowing the creation of a new Eden, whereas allowing the Jews to continue to exist made the totality of the Nazi vision impossible.

Jews were therefore easily identified as the source of liberalism, or of communism, or of capitalism. Nazi propaganda alleged that Jews were planning to use their excessive power to dominate the world. Humanity was divided into several *Volks*—national groups, each with their own distinct spirit and embedded values—and the German *Volk's* superiority, its right to live and vanquish its enemies, validated its moral right to wage war. This, in turn, justified its right to destroy the religion, the depository of the values, of its greatest enemy, the Jews.[6] Germany was in peril, and only the Nazis could save it.

Nazi idolatry was just as opposed to Judaism theologically. The Rabbis of the Talmud categorized idolatry along with two other cardinal sins— murder and sexual violation (such as incest)—as uniquely representing death for the human body or soul. Like murder or sexual violations, idolatry is a threat to human dignity and human life. Judaism insists that just as God loves and nurtures life, so idolatry hates and undermines life. God is a Force, a Presence extending beyond all human limits, not controllable by finite creatures, and therefore any attempt to make a finite human principle absolute is, in effect, an attempt to cut off a piece of reality from the Infinite God. This is why Judaism considered idolatry the anti-God. For idolatry to survive, to make something human and finite appear infinite and absolute, the Infinite God had to be removed from view—eliminated from the picture.

This, then, was the theological agenda behind the Holocaust. To make a human leader and system absolute and unchecked, one had to eliminate the unlimited, uncontrollable God of Israel. To control God and make room for their absolute worldview, the Nazis took over German Christianity as a vassal of National Socialism. They established a racially and doctrinally purified German Christian church, domesticating it, or limiting God's claims, in the hopes of making religion subservient to and supportive of the human absolute. But ultimately, the only way to eliminate the God of Israel was to obliterate the people Israel.[7]

The German Christian theologian Dietrich Bonhoeffer, who was later killed by the Nazis, came to recognize this implicit theological element of Nazi ideology. After Kristallnacht, Bonhoeffer "meditated and prayed" and then came to realize that "the synagogues that had been burned in Germany were God's own. . . . To lift one's hand against the Jews was to lift one's hand against God himself. The Nazis were attacking God by attacking his people."[8]

One need not accept Jewish and Christian theology literally to accept this understanding of Nazi ideology. In secular terms, the Nazis sought absolute control, and sought to make Hitler the ultimate authority. By their existence, the Jews stood for an alternate value system that negated the vision of a homogenized Aryan society. Nazism could not incorporate the Jews into its totalizing vision of redemption, so it needed to eliminate them. Extermination would not only uphold the absolutism of Nazism; the process itself would intimidate any other form of opposition or dissidence.

The Assault of Death on the Jews and Judaism

When the Nazis decided to eliminate the Jews completely, they were mounting an assault on Jewish life, not only on the Jews as individuals. The Final Solution was, of course, an assault of death on Jewish life in the literal sense. The Nazis murdered Jews, first by the slow death of starvation and sickness, then by unleashing the fury of shooting squads, and then in death camps and forced marches. But the Nazi assault of death on Jewish life was broader. Early on, a campaign of humiliation and dehumanization diminished Jewish life by isolating Jews from the people around them, attacking Jewish religion and culture, and targeting Jews when they were most alive—at times of childbirth and infancy. All of these campaigns gave death power over Jews and made them less able to live their lives, even while they were living.

Some of the Nazis' choices, especially toward the end of the war, derived from economic factors: they calculated the cost per Jew killed, and balanced it against the labor value of a Jew kept alive and forced to work. But the Nazis cared more about ending Jewish life than maximizing economic gain. A 1942 ss study on how to maximize profit from using prisoners as workers found that if one killed the prisoner too soon, there was lost output, but if one let the prisoner live too long, productivity dropped from weakness. The conclusion was that a nine-month life expectancy would maximize profit. Yet by the time the largest Jewish deportations and selections occurred in 1943 and 1944, most Jews in the camps were gone within three months—because the ss did not seek to maximize profits by conserving their lives.[9]

Still, killing Jews was not the sole purpose. Well before the mass murder campaigns, the assault on Jewish life began with organized degradation. The Nazis engaged in systematic exclusion, legalized discrimination, and random violence against the Jews in order to remove them from German life, in part by forcing German Jews to leave. Repeated campaigns of degrading propaganda images were meant to humiliate the Jews, validate the Nazi contention that Jews were subhuman, and make them appear so repulsive that there would be less internal recoil at killing them. Joseph Goebbels, *Reichsminister* of Public Enlightenment and Propaganda, commissioned a propagandistic film, *Der eigen Jude* (The eternal Jew), and then declared its content "so dreadful and brutal ... that one's blood freezes. One pulls back in horror. ... This Jewry must be exterminated."[10]

When they turned to systematically exterminating the Jews, the Nazis often chose to do so in particularly painful and humiliating ways, because they wanted to destroy Jewish life and Jewish humanity as well. At Auschwitz, prisoners who were selected for labor—that is, for a temporary life and a painful, grinding death—were tattooed; they would henceforth be identified by a number, not a name. Their hair was shaved off, sloppily and brutally, to be used to make textile goods for German soldiers and civilians. The ashes of their burned bodies were used for fertilizer or traction for roads in winter. Thus human beings were converted into raw materials. Still, the main point was that the prisoners looked degraded, defaced, even ridiculous. The tattered, ill-fitting uniforms they were given often made them look like scarecrows and walk like clumsy stick figures. Drastically limited access to showers, sanitation, soap, and changes of bedding kept the stench of their excrement ever present and choking.

These humiliating conditions made the Jews less alive, even while they were living. Cut off from the population around them, stripped of the legal rights and processes that governed interactions between other people, they soon learned that, while they might get an occasional kindness or help from an individual functionary, in fact those systems of acknowledging basic human dignity no longer had any dependable or enforceable obligation to them.[11]

Mary Gale was a young girl hidden by her parents with a Polish family that saved her life. She concealed her identity as a Jew after the war for more than fifty years. When asked why she did this, she explained: "I became paranoid . . . during the war I couldn't even think of being Jewish because being Jewish meant being dead." She did not want to die, so she totally denied her Jewish identity to herself. The trauma and force of the association was so strong that she could not bring herself to acknowledge the connection for another five decades.[12] Although the Nazis did not kill Mary Gale, their regime of terror and humiliation did kill her Jewish life for most of her years.

In the camps, the assault of death on Jewish life was so strong that the line of demarcation between life and death was eradicated. Life conditions—food, shelter, clothing, work, social activity—were all so warped as to destroy people step by step before they died. The production of "living skeletons" is one of the genuine inventions of the concentration camp.[13] Living Jews began to feel and act like dead ones, as the Final Solution turned into an assault of death on life itself.

The classic expression of this hollowing out of life was the *Muselmänner*, the walking dead in the camps—prisoners so emaciated, their bodies so broken, that their souls collapsed into total apathy and torpor, unable to act. As Primo Levi points out in his memoir of Auschwitz, "One hesitates to call them living; one hesitates to call their death death; in the face of which they have no fear, as they are too tired to understand."[14]

Nazi policy was additionally to assault Judaism and Jewish values. Destroying Jewish values and beliefs was a key part of destroying the Jews. In prewar Germany, assaults on synagogues and sacred scrolls were designed to break Jews' cultural presence.[15] With the invasion of Poland, this turned into a systematic attack on the Jewish religion. Synagogues were bombed, damaged, vandalized, and repurposed into warehouses, stables, and other derogatory uses. Kosher food was cut off. *Mikvehs* were raided or closed. Religious services were forbidden or disrupted. Assaults were commonplace, especially beatings of Orthodox Jews—dressed in traditional garb—that included cutting off their beards. The Nazis then went out of their way to upend the Jewish holy days into days of extra suffering and degradation. There were hangings of groups of Jews on Purim—proclaimed as revenge for the hanging of Haman's ten sons as told in the book of Esther.[16] The edict to establish the Warsaw ghetto was promulgated on October 12, 1940—the day of Yom Kippur. In the camps, the Nazis strangled religious life by killing a higher proportion of traditionally observant Jews and their rabbis and scholars.

By attacking Jewish religious practices, the Nazis saw they could inflict damage on Jewish life far beyond the number of Jews they were able to kill in the flesh. When the Nazis banned Jewish emigration from Nazi-occupied Poland, Reinhard Heydrich, director of the Reich Security Main Office, commented that killing Polish Jews would mean killing "a large part of the rabbis, Talmudic teachers, etc. who are much in demand... in the United States," because "each Orthodox Jew also represents an additional element in their [American Jewish organizations] to effect both a spiritual rejuvenation and further cohesion of American Jewry."[17]

Finally, the Nazi assault focused specifically and horribly on the moments where the Jews were most alive: reproduction and infancy. The ultimate symbol of their hatred of Jewish life was the prohibition of pregnancy in the Kovno ghetto in 1942–43.[18] The secretary of the ghetto's Jewish council, Avraham Tory, reported in his diary: "The Gestapo issued an order: pregnancy in the ghetto is forbidden. Every pregnancy must be terminated. An eighth or ninth month may be completed. From September on giving birth is strictly forbidden. Pregnant women will be put to death."[19] Margita Schwalbova, a Czech Jewish doctor who worked in the hospital in Auschwitz, reported that "every woman found to be pregnant [in Auschwitz] was killed by a phenol injection" and that later, when children were born in Birkenau, "as a rule, mother and child were sent to the gas chamber after birth, regardless of whether they were Aryans or Jews. Auschwitz was a death camp, not a life camp, and there was no need for young progeny."[20] Similarly, in the Kovno ghetto, the Jewish police discovered one consistent policy of selection during deportations: large families were uniformly sent to the left to be killed. The Jews responded by splitting up large families into smaller groups, to help more people get through the checkpoint. While individual Nazi officers may have taken it upon themselves to develop some of these policies, nonetheless, the operations captured the underlying spirit of the Shoah: the absolute hatred of Jewish life, and determination to oppose any new or additional life creation.

The Nazi assault of death on Jewish life raises an important theological problem: if the God of Israel is a God of life, and Judaism is a religion of life, then how could God allow so many Jews to die, and how could the Jews have allowed it? Seeing with their own eyes the fate awaiting them, why didn't more Jews do something? Although there are many possibilities, the first answer is that most humans faced with overwhelming force surrender to it, and the Jews were no exception. Even highly trained Russian soldiers who were taken prisoner by the Nazis and then starved or killed systematically overwhelmingly passively accepted their fate. Second, there are fates that might seem worse than death by shooting—such as being beaten to death or watching one's loved ones suffer as punishment for one's own resistance. And third, the total assault of death with which the Jews were faced made them less able to resist. Rivka Yosselevska, who survived the *Einsatzgruppe* massacre that killed the rest of her family, said later that after hours in the sun without food and water, and with the constant torture of the sounds of death and the children crying out of hunger and fear, she and other mothers trudged forward in the line to bring a quicker end to the suffering.[21]

Even so, even as Jews were largely unable, physically and mentally, to fight against the Nazi assault of death, many resisted by choosing life as much as possible. People did get pregnant—although at the end, in the Warsaw ghetto, the death rate surpassed the birth rate by forty to one. They organized illegal *yeshivot* and *batei midrash* (Torah study groups), underground provision of kosher food, secret *mikvehs* (that quickly closed when the Nazis discovered them), and underground youth groups. As it became clear to many communities that most of them would die, they began to think about what might outlive them. A stunning number of people set about writing diaries and chronicles in the hope that their testimony might survive even if they did not. The historian Emanuel Ringelblum organized the *Oyneg Shabes* project to collect and document what was going on week by week in the Warsaw ghetto by burying documents in milk cans and tin boxes, several of which were found after the war.[22]

In another classic example of the determination to uphold life even in the very jaws of death, Jewish doctors in Warsaw realized they could not stop the mass starvation they were witnessing, but they could study it and record it. Monitoring over 150 patients, they made important clinical and hematological discoveries about the symptoms and treatments of adult and child starvation.[23] Most of the physicians died during the deportations. The surviving doctors managed to complete the study, print it, and send it to the Aryan side in the hope of saving it from destruction. This was a powerful mirror and an implicit rebuke to the Nazi doctors, who intentionally caused suffering in order to study it. The Warsaw ghetto doctors were powerless to stop the deaths by starvation, but to the extent that they could gather future lifesaving information, they still worked in the face of those deaths to strengthen the side of life.

Even when it seemed futile, Jews responded to their impossible situation by trying to live. People tried to feed their families and provide for their children. They struggled for survival in an ever-changing, overwhelmingly hostile environment. This includes the members of the *Judenrat*, the Jewish councils designated by the Nazis and forced to do their bidding—including collecting Jewish funds to be paid to the Germans as fines and penalties, supplying forced labor, enforcing German decrees, and later even participating in roundups and deportations. For the most part, they saw their work, including its horrifying compromises with evil, as the only chance to create a functional society in which the Jews could survive until some future liberation resolved the agony.[24] In the Warsaw ghetto, the Judenrat organized soup kitchens and other welfare programs. Hostels were organized for refugees. Special kitchens and countless classes and schools were set up for children—the most famous being Janusz Korczak's children's home, with its self-government by the child residents. The Judenrat grasped at straws, hoping to stay alive and keep as many of their community alive as they could, while doing the Germans' bidding—resisting the counsel of despair even in situations of overwhelming death. In countless small ways, Jews fought the Nazis by living and helping one another live.

Grappling with the Possibility of
Horror in the Third *Tzimtzum*

As the Jews struggled to find room for life during the Holocaust, they grappled with its theological implications. They, too, wanted to know how a God who loves life and the Jewish people could allow the destruction they saw around them. In many cases, they attempted to answer such questions with theological models adapted from earlier Jewish sources that focused on God's Divine justice, or promised a redemptive value to suffering. Ultimately, these explanations were insufficient. They neither helped those Jews who adopted them to understand the situation and act to save themselves, nor provided a satisfying theological account of God's actions in light of the destruction of so much of God's people.

It was precisely the struggle to honor the reality of God and Divine involvement with Israel as expressed in historical redemptions such as the Exodus, and the manifest absence of such comparable activity in the Shoah, that led me to seek a new understanding of God's behavior. In turn, this led to the uncovering of the *tzimtzum* that underlies the Rabbinic rearticulation of Judaism and the covenant that is the heart of this book. In modernity's *tzimtzum*, God came closer, and humans were handed full responsibility—including, in the end, the full responsibility to stop the Holocaust. What array of forces came together and what humans did (and did not do) in response to the Divine summons is essential to understanding what made the Holocaust possible.

During the Holocaust, one widespread Jewish theological explanation was that the Jews were being punished for their sins. For example, in February-March 1942, the Agudat Israel newspaper, *A Kol in der Midbar* (A voice in the desert) published an analysis of the mitzvah of remembering Amalek that was also, by implication, a commentary on the current situation of Jewry. It said that if, as the Talmud says, Amalek comes because the Israelites "become lax with respect to the Torah," then the response must be to intensify and expand Torah study.

If Amalek's power stems from doubts and carping—"Is God among us or not?"—then in response we must greatly strengthen our faith and trust in God. This article clearly bespeaks a classic traditional analysis of history: God pulls all the strings. God sends the political persecutors of Israel when the Israelites turn away from God; God saves them when they repent.

This explanation fails on a number of levels. It implies that the correct response is quietism, prayer, and repentance, and that political or social resistance to the Holocaust would contradict God's will. For example, as antisemitic violence soared, the rebbe of the Satmar Hasidim, Rabbi Yoel Teitelbaum, insisted that no actions other than prayer, repentance, and strict observance of mitzvot could help; all other protest or resistance was prohibited, as Jewish political action would only interfere with God's plans and punishments.[25] As a member of the Central Bureau, a regional body of Orthodox Jewish leaders in Eastern Hungary, he learned of the extermination of Polish Jewry, but he refused to call on his followers to try to protect their own lives through rescue or emigration. On the contrary, he warned would-be immigrants to Palestine that they would likely harm their *haredi* way of life. As the war intensified, he did take steps to obtain visas that would facilitate escape to Palestine or the United States for himself and his closest circle—yet he vetoed cooperation between the heads of Orthodox communities and Zionist organizations, which had access to some visas due to their connections abroad. Any cooperation with the Zionist movement was prohibited. The Zionist movement had created an escape route from Hungary into Romania that ultimately saved the lives of ten thousand people—but in March 1944, when a group of Hasidim decided to follow this route, Rabbi Yoel refused to join them and the plan was aborted. Eventually, he agreed to cooperate with Zionists enough to be transported himself to Switzerland, and later to Jerusalem and then to the United States, where he rebuilt Satmar Hasidism to the extraordinary extent and power that it has achieved.

Although the Satmar rebbe himself survived, his theological under-standing of the Holocaust contributed to many deaths among his fol-lowers, who stayed in dangerous situations even when they could have left. The traditional views were applied so relentlessly and so pejora-tively to others' lives that they materially added to the losses, and sub-stantively betrayed those who obeyed and trusted their leaders with their lives and their families' fate.

To his dying day, even though his own life had been saved by Zion-ists and their interventionist understanding of history, the Satmar Rebbe proclaimed his theology of quietism and repudiated Zionism. In a treatise written in response to Israel's Six-Day War, he wrote that the Holocaust was God's punishment of the Jewish people for its sins. The primary sin was Zionism, itself a revolt against God and the Jewish people's place in exile. The Zionists not only brought on the Holo-caust by angering God; they made it worse by provoking Hitler with their protests and criticisms of his policies. Moreover, he wrote, the Holocaust was part of the messianic redemption process. The Mes-siah would have come then, but Satan and the Zionists' activities had impeded his arrival.[26]

In addition to its deadly practical results, the explanation that the Holocaust happened because God was punishing Israel's sins fails on theological grounds. For me, the sticking point was and is the impli-cation of the nature of God that follows from holding on to the classi-cal idea that God inflicted the Holocaust on Jewry to punish its wrong behavior. I cannot fathom what sins could ever justify such horren-dous cruelty and extermination. What kind of a Moloch god does this conception turn the Loving God of Israel into? However reasoned, however rooted in the sources or nobly intentioned, such responses are a betrayal of most of what we have known or learned about God over the course of a partnership that has lasted almost four thousand years. There are no sins the Jewish people could have committed that could have justified the Holocaust in response.

Some Jews living during the Holocaust sensed that the intensity of the Nazi assault was straining the capacity of the classical explanation that such evil is a punishment for Israel's sins, and proposed an alternative, also grounded in Jewish text and tradition: the Holocaust and the surrounding war and upheaval were not ordinary punishment for ordinary sins, but were instead the birth pangs of the Messianic Age. For example, Rabbi Isaac Breuer, a leading ideologue of Agudat Israel in Germany, said that the scope of the world wars and the scale of Jewish suffering in the Shoah were so vast that more than ordinary punishment for sins was occurring; these could only be part of the catastrophic end times that signaled the coming of the Messiah. Rav Elchonon Wasserman, himself a martyr to the Nazis, also insisted that this era was signaling the coming footsteps of the Messiah.

While this explanation avoids the theological problems incurred by saying that the Holocaust was a just punishment for Israel's sins, it does not solve other problems raised by that approach. In particular, it maintains the belief in quietism. Wasserman, for example, remained resolutely opposed to any human political activity to bring the redemption. Criticizing Agudat Israel for its involvement with the *Yishuv* in Palestine, he insisted that any activity that helped to build Palestine constituted fellow-traveling with Zionism, and was therefore part of a presumptuous, sinful attempt to take Jewish fate into human hands. "There are two primary false gods whom Jews serve ... Socialism and Nationalism," Wasserman wrote. "In Heaven, those two false religions have been combined into one [National Socialism]. A terrible rod of wrath to punish the Jews has been created from the mix."[27] When Wasserman and a group of rabbis were martyred by the Nazis, he went nobly, assuring his comrades that the death of the righteous was an expiation for the sins of other Jews, and that their sacrifice would bring the Jews to new life.[28]

Understandably, such responses were trying to address the fact that God did not actually intervene and stop the Shoah. Out of profound loyalty to God and the way they understood the tradition, these Jews justified God's actions. The Auschwitz and Buchenwald survivor S. B.

Unsdorfer wrote: "In all actions of His Blessed Name, whether universal or particular, everything is precisely calculated."[29] One can only bow one's head at the loyalty that could evoke such an affirmation in the face of overwhelming proof to the contrary in the form of innocent agony and suffering.

Some religious individuals and groups have sought to fudge the reality of God's nonintervention by focusing on stories of individuals saved or on specific events of deliverance. But if one steps back and looks at the total picture, the sheer sum of six million Jewish dead—along with millions of others—and the infinite experiences of suffering of every type that occurred far outweigh the redemptive moments, and crush the credibility of all such claims.

In the cauldron of agony, many Jews, even religious Jews, broke with the old interpretive framework—and with any religious framework. Hillel Zeitlin, one of the leading religious writers and public intellectuals of prewar Poland, wrote in 1941, "Religious life has sharply declined in the ghetto. . . . A typical response is a mutiny against God, against Heaven, evident among many religious Jews who no longer agree to submit to the Judgment of Providence."[30]

The work of the Piaseczner rebbe, Rav Kalonymos Kalman Shapira (sometimes rendered Shapiro or Szapiro), an important religious leader in Poland before World War II and an innovator in Hasidic education, offers a different model from within the Shoah of the direction Jewish religious thought might take. Shapira lived, suffered, and survived in the Warsaw ghetto until the mass deportations to Treblinka in July and August of 1942, when he went into hiding before being caught and killed in 1943. Earlier that year he had buried notes and transcriptions of his *derashot* (sermons), which were later found and published by Hasidim in Jerusalem in 1960 under the title *Eish Kodesh* (Sacred fire).[31]

In some of his earlier sermons, Shapira invoked classic *middah k'neged middah* (measure for measure) theology, but increasingly over time, he shifted his main thinking in two distinctive directions: on Jewish suffering and on Divine suffering. In a remarkable early *derashah* (November

4, 1939) he turned to our mother Sarah as the incarnation of Jewish suffering. Her suffering is unmerited, he says, not the outcome of a punishment. Shapira cites Rashi's teaching that Sarah died when she heard of the binding and near slaughter of her beloved son, Isaac. He suggests that Moses juxtaposed the story of the Binding of Isaac and Sarah's death in the Torah to advocate on Jewry's behalf, "and to suggest to God that if the anguish is, God forbid, unbearable, then death can result." He adds: The Torah may be telling us that Sarah "died in order to show God that a Jew should not be expected to suffer unlimited levels of anguish."[32] Sarah's experience is a warning that suffering can be beyond human capacity.

Shapira saw that, past a certain point, suffering is no longer useful or instructive. He returns to this theme of Jewish suffering repeatedly, not to justify it as punishment and not even to redeem it as martyrdom, but rather to stress its destructive and depressive effects on human beings.

The other great theme Shapira develops is that of Divine suffering. The beginning point is this: not only when the Jewish people suffer, but when any individual Jew is in pain, then the Divine is in agony.[33] He goes on to say that "because God is infinite . . . God's pain at the suffering of the Jewish people is also infinite."[34] Just as finite humans cannot grasp God's infinite nature, so too the extent of Divine pain may be beyond human comprehension.

Jews may still feel abandoned, as if God is distanced, but this is a false impression—perhaps because Jews in this generation are more self-centered, but also because the Divine pain is so great that God cannot express it openly: God must hide it from Israel and from Creation itself, lest the fullness, the agony and evil, crush them.

Thus, Shapira suggests that when Jews feel *hester panim*, the hiddenness of God's face, typically experienced as a kind of abandonment, they should deepen their faith and look deeper, and they will discover God right there—a discovery that will end the hiddenness and distant feeling.[35] Thinking about God's suffering can allow individual Jews to place their own suffering in cosmic perspective. God's suffering is so great that the faithful Jew is driven to look beyond his own pain and identify with the Divine agony.[36]

Thus, Shapira is thinking about God not as the cosmic puppet master who is controlling history and who must be beating the Jews by means of the Nazi rod, but on the contrary, as the Divine interventionist whose primary act is to come closer to the Jews and suffer their pain even more intensely than they do themselves. As Shapira put it, "When the Holy Temple existed . . . God . . . performed supernatural miracles and wonders for them [Jewry]. That was how the Holy Blessed One unified His name and showed the whole world that He is One. Now, however, when the Jewish people are in exile, the Congregation of Israel is the only one unifying God. In order to unify the name of God, the Jewish people . . . bear the brunt of suffering and even give their souls for the Oneness of God."[37] The pain the Jews are experiencing has nothing to do with punishing the Jews measure for measure. God loves Israel— hence the Divine coming closer and sustaining unlimited suffering. Similarly, Israel loves and remains faithful to God selflessly. Jewry is in fact the unique witness and unifier of God's name by its faithfulness— even when God is no longer showing might or power via miracles or displays of power or control.

I do not claim that Shapira embraces the argument I have developed in this book, that in this era God has chosen by self-limitation to be a Presence, rather than a controlling force. However, I believe that in his spiritual depth and openness, he sensed the cosmic movement of Divine *tzimtzum* that left the Nazis free to do their evil, while bringing God and Jewry even closer together in common fate and mission. This meant that Jewry was testifying to God and covenant in an age when the old displays of Divine might—including measure for measure— were nowhere in sight. Although steeped in the inherited *middah k'neged middah* tradition, Shapira recognized the reality of unlimited and unjustified Jewish suffering, and pointed us in a new theological direction: being faithful to a God who is now more totally close. Israel is not the sinner chastened by God, but the lover who remains faithful because "love is as strong as death" (Song of Songs 8:6). This is the highest level of covenantal faithfulness. This is a fulfillment of the verse, "Though He slay me, I will hope and yearn to Him" (Job 13:15).

Rabbi Yissachar Shlomo Teichtal, a Hungarian rabbi and prewar anti-Zionist, was also jolted by the Shoah into reevaluating traditional theology. He concluded that the catastrophe inflicted on Orthodox Jewry called for self-criticism and reconsideration of the pre-Shoah policies.[38] The Orthodox policy opposing human political initiatives had been disastrously wrong. Had Jewry gone the Zionist route, millions might have moved out of the path of destruction. Moreover, God had wanted human initiative; the proof was that the work in Palestine was flourishing. The extreme suffering in the Shoah could only be accounted for by an out-of-the-ordinary development: a signal of a coming messianic breakthrough. It followed that the Jews were not being killed for their religious shortcomings; nor was the Shoah commensurate with their sins. Rather, many misjudgments and failed policies resulted in increased losses. The sting of these failures should evoke repentance, and a community-wide turn to building the Land of Israel. Thus Teichtal saw that a theology of quietism could not preserve the Jews in modernity. Instead, the Jews' commitment to the God of life now required human action as well as faith in God.

Neither Shapira nor Teichtal survived the war, and neither of their views were adopted widely, during or after the Shoah. The vast majority of Orthodox rabbis clung to the passive theology that all was in God's hands; only repentance and deepened observance would evoke God's redemptive actions. Human activity was prohibited; it would arouse the anger of local authorities who, serving as the rod of God's anger, would inflict further evils on the Jews. These rabbinic authorities, who had chosen to eschew modern culture, had no idea of the vast power amassed in the new culture now in the hands of antisemites. Nor did they fully grasp that modernity had put a terminus on the *haredi* strategy—that Jewry could no longer live self-contained, powerless, and undisturbed in the interstices of modern civilization.

The most disastrous assumption of all was the conviction that God would intervene and save faithful Jews from the coming evil. Eastern European Jewry, including millions of devout Jews, was decimated even more than other European Jewish communities. I have no doubt that under the Nazis' yoke, many of these millions prayed with greater devotion, fasted, and repented during the Ten Days of Penitence with heightened intensity; kept their traditions at great sacrifice; begged God intensely for deliverance—in vain. Even if some of these individuals survived, the sum of death makes clear that the kind of salvation predicated on *haredi* theology and promised by the rabbis did not happen. Going forward, any honest, credible Jewish theology must reckon with this fact.

The Holocaust was all the more devastating because the Divine *tzimtzum* had made redemption dependent on human action, while at the same time giving humans more power to act in evil ways than ever before. Future religious thinking and strategy must draw the lessons of this catastrophe, and rearticulate the Divine and human roles in the covenant going forward. In pursuing this understanding, Jews should be loyal to God and to the covenant, and not to our inherited notions of how the two operate together in Jewish history. Following the model of the Piaseczner rebbe, who saw shared suffering between God and the Jewish people as a way for the Jews to feel closer to God, we can understand that, although God no longer acts directly in the world, our ability and responsibility to act brings God and Jewry even closer together.

12 Responses after the Holocaust

When I first began to respond to the Holocaust theologically, I was under the spell of the traditional view of Divine control of history. I had lived in a universe where God ruled, where every year people were put on trial for their lives, their fate depending on whether they had done more good or more evil in the previous twelve months. Along with Jews worldwide I prayed: "Our Father, Our King, we have no King but You . . . nullify the plans of those who hate us."[1]

These views were pulverized in the Shoah. When I read that in the burning pits of Treblinka, if the "[guard] was kind, he would smash the child's head against the wall before throwing him into the burning ditch; if not, he would toss him straight in alive,"[2] I could not reconcile that with God's Presence in the world. I am an observant Jew, and all my life I have loved doing the mitzvot. But I went through days when I put on my tefillin and such scenes flooded back into my mind. I choked on the words of the prayers and could not say them. I certainly could not accept that this cruel fate was inflicted on the Jewish people because of their sins.

Why did I not let go of my faith entirely? A lifetime of religious observance and experience held me. Also, my most intense years of immersion in the Holocaust were spent in the Land of Israel (1961–62; 1974–75). Every day there I experienced not only the triumph of death in the Shoah, but the power of life. Walking the streets of Jerusalem, my eyes feasted on neighborhoods restored after thousands of years, and my ears heard the prophet's predicted "sounds of revelry and joy of groom and bride" (Jer.

33:10–11). In the renewed city, God's Presence was manifest. I sensed that I was witnessing the renewal of the covenant by the Jewish people and by God. This new birth was reversing the Nazi death blow, and proving that God "had planted eternal life in our very being."[3] In my mind, the twin death star of the Holocaust and life star of Israel were locked in unrelenting combat. I was totally held by both, and mired in a standoff between their two gravitational pulls.

It became increasingly clear to me that this was not only a personal crisis of my own faith. The existing religious and secular understandings of faith and truth would have to be transformed to be credible in light of the Shoah. Religion as it had existed before the Holocaust had been unable to prevent the Nazis; nor could theology explain their regime of death. Heinrich Himmler, the chief architect of this realm of death, insisted to his confidant, Felix Kersten, that ss men must believe in God, otherwise "we would be no better than the Marxists."[4] At the same time, sometimes atheists were more able than religious people to understand and respond to the Holocaust. The philosopher Albert Camus, an atheist, described himself yearning and praying in vain for a word from the pope opposing the Final Solution. He expressed his disappointment and disillusion on realizing that being Christian did not make people more likely to support the Resistance. If the Nazis could see themselves as people of faith and see God as integral to their project, if an atheist could understand the absolute need to oppose the horrors of the Final Solution while the pope himself could ignore it, then something must have been wrong with inherited approaches to religion.

In the same way, in the early State of Israel, religion did not seem to predict people's commitments to protecting the Jewish people. To me, the State of Israel was the most powerful and persuasive proof of the presence of God in history and of the ongoing viability of the covenant. Yet the majority of Jews then populating the Jewish state were nonobservant and secular—and many of them literally gave their lives defending it. In my view, by spending their lives building the homeland, these secular Jews were giving witness and "proving" God's promises were true, regardless of the fact that many of them would have denied they were doing so and would have even rejected belief in God.[5] By contrast, many ultra-Orthodox Jews in the Land of Israel had exempted themselves from the army to study Torah and engage in religious ritual activities. I concluded that in this world, actions speak louder than words. Religious is as religious does. In Israel, as in the Holocaust, Jews' degree of religious conviction did not predict their degree of participation in the causes that advance the goal of life and flourishing for the Jewish people.

Toward Voluntary Covenant, and Beyond It

I struggled to find a conception of religion that would explain how people's relationships with God could so completely fail to explain their behavior in their greatest moral and political test. I was already moving toward understanding the Shoah as reflecting a new age of greater Divine hiddenness and greater human responsibility, yet I remained mired in the traditional framework of covenant, in which Israel witnessed to God and worked for *tikkun*, while God directed history and protected Israel. Ultimately, I had to acknowledge the truth in Elie Wiesel's words: "For the first time in history this very covenant [of reciprocity] is broken."[6] Protestant theologian Roy Eckardt's argument also helped sharpen the nature of the crisis. Eckardt claimed that God must repent—we would say, in Jewish terms, must do *teshuvah*—for having given His chosen people an unbearably cruel and dangerous task without having provided for their protection.[7] Part of me found this compelling. Since God had failed to uphold the covenant by failing to save the people of Israel, therefore, as a just deity, God had to withdraw the covenantal obligation.

It seemed clear to me that, had the covenant between God and the Jewish people been the same as the traditional version, then God's behavior during the Holocaust would certainly have broken that relationship. But even as I developed these thoughts, the evidence around me showed that the Jewish people continued to live in covenant with God. Although the Nazis had killed an estimated 80 percent of the rabbis, scholars, and full-time students of Talmud alive in 1939, within a half century, there were more rabbis, scholars, and full-time students of Talmud than ever before, in any age of Jewish history.[8]

I was inspired by the example of Naphtali Lau-Lavie, scion of a devout Orthodox family in Krakow, grandson of a distinguished rabbi who survived harsh labor camps in Hortensia and Czestochowa. He was liberated in Buchenwald at the age of nineteen, while nearly all of his family had been killed. After his liberation, he spent two weeks without putting on tefillin or engaging in prayers. Then he received a note saying: "You have to say Kaddish because your mother is no longer alive. She died in Ravensbrück." In that moment, he decided that he would live his life and raise his children in the traditions of Israel, and eventually he came to live in Israel as a fully observant Jew.[9] Although its very basis seemed smashed, the covenant was operating at full blast in Jewish life worldwide.

Trying to reconcile these two contradictory understandings, in a 1982 essay I offered the possibility of a *voluntary covenant*: "The covenant ... was broken but the Jewish people, released from its obligations, chose voluntarily to take it on again. We are living in the age of the renewal of the covenant. God was no longer in a position to command but the Jewish people was so in love with the dream of redemption that it volunteered to carry on its mission."[10] According to this understanding, God did break the covenant by allowing the Holocaust to happen — but, in practice, the covenant was still functioning, because the Jewish people had chosen to uphold its side of the terms. The covenant had none of its old obligations and enforcement mechanisms, but it remained a commitment and set of actions the Jewish people could take on to further the dream of redemption through partnership with God.

Still, calling the covenant "broken" troubled me. After all, all around me the covenant was operating in full force, and even blossoming, with astonishing accomplishments unfolding in practically every sphere of human endeavor. Additionally, I feared that, in voluntary commitment, some Jews would interpret the term "broken" to allow for both a lowering of the behavioral and devotional standards required of them and a lessening of their passion for pursuing and enacting those standards. Hence, I added a footnote on the word "broken," clarifying that I did not mean "null and void," but rather that "its brokenness makes the covenant more adequate insofar as it relates more totally to the Jewish condition. This helps account for the extraordinary pull it exerts on this generation of Jews." I also wrote that "no covenant is so complete as a broken covenant."[11] I was beginning to sense that, in the covenantal process, God was wagering that humans operating in freedom would deepen their commitment and achieve far more than they had when operating under orders from a coercive authority.

In my own religious life, thinking about the covenant as broken and about all subsequent Jewish life as voluntary had brought me closer to the Divine Presence. Still, others responded differently. I was pained by the fierce rejection of the idea in the yeshiva world, even in that part of it I still lived in. Many other responses challenged and unsettled me, too, foremost among them Steven Katz's warnings that a paradigm of voluntary commitment undermined the reciprocal dimension of *brit*. By implication, this conceptualization of God and the Divine activity in history could well undercut the *brit*'s capacity to compel redemptive behavior and evoke loyalty and faithfulness.[12] For myself, the voluntary covenant moved the needle that oscillates between faith and void toward the positive side: a much greater number of my days and nights were experienced in connection with God's Presence. Nonetheless, I took seriously the dangers my understanding could generate in others.

Indeed, as I wrestled with these responses, I found my thinking developing in other ways as well. I felt that viewing the Holocaust as *the* defining turning point in Jewish history, where the covenant was broken and had to begin anew, risked recalibrating Judaism around a moment of death, instead of around Judaism's primary focus: working toward redemption. I was committed to upholding the centrality and focus on life in the Jewish tradition and determined not to let the immersion in death, in the Shoah, take over my religious worldview. It helped that, just as the Shoah crashed my world, Israel became a vital force in my life and thought. In addition, our five children were born during the years in which I came closest to falling into despondency under the accumulating weight of knowledge of the catastrophe. Their burgeoning lives proved to me the supremacy of life. Despite the need to incorporate the Holocaust into Judaism's sacred narrative, then, I came to understand that the focus should not drift from redemption and *tikkun olam* to death and martyrdom. Nor should one hand Hitler a posthumous victory by shifting the motivation for covenantal loyalty from advancing life and love to fighting back against evil.

Perhaps in response to swimming in the ocean of death and pain, I began to actively develop the course on "the triumph of life" that was the origin of this book. Over time, I continued to affirm the primary insight articulated in *voluntary covenant*—that this is the age when humans take full responsibility for carrying out the covenant—but I came to retract the specific formulation that God's commanding authority was broken and that the Jews were now bound by a purely voluntary assumption of the *brit*. Instead of thinking of the covenant as broken, I came to think of it as *transformed*. God and the Jewish people continue to be bound by our shared covenant, but that covenant is in a new stage: one where God has invited humanity to become the "managing partner" in our relationship, so that we now bear the responsibility for how our choices affect world developments.

Additionally, I came to see that understanding modernity in terms of this new *tzimtzum* preserved the conceptual benefits of the broken covenant idea, while avoiding its theological and communal pitfalls. Thinking about the covenant not as broken but as *transformed* by God's *tzimtzum* helped me bring my theological intuitions back into conversation with my communities.

All the more, I realized, focusing on the renewed covenant as a force for life in modernity can help the covenant become a force for good in the world. The mechanism of covenant as *the* method of *tikkun olam* became central as I turned to a new exploration of the goal of the *brit*: to honor and draw human freedom to the work of *tikkun*.[13] The narrative of the original biblical covenant, the Noahide, revealed a fundamental Divine shift from authoritative power and human obedience to persuasion and human education. Upon closer inspection, there was a fundamental Divine pedagogy intrinsic in *brit*. Humans would not be pressured to do the right thing but educated and inspired to work on the side of life. The goal was for them to grow into identification with the aspiration of *tikkun olam* and the love of God, so as to willingly take on a covenantal way of living. Only in this way could they mature into infinitely valuable, equal, unique beings.

As a religious community, we must take the Shoah seriously to heart—and grow up. God is asking us to switch from a quid pro quo contract to a covenantal commitment based on love, relationship to God, and a common vision of *tikkun olam*. God is profoundly hiding, so that we will put less energy into proclaiming God's greatness and more effort into serving the Lord by redeeming the world and healing God's creatures. We have to dig deeper into existing channels of connection to God, and develop new ones that follow and relate to the Deity in the depths of hiddenness. When we recognize the call to become fully responsible for the outcome of the covenant, we will be set free to fully realize our own image of God. We will be inspired to work harder to create a world that respects everyone else's image as well. If we are willing to make the same wager that God did, on human goodness and decency winning out, then we may be able to move the planet and all of humanity toward the side of life.

I submit that this is the proper role of the current generation of the Jewish people, who have gone the whole covenantal way with God. Jews are called to testify to the world that the profoundly hidden God is neither absent nor uncaring. From our historic experiences, we know that humans are not alone, yet evil will not be stopped by any power but themselves. God's deep concealment is a call to seek out the Divine

Presence at a deeper level, a plea to us to work at a higher level for *tikkun*. The covenantal goal is not abandoned; to realize it is our human calling. The road ahead is harder and more dangerous; the record of the Holocaust is a continuing countertestimony to our dreams. Nevertheless, the Infinite One believes in us and in our capacity to meet this challenge, and will accompany us all the way.

Human Agency and Power in Modernity

After the Shoah, a growing number of Jews understood that, in the new situation, they had to strive to take power and accept responsibility for their lives. They had to renew the covenant on terms of much greater responsibility. They had to accept the staggering risk in a mission in which God would only promise to share, to suffer along, to sustain, but not to control and guarantee victory. This heroic maturation liberates us from the confines of the bubble of self-centeredness that most people inhabit.

If we look around, we can see that we are living in a time of world redemption. Many people and forces are out there working for the same goal. We need to accept full responsibility and affirm that a Divine redeemer is not going to come save us; it is too late for that. But we have a real chance to bring the redemption, for God's sake and for ours.

The Human Power to Act in the Face of Evil

The best proof of this thesis—that human agency is the most important piece of the covenant of life in modernity—is the actual record of Jewish death and Jewish survival during the Holocaust. In 1941 Hitler unleashed the full fury of industrialized extermination on the Jews. Thousands of German soldiers participated. Hundreds of thousands of people joined in or watched the *Einsatzgruppen* shootings and the life-crushing ghettoization of Eastern European Jews. Ordinary people built the death camps, managed the bureaucracy that organized roundups and transports, and played other roles on the side of death, including through inaction. The general population neither resisted nor condemned the Nazis' policies of death and destruction. Unchallenged antisemitism provided the atmosphere and cover for this ultimate crime. Organized solidarity with Jews was almost unheard of.

Throughout the Hitler regime, only one public demonstration in Germany protested anti-Jewish actions. When the Gestapo arrested eighteen hundred Jews married to non-Jews, the non-Jewish spouses—primarily women—demonstrated for a week. Hitler feared a negative popular reaction. The imprisoned Jewish spouses were released; the other Jews arrested at the same time were deported to Auschwitz.[14] The fact that this protest was successful only highlights its uniqueness. If a small number of non-Jewish family members could protest for a week and win their partners' safe release, it seems possible that, had more Germans protested, thousands or even millions of lives might have been saved. The Nazis' individual choices gave them the power to kill; ordinary citizens' choices gave them the power to save.

The same was true in the countries the Nazis occupied. In places where the local population showed solidarity with the Jews, where they rejected Nazi efforts to separate the Jews' fate from others, more Jews survived. When the local population helped the Nazis, when governments treated Jews as foreigners in their midst, survival rates went down. In short, the variation in Jewish survival rates was not primarily due to murderous Nazi behaviors or to Jewish efforts to survive, but due in large part to the behavior of the *bystanders*.

Four countries—Bulgaria, Denmark, Finland, and Albania[15]—saved almost their entire Jewish populations. Bulgaria's case is particularly striking, as the Bulgarians were allies of Nazi Germany. Still, the Bulgarians saved their native Jews, refusing to hand them over to the Nazis, which saved them from death in Auschwitz. By contrast, when the Nazis put the Greek provinces of Thrace and Macedonia under Bulgarian jurisdiction, the Bulgarian authorities did turn over the Jews there (who were not citizens of Bulgaria) to the Nazis, who sent them to the death camps.

In Denmark, citizens banded together to prevent the deportation of Danish Jews. When the Germans came to arrest Jews in their homes, only four hundred were found; all the rest had already hidden or escaped. Three days later, a letter from the bishop was read in Danish churches calling on citizens to obey God and not unjust human laws. Over the next two weeks, the Danish Jews were ferried to Sweden by an impromptu fisherman's fleet. When Jewish refugees flooded the trains to the seaport, the employees and police looked away. At the Danish government's insistence, those few Jews rounded up were sent to Theresienstadt—not Auschwitz. The government continuously pressed for their return. Of the 472 Jews deported, 423 returned safely after the war. Individual Danes, from the bishop to the owners of small fishing boats, had provided a shield for the Jews, and kept them alive in the face of the Nazi onslaught.

In contrast, in countries where the local population chose to help the Nazis, Jews were murdered at higher rates than the Nazis ever could have managed alone. For example, in Lithuania, even before the German army arrived, Lithuanian nationalists carried out violent pogroms and local massacres. Thereafter, local auxiliaries participated in German *Aktions* that murdered the Jews, mostly by shooting. By the end of 1941, of more than 220,000 Lithuanian Jews, only forty thousand were still alive. Fewer than fifteen thousand Lithuanian Jews survived the war.[16] The deeply antisemitic culture that had existed before the war led many Lithuanians to murder Jews themselves or support their murder by the Germans. Meanwhile, Lithuanian Jews were much more religious than Danish Jews, so it is clear that devout religious practices were not protective against the Nazi assault. Rather, individual people across Europe made choices that could kill—or save—their neighbors.

One can point to countries with mixed records. In France there was both a Vichy collaborationist government and a strong underground resistance. Of seventy-six thousand Jews deported to the killing camps, only about twenty-five hundred survived. Yet despite the devastating death rate of those deported, between 70 and 80 percent of prewar

French Jewry survived. In Belgium, 60 percent of the Jews survived. An estimated thirty thousand Jews went into hiding, helped by neighbors. In the French-speaking, more liberal Walloon province, 75 percent of the Jews survived. In Flemish-speaking provinces, where conservative and antisemitic attitudes were endemic, 75 percent of the Jews died.

The Allies, too, had the opportunity to make choices that would have saved Jewish lives. Instead, they prioritized other objectives and allowed Jews to be murdered. The Allies never confronted—or countered—the Nazis' primary focus on destroying the Jews. They never set the rescue of the Jews as a major war aim. Both Great Britain and the United States impeded Jewish emigration efforts and chose not to bomb Auschwitz to force it to shut down. As in Germany, the isolated instances of attempts to save Jewish lives often did succeed, but these were few and far between, and not on a scale that compared to the Nazis' scope of destruction. The Allies' effort to win the war was used as an excuse not to devote serious resources to foiling the Final Solution. Standing before the bar of history, the local populations can plead guilty, with extenuating circumstances: they were under Nazi control and constant pressure to carry out the genocide. In contrast, the Allies had both power and freedom of action, but they chose not to take responsibility.

In sum, Jewish survival rates strongly suggest that Divine *tzimtzum* and full human responsibility are the prime forces operating in history. The Holocaust was the outcome of human power, gathered and dedicated to an evil purpose, and operating without moral restrictions. After the Holocaust, any assessment of humanity's moral condition must be built on a foundation of despair and remorse. The sadness is only increased by the realization that God was incessantly calling, pleading, begging humanity to be their brothers' and sisters' keepers— largely in vain.[17] The God of *tzimtzum* did not miraculously save the victims. Heartbreakingly, God's designated agents for rescue (or those we might think of as such) were overwhelmingly missing in action.

To take up our responsibilities and move forward after the Holocaust, humanity must come to understand how badly things can go wrong: how horrific were the behaviors and how colossal were the failures and breakdowns—political, moral, and cultural—that made the Shoah possible. Proper response to the Holocaust demands a genuine self-examination and critique by every group, nation, religion, political party, and profession—and, from there, repentance and turning from the failed values and policies toward a new understanding of the relationship between God and humanity. Instead of using God as a crutch, and religion as a shelter or self-aggrandizing network, humanity finally has to take full responsibility for repairing the world.

The Ethical Obligation to Hold Power

In order to respond to the Holocaust and begin to repair the world, humanity must understand the incredible increases in power generated by modern culture and think carefully about how it is distributed. If you want to be safe from unlimited aggression, you must obtain sufficient power to protect yourself. Implicit in this finding is the recognition that one cannot depend on the goodwill of others—or on legal or constitutional rights written on paper.

This lesson was not lost on most people worldwide. Subjugated communities, minorities living among unsympathetic majorities, and groups already bearing the stigma of being outsiders came to understand that they must gain power—or else. There was no other reliable limit on their potential mistreatment except for self-defense.

In the postwar period there arose a worldwide anticolonial movement among groups in the developing world. The Holocaust was not the only impetus. A wide range of factors, including inherited cultural and religious traditions, diverse liberationist ideologies, emerging conceptions of democracy, and a growing awareness of the racist ideologies and abuses of power that undergirded imperialism, played major roles. Still, for many nationalist movement leaders, the lesson that only members of one's own group could be trusted to rule over and secure its people—illustrated so powerfully by the Holocaust—proved vital.

In Palestine, *Yishuv* leaders grasped the message that they could not rely on global powers to protect Jewish interests. Consciousness of the Holocaust became a driving force among the Zionist groups that moved to declare a Jewish state. The Jews of the world were also profoundly stirred. They shifted overwhelmingly to support Zionism, statehood, and the Jews of Palestine. At the same time, in India, what had been a much smaller prewar independence movement grew into a widespread revolutionary movement. Its leadership had been fully exposed to what happened in Europe. Many revolutionaries in Asia and Africa were also deeply influenced by these developments. Over the following decades, parallel movements unfolded across the world. The conclusion: to look out for ourselves, I and my people must take charge.

Within a generation, national liberation movements were matched by cultural liberation movements. These, too, were the products of a growing awareness that marginalized groups had to take power for themselves. In the United States in the 1960s, an explosion of Holocaust consciousness emerged side by side with a series of liberation movements. Hitherto oppressed groups demanded the power that would enable them to end their subjugation and throw off their second-class status. First came movements for civil rights and Black liberation. Activists demanded an end to Jim Crow laws and discrimination, the protection of voting rights and other freedoms, and Black power. They demanded and organized to get Black people included in the governing establishment, and they exposed and disrupted invidious stereotyping (for example, through the "Black is Beautiful" movement).

In the late 1960s, I heard a presentation by the writer and political activist Eldridge Cleaver, an early leader of the Black Panther party, arguing for Black power as the goal of the Black liberation movement. Growing up, he said, he had been taught to be "good" and submit to white power structures. Then, he said, "I read about the Holocaust. I said to myself: Go along? Don't make trouble? My God, there is no limit.

They will round you up, transport you and gas you! There is only one way to be safe: Black Power!" His words crystallized how the Holocaust teaches people to take power themselves.

Next came the movement demanding an end to the oppression of women.[18] As in the case of other groups, one of the women's movement's insights was that no one's status and well-being should be dependent on the goodwill of others. Dignity and status must be embedded in a power base of one's own. The LGBTQ+ liberation movement followed, and movements of cultural minorities and people with disabilities—each insisting that only the marginalized group itself could fully understand its own pain, and that only direct representation and power held by its own members could achieve security and dignity.[19] Over the next few decades, notable victories have been won toward their goal of equal treatment in American society, even as much work remains.

Jewish cultural movements also responded to the Holocaust by reinforcing Jewish culture. In the Soviet Union, many grasped that the Nazis had defined as Jews even those who did not self-identify as religious, or even as Jews—and then killed them. This drove home the message that being Jewish—even if only by birth or ethnicity—was more decisive in determining one's fate than all of one's beliefs or activities. Some Soviet Jews responded in the manner of Yosef Mendelevich, later a pioneer in the revival of Soviet Jewish identity, who concluded: *If I can be killed for being Jewish, then Jewish is a category of ultimate meaning, literally a matter of life and death. Then I choose to live as a Jew.* Since Jewish culture, religion, and education were suppressed in the Soviet Union, Mendelevich set out in an underground search for Jewish living, and eventually began agitating to be allowed to emigrate to Israel.[20] Denied an exit visa, Mendelevich joined other so-called refuseniks, whose movement to be allowed to leave the country captured broad attention and inspired protests by Jews worldwide. For some refuseniks, Holocaust consciousness and ongoing Soviet repression evoked a desire not only to emigrate but for cultural power as well—both in the Soviet Union and in Israel, where they hoped to go.

In America, especially after Israel's 1967 Six-Day War, broad-based movements to define and defend Jewish interests, reassert Jewish distinctiveness and values, and assert Jewish power flourished. Beyond the "free Soviet Jewry" movement, Jews campaigned to include Jewish Studies (like Black Studies and Women's Studies) in the course offerings of secular universities in America, and developed more Jewish agendas for communal life, such as priority funding for Jewish day schools. This led to the growth of a political activist culture to uphold Jewish interests, especially to gain support for Israel's right to sovereign self-government. Over the next two decades, AIPAC, the American Israel Public Affairs Committee, grew from a mom-and-pop operation essentially run by one man to what came to be called, and to be attacked as, the most powerful lobby in America.

Holding power can be seen as an ethical obligation. The notion of resisting evil with nonviolent submission or resistance, thus vanquishing evil by moral witness, was shattered by the murder of countless Jews who did not engage in violent resistance. George Orwell made this point in a cutting review of Mahatma Gandhi's memoirs. Gandhi—who prided himself that his *satyagraha* (nonviolence) philosophy defeated the armed might of the British Empire—criticized Zionism, and said that Jews should react to the Nazis only with *satyagraha*-type policies.[21] However we assess Gandhi's own efforts, Orwell's point was that Hitler and other tyrants would have ended Gandhi's defiance of the Empire's troops by silencing or executing him. An ideologically driven policy of Jewish passive resistance to Hitler's assault would only have facilitated the genocidal mass murder that followed.[22]

Sadly, the Holocaust showed that the power available to evil is limited only by the capacity of the evildoers when the will to use it is unlimited. Up to 1945, the Axis forces of evil won repeated, massive victories. They would have claimed millions of additional victims had the Allied nations not opposed them with their military might. To put it another way: henceforth only power was capable of restoring freedom and human dignity where tyrants were determined to crush it.

Pluralism and the Limits of Ethical Power

In the latter part of the twentieth century, increasing numbers of people understood human beings taking power as the key to a better world. The postwar world—especially the West—set about increasing human power and capability in every field of endeavor. Power then built on power; with every advance, ever-greater combinations of energy and resources could be employed. People understood that there were unplumbed possibilities to accomplish—specifically, to do good and advance life—in every area of living, from global poverty reduction to medicine and technology. These developments of power in industry, commerce, science, and medicine have yielded remarkable achievements in advancing life.

This embrace of power, however, comes with its own risks. An emphasis on sheer growth has strained the capacities of governments and nations to uphold adequate limits. Now the sum of improvements in life is starting to threaten life itself. Even as government regulations and professional and industry associations have developed ethics, rules, and best practices to prevent abuses in many fields, nevertheless, in the macro picture, increased pollution, global warming, and habitat and species destruction threaten to override present limits and even to outstrip the planet's ability to protect and regenerate itself. Humanity has not done enough to rein in the exercise of power. The profit motive and the drive to control have all but nullified the sense of being covenantal and accountable. Moreover, the weakening of religious influence—in part due to religious reactionaries insisting that past traditions, established in days when the human capacity to do evil was significantly more restricted, are Divinely mandated—has further undermined humanity's sense of being partners in the world.

In general, power corrupts. Absolute power—even when well-intentioned—is guaranteed to turn pathological. Therefore, since power is needed to operate any society or system, checks and curbs are crucial. In particular, political, legal, economic, and societal pluralism becomes essential. Only decentralized, multiple power centers can generate sufficient balance and offsetting checks to prevent strong forces from spiraling out of control. In Nazi Germany, the overwhelming imbalance of power between the perpetrators and the victims sealed the outcome. The most important foundation for preventing future Holocausts is to break up all excessive concentrations of power.

In healthy democracies, policy formation and decision-making are widely distributed, and constitutional or institutional checks and balances are in place in order to make the creation and execution of any far-reaching plan difficult to achieve. Indeed, no genuine multi-party democracy carried out a genocide in the twentieth century.[23] Of course, many competing centers of power can lead to gridlock and political stress. But democracies usually manage to muddle through. The redeeming side effect is that it is harder to harness the society for unitary, totally evil programs.

Similarly, a large private sector in the economy can reduce the danger of totalitarianism and tyranny, and the growth of checks and balances in all aspects of society and culture can help lead to a safer, more humane world. Post-Holocaust genocides have taken place largely in places marked by concentrations of one-sided power, and preventing such phenomena is pluralism's unfinished agenda.

Pluralism in religious, educational, and cultural spheres is also important in avoiding excessive concentrations of power. Dominant cultural and religious paradigms generate great force that can decisively shape political landscapes, while limits and boundaries on them express both cultural and political pluralism. The Nazis succeeded in part because they took over the universities, the media, the Protestant church, and the unions—institutions that in a genuine democracy could have challenged governmental policies and actions.

The commitment to pluralism that flows from the implications of the Holocaust is more than prudential. The way rhetoric both articulated and euphemistically covered up this horrific crime, the way words were inadequate to capture or represent what unfolded, left a widespread sense in European culture that truths, concepts, and categories that had once appeared absolute and beyond question had been revealed as sources of evil or, at best, as inadequate to check them. Therefore, all totalizing ideas appeared to be untrustworthy or, at best, of limited usefulness. One had to establish their limits before using them again. Two dominant paradigms—modernity and established traditions—proved unable to cope with or prevent the Shoah, so they had to be taken down from their cultural thrones, to assure there would be no recurrence.

Considering that cultural hegemony and moral centralization are potential threats to liberty and dignity, it is no accident that postmodernism has been one of the strongest cultural trends in the post-Holocaust period. Postmodernism rejects the certainty of modernism's universal claims and grand ideologies; it tries to overthrow unitary canons in literature and philosophy. Essentially it is disillusioned by the failure of modernity's pure, abstract reason to deliver on its methodological and utopian claims. The Enlightenment had promised to deliver a more solidly grounded truth, established by reason and scientific inquiry and free from the weight of inherited traditions—and, moreover, to bring utopian achievements in its wake. But the Enlightenment's great promise was undone when it met the real world of the twentieth century.

Postmodernism offers a relational logic that acknowledges significant overlap and intermix in dichotomies in general and that of modernity and tradition in particular, and seeks to bring these elements into dialogue with each other. Postmodernism also insists on contextualizing all values and statements, and on grounding all narratives in specific points of view—thereby limiting the authority of any one overarching ideology or viewpoint. As against authoritative, established voices, postmodernism looks for and highlights overlooked, neglected, absent voices. Hence postmodernism is valuable in helping to establish pluralism, and preventing a single perspective, narrative, or ideology from achieving hegemony.

However, postmodernism itself can become a form of hegemonic thinking, and lead to a new false universality that denies there can be any valid truths at all. A person who has assimilated this mode of thought too deeply might come to believe that no truth and value claims are more than assertions of group interest, that any narrative is simply a front for a group, and that a value is nothing more than the self-interest of the groups upholding it. Many people who have rejected postmodernism claim that it is predicated on relativism and denies the existence of any transcending truths.

I believe, however, that relativism is not the essence of postmodernism, but rather the result of an overreaction to the past excesses of absolute systems and universal narratives. This very overreaction leads in turn to negative absolutes, such as the assertion that independent moral standards do not exist, and that no universal stories or rights are valid. If these negative absolutes triumph, then we have not solved the problem of past abuses that flowed from prior claimed absolutes; we have only continued the harm in a new form. Thus this dark side of postmodernism must be taken in hand and neutralized so that its pluralistic core value of setting limits on even valid truth claims can be adopted. Insisting on the need for broad-based, diverse forms of dialogue in addressing these issues will enable us to recognize and preserve the most valuable elements of inherited values and traditions, while identifying and averting excess.

The true alternative to absolutism is not relativism but pluralism. Pluralism does not represent the denial of truths; rather, it places limits and checks on truths. Once we recognize how the established values and powerful assumptions of modernity were exploited to commit terrible crimes, and we see how the new relativism, too, can lead to new catastrophic outbreaks, then we can stimulate cultural immune systems to check the tendency toward new excess. If this adjustment can be made, it will become clear that the real goal of postmodernism is to create a balance in which multiple truths and systems can coexist, even conflict, without invading or destroying each other.

Another way of stating the grounds of pluralism is to say, all truths are broken truths. All systems are intrinsically—by dint of being rooted in human reality—partial and flawed.[24] Post-Holocaust theologians and philosophers who make this claim are recapitulating the development of Lurianic Kabbalah in the wake of the expulsion of the Jews from Spain: after reflecting on a far-reaching catastrophe, both groups concluded that the governing paradigm of wholeness and perfection (rooted in the Divine ground and source) must be put aside. Even a Divine absolute—and, by implication, any and all absolutes—integrated into the human ecosystem will perforce crack and become flawed, broken, and partial. Paradoxically, the recognition and admission of brokenness makes any system safer and more usable in the human context. As the poet Leonard Cohen put it: "There is a crack in everything; that's how the light gets in."[25]

One must acknowledge the limitations of all truths. Then one must spell out, in every case, the range of an individual truth's validity, the context of a particular system's credibility, the limits of all claims. In developing these more bounded and partial articulations, one does not relinquish the drive to ascertain objective truth, or to establish the existence of absolute values. One strives for the ultimate goal—but acknowledges that the quest will fall short. Consequently, one is to employ and apply all truths with restraint and caution, which in turn makes their operations safer in the context of human cultures.

In the end, an approach that encourages mapping the limits of every claim protects against excesses. In a world where systems have limits and multiple alternate voices exist, a totalizing, destructive vision cannot assume universal credibility. It follows that even religions and other systems that believe they are directly rooted in the Divine and are, therefore, entitled to priority or dominance should welcome the mechanisms that put limits on them. In fact, they themselves should act to generate or welcome countervoices. In this way—perhaps only in this way—they can protect against their own ingrained flaws. They will also be saved from extending a truth, an achievement, a success, further and further until it overreaches or operates in realms where its validity does not hold.

Elsewhere I have articulated this matter this way: "All truths are moment truths. They will remain that way until the coming of the Messiah, that is, as long as the world is flawed and fragmented."[26]

This acknowledgment of being true for a moment should not be confused with relativism. A truth's moment may last for millions of moments, which add up to thousands and thousands of years. On the other hand, the truth may not work, may not be credible or correct, at certain moments within this period. Each group should welcome the countervoices to itself, for these can help alert members to the limit or boundary beyond which the deeply held truth is invalid or counterproductive.

Interreligious dialogue is a good example of how to carry this out. On its face, it might seem incoherent for people who are deeply committed to the truth of their religious beliefs to engage in dialogue with people who hold opposing beliefs. But in fact, in the decades after the Holocaust, Jewish-Christian dialogue has been a particularly powerful force in reconciliation and ameliorating centuries-old tensions. Respectful dialogue opened up both Jews and Christians to the truths operating in the other tradition and to the achievements and contributions of the other. Each religion was able to see qualities present in the other that could be learned from, and even incorporated into, its own faith system. This also led to a recognition of the ways in which each tradition had libeled, demonized, and degraded the other. On the whole, this dramatization of the flaws in both helped to break each participant's internal sense of being absolutely right, combat dissemination of hatred of the other, and reverse millennia of oppression and mistreatment of the Jews.

This process takes the poison out of many aspects of one's faith. Each religion gains a constructive sense of its own limitations, and this attitude has a moderating effect, restraining interpretations that would otherwise dismiss the other. Each religion is enhanced in accordance with its own best values, as well as with content contributed by the other. This paves the way both to partner with each other and to contribute more to the whole world.[27] The result is pluralism at its best: each religion maintaining its own truth, but understanding the other, and valuing living in a world with multiple truths.

Repairing the World after the Shoah

The Shoah assaulted Judaism's assertion that life is stronger than death and that humans are tasked to strengthen and increase life in the world. Ultimately, responding to the Holocaust demands that we restore the image of God in the world, and that we rebuild the covenantal consciousness that will allow our world to grow toward its messianic *tikkun*.

Restoring the Image of God in the World

The Talmud states: "One who spills blood, reduces the image of God [in the world]."[28] The Nazi murder of six million Jews constituted a massive removal of the image of God from the world. The removal of the shield of awe and dignity surrounding every person rendered the murderers unable to recognize the infinite value of each life and set them free to kill; each individual act of killing further devalued the image of humanity as a whole. Moreover, many more images of God were never born: as the Holocaust intensified, with no hope for a future for any Jewish child that would be born, Jewish birth rates in occupied Europe plummeted.

One of the central and most important postwar responses to the Holocaust was having children. This counteraction started with the survivors themselves. There was a frenzy of marriage, recreating family, and having children in their ranks. Birth rates soared in the DP (displaced persons) camps, where from 1946 to 1948, the birth rate was the highest in the world.[29]

This is a classic human response to untimely death: throughout the world, birth rates tend to rise in the aftermath of war. The survivors, having been immersed in death and in many cases left alone with little or no surviving family, tend to respond even more intensely with an outburst of life. Still, the Jews' reaction was not a given. They might well have despaired and given up on life altogether. Instead, in a heroic affirmation of life, they created life at a remarkable rate. The image of God in the world, having been diminished by the loss of millions of images of God, began to be rebuilt as people continued to populate the world. I call this an act of religious witness. Whether the survivors were religious or not, they provided the most powerful testimony to the bottomless nature of the well of life, by replenishing it. Perhaps this is the only credible way of speaking of God after the Holocaust: not by speaking, after all, but by giving birth to images of God.

However, restoring the image of God requires more than births and increased numbers. The Nazis also diminished the image of God by dehumanizing people, by making them appear to be less created in God's image. The Nazis prefaced their systematic killing campaign with relentless denigration of the victims—Jews, Roma, Slavs, people with disabilities, gay people, and others—as subhuman. This dehumanization enabled the murderers to act freely and unashamedly, and others to stand idly by. By contrast, the single most reported characteristic of righteous gentiles who saved Jews was that they felt a human connection; they recognized the image of God in the other. The victims had a claim on them as human beings; therefore, they could not abandon them to their fate.[30]

The most powerful response to the Nazi dehumanization campaign is the determination to uplift the image of God of potential victims. In the decades since the Holocaust, the pursuit of equality among humans as a fundamental legal, political, and social norm spread rapidly worldwide. On December 10, 1948, the United Nations General Assembly adopted the Universal Declaration of Human Rights. In the words of its official history: "The international community vowed never again to allow atrocities like those of that conflict" (i.e., World War II; a euphemism, primarily, for the Holocaust). The declaration's article 1 states: "All human beings are born free and equal in dignity and rights." Article 2 states: "Everyone is entitled to all the rights and freedoms set forth in this Declaration, without distinction of any kind, such as race, colour, sex, language, religion, political or other opinion, national or social origin, property, birth or other status."[31]

Of course, this changing norm has not resulted in the disappearance of all forms of bigotry. The Universal Declaration of Human Rights was ratified and signed by dictatorships and slave-holding member nations as well as nations that rejected such practices. Racism and xenophobia continue to be significant problems throughout the world. Nonetheless, these proclaimed norms can sometimes be deeply meaningful. Every step forward in the battle against racism and xenophobia represents progress in restoring the image of God that the Nazis debased.

Within Jewish culture, Jews, too, have been learning to see the image of God in potential victims. Since its inception, a central goal of the State of Israel has been to remember the potential victimhood of Jews and help keep them safe. After the war, in reaction to the Shoah, the newly established State, with a Jewish population of six hundred thousand, took in 250,000 survivors and, shortly thereafter, more than seven hundred thousand Jews expelled from, or otherwise driven to leave, countries across the Middle East and North Africa. On July 5, 1950, Israel passed the Law of Return, guaranteeing any Jew anywhere in the world automatic admission and citizenship in the Jewish state. In the 1980s, hundreds of thousands of Jews in the Soviet Union responded to the openings made possible by the movement to free Soviet Jewry by flooding into the State of Israel. In the 1990s, tens of thousands of Ethiopian Jews were airlifted to Israel to escape Ethiopia's civil war.

Israel now has the power to protect the image of God within each Jew in a way that Jews were tragically unable to do for one another during the Holocaust. A striking indication of this new reality followed Russia's 2022 invasion of Ukraine. In contrast to what they would have faced during the two millennia of exilic existence, Jews fleeing Ukraine had a guaranteed place of refuge in Israel and as refugees were in consequence more, rather than less, likely to be helped than their non-Jewish peers.

The more I wrestled with the Holocaust—and met people seen as the "other" by my own tradition—the more I concluded that my wonderful, sustaining community had internalized violations of the image of God that had to be corrected. To me, many forms of women's exclusion from Judaism (including from public leadership and advanced rabbinic Torah learning)—and also their exemption from time-bound commandments and, therefore, from liturgical roles—reduced women's image of God. Rabbi Joseph Soloveitchik had written unequivocally: "This Divine gift [of being in the image of God] was given to both men and women. . . . In their spiritual natures, they were equally worthy. . . . They do not differ axiologically, as regards their worthiness before God." Thus he rejected "the perverse notion that Judaism regards woman as being inferior to man." Nevertheless, he claimed that the two differed in their psychical natures, this accounting for their different halakhic assignments.[32] In other words, women were separate but equal. He did not acknowledge—because he was not ready to deal with—the reality that, in Orthodoxy, women were separate but unequal.

More than that, women were marginalized. In public Orthodox society, women were second-class citizens. In the *haredi* Orthodox community, this inferiority was understood and taken for granted. The Modern Orthodox community, however, was saturated with the principle of equality due to its immersion in modernity, so it had to offer rationalizations, like Rabbi Joseph Soloveitchik's comment above, or even apologetics, as in Rabbi Ahron Soloveichik's claim that women are spiritually *superior*, so they are excused from various liturgical roles and time-bound commandments because they do not need them.[33]

After the Holocaust, with its implied message that the image of God in all had to be acknowledged and honored more vigorously, I could not convince myself that women in the Orthodox community were being treated as anything other than separate and unequal. To my surprise, this conclusion did not destroy my identification with Orthodoxy. I concluded that the situation could and should be improved in true covenantal fashion—including learning from liberal Jews and others where they had correctly gone before us. In all these matters, the thinking and teaching of my wife Blu, an author and activist, pointed the way and, simultaneously, sustained my loyalty to the system with all its limitations.[34] I came to see that there was both need and room for improvement in the halakhah regarding the condition and treatment of many others: non-Jews, gay people, people with disabilities, female converts, adopted children, and adopting parents. In light of heightened awareness due to the Shoah, the halakhah necessitates correction in all such areas, to come closer to its own ideal standards.

Happily, many in the halakhic community recognize these new urgencies. Major steps have been taken to upgrade women's Torah education and religious roles. Smaller but nevertheless real steps have been taken in the other areas as well. Several of these steps have been resisted, and the bona fides of the pioneers challenged, but the process continues. Accomplishments in the next generation will be even greater, and halakhah will be even more able to fully realize the image of God in each person.

Similar progress has been made in some of the ways Jewish culture relates to non-Jews. In Jewish-Christian dialogue, for example, the focus, appropriately, had long been on addressing Christian terminology that degraded Jews. With newly heightened sensitivity to the role of language in degrading outsider minorities, our Christian dialogue partners recognized that "othering" language paves the way to mistreat others, and largely came to apply a hermeneutic of suspicion to inherited categories of classification—particularly where such categories excluded or reduced others. At some point, though, it occurred to me to ask myself: Is there anything in my own tradition that misrepresents or degrades my dialogue partners—or anyone else? I concluded that sometimes Jews failed to acknowledge that non-Jews are created in the image of God as well. Anger at gentile cruelty and mistreatment had led many Jews to stereotype non-Jews, often dismissed as *goyim*, as morally clueless, violence-prone believers in irrational and superstitious religion. Christianity was dismissed as idolatrous because it worshiped a human being, or honored statues and icons of human beings. These depictions needed to be addressed.

Most Jews have since moved away from these stereotypes—thanks to liberal, democratic values in the general culture and to positive personal contact with gentiles. However, in the Orthodox community, where the inherited narrative still holds substantial influence, these stereotypes have persisted. Just as Orthodoxy is learning to see the image of God in women, gay people, converts, and other members of the Jewish community, it must do the same with non-Jews.

Restoring Covenantal Consciousness

Another critical post-Holocaust response is to restore covenantal consciousness—a committed approach to world repair in the spirit of partnership. Like the BRCA gene, which makes Ashkenazi Jews more prone to develop cancer, the gene of runaway power is present in modern culture. Unless it is controlled—turned off, if you will—by the mechanism of covenantal consciousness, it is liable to develop lethal metastases.

In every area of life, growing human competence must be brought within covenantal containment, to keep it healthy and life-affirming before it breaks all limits and threatens life itself. Proper limits must be imposed to prevent humans from acting as masters of the universe, exploiting their control—say, in increasing meat production—for immediate self-interest and thereby threatening the world's climate. We cannot count on industry and other leaders to recognize themselves as partners accountable to a higher authority—God, the true Master—or to see themselves as sharing ownership and responsibility with past and future generations.[35]

The Divine *tzimtzum*—the total hiddenness of God—can be wrongly interpreted to mean that there are no limits or any authority to impose controls on humans. The Jewish people, who inherited the covenant from an earlier age, when its Master and Partner was more apparent to all, needs to step up and model covenantal consciousness for those who have not encountered a display or demonstration of Divine authority and limit-setting. People are grasping that taking power and transforming culture are necessary to achieve what the Jewish tradition calls *tikkun olam*. Covenantal consciousness can help show the value of built-in limits for restraining, rather than forgoing, welcomed innovations. Covenantal accountability can help channel power, as it develops, toward life and *tikkun*, and stop it from spreading out of control and engendering harm.

I would suggest, in fact, that such covenantal consciousness will work better than past understandings embedded in an ethos of reward and punishment, which, as we have seen, can fail when the quid pro quo fails to materialize — or when evil forces offer more compelling rewards and punishments. In contrast to those who come to the covenant out of fear, people who come to the covenant out of a sense of empowerment and capacity are better able to enter into positive partnership. They are more capable of connecting to *brit* out of a common vision. This outcome responds to God's purpose in the *tzimtzum*. By allowing humans free choice, God hopes that we will carry out our obligations to build a better world more creatively and more fully than we would if we were only responding to our fear of punishment for our failures.

The same, more mature consciousness must be quickened in religious Jews, who carry on the *brit* out of their religious inheritance and loyalty. In their case, the instilling of covenantal consciousness must take the form of reminding them that they must fully participate in the work of *tikkun olam*. *Tzimtzum* is a call to take a more responsible role in the world as well as to assure that all covenantal actions, including ritual, live up to the best standards of *tikkun olam*. Present religious standards, especially the inherited compromises with inequality, need to be recalibrated and deliberately moved closer to the messianic ideal — even if only incrementally. The religious way of life should be generating more committed, self-sacrificial, and energetic work for *tikkun olam* in every area of human existence.

The Messianism of Human Life and Dignity

The only way to reestablish the covenantal promise of redemption and the credibility of classic Jewish teachings in light of the Holocaust's devastating blow to the moral economy of humanity is by countertestimony: breakthroughs for life and human dignity now. Seen in the global, or even cosmic, view, restoring balance requires a *tikkun* of overwhelming proportions. The requirement to work for new breakthroughs in human life and dignity translates into accomplishments of such scope and intensity as to be messianic.

Awareness of this need seems to have emerged quickly within the Jewish people in relation to the reestablishment of a Jewish state. The Israeli rabbinate was correct in calling this development "the beginning of the flowering of our redemption."[36] The term "redemption" captures the messianic scope and import of the successful creation of the state and its fulfillment of ancient messianic prophecies. The phrase "beginning of the flowering" captures the limited nature, the flawed and complex process of state-building itself, as well as the fragile and unfinished nature of the work. The same spirit ought to be applied to other new developments. Humanity needs a redemptive vision, combined with the humility to know that redemption is gradual and incomplete.

For most of the twentieth century, there was very little explicit Jewish messianism. Zionists rarely invoked messianic imagery in setting up the state. Mostly, they employed the terminology and methods of business as usual—especially compared to the Jews of the past, who more than once had begun messianic movements in the wake of great moments of catastrophe. In 1966 I complained about what I saw as the absence of Jewish messianism in modernity, mainly out of frustration that the Holocaust was not being recognized as transformational for Jewish history and religion. I wrote then that this lack of messianic activity was due to "the tyranny of modern categories and sheer lack of feeling."[37] I thought that modernity itself had made the messianic impulse too hard to access. I lamented the potential transformations lost in that change.

I was wrong about the Jewish people's capacity for messianism in modern times. I assumed their messianic impulse was dead and I missed their pent-up spirit waiting to explode and reenergize Jewish history. Over the next few decades, both Chabad and Gush Emunim (Bloc of the faithful), a right-wing activist movement based in the West Bank, began significant messianic movements.

Yet, I believe that both of these movements were wrong, because they misinterpreted history. They were right that now is the time for achievement on a messianic level. But they missed the implications of the Divine *tzimtzum*: they both proclaimed an absolute messianism, not one tempered by an acknowledgment that it is incomplete.

More dangerously, they acted on the assumption that their messianism was bestowed and guaranteed by God. In their minds, this supernatural backing absolved them from reckoning with political or diplomatic realities, military balance, or moral issues. Gush Emunim pressed for settlement in all areas of the West Bank, in ways that most of the world, including many Israelis, understood as a rejection of peace and oppression of the territories' Palestinian inhabitants. The ethical and political costs of these settlements far outweigh their value. In short, the radical settler movement has lost sight of the covenantal principles of limits, realistic and modulated human efforts, and incremental achievements.

The same can be said of Chabad. Despite the fact that the Chabad movement actively engages with Jews of many backgrounds, it became intellectually self-enclosed, and many of its members eventually came to believe that its most recent rebbe, Menachem Mendel Schneerson, met the Maimonidean standard of being the Messiah, a person who brings all of Israel back to the Torah. This assertion is first of all questionable on demographic grounds: Chabad has tried hard to fight the widespread assimilation of diaspora Jews, but its impact on this trend is unclear. Moreover, it's questionable on religious grounds: some streams within this movement continue to uphold and proclaim the rebbe's messianic status despite his death. Additionally, the movement has played a problematic role in Israel. Guided by his belief that God makes all important decisions and bestows all victories, the rebbe proclaimed that Israel should not give back an inch of land for the sake of peace, and that human political considerations had to be dismissed in forming policy. Chabad political activity has often been on the side of extreme right-wing, irredentist political forces heavily tilted toward anti-Arab attitudes and values. This type of messianism is ethically and politically damaging to Israel and the Jewish people.

The failures of these two significant postwar Jewish messianic movements leads us to ask whether modern Jewish messianism has any potential for good. David Hartman, for one, argued that it does not. Such movements, he observed, have not only failed to achieve a redemptive future; they have also exacerbated some of the very problems they were trying to solve. In Israel, he believed, messianism has become a dangerous attitude that brings out fantastical thinking and irresponsible behaviors. Hence, the messianic idea ought to be put aside (at least temporarily) in order to assure the constructive performance of halakhah and Jewish tradition in a functioning state.[38]

Nevertheless, I continue to believe that messianism, fulfilling the vision of *tikkun olam*, is the galvanizing force of Judaism and the Jewish people. Therefore, it should not be given up. Rather, it must be brought within limits—oriented back to reality and harnessed as a force for incremental, covenantal progress. The dialectic of perfection and realism-with-human-responsibility is the right combination of power to move the world and Jewish life forward. We need a chastened, "broken" messianism, aware of its limitations, to be an inspiration and motor for the Jewish people's *tikkun olam* efforts. In Israel, this approach should be applied concretely, by seeking political, economic, and social improvement focused on equality and quality of human life, side by side with serious outreach to help the rest of the world, especially the developing world. Similarly, a policy of messianic scope can be undertaken in seeking rapprochement and partnership with Christianity and other religious traditions.

In the internal world of halakhah, messianism should express itself in vigorously elevating the status of all neglected or discriminated groups, and in nurturing *tzelem elohim,* the image of God, in all areas. Central to this approach is the idea that in the Messianic Age, all of the Earth will be full of knowledge of the Lord (Isa. 11:9). Therefore, the religious challenge is to push forward the frontiers of *tikkun olam* — to advance morality and covenantal values — even, and especially, in secular domains. In our times, secular activity has unparalleled potential for protecting and elevating life, and it is our covenantal responsibility to fulfill that potential. Thus the messianic impulses generated by the Holocaust should inspire ever-greater ambition for worldwide *tikkun* — a *tikkun* of life and a truly healing response to the Shoah.

13

The State of Israel

The fundamental Jewish response to the devastating death blow inflicted by the Shoah was to create the State of Israel. In this extraordinary assertion of its determination to live, Jewry reached for two key initiatives to counteract the trauma of the Holocaust: the assumption of power and the restoration of the dignity of the image of God. This action was no less an intuitive commitment to activate the millennia-old attachment to Zion and renew the covenant in the manner proclaimed by the prophets: to return to the homeland, ingather exiles, and build a flourishing national life.

The creation of the state ensured that the next era of the covenant would unfold importantly in the Land of Israel—as it had not done in two thousand years. Restoration of the Jewish people as the primary force in determining Jewish fate required both developing power and developing guardrails to prevent abuse of that newly acquired power. Yet state-building released powerful messianic impulses within Judaism and Zionism that encouraged overreach. The outcome of the tension between these dueling polarities—limits versus overreach—will answer the central challenge of this era: Can the Jewish people become a fully responsible partner in the *brit*?

The Responsibility to Assume Power

For most of Jewish history, Jews have been in exile, powerless, with no army or government, living on sufferance amid non-Jewish populations.

Rabbinic Judaism developed a way of life that could be carried on in the Diaspora. A great expansion of mitzvot in the home and of the *halakhot* of daily life made up for the loss of commandments specific to the land. The deeper lesson of living in diaspora was that existence is rooted in God and not just in geographic space or physical land. The infinite ground of the Divine sustains, wherever one is.

This absence of rooted space is not inherent to Judaism. The founding stories of the covenant center on the promise of the Land of Israel, and on Jewish sovereignty there. In the Bible, Abraham and Sarah were summoned to go to the land that their descendants would inherit, to enter into a covenant with the Lord that would be a blessing for them and for the world (Gen. 12:1–3). A central component of the liberation from Egypt was God's promise: "I will bring you into the land that I promised to Abraham, to Isaac, and to Jacob and will give it to you as a heritage" (Exod. 6:6–8).

Even as the Rabbis developed practices enabling Jewish life in the Diaspora, they suffused the sacred moments of life with the dream of returning. Weddings, birth ceremonies, funerals, shivah, the Passover seder, Sukkot liturgy, and prayers for rain placed great emphasis, and in some cases were even centered, on the Land of Israel and its seasons. "Next year in Jerusalem" became the end cry of the most important rituals. Israel became the future paradise regained. Of course, some Jews resided in the Land of Israel always. The bulk of Jewry adjusted to living in exile.

The adaptations Judaism had been making since antiquity enabled it to survive in diaspora but left it unprepared to survive in a world where enormous power was consolidated in the hands of governments bent on their destruction. From the beginning of the State of Israel until today, Jewry had to develop new ways of obtaining power to protect itself—and take fuller responsibility for the covenant with God.

A Response to the Message of Modernity

Rabbinic culture relocated Judaism to the spiritual world. It taught that God had only "the four ells of halakhah" (BT Berakhot 8A) for the

Divine domain and that Jewish mystical and religious behaviors drove the cosmos. This theology saved Jews from internalizing their powerlessness and their neighbors' contempt. But their political culture turned increasingly passive. They waited, without acting, for a Divinely sent redeemer to rescue them from exile.

Zionism—Jewish nationalism—reemerged in the nineteenth century as a Jewish response to the Divine *tzimtzum* that led many peoples the world over to take control over their own destinies, especially through nationalism. The Zionist movement called for a return to Jewish dignity through self-government in the ancient homeland. The key visionary for Zionism as a political movement, Theodor Herzl, viewed nationalism as the vehicle for human progress in modernity. He judged that the countries where Jews lived would not end antisemitism, nor let Jews assimilate. Jews had to establish their own dignity and fate by creating their own state.[1]

Those who responded to modernity's call to take power were disproportionately people who had absorbed the values of this new era and discarded the Jewish narrative of passivity. Some secular Zionists talked of creating "new Jews," unburdened by a rabbinic tradition that cut them off from the body, physical labor, and rootedness in nature.

The Orthodox establishment counseled waiting for the Messiah. Still, a religious minority joined the Zionist movement. Allied secular and religious Jews continued the covenant by taking responsibility for Jewish fate. They set about building a new society.

In a historically unprecedented action, a people driven from its homeland returned and rebuilt a national infrastructure and culture. As these *halutzim* (pioneers) cultivated the land, they often uncovered past Jewish history. They recovered the Hebrew language that had been the literary dialect of the sacred and made it the medium of daily communication. Daily life (even of secularists) was infused with classic sources and intertwined with historical places. Thus Jews gained access to the tradition. Many saw themselves as continuous with it.

None of this was easy. The *ḥalutzim* committed their lives to renew national life in a rocky, swampy land ruled, first, by the hostile Ottoman Empire and then, after World War II, by the colonialist British Empire. Jewish farmers formed collective settlements to sustain each other and introduced new methods that improved crop cultivation. Thousands died of illness associated with the harsh conditions or gave up and returned to Europe.

Many Arabs already living in the land were hostile to or uncooperative with Jewish development. Such groups waged anti-Jewish pogroms in 1929 and 1936. In spite of Britain's 1917 Balfour Declaration committing them to support for a Jewish national home, the colonial British government wagered its future in the Middle East on the emerging Arab nations. They restricted Jewish immigration, and in 1939 Britain's Peel Commission repudiated the Balfour Declaration.

Tormented by Jewish powerlessness, Zionist leaders such as David Ben-Gurion nevertheless persisted. In 1942 he wrote: "We are the only people in the world whose blood is allowed [to be shed] . . . because the Jews have no state, no army, no independence, and no homeland."[2] In 1947 the *Yishuv* won an improbable United Nations resolution authorizing partition of the land into Arab and Jewish states. The neighboring Arab nations swore to invade and destroy the Jewish state. British and American general staffs estimated that if independence was declared, the Jews would be "driven into the sea." U.S. secretary of state George C. Marshall warned Ben-Gurion that America would not intervene to save Israel. At the decisive meeting of the Provisional Council to decide whether to declare a Jewish state, Haganah (Zionist military force) leader Yigael Yadin told Ben-Gurion: "At this moment our chances are about even [to win the war]. If I wanted to be more honest, I'd say that the other side has a significant edge."[3] Ben-Gurion, and eventually the council, concluded that there was no alternative. After the Holocaust, the Jews had to have a state. Otherwise, whether out of persecution or despair, the covenant people might well come to an end.

Ben-Gurion and the leadership were prepared to fight and die rather than give up on the Jewish fate. Furthermore, 250,000 survivors of the Shoah had no other place to go. On May 14, 1948, the *Yishuv* leaders proclaimed independence. The modern State of Israel began with the risky bet that even an endangered and precarious Jewish state would be safer than a world with no Jewish sovereignty at all.

The next morning, six Arab states invaded. Israel was hamstrung by shortages of arms, trained officers, soldiers, and battle experience. A staggering 1 percent of the *Yishuv*'s population was killed in the War of Independence. However, the Jews' determination overcame these obstacles. In the end, the Israelis conquered more territory than the enabling United Nations resolution had assigned to them.

Even as the invading nations were defeated, they refused to recognize the Jewish state. For the next half century, they would wage political and economic war on Israel. Outrageously, the state's very right to exist continued to be denied and directly threatened—only a generation after Jewry had experienced the total assault on its life that was the Holocaust. Even with this history, Israel was mostly left on its own to defend its right to be.

The New State and the Jewish Past

In the new state's declaration of independence, the Zionist leadership made clear that Israel was to be a democratic, not a theocratic, state. Nevertheless, Israel saw itself as continuing Jewish history and fulfilling the goals of the covenant: "The State of Israel will be open for Jewish immigration and *the ingathering of the Exiles*. . . . It will be based on freedom, justice, and peace *as envisaged by the prophets of Israel*."[4] In part in response to the Holocaust, the Law of Return (1950) granted any Jew anywhere in the world a haven and automatic right to citizenship.

As new immigrants arrived in the 1950s, the Jewish population exploded: 600,000 residents unbelievably absorbed 250,000 survivors and 850,000 Jews from Arab lands. This precipitated a period of severe austerity, including housing and food shortages. The resident population accepted this deprivation partly because, in a hostile Middle East, the Jewish state needed a larger population to defend itself. But the primary policy drivers were taking responsibility for Jewish history and assuring the fate and security of the covenant people.

Throughout Israel's history, the secular leadership's actions spoke louder than their vocal dismissals of Jewish religion. Step by step, a richly Jewish environment emerged. The Sabbath became a national rest day. Jewish holy days became national holidays. Kosher food was served in public institutions and the army. Marriage, divorce, and conversion were given over to the religious establishment. With the arrival of Sephardi and Mizrahi Jews, the daily culture of music, food, and popular media became even more suffused with Jewish tradition. Looking more deeply, the creation of the state confirmed God's presence in the world. The ingathering of the exiles was the prophetic sign that the covenant was still alive, and that Jewry was continuing in its path toward fulfilling the vision of *tikkun olam*.

An Ethic of Power

Winning independence meant that a Jewish government would administer justice, control the economy, and divide wealth. Initially, Israel's socialist leadership strove to reduce inequality and distribute the burden of running the state fairly among the whole population. The socialist policies honored the classic Jewish idea of a minicosmos: the national state would be an exemplar of the ideal world, with egalitarian living and justice for all. Nevertheless, extensive regulations, high taxes, and governmental control of industrial development also impeded economic productivity and growth. In the initial decades of the state, the joke went: "How does one make a small fortune in Israel? Bring a large one!" The electoral overturn of 1977, which ended three decades of governments led by Israel's socialist political left, eventually led to a freer economy and heightened economic growth. Israel became a "start-up nation"—an extraordinary achievement, though at the cost of greater inequality.[5]

From its earliest days, it was clear that military force would be critical for Israel's survival. The Israel Defense Forces (IDF) would have to prepare for war at any time and punch above its weight to neutralize its enemies' larger numbers of soldiers and arms. A near-universal draft for the state's Jewish population—with notable exemptions for *haredim* and Arabs—ensured that the army and the people were one. A people without tradition of warfare or a warrior class (in medieval Haggadahs, the wicked son is illustrated as a *soldier!*) had to generate a culture that would inspire military service and heroism. It is hard to say which was the greater miracle: that this people developed a technologically advanced, superior fighting force ranked, as of 2023, the fourth strongest military power in the world, or that they did so without turning into a Spartan, militaristic society.[6]

From the beginning, the IDF emphasized the sanctity of life and a strong moral code, believing that soldiers convinced of the righteousness of their cause fight better. The principle of *tohar haneshek*, purity of arms, was stressed and, since 1994, has been core to the ethics code, *Ruach tzahal* (Spirit of the IDF), distributed to every soldier. Under the fundamental value of "human life," clause 1 states the principle of *necessity*: "The soldier will protect human life in every way, out of recognition of its ultimate significance, and will endanger himself or others only to the degree necessary to fulfill the task." Under "purity of arms," clause 2 authorizes using "force and weapons only to the degree necessary to defeat the enemy," which should be "without unnecessary damage to life, body, dignity, or property of the other, be they soldiers, noncombatants, and especially those who are defenseless."[7] Additionally, only if the enemy soldiers are embedded among civilians, and only if there is no other way of defending Israel, may soldiers jeopardize civilians. If attacks will cause disproportionate losses to civilians, they may not be launched—a criterion of proportionality. Authorities regularly discussed and refined the guide; an IDF judicial advocate's office investigating cases of civilian deaths backed its use; Israel's free press highlighted violations; and Israel's Supreme Court took on the power of final and independent review of the country's military actions.

When Israel's wars came to include asymmetrical conflicts facing irregular or terrorist groups embedded among civilians, the IDF developed tactics often used to minimize civilian casualties, such as dropping leaflets, making mass phone calls, or using dummy ("knock on roof") shells to warn civilians at risk. Many attacks were aborted when at the actual moment of contact, there were too many potential civilian casualties near the military target. The IDF continued to innovate new methods to reduce its civilian casualties, including networks of shelters, Iron Dome batteries, and the West Bank separation wall—built during the early 2000s to cut off infiltration routes for terrorists and weapons. Even though Palestinians and some Jews denounced it as the "apartheid wall," the wall reduced Israeli casualties and importantly reduced pressure on Israel to strike back at Palestinian civilians—even as the limits of barriers on Israel's border with the Gaza Strip became painfully apparent after the Hamas attack of October 7, 2023.

Colonel Richard Kemp, head of the British forces in Afghanistan, offered a powerful illustration of the ethic of power long associated with the IDF. By extraordinary efforts, he said, Western armies reduced Afghan civilian casualty rates to three to four civilians killed for every Taliban fighter eliminated. In contrast, an IDF analysis of the 2,125 Palestinian casualties from Operation Protective Edge in 2014 showed 761 were civilians and 931 were Hamas and PIJ (Palestinian Islamic Jihad) fighters (with 433 undetermined)—in other words, incredibly, fewer than one civilian for every fighter killed.[8]

This is why I have long called the IDF the most moral army in the world. It is heartbreaking that the definition of a moral army means it kills fewer innocent civilians than do other armies. But in the real world, taking up arms to defend the state is the price of staying alive. Moreover, given that constant war often leads to reduced efforts to minimize collateral damage to the other side, I believe the IDF's persistent efforts to improve and refine its ethical standards over these years exhibits a dimension of moral heroism.

Because of the continuous denial of Israel's right to exist, wars have played an outsized role in the history of the state, and as a result these conflicts have become part of a broader story. For example, the War of Independence fused a disparate conglomeration of communities and values into a patriotic Israeli public strongly committed to maintaining a Jewish state. Nearly two decades later in the Six-Day War, it seemed to many within Israel and beyond as if the Holocaust was about to be reenacted. Arab nations spoke openly of "pushing the Jews into the sea," foreshadowing a repeat of the 1940s, and President Charles de Gaulle withdrew France's support for Israel in what seemed an ominous repetition of Allied indifference and studied inaction in the face of Jewish catastrophe. The Israeli Defense Forces appeared to be outmanned and outgunned by the combined Arab armies. In light of this, the actual war, with Israel's lightning victory, seemed nothing less than a miracle, a victory of biblical proportions, a validation that the arc of history bends toward the just. The recovery of the Temple Mount, the return to (Mount) Zion, closed a circle of Jewish history—a two-thousand-year cycle of destruction and suffering. In the eyes of many, the prophetic promise of return was being fulfilled. The age of redemption was dawning.

The IDF's doctrine remained focused on defense of Israel's existence rather than expansion or using military might to browbeat neighbors into submission. The one exception was the First Lebanon War, in 1982, undertaken to stop the constant terrorist incursions on the northern border, and out of the mistaken belief that Israel could shore up the Christian president of Lebanon's rule and his plan to make peace with Israel. This first "war of choice" split Israeli public opinion sharply. Significant parts of the population decried the incursion as a strategic war of aggression to advance Israel's long-term political and security interests rather than a just war of self-defense. Furthermore, the IDF stood by as a Christian militia responded to the assassination of Lebanon's president-elect, Bashir Gemayel, by massacring Palestinians in the Sabra and Shatila refugee camps, provoking a worldwide outcry, particularly among Jews. The government's Kahan Commission condemned the IDF's moral failure to intervene and forced the resignation of Israel's defense minister, Ariel Sharon. Israel continued to play a role in Lebanon, through the IDF and then through Lebanese allies. Ultimately Israel failed to secure its own interests and prevent the rise of Iran's terrorist ally, Hezbollah. Eventually, Israel withdrew completely from Lebanon, but that country spiraled down into a failed state and a base for Hezbollah, which continues to threaten Israel.

A Growing Israel

The story of modern Israel is also a story of growth. By 1945 more than five hundred thousand Jews lived in Palestine. After 1948 hundreds of thousands of European survivors arrived, followed by triple that number of Jews from North Africa and the Middle East. Many of them had been stripped of their possessions and expelled, or evacuated to Israel, because hostility and antisemitism endangered their existence. Israel kept its promise of providing a haven for Jews in jeopardy, regardless of the risks or costs involved. Israel willingly paid cash for every liberated Jew when certain Communist governments in Europe demanded money to allow their Jewish residents to move there.[9] Absorption efforts continued even as the Israeli public split over whether to accept reparations from the West German government for Jewish lives and property taken in the Holocaust, which could help alleviate economic austerity in the Jewish state. Future prime minister Menachem Begin intensely opposed reparations as "blood money," in direct violation of the Torah's exhortation, "You shall not take ransom for the life of a murderer" (Num. 35:32). Prime Minister Ben-Gurion, however, insisted that the Jewish state was the logical and moral inheritor of murdered European Jewry. It was better that the money be in Jewish hands and used to rebuild Jewish life and society. The flow of reparations began in the 1950s. Although Israel continued to be dependent on diaspora Jewish philanthropy and foreign aid, in time the state achieved cumulative economic power as well as demographic growth.

Over the next decades, Israel spent millions of dollars to rescue almost 150,000 Beta Israel from Ethiopia. They came from a region plagued by poverty, hunger, diseases, internal violence, civil wars, and government neglect. However, Israel and world Jewry would leave no stone unturned to save fellow Jews and thereby restore the value of Jewish lives. In Israel, Ethiopian Jews often experienced discrimination and bigotry; they suffered cultural and religious disruptions. To this day they lag in educational and income levels. Yet they are making great progress and there is broad support and significant ongoing investment to bring them up to full parity.

After World War II the much-depleted Russian Jewish community was persecuted. After the Six-Day War the Soviet government, infuriated at the defeat of its allies, broke off diplomatic relations with Israel and increased discrimination against Russian Jews. However, a wildfire of Jewish pride, self-assertion, and Zionist awakening burned through Soviet Jewry. In the aftermath of these efforts, 250,000 Jews demanded and were granted permission to leave. Most went to Israel.

This left many Jews languishing in a Soviet society where they faced intense discrimination and limits on immigration. A worldwide Soviet Jewry liberation movement was launched. After the Soviet Union's collapse in 1991—the dictatorial governing power eroded in no small measure by the Jews' successful defiance of government intimidation—restrictions on Jewish immigration were lifted. Over a million Soviet Jews immigrated to Israel, among them hundreds of thousands who were not Jewish by rabbinic law but were eligible for Israeli citizenship. Under the Law of Return, Israel upheld its commitment that any person endangered for their connection to Jews would be given haven.

Israel's Jewish culture treasured family. Great value was ascribed to having children. In 2016 Israel had the highest birth rate of any nation among the highly developed countries in the Organization for Economic Cooperation and Development.[10] The birth rate plus repeated waves of immigration raised Israel's Jewish population in 2023 to 7.1 million, about 46 percent of the total world Jewish population.[11]

Israel's growth has been more than demographic. Its productivity has increased exponentially. From 2001 to 2021 its gross domestic product rose from $137 billion to $437 billion; in the same time period, per capita GDP multiplied from $21,000 to over $47,000.[12] Israel has become a major world power in high technology and cybersecurity, as well as a leader in the frontiers of medicine. Welfare capitalist Israel, with its markets freed, restored the good reputation of Jews as a people successful in commerce and finance.

Israel also generated a robust Jewish culture. Hebrew language, literature, and the arts are flourishing. Mizrahi cultures have turned traditional music and *piyyut* (devotional poetry) into popular art forms. Israeli cuisine has been incorporated into the international "foodie" revolution. Daily Jewish discussions enliven a range of media. Israeli films and television productions are in demand worldwide. Rates of interfaith marriage are very low and Jewish observance is high: in 2000, 98 percent of Israeli Jewish homes had a mezuzah, 85 percent said they always participate in a seder, and 67 percent fasted on Yom Kippur. (Not driving a car on Yom Kippur has become almost universal.) Fifty-eight percent of Israelis also reported refraining from eating nonkosher foods — a rate almost triple that of the American Jewish community.[13]

In retrospect, we can identify two major strategies that emerged to deal with the danger of dissolution and assimilation stemming from the modern emancipation of world Jewry. The dominant response was to modernize Jewish religion and modify Jewish identity to maintain Jewish existence while integrating into modern culture — an approach manifest in religious denominationalism, secular Judaism, nationalism, socialism, and Yiddish culture, among other developments. While this modernization identity model has remained dominant in diaspora Jewry, the general society has been so welcoming that assimilation and intermarriage rates have soared. Despite important pockets of strength in various diaspora groups, the center of diaspora Jewry has weakened. The stability and future development of integrated diaspora Jewry remain uncertain.

The second alternative—in the early days chosen by very few—was to go back to the homeland and create a Jewish society and culture there. As it grew, it would pass on identity and religion (as most religions do) by personal interaction, cooperation, civic culture, and educational transmission. At this point, the Zionist solution is working better than the alternative. Admittedly, modernizing identity seemed to be working better a hundred years ago, and a century or two is a blink of an eye in Jewish history. Nevertheless, the State of Israel appears destined to play the principal role in providing for the future of the entire Jewish people.

The Struggle for Democracy

One of the great miracles is that Israel emerged as a democracy. Neither the old *Yishuv* nor the new *yishuv*'s pioneers and farmers had lived under robust democratic regimes.

How then did the Jewish state end up being a democracy in a neighborhood of dictatorships and monarchies? Partly because the values of the early secular socialist Zionist leadership were shaped by democratic traditions imbibed from modern culture. Herzl established democratic elections for the World Zionist Organization; the preparatory committee for the *Yishuv*'s National Assembly decided in 1898 that women should have the right to vote; Great Britain's parliamentary governance model influenced the mandate period. Finally, there is resonance between democracy and Judaism. Although there is no political culture of democracy in the tradition, democracy resonates with Judaism's humanist and egalitarian foundations as a political system doing greater justice than its rivals to the equality of each image of God.

Despite hostile forces surrounding it, for most of the modern state's history, democracy has only grown. Despite constant war between Israel and Arab nations and considerable challenges in education and economic life, Israel's non-Jewish Arab minority experienced steady progress. Israeli Arabs moved from military government to full citizenship and democratic voting rights. Perhaps most strikingly, 2021 saw the first incorporation of an Arab party into the governing coalition—a move that generated a backlash from ultra-nationalist, ultra-religious, and religious Zionists, but represents a genuine advance for a vibrant Israeli democracy.

Another chapter in the story of Israeli democracy is the development of an independent judiciary. Despite not having a constitution, the Supreme Court took the initiative to begin declaring laws "unconstitutional" for breaking fundamental norms, using failure to meet the standard of Israel's Basic Laws as the criterion. The court became the primary force for protecting minorities and tackling discrimination. Public values combined with judicial activism in Israel led to steady advances in the rights of women, LGBTQ+ people, and people with disabilities.

Although Sephardi and Mizrahi Jews were initially subject to considerable mistreatment by the Ashkenazi establishment, in time the newcomers were increasingly integrated, achieving social and economic progress and, eventually, political power. One of the great breakthrough moments for democracy was the 1977 election. For the first time, the socialist parties and the Ashkenazi establishment were beaten by the combination of bourgeois opposition parties and the energized Sephardi vote. Paradoxically, this advance for democracy also brought antidemocratic politicians such as *haredim* into power.

Haredi religious parties leveraged their power under the parliamentary system to secure major government funding favoring their institutions and community, but they sought to deny such funding to other religious communities. Thus, greater democratization of politics weakened the base of Israeli democracy. The Supreme Court has at times pushed back, disqualifying antidemocratic legislation favoring the Israeli rabbinate and the settlement enterprise. This, too, evoked right-wing counter reactions, including campaigns by Israel's far-right governing coalition to revoke the independence and review power of the judiciary.

In December 2022—as happened in other Western countries—Israel's democratic system came under attack, here accelerated by extremism in the religious Zionist community. The extreme religious/nationalist right's legislative agenda favored its own interests to the detriment of women, Israel's non-Jewish Arab population, gays and lesbians, and other minorities. These extremist forces sought to expand the jurisdiction of rabbinic courts at the expense of independent oversight, despite the fact that many of those bodies have been marred by corruption, sexism, and intolerance for other religious views. The most extreme nationalist, ultra-Orthodox parties in the governing coalition, together with Prime Minister Benjamin Netanyahu, proposed judicial legislation designed to end the judiciary's independence—a clear and present threat to Israeli democracy. Democratic forces pushed back, generating months of the largest protest demonstrations in the history of Israel. An overwhelming number of leaders, in the economy, in the IDF and security agencies, in media, culture, education, science, and medicine, joined the fight to uphold democracy. The democratic forces proved to be so strong that they forced a coalition led by MKs who had no scruples about overriding democracy—headed by a prime minister desperate to destroy judicial independence in the hope of escaping conviction for his own corruption—to stand down.

On October 7, 2023, Hamas, the terrorist group ruling Gaza, launched a surprise attack massacring 1,200 civilians and soldiers, devastating nearby Jewish communities, and smashing Israel's image as militarily dominant and almost invulnerable. In response, Israelis came together, overriding the societal divisions that threatened to tear their nation apart in the fight over democracy. Diaspora Jewry largely rallied to support Israel. The government of Israel—now run by an emergency unity coalition—launched a war to eliminate Hamas and restore security and deterrence. Meanwhile the strategic and intelligence failures that enabled Hamas's shocking success upended credibility in the ultra-nationalist government and Prime Minister Netanyahu. This considerably strengthened the probability that the forces pressing for a more democratic and liberal Israel might come to dominate Israeli life post war.

The sobering lesson is that, once human beings took full charge of realizing the covenant, there were no guarantees (or divine controls) to assure the ideal outcome. After October 7 much of world Jewry, standing by Israel despite its being led by an extremist government, has wagered its fate on the vision that those upholding freedom and human dignity would win out. Covenantal loyalty to Israel meant standing with it — albeit working for correction — even if Israel fell into the hands of wrong leadership for a period.

As I write these words in December 2023, I believe that Israel's record and performance since its birth justifies this faith. With the passage of time, the classic Zionist narrative will win out. The vision enshrined in Israel's declaration of independence, of a state that guarantees "full freedom of conscience, worship, education, and culture," is stronger than the discriminatory ethos of any one ruling coalition.

Israel and the Palestinians

The United Nations resolution that validated Israel's birth also authorized creation of an Arab state. Zionist leaders accepted the resolution. The neighboring Arab nations rejected the resolution. Between 1948 and 1967 they chose not to establish any state for the Palestinians living under their control. Eliminating Israel had priority over giving the Palestinians their own state. They focused on destroying Israel by war, relentless economic boycotts, and diplomatic isolation. After Israel's capture of the West Bank and Gaza in the 1967 Six-Day War, United Nations ceasefire resolutions called for Israel to return some conquered lands for peace. Israel was willing. The Arab nations responded with three no's: "No peace with Israel, no recognition of Israel, no negotiations with it."

Six years later, the Yom Kippur War almost brought the Jewish state to its knees. The United States then facilitated a peace treaty between Israel and Egypt, with Israel returning the Sinai Peninsula. It was a cold peace, but Egypt was removed from the cycle of endless war on the Jewish state.

The whiplash between the glorious Six-Day War and the nearly catastrophic Yom Kippur War released religious currents in Israeli society that envisioned possession of all biblical lands. The Gush Emunim movement pushed for Jewish settlement in Judea and Samaria (the West Bank) while the Israeli government envisioned the possibility of trading territories for a future peace. Secular Israelis also joined the movement to achieve *eretz yisrael hashleimah*, "the whole Land of Israel." The fact that dwellings in the settlements were cheaper and more luxurious gave impetus to the movement. From 1977 on, rightwing parties frequently ruled the government and supported settlement building. By 2023 over four hundred thousand Israelis lived beyond Israel's 1967 borders, creating a considerable interest bloc that was skeptical or opposed to a Palestinian state.

Israel began governing the West Bank in 1967. Palestinian life improved in significant ways. The gross national product of the West Bank grew by 12.9 percent annually from 1968 to 1978. Cars increased tenfold, telephones sixfold, tractors ninefold. In 1967 there were no Palestinian universities; two decades later, there were seven. Civic life expanded. Ironically, the most powerful outcome of Israeli control—in no small measure due to exposure to Israeli life—was the deepening and further crystallization of Palestinian national identity. This turned Israeli control—won in a war of self-defense—into an occupation, deeply resented by the local population. Fatah (the dominant PLO faction) and Hamas (more radical, religious, and violent) grew stronger. These groups and the Palestinian population increasingly demanded a state of their own. Millions of Palestinians found themselves in limbo, without citizenship, either in Israel or in their own state. To Palestinian nationalists, Israel's control of the West Bank amounted to an occupation. A majority of Israelis supported a two-state solution then, but no

Palestinian leadership emerged to make a deal to end this occupation. In time, the explosive mix of growing Palestinian nationalism, increasing settlements, terrorism, resistance, and suppression resulted in outbreaks of terror and violence such as the First Intifada.

The First Intifada was ultimately suppressed (mostly by force), but at the cost of a vast outlay in time, energy, money, and lives. It also made clear that the Palestinian national issue could not be ignored. The U.S. offered recognition to the PLO on condition that it renounce terror, revoke the clause in its charter calling for the destruction of Israel, and affirm a two-state solution. The Palestinian National Council eventually voted for these steps, but in such an ambiguous and evasive manner that most Israelis did not believe it was acting in good faith. Despite regaining their voice in the international arena from other Arab nations that had spoken for it previously, the Palestinian national movement failed to decisively turn away from a focus on the elimination of the Jewish state.

By the 1990s a new narrative of the Middle East emerged. Hitherto, Israel, sitting on 1 percent of the landmass of the region, with a population of eight million amid four hundred million Muslims in the Middle East, was seen as an embattled David holding off a hostile Goliath. Now the Palestinians were presented as a scattered, oppressed people, facing a larger Israeli population that ruled them with an iron hand—recasting Israel as Goliath.[14] Elements of world opinion, especially on the left, increasingly turned against the Jewish state.

In 1993 back-channel contacts between Israel and the PLO culminated in the Oslo Accords—mutual recognition by Israel and the PLO and a peace process, based on UN resolutions 242 and 338, to fulfill the Palestinian people's right to self-determination. The Palestinian Authority (PA) was to govern two areas in the West Bank (Areas A and B), whereas Israel would initially control the remainder (Area C) but transfer it in stages as negotiations progressed; Israel, in fact, redeployed its troops to give the PA autonomous control over Area A. However, amid delays in changing the charter, incitement and use of language calling for Israel's destruction, and its ongoing toleration and rewarding of terrorist violence—even as the PA cooperated on security with Israeli authorities—negotiations ultimately went nowhere.

With every passing year, Israeli disillusionment grew, with more Jews moving to the political right and Palestinian leaders continuing to impugn Israel's legitimacy. Despite active U.S. intervention, PA leaders rejected peace offers, including by Israeli prime ministers Ehud Barak in 2000 and Ehud Olmert in 2008, that would have established a Palestinian state on 95 percent of the West Bank. The sticking point was the PA's unwillingness or inability to recognize Israel's existence as a Jewish state. The Palestinians correctly describe the creation of the Jewish state as their *nakba* (catastrophe). However, they fail to acknowledge their responsibility for this outcome, either by their own negative decisions or for those of surrounding Arab nations.

The savagery of the October 7, 2023, Hamas attack—in which 1,200 people were murdered (the most Jews killed in one day since the Holocaust) and 240 people (including babies and elderly) were abducted—traumatized Israel. The atrocities—families burned alive, numerous rapes and instances of sexual abuse, babies beheaded, communities devastated—convinced the nation that Hamas's commitment to destroy the Jewish state was deadly serious. Together with Iran and Hezbollah's military capabilities and their determination to destroy Israel, Hamas posed an existential threat. A ground war was launched to eliminate Hamas by destroying its military infrastructure.

October 7 unleashed a worldwide wave of antisemitism, including support for Hamas and even celebration of its crimes as "resistance" to colonialist occupiers. Especially on the radical left, Israel was demonized.

The Israeli counterattack devastated much of Gaza. Hamas had emplaced its operations and vast military tunnel system in civilian settings—hospitals, mosques, schools—complicating Israeli military efforts to reduce civilian casualties. Thousands of Gazan civilians died. In what I see as a posture tantamount to siding with Hamas, some United Nations resolutions and many demonstrators worldwide did not condemn Hamas's atrocities, demanding instead an immediate ceasefire that would end the deaths of innocent Palestinians yet also leave Hamas in power. Hamas had already made its intentions clear: to repeat the trauma of October 7 on Israel.

As I write these words, thanks to United States backing, Israel has been able to continue its fight to end Hamas's power and threat. Still, especially on the left and in academia, anti-Zionist, antisemitic sentiment has spiked. World Jewish communities have largely stood fast with Israel, albeit with some slippage of support especially among younger Americans (Jewish and non-Jewish); all the while antisemitic, anti-Zionist threats and acts have multiplied and scathing criticism of Israel in the name of human rights persists. In a climate of outright lies and constant demonization, the Jewish state continues to be compared to rogue states like Iran, North Korea, and Pakistan.

Still, there are signs of hope. The Abraham Accords (2020) with the United Arab Emirates, Bahrain, and Morocco represent a breakthrough in legitimizing Israel and overcoming the Arab denial of its right to exist. On the other hand, as I write these words, the Gaza war has stopped the process of normalization with Saudi Arabia and placed great strain on Israel's existing Arab peace partners.

The Talmud says that prophecy has ended but the predictive power has passed to children and fools.[15] I predict that Israel will persist and end Hamas's power. Its population, united by lives sacrificed and suffering in war, will arise, change leadership, and strive to create a more ethical, inclusive society. I even believe in a long-term process in which militant Palestinians turn from undermining the Jewish state toward more democratic, societally constructive, autonomous self-rule. Following this path can win back the trust of Israelis and open the door to a Palestinian state that could live in peace with Israel.

Religious Pluralism

Israel faces other challenges. Early in its history, the Israeli government adopted a model for religious life based on the Ottoman and

British systems of multiple religious establishments (as opposed to an American-style separation of church and state). The state agreed to provide support for religious services and offered public education for secular Jewish and religious Zionist streams while substantially supporting an ultra-Orthodox educational system.

Since the 1980s *haredim* have come to dominate the Jewish religious functions of the state, carving out independent authority and substantial financial support for their institutions and way of life. Consequently, *haredi* views determine many of the most important aspects of Israelis' personal lives, such as public transportation on Shabbat (forbidden in most of the country) and restrictions on marriage, divorce, and religious conversion.

Can Israel broaden religious freedom and bring all its religions and Jewish denominations to full equality? Progress in religious pluralism has been glacially slow. The Supreme Court of Israel has been a major force for equalization and extension of freedom for all groups, but has also itself come under pressure to desist. Israel desperately needs a progressive Orthodox renewal movement (currently a minority in the *dati leumi* sector) to enable the religion to become a force for pluralism, peace, and cultural and ethical cohesion.

I believe we will see the long-term victory of the better angels of Israeli nature. The country will not turn into a theocracy. At the same time, disestablishment of Jewish religion is a bridge too far for most Israelis. Therefore, short term, Judaism will continue to be a source of internal conflict, both inspiring reengagement with the tradition and spurring undemocratic behaviors that offend many Jews in the Diaspora and weaken international support for Israel.

Diaspora Relations

Most Jews in the Diaspora are not Orthodox. The Israeli religious establishment refuses to recognize non-Orthodox denominations as valid. For some American Jews, this painful rejection of their Jewish identity has distanced them from Israel. There are also signs of "Israel fatigue": some Jews are tired of defending Israel in the face of unrelenting criticism.

Israel has paid a price for being a Jewish state. Much of its international opposition is based on antisemitism. By the same token, diaspora Jewish communities have come under attack for standing by Israel. The Gaza war has deepened the sense of a unity of fate, but this is not yet the dominant force regulating policy. In the twenty-first century Israel has moved to give back to the Diaspora, especially through its partnership in programs like Birthright Israel and recent initiatives to support diaspora Jewish education. Israel has become a key element in the Jewish identity of millions of diaspora Jews, intensifying their commitment to Jewish culture, religion, continuity, and fate. Israel also supplies security aid and unofficial protection to many diaspora Jewish communities.

Despite the fact that world Jewry's needs are not yet given full weight in Israel's policy making—a standard truth in a democracy holds that domestic groups and needs outweigh foreign interests and justice—I am convinced that Israel's powerful sense of Jewish peoplehood will eventually triumph, embracing solidarity with Jews worldwide and consequently regulating domestic policies to strengthen the unity of the Jewish people worldwide.

An Era of Hope but No Certainty

In the age of the third *tzimtzum*, we have no guarantees. Foreign threats such as a threshold nuclear Iran and its proxies are an existential threat to life in Israel. Internal radicalization may lead to amoral policies that betray the covenantal goals. There is no certainty that covenantal ideals will win out, or that the morally restrained will be rewarded with victory.

Successful covenantal living requires living in the tension between the real and the ideal. Given how far we have come, I believe the forces of religious humanism and world repair will win out.

In Israel, messianic religious currents have often been a force for overreach. But there is also a covenantal messianism within Zionism—an aspiration for a responsible State of Israel to play a realistic, formative role in an ethically perfected world. In fact, Israel already has transformative—I would say redemptive—impacts, serving as a "light unto the nations." It is a living laboratory for developing an economy from scratch. It demonstrates how to enact the values of modernity and even postmodernity while also preserving its Jewish heritage and upholding the dignity of the past. Its high-tech sector has brought great advances to humanity; its medical startups have generated breakthroughs and lifesaving treatments for millions. It is a global leader in desalination and water efficiency, offering its improved agricultural practices and technologies to countries worldwide.

A final redemption will not happen in one dramatic swoop. The global Jewish prayer for the State of Israel describes it as "the beginning of the flowering of our redemption." As Israel continues to grow and develop in its covenantal relationship with Jewry and humanity, we can look forward to transformations that pave the way to the greatness, national achievements, and true messianic possibilities of our era.

14 Judaism in the Third Era

In the Third Era, as God's *tzimtzum* calls on humans to take full responsibility for the covenant in partnership with the Divine, the Divine role transforms as well. As the German Christian pastor Dietrich Bonhoeffer pointed out, the Deity is no longer the "God of the gaps," to whom humans turn out of insufficiency, or to explain the inexplicable.[1] Instead, God is the Lord to whom one turns out of strength, common cause, and love.

First and foremost, despite this era's *tzimtzum*, God is totally with each individual in every moment and place of life. Loving people, God shares joy and expands it exponentially. God elevates our spirits from the depths, raising the poor and moderating the mighty. God absorbs pain, making it more bearable. This closeness sustains us: "Though I walk in the valley of the shadow of death, I fear no evil for God is with me" (Ps. 23:4).

This sustenance is not to be confused with the magical idea that I cannot be harmed because God will shield me from bullets. The natural order operates. However, rooted in God, I have the strength to take up my intended role, confident in God's presence and partnership.

God continues to guide, urge, and persuade in every moment of life—through Torah and memory, through human interpreters and hidden Divine agents. The heavenly voice speaks from Sinai not just daily,[2] but at every moment. We must listen and hear it from whatever source or direction it comes.

Believing that, despite *tzimtzum*, God still judges and holds us accountable continues to be a powerful driver of behavior. The standard set by God, "who does not play favorites or accept bribes"

(Deut. 10:17) and may rebuke our behavior even as the world applauds our success, motivates us through shared values rather than coercion.

The Human Role

The third Divine *tzimtzum* calls all human beings to greater partnership—that is, to intensify human activity toward Judaism's messianic goals: in economics, to overcome poverty and hunger; in politics, to overcome oppression and war; in life sciences, to cure sickness and roll back death; in religion, to raise norms and behaviors to ideal standards, uncover new channels of connection to God, and turn to God out of human capacity, not incapacity.

As humans become increasingly capable, prayer shifts from dependency—requesting supernatural interventions—toward expressing relationship, gratitude for life, and wonder at Creation. Prayer becomes the invocation of the powerful, not the plea of the powerless. The surgeon does not ask God to zap an incurable malignancy with a magical reversal of nature but prays: May God guide my hand. The oncologist prays: May I grasp how to work with this patient's immune system to destroy the invader. The scientist prays: May I uncover and rightly apply all the miraculous properties in matter. The political leader prays: May I calculate responsibly, aware of my limitations and accountability, and marshal the needed resources to ensure victory for life and human dignity.

The Jewish People's Contribution in the Third Era

In the global work of *tikkun olam*, two distinctive Jewish paths have emerged. In the State of Israel, a Jewish majority can strive to build a society that is a microcosm of a repaired world. In the Diaspora, especially in the United States, Jews can lead in advocating human rights, welfare capitalism, and other efforts to promote life.

Jewish religion and culture can contribute by upholding the covenantal partnership model as the method of redemption, showing that, where humans operate as God's representatives and partners, their work will be a blessing. Jewish witness can include the memory of past redemptions, to help others grasp the continuity of the covenant. In this age of Divine invisibility, a growing secular outlook risks rejecting limits and so becoming idolatrous, as Nazism did and was. In teaching covenant's value, Jewish witness models the importance of setting limits on human power, in order to protect life and preserve the world.

Toward an Ethic of Power

The augmented human role in world redemption requires developing an ethic of power across diverse fields. Many inherited moral codes reflect ethics of powerlessness and scarcity of resources. For example, given the universal devastation of poverty, the Torah mandates giving *tzedakah* to people with insufficient resources. The status quo inequitable distribution of wealth is assumed, but the wealthy are charged to share. Today, however, given major economic developments capable of actually ending poverty, an ethic of power can, and ought to, prioritize not just charity but mechanisms of fair distribution.

The key to keeping life uppermost lies in upholding limits. Inherited ethical systems can shed light and offer precedents, but must be adapted to modern capabilities and enable advances in dignity and equality for previously suppressed groups. Jews—who learned from the Holocaust that passivity is no longer practical or moral, for there is no limit to the catastrophes that may be inflicted on the powerless—can urge humans in every field to take power for the sake of advancing life. Ethicists can teach that greater power spells greater capacity both to do good and to inflict evil: human productivity can now end poverty—or destroy the planet. Humans exercising their new power must mimic God's ethical role, offering a holistic vision of justice not controlled by any one interest group. Even those who seek to do God's will cannot escape the self-centered nature of being a human being, and must fight against their own self-righteousness or sense of infallibility by welcoming ethical input and critique from many sources.

Jews can also be a light to the nations by making the positive case that humanity is called to strive toward *tikkun olam*. To recapture the wholly necessary awareness of covenant, they can teach both accountability to and partnership with God, as well as embark on joint ventures with all of humanity's peoples, religions, and value systems. They can work to further a covenantal ethic of limits, restraint, and step-by-step world repair, hand in hand with structures of balance and moral critique in every field.

Judaism in the Third Age

Judaism itself, as a religion, is subject to these challenges in the Third Age, too. Here, we can learn from the ways the Rabbis responded to their *tzimtzum* two thousand years ago. Despite great historical upheavals and Jewish defeats, the Rabbis believed the covenant of redemption was still valid. Despite living in changed locations and encountering different civilizations, they saw themselves as the descendants of those Jews who took on the covenant of Sinai. As its inheritors, charged with carrying the redemptive task to completion, they felt empowered to move beyond past practices to come closer to God. Their work led to three great achievements.

First, they expanded the zone of holiness immensely by teaching Jewry to seek out the hidden *Shekhinah* in every area of life. Guiding behaviors toward heightened life, they uncovered the presence of the hidden God in every aspect of living. In synagogues everywhere, the *Shekhinah* joined the congregation of Israel. The people matured spiritually and internalized covenantal values. New moments of sacred time and expanded prayers and blessings brought countless encounters with God every day.

Second, the Rabbis renegotiated many significant covenantal compromises, because, in their new circumstances, the gap between the ideal and the real had changed. They improved women's conditions by instituting the *ketubah*, guaranteeing a wife's rights in marriage and legislating a financial settlement to help protect against one-sided divorce that would leave her penniless. Without eliminating the death penalty or the enslavement of fellow Jews, they restricted both. To advance prosperity for all, they also bypassed provisions that might have restricted commerce, such as the biblical forgiveness of loans in the sabbatical year.

Finally, the Rabbis tremendously expanded both the ranks of religious leadership and the levels of participation of the masses. Leadership expanded beyond the aristocracy and priesthood to encompass anyone engaged in *talmud torah*—the study and teaching of Torah—which the Rabbis made into a broad norm. Education was implanted deeply in Jewish culture and glorified as a value. The Rabbis also developed new institutions, including synagogues and houses of study, to involve more people in the work of Torah and covenant.

These changes resulted in a fuller Jewish way of life, engaging more people and enhancing their connection to the hidden God. The Jewish people overcame the trauma of losing their homeland and becoming an outsider minority where they dwelled. They remained faithful to the covenant in the face of centuries of persecution. They retained their sense of being blessed in their chosenness, even while living among majorities that claimed God had replaced Judaism with other religions. For centuries Jews maintained a vibrant religious life and a society with strong social solidarity. The Rabbinic second stage of the covenant kept the covenantal dream alive.

In our era, Judaism will need to carry the Rabbis' accomplishments forward in these same areas: expanding the zones of holiness, renegotiating the compromises of the past, broadening leadership and institutions, and embracing the challenges of pluralism.

Expanding the Zone of Holiness

The Divine movement into total hiddenness plunges us into a world of global secularity—yet the Rabbis' insight that God has come closer and is totally present relieves this cosmic absence. The single most potent way to come closer to the hidden Divine is to seek out or deepen the presence of life, especially in its more intense forms, whether in quantity or in quality.

In the Third Era, all human actions should strive more intensely to make the Earth more hospitable to life and more sustaining of a higher quality of life. Every covenantal action should focus on maintaining or repairing life or, if necessary, be redesigned to uphold life in all its dignity. Every interpersonal ethical action should represent the appropriate response evoked by a creature of infinite value, equality, and uniqueness. Every action affecting the environment and other species should reflect recognition that the planet and all biota, the dwellers therein, are representatives of life. No less should every ritual action nurture life and every encounter with the Divine strengthen reverence for life. When our personal actions increase the quantity or quality of life, we make God manifest. Ritual confirms and blesses this development. In every place where we cause God's name to be pronounced, "I [God] will come to you and will bless you" (Exod. 20:21).

Expanding Holiness in Eating

Eating is a central human activity. One cannot live without an adequate diet, and much of the quality of life is shaped by practices and social interactions connected to food consumption. So too, biblical and Rabbinic systems for ritual associated with eating reflect the irreplaceable sacredness of life. Acting on the third-stage covenantal principle of finding the holy in the secular, we need to expand the *halakhot* of kashrut to intensify respect for life, both among those who do not keep traditional kashrut and among those who do.

Given the broad rise in standards of food adequacy, we might reassert the classical Edenic push toward vegetarianism or even veganism. Modern industrial farming and animal husbandry have broadened the availability of food at a reasonable cost, but they have also led to exhaustion and erosion of soils, deforestation, and animal crowding and cruelty. Reversing these trends is a first priority.

Classically, failure in the preparation process makes an otherwise kosher animal unfit for eating. Extending this model, making veal more tender by starving calves to make them anemic should be prohibited— the calf rendered unfit for eating—as an assault on the dignity of animal life. Raising chickens in crowded conditions so that they cannot move is a violation of the prohibition of causing pain to animals. Overfishing and eating endangered species should be prohibited, for this pushes the planet toward death instead of life. We should designate such foods unfit for human consumption. God, whose "compassion is on all God's creatures" (Ps. 145:9), is driven out by such cruelty. On the other hand, practical steps to improve conditions—organic farming, expanded use of plant derivatives and equivalents, individualized slaughter, humane husbandry—bring us closer to God.

We also must look to the image of God of those who prepare the food. Are the working conditions degrading or dangerous? Exposure to pesticides and weed killers endanger the health of food workers. When we respect life more intensely, such violations disqualify much of conventionally farmed food.

Reverence for life should extend to the act of eating as well. Choosing healthy food is a rigorous requirement of holy eating. Choosing wholesome ingredients, avoiding those that harm us, adding elements like iodine or folic acid to prevent illness and birth defects directly fulfill the command to "choose life." In preparing food, we can apply the halakhah of increasing quality of life. A chef who brings out deeper flavors in food brings us closer to the One who generated this wondrous food. This helps us pass the talmudic test that each of us will be held accountable in the afterlife for every permitted delight that we passed up.[3] Embracing life through joy will be a hallmark of finding the holy within the secular in this new era.

Eating together, conversation, and fellowship in dining lead us to know the image of God of the other. Preparing food for others as an act of service, of commitment, or of love is a way to savor life and deepen relationships. Special meals, such as religious, national, or communal celebrations, add a connection to a higher cause, reminding us of our group commitment to move the planet toward freedom and perfection.

All of these considerations expand the covenantal parameters for those who observe the laws of kashrut. However, in accordance with the third stage's universalistic focus, they apply to all people—Jews and non-Jews alike—as well as to all foods that are eaten. Thus, this secular realm is suffused with sacred values and lifted toward God and life.

Expanding Holiness in Interpersonal Relations and Sexuality

Respecting the infinite value, equality, and uniqueness of the other is the highest thing one can do to intensify life. The encounter with the image of God in the other is the most powerful way to connect to God.

The human being has an innate need for connection. The Bible expresses this as a dictum: "It is not good for the human to be alone" (Gen. 2:18). In childhood, healthy connections to family and caretakers can confirm our sense of human equality, value, and uniqueness; friendships broaden our circle and confirm that each of us is an image of God. Maturing, we develop the capacity to focus on one relationship that can become total. There, nothing personal need be held back, because each of us is secure in being infinitely valued; we can each be ourselves, confident that the other respects our uniqueness. A lifetime commitment becomes possible, one in which we might exercise the Godlike capacity to create a life, and in which the stability and dependability of marriage offer the strength to raise an image of God over the decades it takes us to accomplish this miracle.

A central part of growing together is expressed through sexuality. Touch, hugs, intercourse express emotions that sometimes words cannot. Such sexual expression of self is both natural and powerful. It is a central (but not exclusive) element in connecting and growing in relationship. Sexuality is more than a physical need or a neutral bodily act: it has consequences and emotional outcomes, and hence should be neither casual nor exploitative. When the physical encounter is true to the actual intimacy, bond, and caring for the other, I call this authentic sexuality. Sexual encounters that nurture human dignity can be peak moments of discovering the image of God of the other, as well as of revealing one's own. In such encounters, we can experience this Divine ground in which we are embedded.

In earlier eras, Judaism often distanced the sexual aspect of life from holiness. In the biblical code of life and death, menstruation was treated as a moment of death, precipitating withdrawal from sexual activities for a week, a time later authorities would extend. Medieval codes, including R. Joseph Karo's Shulḥan Arukh, pitted flesh and desire against soul and spiritual discipline, urging restriction and reduction of even permitted sexual activity. Holiness in sexuality was defined by its withdrawal and restriction periods, including intricate *harḥakot,* "distancings," introduced to prevent sexual attraction or activity during menstrual impurity. In certain strands within the tradition these tendencies have led to reducing permitted sexual activity within marriage to an absolute, non-pleasure-oriented minimum out of the belief that human sexuality is spiritually degrading and threatening to holiness, so defined as transcending the body to be with God through spiritual activity.

The Third Era expansion of holiness will move toward affirmation of the body and of physical pleasure. Contemporary science and culture stress that much of one's humanity is anchored in the body and expressed through it. Consciousness is not a separate force, nor is a soul an entity made of different material, temporarily trapped in the body. Rather, it is rooted in the body, reflecting the Bible's affirmation of the human as a body-soul unity. Channeling life forces and sexual activities toward enriching life will be a sign of intensified holiness. Rav Abraham Isaac Kook, the great theologian of pre-State Israel, suggested that sexuality is the sacred expression of the life force that courses through each generation and links it, through life creation, to the next generation in the covenantal chain. He argues that, in the past, the tradition inculcated holiness mainly through restriction in order to curb the animal tendencies in human beings. Now the time has come to uplift sexual passions by directing them toward expression in joy and fulfillment. Religion connects these behaviors to the Divine image in us and to the Divine itself.[4]

When we affirm the beauty and spiritual dignity of the body, all the techniques and practices of love—physical, verbal, sexual, emotional—become covenantal actions. If a person discovers that this image of God is particularly responsive to a certain kiss or to the stroking of a specific part of the body, and if a person honors this uniqueness by expressing love through giving that pleasure, then that person is nurturing an image of God. Similarly, to express love verbally or nonverbally in a way that confirms the great worth of the other constitutes imitating God by sustaining a human fully in the image of God.

Critics may decry this approach as giving in to a culture that recklessly disseminates and commercializes sexual messages and promotes promiscuity and pornography. Promiscuity is the futile pursuit, by an impoverished image of God, of self-confirmation that is never achieved, because the sexuality is not embedded in relationship. It is no accident that promiscuous sexual activity is often connected to a weak self-image. Feeling unworthy and unequal, the individual image of God seeks out confirmation from another, but in the absence of relationship, the sexual act is empty and transmits none of this message. The participant lies (or accepts the lie) in the act, for a moment, and the hunger remains unsatisfied. By vitiating the sexual interaction's weight and depth, hookup culture as a whole lies to its participants, leaving them emotionally malnourished. Often the underlying self is robbed of value in each emotionally empty encounter.

Even worse are abusive or exploitative sexual encounters, where an individual turns sexual activity into a (one-sided) demonstration of power, instead of an expression of connection and relationship. Preventing such behavior requires both legal protections and norms of respect that foster equality—and not, as some groups today seem to think, devaluing sexuality or claiming to "protect" individuals, often women, by placing them in segregated or sheltered settings. Many of those allegedly "protected" settings are actually based on (and reinforce) a belief in the secondary status of women, which in turn puts them at heightened risk of abuse. By contrast, an authentic act of sexual expression confirms that I am an image of God. The message is: this person values me and my uniqueness; this person is responding to my body, my magnetism, my arousal.

Because of this, I am less concerned about the dangers of easily available sex undermining marriage and family. A full-throated affirmation of God's gift of body and mind, the wholehearted embrace of the joy and pleasure of a life well lived, give couples fulfillment in living as no other medium can. Loving spouses will discover the difference; gravitating toward the covenantal limits that sustain worth without limit, they will encounter the depth of life where the hidden God is present. They will experience for themselves the fulfillment of the talmudic promise that in sexual intercourse, when a covenantal couple is worthy—that is, when they recognize the image of God in each other—the *Shekhinah* is between them and with them.[5]

In this Third Age, these truths of human sexuality must come to apply equally to heterosexual and homosexual relationships. I believe the Torah's bitter opposition to sexual intimacy between men reflected a time in the ancient world characterized more by an antilife culture of dominance than by an emphasis on relationship.[6] Later, the widespread premodern assumption that homosexuality represented a perverse desire to reject relationship and family to experience a different sensation emerged based on ignorance of the fact that a human minority experiences desire and intense physical and emotional responses to people of the same sex. It has since become clear that same-sex attraction is part of the natural spectrum of sexual activity.

The same covenantal demands of relational sexuality between men and women apply to same-sex couples. Authentic sexuality for them, too, is rooted in relationships. To use covenantal terms, the deeper the relationship, the deeper the sexuality. LGBTQ+ people who emphasize deepening relationships and faithfulness in order to know the image of God of the other equally desire covenantal, long-lasting, committed, and dependable love. This leads to family, the sacred, life-affirming work of creating and nurturing images of God. Finally, this leads such loving couples to affirm their role as a link in the covenantal chain. The home becomes an island of holiness—a place of faithful relationship where the image of God of each partner is nurtured and the *Shekhinah* comes to dwell.

I believe that in the third stage of covenant, the tradition will come to this understanding of LGBTQ+ people's needs and desires. A whole sector of humanity once banished and mistreated as the enemy is now recognizable as part of the forces of life advancement. A new zone of holiness has been revealed.

Expanding Holiness in Work and Daily Life

In the second stage of the covenant, the Rabbis expanded the locale of holiness beyond the Holy Temple's walls. Embodying it in one whole day of the week, Shabbat, and in the Festivals, they suspended all work on Shabbat (and most work on the Festivals), in order to immerse completely in the realm of holiness. Refraining from activity evocative of the ordinary enabled deeper focus on being present with people and with God.

The Rabbis' definition of work, however, paved the way to expand holiness into the realm of work itself. In fact, to be prohibited on Shabbat, work had to be *melakhah*, dignified labor of highly creative accomplishment. Merely expending energy to attain a change in the external world did not qualify. The prototype categories of *melakhah*, derived from activities used to build the *mishkan* (Tabernacle, the portable Divine dwelling used before the Temple was built), included all the work of civilization: growing and preparing food, producing clothing, writing Torah scrolls (representing the creation of culture), providing shelter and fire, and transportation and carrying (which I interpret broadly as commercial exchange and entrepreneurial activity). Since God's House was intended to be a microcosm of the future messianic world, the Rabbis were saying that higher-level human activity constituted holy work, analogous to the building or completing of the perfect world.

In the Rabbinic treatment, daily work itself is not yet a mitzvah. In the third stage, however, we are called to imitate God's creative activity in work as well as in rest, and thus expand the holiness zone into all seven days of the week. We do this by reshaping work into a covenantal action or mitzvah, using the same six criteria the Rabbis employed to define *melakhah*, holy work:

It must be *melekhet maḥshevet*: planned and intentional, with a clear purpose and intended product, fully engaging and upholding the dignity of workers.

It must be *metakein*, an act of constructive accomplishment that upgrades the world.

It must be *tzarikh legufah*, necessary, because its product is needed and because this work is the activity needed to effect that result.

The workers must themselves be *mitkavein*, acting intentionally to produce an outcome, and thus dignified, because the work accomplishes their goals.

The physical work must be done *k'darkah* with normal, natural, and efficient motions that do not strain or injure the body.

The final product must be *mitkayyeim*, of some utility and longevity, and hence stand as a beneficial use of the world's resources for creation.

In the Third Era, we need to apply this Rabbinic model to *all* work. The goal of all work is to increase the quantity and quality of life in the world.

Work must be redesigned to repair the world. Workers in every field should see themselves as God's human partners in *tikkun olam*, making the effort to ensure their work improves the world and adds to life. Human and artificial intelligence, and every available technology, must aim toward this upgraded world. Eschewing the sins of exploitation—of both nature and people—work must also end abuse of other life-forms and species destruction, and reduce pollution and waste.

Additionally, work must be redesigned to maximize the image of God in all workers, according them their value and equal dignity. Anonymous, atomistic, repetitive work must be designed out—perhaps replaced by robots and automation—and substituted with work in which laborers fully understand the total conception of the outcome and their responsible role in the creative process. Workers who are respected and given responsibility experience more value, equality, and uniqueness in action, and respond in turn with more productivity and conscientiousness, thus fulfilling and enriching each one's image of God.

The workplace, too, must be redesigned to make work constructive and intentional. Rules and procedures must ensure healthful and fair work, not overwork or unreasonably paced activities. Individual autonomy and ownership of work in cooperation with others must become standard procedure, and so support the goal of making the workplace a locus of life-affirming holiness and Divine Presence.

A holy workplace will incorporate just work policies and fair wages, paid on time. Forced labor, predatory working practices, unjust tactics, and violent discipline are all violations of the image of God of the worker. In this era, business leaders who take advantage of workers in order to maximize their own profits will be seen as violators of the sacred who drive out the presence of God.[7]

In the postmodern global economy, special protection must be written into trade treaties, lest developing nations feel pressured to betray these standards in order to attract investment. In real estate development, shelter and commercial spaces must be qualitatively upgraded, with architectural sensitivity to location, nature, and human scale, all to add holiness. By contrast, exploitative development, shoddy construction, inhumanly scaled construction, and predatory lending and sales all damage the image of God of the victims and drive out the Divine Presence.[8]

Government regulation and legislation have to level the playing field as well, by advancing transparent business practices and penalizing exploitative ones. The process pays off in living conditions that enhance the image of God of all involved. As the holiness quotient goes up—by upgrading housing and neighborhoods—the benefits spill over in ever wider circles. Jews can contribute not only by supporting such legislation but by developing a rating system for "kosher" housing, office, and real estate development, as well as prohibiting projects that violate these norms.

Personal activities can similarly be redirected toward secular holiness to maximize life. For example, private cars, a hallmark of affluent society, give workers better access to employment and entertainment, and expanded living options. However, growth without limits has degraded quality of life: in air pollution, accidents, property damage, and deaths. With improved mass transit, safer car design, and less-polluting electric cars, travel will become an expanded zone of holiness.

In the same spirit, consciously strengthening the body turns one's personal habits into covenantal activity. Nachmanides translated the Torah's clarion call, *kedoshim t'hiyu!*—be holy!—as an instruction to turn regular daily physical activities into higher levels of quality of life. In this stage of the covenant, disciplined eating, physical activity, and healthy sleep habits become halakhic behaviors, part of the covenantal call to act on the side of life.

Renegotiating Compromises and Reaching for Messianic Standards

In this third major Divine self-limitation, delegation of power and responsibility to the human partner should go beyond that of the Rabbinic era. Humans have all the power and authority necessary to redevelop religious law in order to further realize the covenant. The primary use of this increased power should be to honor the dignities of the image of God in every human being to the greatest extent possible. This includes renegotiating inherited historical patterns that compromised the dignity of various groups.

Three factors compel this religious response. The first is the almost godlike development of human capacity. Since in this era humans are reaching for the highest goals of *tikkun olam*, religious behaviors, too, should be upgraded, to move the point of reconciliation between today's real and ideal closer to the ultimate standard—especially where religious standards reflect prior compromises made on the covenantal journey.

Second is the fundamental religious response to the Holocaust: to increase the value of the image of God. Every halakhah where human equality or uniqueness has been compromised or insufficiently realized—such as with women, or people with disabilities, or gentiles—should be upgraded. As seen below, transformations in Jewish life have already begun in these three areas. This sacred work must be carried forward to reflect a higher commitment to the dignity of these images of God.

Third, now that the steady growth of human capacity has suffused the general culture with the assumption of broader equality, as the halakhah negotiates the gap between the long-term ideal and the present real, it needs to demand a closer approximation to honoring the full dignity of the human image of God in all areas of life. Even as the covenant mechanism brings the whole past with it and reveres that past, it must reject the fundamentalist claim that current generations have no authority to change past policies. The Divine delegation of power to humans says the very opposite. Human actions must be rooted in the past, but cannot be anchored by it to the point of immobility, especially at a time when humans are called to pursue the perfection of the world.

The Status and Roles of Women

The status of women is the classic expression of unfinished business in advancing messianic standards. In the Torah's primordial vision, all human beings are made in the image of God. "The Lord created the human in God's image; in the image of God, God created the human; *male and female, God created them*" (Gen. 1:27). All people, regardless of gender, are to be treated as infinitely valuable, equal, and unique. Yet women have widely been considered the second sex, too often treated as chattel, or as enablers or wards of a beneficent patriarchy.

Just as women were denied full equality as citizens and voters until the nineteenth and twentieth centuries, so were women not treated as full citizens in Jewish religion. Although the Rabbis expanded their rights, women were exempted from time-bound commandments and not counted as members of the minyan for prayers. They were not eligible to serve as witnesses in rabbinic courts, or as judges or spiritual leaders.

In Jewish communities that have integrated into modern and postmodern life, the principle of women's equality has become increasingly accepted, even as reality lags behind. Traditional and Orthodox circles, however, have moved more slowly. Modern Orthodox institutions—coeducational day schools, girls' schools and seminaries, and, eventually, higher educational institutions for women—have increasingly offered Torah learning, and even ordination (or its equivalent).

Still, the *haredi* community has opposed any change in women's religious status and roles. Bais Yaakov schools and other *haredi* girls' educational institutions taught, and still teach, that women's primary religious roles are as mothers and homemakers, deliberately avoiding teaching women Talmud to make clear their continuing secondary status. As women's learning and leadership became more strongly demarcated as the front line of modernity, *haredi* and even many "centrist" Orthodox institutions have closed ranks to deny legitimacy to Orthodox groups supporting liberalization. In the United States, for example, a rabbinic panel of the Orthodox Union ruled in 2017 that women may not carry rabbinic titles or serve clergy functions in synagogues. Rather than openly deny women's equality, a democratic value modern Jews overwhelmingly hold, the panel insisted that women's status in Judaism is equal but expressed in distinctive roles—from which religious leadership is excluded. They relied heavily on medieval sources stipulating that women cannot rule over men, regardless of the fact that the medieval exclusion could only be justified by women's secondary status.[9]

The irony is that egalitarianism is sweeping the entire Jewish community, and is eventually likely to win out in any part of the Orthodox world integrated into modern life. Upholding distinctive gender roles could be an important contribution for Orthodoxy to make, but at present the "distinctive role" idea is so intertwined with an insistence on women's secondary status that it has no credibility outside centrist and *haredi* circles. Until Orthodoxy moves away from marginalizing and exploiting women, it will have no influence on how gender interactions unfold in the broader Jewish community.

I believe that the entrenched Orthodox denial of women's full equality will not stand. Judaism's contribution will be reduced if the ethical standard of full human dignity continues to fall short for half of its most committed followers. I wager that new leaders, including women, will step forward to take responsibility under the *tzimtzum* and insist on the messianic standard: "All your children will be learned of the Lord" (Isa. 54:13).

The prophet Hosea wrote that, when the redemption comes, the woman will call her consort "my man and not my master" (2:18), a process already in full swing in general society. The daily sight of women working on an increasingly equal plane in every field, and often leading men, has broken down fixed assumptions about women's traditional roles. At some point, the reality of women being as learned and religiously engaged as men, of women being economically self-sufficient through their work and not wards of husbands or fathers, will lead to their full acceptance in the religious community as well. Rabbi Soloveitchik suggested (in the context of discussing slavery in Jewish historical tradition) that halakhah releases those who are not free and equal—who are not masters of their own time or truth—from time-bound commandments, and bars them from serving as witnesses.[10]

This suggests to me that women's historically second-class social and economic status accounts for the religious limitations imposed on them. As women attain full equality and mastery of their time, then, they become able to fulfill time-bound commandments for themselves and others. Similarly, their right to witness—and judge—in halakhic courts must come to be recognized. Recognizing this, the way will be cleared to remove religious exclusions and injustices inflicted on women, and to allow them to contribute all their talents and insights to enrich Jewish life.

As women's participation in religious life rises, the expressions of lesser dignity that have crept into the tradition have come to be identified as dissonant. Some communities have replaced blessings such as thanking God "for not having made me a woman" with positive affirmations, such as "who made me in God's image." Liberal halakhic circles are already experimenting with egalitarian wedding ceremonies and documents, in which both spouses are active and protected. I believe this trend will continue and intensify as women's dignity moves through the halakhic world. Liturgical experimentation and creativity will develop to celebrate women's lives, spilling over to enrich and renew traditional life ceremonies. As my wife, Blu, jokingly said decades ago: If rabbis gave birth, by now we would have one humdinger of a blessing to recite.[11]

Disability Inclusion

Moving closer to messianic standards requires us to uphold the image of God in every person, including those with disabilities. In the Bible, only animal specimens seen as perfect could be sacrificed to God (an expression of respect), and only priests who were seen as perfect human specimens could serve before God in God's House. This notion of priestly physical perfection foreshadowed the future repaired world, in which all disabilities would disappear. Isaiah prophesied: "The eyes of the blind will see and the ears of the deaf will open [and hear.] The lame will leap as a deer and the tongue of the mute will sing joyfully" (Isa.

35:5–6). However, biblical and Rabbinic cultures were not attuned to the loss that people with disabilities experienced in exclusion, or to the larger community's loss in their marginalization. The uniqueness and diversity of God's creatures were overlooked—slighted—by the collective failure to recognize this exclusion or to secure their place in social and religious life.

The Talmud spoke of deaf-mutes, the cognitively disabled, and minors as not responsible for their actions because they lacked understanding.[12] In fact, people who are deaf are just as likely as hearing people to have full mental faculties, yet their lack of access to learning the oral tradition prized by the Rabbis was interpreted as mental incapacity. Sign language, technology, and changed attitudes have now led to their increased participation in culture and society. Halakhic writers have begun to address their religious status, but not quickly enough. Failure to include them religiously contradicts the Divine gift of image of God to all humans.

Inclusion is one of the glories of contemporary culture. A culture of empathy for human diversity has grown steadily. Greater accessibility for people with disabilities has become the legal norm. In the third stage of covenant, then, medical and pedagogical efforts to heal disability where that is possible, and to accommodate and value the range of human beings, must be matched by efforts to include all people fully in religious events and private occasions. Updating inclusion to bring the halakhah into compliance with the standards of dignity to which all people are entitled will be rewarded by letting us meet the hidden Lord in new places.[13]

The Status of Gentiles

In the story of Creation, the Torah states unequivocally that the Lord created Adam, the human, in the image of God, and that Adam and Eve are the parents of all humanity (Gen. 5:1–2). This is the great principle of the Torah; all standards and obligations for treating humans are shaped by this criterion.[14] Nevertheless, in the course of history this principle became compromised in the tradition's attitude toward non-Jews. In early manuscripts, a *mishnah* establishes that any and all human lives are in the image of God and of infinite value—"One who saves one life, it is as if he saved a whole world"—but in the Middle Ages, the scope of this teaching was limited to "one life of Israel."[15] Later, others suggested that ethical obligations such as returning lost property and even refraining from stealing do not apply to Jews' treatment of gentiles.

Why had Jewish attitudes toward gentiles deteriorated? In the early clash between Judaism and paganism, pagan religions were understood to violate fundamental norms of morality and decency. Idol worship was labeled *avodah zarah*—strange, alien worship, without socially redeeming value. Just as the Torah preached that the Israelites should fully extirpate idolatry from the holy Land of Israel (Deut. 7:1–5,24–26; 12:1–3; 13), the Rabbis forbade entering a house of idol worship or recognizing its religion in any way. Because idolatrous religions were seen as degraded, their practitioners came to be viewed as less than human. In a climactic outburst of anger, the Talmud says: *atem* [you Jews] are called *adam* [human], but idolators are not called *adam* [human].[16]

The demotion of gentiles from a status of full equality also reflected a reaction against the relentless degradations and injuries inflicted on Jews by many Christians and Muslims over millennia. Christianity's longstanding teaching of contempt for Jews—its theological demonizing of the Jews and their religion as cruel and inhuman—was particularly harmful, injecting loathing and alienation toward Jews into European culture. Religion-based hatred of Jews was the bane of their existence in Europe for centuries. Because gentiles often justified cheating Jews or repudiating debts owed them, Jews felt no moral reciprocity. In medieval halakhic codes, moral obligations to gentiles were often upheld prudentially, to maintain good relations while Jews and gentiles lived in proximity to one another, or to avoid backlash (should it come out that Jews considered gentiles degraded or less than human). Still, the foundation of true relationship and loving responsibility, recognition of the image of God of another person, was undermined in the case of gentiles.

The Rabbis extended ritual categories to distance Jews socially from gentiles. A prohibition against drinking wine that might have been poured for libations before idols was extended to proscribe drinking any wine touched by a gentile (*stam yeinam*). Similarly, eating kosher food cooked by a gentile (*bishul akum*) was disallowed in many cases. These arrangements imputing social "impurity" to non-Jews are still typically in force today in modern kashrut supervision.

Modernity ended the wall of legal and social isolation around Jews. The emerging democratic ethos affirmed the humanity of the other and increasingly offered full citizenship to all. More social interaction with gentiles induced Jews to imitate and integrate with the majority. Because food restrictions were obstacles to taking advantage of opportunities in the new society, many Jews dropped kosher practices. Moreover, the perceived disrespect for gentiles and the hostility embedded in these practices backfired. Modernizing Jews tended to ignore or reject the restrictions; only the most traditional Jews, who had least social contact with gentiles, maintained them.

The third stage of the covenant requires a systematic halakhic correction: the full recovery of the image of God of gentiles. Recognizing the full image of God of all leads to upholding the value, equality, and uniqueness of every person, politically, economically, and culturally. Jews are major beneficiaries of such trends; morally, they owe reciprocity to non-Jews.

The implications of the Holocaust also necessitate such changes. The Final Solution showed that systematic degradation of the image of God of any people weakens their most important shield—their humanity—in the eyes of others. This may start with stereotypes and put-downs, but it can end with total exclusion and genocide. Hillel said: "What is hateful to you, do not [allow anyone to] do to others."[17] The post-Holocaust commandment to restore the sacredness and inviolability of the image of God of all humans also calls for an end to devaluing other religions, lest this turn, as it inevitably does, into devaluation of those faithful to that religion. Every degradation must be fought.

The focus of diverse religions on what Judaism calls *tikkun olam*, and on joint action to achieve it, is strengthened by the growth of mutual respect between religious traditions. Judaism's ability to participate in intensified campaigns for *tikkun olam*, and to inspire and serve as a light for nations, depend on recovering the unqualified principle that every human is an image of God. Judaism must lead in making this principle emotionally real to all Jews, and this in turn will motivate acts of aid and justice inside and beyond the Jewish community. The prophet Isaiah suggested that in the Messianic Age, Jews will recognize that gentiles also can serve as priests and Levites, serving God (Isa. 66:20–21). When all humanity, including Jews, works side by side to perfect the world, when evil and destructive acts are challenged and repaired, then the whole world will be filled with knowledge of God, "as the waters cover the sea" (Isa. 11:9).

Given soaring Jewish assimilation and skyrocketing interfaith marriage rates, some argue against bringing Jews and gentiles into closer, more loving connections. But social exclusion does not work in an open society. Ethical people are appalled by the moral price of degrading others for the sake of putative survival, but galvanized by creating a community of love and solidarity free of "othering" others. The ethical alternative for Jewish continuity is to develop a powerful distinctiveness in the presence of the other — one encompassing full-hearted respect for the other's life and faith. Forging a healthy, vital Jewish community that brings its unique covenantal commitment to *tikkun olam* to its participation in general society is a central religious challenge of our time.

Expanding and Enriching Jewish Leadership and Institutions

Successfully executing the third stage of covenant will require a massive expansion of lay and professional Jewish understanding and activity. In postmodern culture, where alternatives to Jewish involvement are ubiquitous, every Jew is a "Jew by choice." Yet Jewry cannot play a role in the world's redemption unless Jews choose to remain Jews. Distinctive Jewish religion, culture, and identity, at home in postmodernity, must offer everyone access to meaningful Jewish experiences at the highest level. Judaism in this new era needs a new flavor—of activism, of conscious choice, of being applied to all of life. The community must refine and redesign itself with a host of new receptors—people, institutions, experiences—to which Jews can compellingly connect.

Jewish Leadership for the Secular Age

The success of the response to the third *tzimtzum* will depend on the community's ability to generate a leadership movement parallel to that of the Rabbis in the first millennium. Rabbis today offer content, experiences, and personal models, but most have been trained with an understanding of God and Judaism drawn from the second stage of covenant. Many people feel dissonance when they hear rabbis speaking of God as a self-evident fact, or offering a more sacramental and authoritative worldview than they believe is plausible. Our new leaders must be able to speak of a God who is totally hidden or more subtly present, whose very Presence can be experienced only as episodic, even uncertain.

Along with male and female clergy trained in new ways, then, we need people on the frontiers of *tikkun olam* who will lead the battle for life in every field of (secular) holiness. If they can testify that, in taking responsibility, they experience the covenantal Partner's sustaining power, then their witness to the hidden God is especially persuasive. Jews who do not experience the Divine Partner, but do feel responsibility and a sense of belonging to a self-transcending covenant dedicated to *tikkun olam*, will also be among this era's religious leaders.

For these people, Judaism must offer enriched understanding of the Jewish tradition and its treasury of past covenantal models. Traditional texts and models will not always be enough. For example, blessings may need to be supplemented (or replaced) by *kavanot* (intentional reflections) to uncover the holiness in new secular areas; prayers may be extended by silence, meditation, music, and other means to reconnect to the hidden God.

Scripture will need to speak in new voices, too. In the first era, the Exodus was narrated as the manifest, miraculous Redemption we know from the Torah. In the second, the Rabbis emphasized a different way of experiencing God—choosing to include in the Bible, from among many versions, a telling of Esther's story in which a more hidden God saved the Jews, acting through human partners.[18] Strikingly, the generation that experienced the Shoah continued this development, giving their own testimony without a formal religious framework. Elie Wiesel's classic *Night* inverted the Exodus narrative as a catastrophe narrative, from freedom to slavery. In his *Megillot Ha-Edut* (*Scrolls of Testimony*), Abba Kovner, a partisan and a resistance leader in the Vilna ghetto, presented himself as a secular, nonbelieving witness, but his account includes powerful representations of every kind of Jew, including individuals who served as representatives of the Present/Absent Lord.[19] Such resonant accounts carry on the scriptural tradition of the covenant in credible, hidden fashion.

New leaders may bring models from their fields that past generations had not imagined for connecting to the Divine infrastructure of existence and to fellow human beings.[20] The numbers of people inspired by these new leaders to enter into this new stage of the covenantal journey will determine the quality of the Jewish contribution to the emerging high-risk, high-gain postmodern culture.

The average layperson will have to reach a level of understanding of Jewish living as to willingly choose to live it, day after day. Hence, education that empowers Jews—including Jewish programming in the secular landscape—must be expanded to offer immersive, meaningful Jewish experiences. Everywhere, Jewish educational initiatives—like the ones highlighted below—must wrestle directly with the "hidden" dimension of holiness and seek alignment and advancement with the covenantal mission.

Retreats and Retreat Centers

In America, where 25 percent of people change their religious orientation or affiliation in their lifetime, adults in recent decades have grown more open than in previous generations to identity-transforming experiences.[21] Retreats provide multiday encounters with Judaism, away from familiar locations that anchor and fix our identities. They offer adults a total environment in which Judaism is central; peers with whom one can bond into a connected Jewish community; respected leaders who can transmit substantive, exciting Jewish wisdom and serve as role models; and a range of experiential as well as intellectual content (lectures, workshops, small groups processing, ritual and religious elements, music and singing, sometimes dramatics and dancing)—food for the soul as well as the mind. I have witnessed participants' Jewish identities transformed from a potpourri of inheritances, memory, habit, and knowledge into a coherent frame of reference: a Jewish lens that can filter and shape life's meaning. The retreat is a Third Era ritual that enables encounter with covenantal redemption in just a few days.

Retreats can be held anywhere. A dedicated space, however, can be turned into a total environment that multiplies a program's impact. Cultural and artistic aspects can augment its attraction to disaffiliated or secular Jews. As Third Era institutions, retreat centers are perceived as neutral, just the right place for secularly oriented Jews to be inspired—even, potentially, to meet the hidden God.

Going forward, retreats built to communicate the Jewish narrative, including the Jewish version of *tikkun olam* for all humanity and its method of covenant, should be offered as a free gift from the Jewish community to young adult Jews. Presented in pluralistic fashion, such retreats could include introductory and intermediate-level workshops on how to create a Jewish home. I believe no other program could do more to assure Jewish continuity and renaissance in an open society.

Holocaust Education Centers

In Jewish history, great orienting events of the covenant, such as the redemptive Exodus and the catastrophic destruction of the Temple, led to the development of institutions of remembrance and transmission. In the aftermath of the Holocaust, a growing consensus emerged that remembering the Holocaust was a central norm of being a Jew. In 1953 the Israeli government established the Holocaust memorial center Yad Vashem to bring together records and evidence, and to present the lessons of the Shoah in an all-encompassing environment. Since that time, major Holocaust museums have been established around the world, including one in Washington DC.

A commemorative museum, dense with Holocaust artifacts, photos, and other records, can convey some fragment of the experience — enough to transform a visitor's understanding. Moreover, such museums are secular, not suffused with traditional religious assumptions or denominational concerns. All Jews, and non-Jews, can enter without feeling out of place. Paradoxically, the secularity of their presentation and the universal human aspect of the Holocaust have made such institutions appropriate and resonant places to wrestle with Jewish fate — and with Jewish faith and its meaning. Thus Holocaust education and Holocaust memorial centers have become crucial parts of integrating Jewish identity in the Third Age.

Holocaust museums reach tens of thousands of Jews who no longer come to synagogues or traditional Jewish institutions. Religious visitors often have religious experiences in navigating a Holocaust memorial center, even as secular visitors feel that it does not force religion on them. Counterintuitively to expectations of what will happen when one encounters stark expressions of cruel, almost senseless attacks on Jews, some Jews have discovered that the Holocaust museum experience sets in motion a journey toward deeper Jewish identity or religious meaning in their lives.

Federations and the Jewish Philanthropic Sector

Among the institutions that have emerged in modernity, one more has great potential to enlarge Jewish life in the Third Age: the Jewish Federation system.

Philanthropy—protecting the needy at home and abroad, and making a society that better protects every human image of God—is a secular act of world repair. Framed within Jewish community and tradition, it can be a meaningful way to join the covenant of world redemption for secular as well as religious Jews.

In North America, the Federations began in the late nineteenth century as local welfare funds, caring for poor Jews so they would not become public charges, with a strong policy bias toward facilitating Americanization and providing nonsectarian services, such as hospitals. In reaction to the rise of Nazism, they became central fundraising organizations for Jewish welfare at home and abroad. After WWII, together with the United Jewish Appeal, they focused on caring for Holocaust survivors and supporting the emergent State of Israel, and after the Six-Day War, consciousness of the Holocaust and Israel as reflecting the distinctiveness of Jewish fate became core to their identity and mission.[22] The Federations' narrative of "from destruction to redemption," taking responsibility for Jews in danger, became a secular, holy way of connecting Jewish history to *tikkun olam*. Though the Federations' energy and their share in American Jewish philanthropy have waned since the decades when a large proportion of American Jewish households made gifts, they remain powerhouse institutions.

Nowadays, when many Federations exist primarily as fundraising and distribution agencies, they are liable to become simply ethnic network organizations, which, among most Americans, fade as the immigrant experience recedes. To remain magnetic, Federations must embed their Jewish identity in a higher cause or purpose. They must rearticulate Jewish philanthropy as the kind of secular activity where one most intensively meets the hidden God. To enable secular Jews to attach their commitment to a Jewish community that holds a higher standard in philanthropic activity, they should ask Jews to give—in proportion to their means—more than the average population in both money and time. While the greater demand will scare off some people, this higher expectation will show that being Jewish is the way to make a higher-level contribution to the universal cause of a better world. Of course, Jews will give to universal channels and general causes, too. But with an invigorated Jewish philanthropic sector, giving through Jewish channels will be associated with higher goals and with the covenantal goal of *tikkun olam*.

Existing Immersive Options

Jews can also build upon the educational institutions that initiated immersive Jewish experiences mostly in the late twentieth century. Day schools offer intensive Jewish learning alongside general studies. Summer camps combine a total Jewish experiential environment with secular sports, arts, and other activities. Gap year study programs in Israel (between high school and college) can be vital Jewish growth experiences for diaspora youth. In the secular universities chosen by the vast majority of North American Jews attending college, Jewish studies courses offer the tradition in sophisticated fashion, introducing students to instructors who constitute a cohort of Jewish intellectuals and role models, "secular rabbis" for the Third Era. Intensive Jewish community on campus, including through Hillel or Chabad, drives Jewish connection. In particular, the Taglit-Birthright Israel program, which runs trips to Israel for thousands of young adults, has resulted in measurably higher levels of both identification with Israel and the Jewish people and subsequent marriage to other Jews. Because Birthright presents as both secular and pluralist and offers Jewish experiences through an accessible lens, it has the potential to be a fundamental rite of passage: a holy secular mitzvah of Third Era Judaism.

Embracing Pluralism

Pluralism is a natural outgrowth of the process of Divine *tzimtzum*. More humans participating and taking authority leads to greater diversity of actual practice. People must learn to respect each other and to live in the presence of conflicting claims and practices, without giving up their own distinctiveness. Pluralism in interpretation and religious decision-making is an intended outcome of human maturation.

In the biblical period, when God was the dominant partner, God's word was to be followed exactly, neither added to nor diminished (Deut. 13:1–12, 18:15–22). False prophets had to be identified and rejected. There could not be two contradictory messages or policy instructions from God.

The Rabbis, called to take on authority and responsibility in the covenant's second stage, developed the Oral Law to uncover God's word and instructions.[23] They uncovered new layers of meaning in the Torah's inherited revelation and derived new laws.[24] Soon, a host of alternative readings or contradictory rulings developed. People and schools of thought operating with good faith and intentions and common assumptions came to different, sometimes contradictory interpretations of God's word. People were becoming more mature in the covenant, not merely taking orders but identifying with covenantal purposes and applying their minds to their best realization. In summoning the people to act as partners in the *brit*, the Lord was inviting people to use their best judgment, and to speak up even where they differed. The Rabbis came to affirm the method of debate and disagreement as a better way to get at the variegated meanings in the word of God. Minority views were recorded in the Talmud and studied alongside the majority ruling, available in case of a future recalibration of the best possible reconciliation of the ideal and the real. "Any disagreement for the sake of Heaven"—in which both sides desire to hear and understand the Torah properly—"will have a lasting outcome."[25]

Nevertheless, the invitation to partnership in the second stage of covenant was limited. The Rabbis defined their authority as less than that of the first stage of sacred Scriptures, given directly from God. New commandments they created, such as reading the Megillah of Esther on Purim, included a blessing of God "who sanctified us with His commandments and commanded us to do [those Rabbinic enactments]"[26] — but those laws were of secondary authority to Torah laws. The Rabbis could apply the law differently, extend it, or limit it, but the biblical commandments were sacrosanct. Nor could one deny that God had created the world, or chosen the Jewish people and entered into covenant with them. The range of pluralism was also accordingly limited: the opposing schools of Beit Hillel and Beit Shammai, for instance, accepted many of the same theological and practical norms without qualification. The Rabbis rejected competing sects such as the Sadducees, who denied that the Oral Law was revealed at Sinai; Jewish Christians, who often repudiated various commandments (and would later ascribe divinity to a human being); and Epicureans, who denied God's Providence and deep involvement in human history and culture. These groups' rulings were not considered part of Torah.

The third *tzimtzum* goes significantly beyond the second. Since God has now chosen to be completely hidden in order to give humans full responsibility for realizing the covenant, the pluralist understanding of the range of human judgment must be expanded to incorporate today's much more divergent religious groupings. God is widening the parameters of pluralism to encompass new people, understandings, strategies, and tactics. The Lord is authorizing human beings to innovate without hesitation in order to realize God's vision. This is why I believe that pluralism will be a standard norm in the religious world generated in the third stage of covenant.

Pluralism among Jews

In 1965 my friend Rabbi David Hartman invited me to help plan a summer institute with as many rabbinic colleagues as we could afford to bring. After we had exhausted the list of Orthodox rabbis with whom we had an appetite to learn, we invited another minyan of Conservative and Reform rabbis, including Jacob Neusner, Emil Fackenheim, and Jakob Petuchowski.

For me, the encounter with a high-powered group of liberal rabbis who were such serious Jews was transformational. They were religiously vital, ethically powerful, wrestling with many of the questions that concerned me. I will never forget a long walk with Jakob Petuchowski in which we talked about halakhah and, in particular, about Jewish divorce law. I had never had a long conversation involving Talmud and halakhah with a Reform rabbi who was so knowledgeable. Even more stunning was my realization that his critique of divorce law was right, and that the halakhah, which I loved and upheld, was in need of *tikkun*. Thus, I learned a foundational principle of pluralism: recognition that one's own tradition, however valid and sacred, contains flaws that need correction.

That summer institute taught me that the Conservative and Reform movements were valid interpretations of Judaism, channels to connect and partner with God. I still believe that my Orthodox movement, with its mix of strengths and weaknesses, contributes more to my own religious life, and, on balance, perhaps to Jews overall. But it, too, can do better if it learns from the others, and if all work together for the greater good.

The experience, which deeply altered almost all the participants, inspired me to found CLAL: The National Jewish Center for Learning and Leadership, to address Jewish community leadership and education as a pluralist institution, where all people could feel that they were at home, not the guests of members of one preferred worldview. A kind of minicosmos, CLAL brought together diverse systems and viewpoints under ideal circumstances to explore how we might function together and learn from one another. *Haredi* Jews never came, because treating the liberal movements as equals was against their basic principles. Still, the Torah studied was richer because of input from a wide variety of teachers and students, and the ability to look beyond one's own group to grasp what *klal yisrael* (the totality of Jewry) needed was consistently enhanced.

Most exciting to me, many participants were set in motion by their encounter with the others. This opened them up to grow in Jewish living. In my nightmares, this pluralism might have produced negative interchange: Orthodox Jews, seeing good Jews and attractive people do just fine without observing traditional behaviors, might have decreased their own observance. Liberal Jews, seeing good Jews who lived Jewish lives without extraordinary intensity in *tzedakah* or social justice activity, might have done less. But in fact the opposite happened. Each group saw what the other lived and treasured, and imagined taking it on to enrich their own experience and commitment.

As an Orthodox rabbi, I have struggled to articulate the rationale for pluralism by Orthodox standards. How can I sponsor programs with liberal prayer services that I would not attend, or equate a rabbi who believes in *Torah min hashamayim* (the divine nature of the faith) with a rabbi who affirms that the Torah is sacred but was—in part or altogether—created by humans? I have come to understand that when liberal religious Jews drop certain classical observances—or when they bring new commandments, such as imperatives to save the environment or honor people hitherto marginalized—they should not be dismissed as antihalakhic. Rather, they are using their autonomy to spell out additional obligations to achieve *tikkun olam*. How do they claim the right to abrogate laws that Hillel and Shammai deemed beyond their capacity to question? By saying: as much as we love and respect the inherited tools of redemption, in our judgment, using these new tools—or not using some of the old tools—will be even more effective in reaching the redemptive dream.

When contemporary Jews generate new religious leadership roles for women, they are not violating the covenantal tradition; they are seeking to apply it anew as part of a dynamic process of redeeming the world. When rabbis use academic and critical scholarship to study canonical texts, they are trying to grasp the tradition in all its original context in order to develop an understanding of the connection between the Divine and the human—and the communication between Infinite and finite—that is more credible in our time.

The Divine delegation of authority does not mean that all changes are improvements. I personally believe that the liberal movements' abandonment of many covenantal behaviors has eroded the power of the religion. The current decline of loyalty and widespread assimilation in liberal communities should be a signal to learn from Orthodox intensity and strengths and to deepen their roots in tradition, even as they seek to move it forward. Orthodox innovators and critical scholars, too, should fully understand the risks of being absorbed into the present culture. They need to constantly expose themselves to intense religious voices and holistic readings of Scriptures. Indeed, traditional or *haredi* Jews who uphold the inherited halakhah as it is should not be asked to relinquish their mission to sustain Torah unchanged. Rather, they should see their role as a counterculture that keeps the present generation from being swallowed up in the maelstrom of postmodern culture.

At the same time, traditionalists must constantly check themselves to make sure they are not willfully closing their ears to new revelation. When liberal rabbis conceive of God in far less personal terms, they are not to be dismissed as breaching the commandment to believe in God. When secular thinkers identify the Divine with basic cosmic processes (such as the expansion of the universe or the evolution of life), they should be recognized as trying to make belief in God fully available, within the cultural consensus of the unbroken operation of natural laws—in other words, trying to extricate the inherited concept of God from utilitarian or magical understandings of the Divine. As science gives us better understanding of Creation and better capacity to heal the world, it is our responsibility to make the religious dimension of

Being credible in its presence. The range of Jewish voices teaches us how to do so.

Pluralism and Being in the Presence of the Others

A postmodern civilization in which every faith and lifestyle lives in the presence of the other offers the opportunity to bypass stereotypes embedded in one's own tradition. One encounters the actuality of the other and comes to appreciate it in all its distinctive reality.

I came to this pluralist understanding emotionally before I could justify it logically. It was the outcome of an early involvement in dialogue—in itself the outgrowth of my response to the Shoah.[27] Shocked by the catastrophic cruelty of the Holocaust and believing that traditional Christian antisemitism had provided a foundation for the Nazis' singling out the Jews, my wife and I joined a Jewish-Christian dialogue, intending to convince Christians that the Gospel of Love was serving as the seedbed for antisemitism.[28] In the process of dialogue, however, we met remarkable human beings who were as determined as we were to see Christianity live up to the standard of love that it proclaimed, so that it would never again give aid and comfort to Jew hatred. As I came to know their ethical intensity and passion for redeeming humanity, I ultimately saw that Christianity deserved credit for being a primary nurturer of people of such moral grandeur. In the backwoods of Sri Lanka, I encountered a whole community of Christians who had left a life of wealth, ease, and fame in Norway to follow Jesus Christ and take up the cross. They cared for a village of children suffering from brain injuries, abandoned by their parents in this poor and rural setting. I was stunned by the raw encounter with the Divine One "who dwells with the oppressed and lowly in spirit" (Isa. 57: 15). I was moved by the power of Christian faith to inspire unlimited sacrificial love. Out of such experiences and further exposure to Christian religious life I came to see that, in parts of the Christian community, "surely the Lord is in this place; and I did not know" (Gen. 28:16). Christian ethics were guiding people to work for redemption. They were living a covenantal relationship with God.

Revelation comes from an Infinite Boundless One, who transcends all capacities of finite mortals to grasp. All Torah reflects a Divine self-limiting in its outreach to humans. Inevitably, humans are able to grasp only some fraction thereof in their understanding. It follows that the disagreement between Christianity and Judaism is not a war between idolatry and monotheism, or a fight between truth and error. It is an argument about the boundaries and actual experiences within the loving, covenantal contract between God and humanity, as experienced in these two communities. If we treat the issue this way, we can differ even as we come closer—even as we work together to achieve the ultimate goals of redemption that we share. We can see Christianity as a vehicle for encountering God, and as a Divinely intended partner with Judaism in the cause of *tikkun olam*, even as we experience Judaism's vitality as strongly as ever. God has entered into relationship with other faiths and communities. This connection need not undercut my people's covenant.

The common refocusing of all religions on the goal of *tikkun olam* also encourages pluralism. In the past, absolutist claims in the name of God and the rejection of others for differing practices turned religions into enemies. Pluralism ends that pattern. Pluralist attitudes enable groups to learn from each other.

Religious traditions, now increasingly exposed to each other in daily contact, need to take up the blessings and challenges of pluralism. Pluralism follows God's *tzimtzum* by retracting claims of exclusive dominance. Pluralism is at once a positive response to a Divine initiative and a needed corrective to keep human growth healthy. Emphasizing the shared goal of *tikkun olam* can also provide a greater platform for specific religious goals, be they union with God, attaining internal enlightenment and nirvana, or harmony with nature.

This focus highlights the great unfinished tasks standing before all religions. No one faith community can realistically hope to achieve world transformation by itself. The status quo is too entrenched; the potential disruption from opponents is too great. Maturation—a realistic sense of one's capabilities, together with an acceptance of one's own limits — plays a more constructive role. Maturation leads to humility, a willingness to serve God's purposes as one of many messengers or constructive partners in realizing the greater goal. Religious groups should show equal respect and openness to secular groups seeking the same outcome of repairing the world. At every step of this way, a pluralistic attitude will improve each group's own capacity and credibility.

In this era, we need every possible means of exploration, precisely because the goals of redemption are lofty — and potentially accessible. Meanwhile, the greater the range and scope of the worldwide search to realize redemption, the more all participant groups need critique and exposure to alternate models of living. Continuing division of activity assures that no one group gains a monopoly on power and applies it destructively. The pluralistic distribution of power is yet another moral necessity in the Third Era.

A Message for Humanity

In this chapter, I have tried to describe the face of Judaism in this third stage of covenant, but I am not God, nor a prophet from God. The reality may differ greatly from these projections. Nevertheless, I close with the main thrust of the third *tzimtzum*, hoping that, as people understand it, they will respond to the opportunity to actualize it.

God has become totally hidden in order not to force or coerce people to do the right thing. The third *tzimtzum* shows the Lord's confidence that, with teaching and guidance from human models past and present, humans will reach for greatness. They will perform miracles and bring the Messiah, or a Messianic Age, or something close to that. With this grant of power, anybody who responds to this summons, consciously or unconsciously — that is, anybody who takes on the task of repairing the world — becomes a legitimate partner in the work of finishing Creation. Those who devote themselves to this mission become cocreators of the Torah, valued collaborators in the never-ending task of reconciling present reality with future perfection.

At this historic juncture, Judaism and Jews have a message for humanity. There should not be one dominant religious or secular model of meaning. Each group should build microcosms of redemption. Then they should learn from one another and work together for the greater good. Jews need to testify to humanity that the greater the power exercised, the more it must be matched by humility. Jews can bring to humanity the promise that it has a Partner to Whom it is accountable. It has a Partner Who, out of infinite love and trust, has wagered the fate of the world on that partnership. If humans respond with all their spirit and talent and love, then the dreams and actions of all the preceding covenantal generations will be realized: the planet will become a paradise for all its inhabitants. Together we can bring the world to the dawn of the triumph of life.

The Three Great Eras of Jewish History

	FIRST ERA — BIBLICAL	SECOND ERA — RABBINIC	THIRD ERA — LAY
Time	(Prologue: 1800 BCE — Abraham) 1250 BCE — Exodus; Kingdoms of Judah and Israel; 587 BCE — Destruction of 1st Temple	(Prologue: 515 BCE — 2nd Temple constructed) 70 CE — Destruction of 2nd Temple; 135 CE — Bar Kochba Revolt; 700–800 CE — Completion of Talmud; 900–1100 — Golden Age of Spain; 1500–1939 — Eastern Europe (communal growth and development, Hasidism and Mitnagdism, Yiddish civilization, modernization and secularization)	(Prologue: 18th–19th century — Emancipation) 20th century — America (Jews attain power, influence, freedom); 1933–1945 — The Holocaust; 1948 — Establishment of the State of Israel; 1967 — Six-Day War; Present day
Key locations	Land of Israel (and the Near East)	Babylonia and the Land of Israel; Diaspora (Europe, Middle East, North Africa)	Diaspora (especially Europe) North America and the State of Israel
Redemptive event	Exodus	Purim	Establishment of the State of Israel
Counterevent	Destruction of 1st Temple	Destruction of 2nd Temple	The Holocaust

327

	FIRST ERA — BIBLICAL	SECOND ERA — RABBINIC	THIRD ERA — LAY
God's role	Dominant, visible Operates in the supernatural Extraordinary intervention	More hidden Operates in nature in cooperation with human partner Hidden intervention	Most hidden Operates in nature only through human agents Intervention infused in natural process, itself the miracle
Humans' role	Passive, receptive Junior partner Genetic elite	Active, participatory Equal partner Psychic elite (broader)	Fully responsible Managing partner Full democratic leadership
Religious leadership	Priests, prophets	Rabbis, rebbes, scholars (Emerging laypeople)	Laypeople Educators, influencers, role models
Religious lifestyle	Sacramental, sacrificial Family ritual, passive worshipers (not educated) Agriculture, nature-oriented, set aside sacred space and sacred time	Synagogue and home Prayer, holiness, learning, and law More individualistic, history-oriented, particularist, antigentile Much less sacramental, less demarcated sacred space	Lay institutions Secular holiness, holy secularity Jewish ethnic identity and values oriented to world repair

Institutions	Temple, sacrifice Prophecy, monarchy	Synagogues, prayer, human interpretation of revelation Community elites	Democratic institutions State of Israel, including representative government and army Widespread general and Jewish education and media Communal, social, educational, cultural, and social justice organizations
Core challenge	Build society *Mishpat* (justice)	Reconcile powerlessness, dependency with covenant Covenantal values	Reconcile power, freedom with covenant
Core tension	Covenantal values vs. power politics	Chosenness vs. powerlessness	Distinctiveness vs. assimilation
Secondary challenge	Maintain Jewish identity in international setting	Maintain Jewish dignity and significance in diaspora	Maintain Jewish identity in context of greater societal engagement, influence, and assimilation

Notes

Introduction

1. Bible translations here and throughout the book are the author's own.

1. Creation and Dignity of Life

1. *Tohu vavohu* suggests an empty void that is nevertheless full of clashing, contradictory, unregulated forces.
2. Shabbat is a world at rest in perfect balance, expanding in dynamic harmony, at peace with itself. Gen. 2:1–3,4–25. Compare these to the summary picture at the end of the sixth day in Gen. 1:28–31.
3. Philip Birnbaum, ed., *High Holy Days Machzor* (New York: Hebrew Publishing Co., 1951), 81, 213, 233, 327, 351, 359, 439, 503, 605, 625, 715, 765, 899, 917, 963, 979.
4. See John D. Barrow and Frank J. Tipler, *The Anthropic Cosmological Principle* (New York: Oxford University Press, 1989).
5. The 50 percent divorce rate in the United States (2013) is proof enough that even great human love is finite—albeit often rising to Godlike levels.
6. This is not to deny that there may be departures from this principle, in two ways. First, sometimes one may need to break order or attack it in the short run for the sake of increasing it in the long run or on balance. Second, the commandments may be applied wrongly, or interpreted or misapplied in a changed context. The tradition must be continuously interpreted to apply correctly to an ever-changing reality. Sometimes, corrections are needed in order to uphold order, life, and quality of life.
7. The dominant Jewish position has been affirmation of human action. As the Rabbis say, "he shall surely heal" (Exod. 21:19) means that physicians have been empowered to use their skills to heal (e.g., to act on the side of life). BT Bava Kama 88A.
8. Joseph B. Soloveitchik, "Shlichut," in *Yemei Zikaron* (Jerusalem: Department of Education and Culture, 1996), 9–15. Compare Joseph B. Soloveitchik, "The Lonely Man of Faith" in *Tradition* 7, no. 2 (Summer 1965): 11–16.

9. Deut. 20:18 prohibits cutting down fruit trees to use them for ramparts during a siege. Only non-fruit-bearing trees are permitted to be harvested. The implication is that destroying food-providing capacity was not necessary to win the battle; hence, this was a needless waste of God-created object or capacity. The Rabbis generalize this. Nothing that God created should be wasted, e.g., used in vain.

10. This is hinted at in the scriptural statement: "The Earth is the Lord's" (Ps. 24:1). Compare to Ps. 104, which celebrates the splendor of daily natural processes as a radiance of beauty and the glory of God.

11. Kashrut has been interpreted as a restriction on killing living things by sharply reducing the number or types of living things one is allowed to eat. There are no dietary restrictions on eating any mineral or vegetable. Within the limited number of living species permitted to eat, *shehitah* has been interpreted as the most humane form of killing animals for food because by cutting off the flow of blood to the brain through the single permitted knife thrust, the animal loses consciousness, ending its suffering. See Jacob Milgrom, *Leviticus 1–16*, Anchor Yale Bible Commentaries (New York: Doubleday, 1991), 704–42, esp. 713–18.

12. This is said although the author disagrees with a trend that insists that humans should not be privileged and animals should not be used or subordinated for human benefit (e.g., Peter Singer on speciesism). The author acknowledges that in the messianic reality that is Judaism's ultimate goal, humans will not use or kill any form of life, but we are now living in an imperfect, unredeemed world. The covenantal morality of Judaism permits a hierarchical moral priority that valorizes the needs of the highest forms of life, especially humans, over other forms of life.

13. The halakhic maxim is *"beriah afilu b'elef lo batel."* A whole organism, even if it is mixed into an amount of food a thousand times larger (e.g., one part in a thousand) is not nullified. BT Ḥullin 100A, Tosafot d.h. *beriah sha'ani;* Shulḥan Arukh Yoreh De'ah, ch. 100, esp. par. 1.

14. The term is used for sexual intercourse for the same reason.

15. Because of historical and sociological factors, the attitude to animals in the traditional Jewish community is considerably more negative. Gentiles used dogs against Jews, etc. Hopefully a new interaction between Jews and animals will enable a recovery of deeper religious attitudes and values.

2. In the Image of God

1. Mishnah Sanhedrin, ch. 4, m. 5.

2. The *mishnah* starts: *Ketzad me'ayemin et ha'edim al edei nefashot*—literally: how do (we) threaten / make the witnesses feel awe before they testify in a capital punishment case?

3. In *Halakhic Man* Rabbi Joseph B. Soloveitchik writes: "The Scriptural portion of the creation narrative [Gen. 1] is a legal portion, in which are to be found basic, everlasting halakhic principles, just like the portion of *Kedoshim* (Lev. 19) [containing "love your neighbor as yourself" and other core commandments] or *Mishpatim* (Exod. 21) [containing the core of Jewish civil law]." Soloveitchik, *Halakhic Man* (Philadelphia: Jewish Publication Society, 1983), 100–101.

4. The text of the most widespread printed edition (Romm, Vilna) states: one life of an Israelite. However, JT Sanhedrin, ch. 4, h. 9, earlier Babylonian Talmud manuscripts, and the best manuscripts of the Mishnah read: one life. Of course, Adam in the Torah is the ancestor of all humans and is not Jewish and so this is the correct and appropriate version.

5. Moshe Greenberg, "Some Postulates of Biblical Criminal Law," in *Yehezkel Kaufmann Jubilee Volume: Studies in Bible and Jewish Religion* (Jerusalem: Magnes Press, 1960), 5–28. Despite the profound problem of slavery in the Bible—including that slaves were legally defined as property in that culture, rather than treated as images of God—it is noteworthy then that when a master beats a slave and kills him, he is punished as a murderer (Exod. 21:20). The influence of treating the slave as property is addressed in Nahum Sarna's commentary on the next verse, Exod. 21:21. See Nahum M. Sarna, *The JPS Torah Commentary: Exodus with Commentary* (Philadelphia: Jewish Publication Society, 1991), 124.

6. International Drug Price Indicator Guide, "Oral Rehydration Salts," http://mshpriceguide.org/en/single-drug-information/?dmfid=572&searchYear=2000. Reflects prices from 2000.

7. Alexandra Peers, "Qatar Purchases Cezanne's *The Card Players* for More Than $250 Million, Highest Price Ever for a Work of Art," *Vanity Fair*, February 2, 2012.

8. Mishnah Sanhedrin, ch. 4, m. 5.

9. To clarify: the Torah uses a language of metaphor and poetry in which the number seven signifies a state of perfection. The number seven times seven (forty-nine) implies that the excellence or perfection has been raised to an even higher level (metaphorically). Similarly, the number eight is a covenantal number. It signifies that while God has created a seven, some state of perfection and excellence, the human partner joins in the work, adding

a one to God's seven and making it even better. For example: the human body is an extraordinary mechanism whose excellence can be rated as seven. However, the human covenantal partner can improve it, making it an eight. This process starts at birth, when on the eighth day, the male body is "upgraded" by circumcision—a covenantal removal of foreskin.

10. Midrash Tanhuma, Pinhas, par. 10, and BT Berakhot 58A record a special blessing to be said upon seeing a crowd. God is to be praised "for discerning secrets"; each person in a crowd is different and distinctive, so only God can know the never-fully-revealed unique mind, thoughts, and values of every person in a diverse crowd.

11. Research by Paul W. Eastwick and Lucy L. Hunt suggests that when people first meet other humans, they tend to judge them by the society's consensus standards of human attractiveness. However, as people establish relationships and get to know the other, the more the unique qualities of the other are discerned. The deeper the friendship and knowledge of the other, the more the uniqueness of the other becomes the basis of judgment. Paul W. Eastwick and Lucy L. Hunt, "So You're Not Desirable . . . ," *New York Times*, May 16, 2014.

12. Mishnah Avot, ch. 3, m. 14.

13. Mishnah Avot, ch. 3, m. 14.

14. Joseph B. Soloveitchik, "Imitating God—the Basis of Jewish Morality," in Abraham Besdin, ed., *Reflections of the Rav: Lessons in Jewish Thought* (Jerusalem: Department for Torah Education and Culture in the Diaspora, 1979), 23–30.

15. BT Sotah 14A; Joseph B. Soloveitchik, "Shlichut," in *Yemei Zikaron* (Jerusalem: World Zionist Organization, 1986), 9–10.

16. See Maimonides, *Mishneh Torah*, Hilkhot Yesodei ha-Torah ch. 2, h. 1–2ff, 9ff.

17. Joseph B. Soloveitchik, "The Lonely Man of Faith," *Tradition* 7, no. 2 (Summer 1965): 13.

18. Soloveitchik, "Lonely Man of Faith," 14.

19. Soloveitchik, "Lonely Man of Faith," 16.

20. Soloveitchik, "Lonely Man of Faith," 14.

21. This community includes God. See Soloveitchik, "Lonely Man of Faith," 28.

22. Interestingly, the Bible does not focus on the fact that the profusion of life leads to the population of predators that feed on other lives—but rather on the vegetation available to all.

23. BT Ta'anit 16A.

24. Desire (*ḥashak*): The Jewish Publication Society Bible translates this as "set one's heart upon" (Deut. 7:7) and "was drawn to" (Deut. 10:15).
25. See Hosea, chs. 1–3, especially 2:18,20–22.
26. Soloveitchik, "Lonely Man of Faith," 29. Italics added.
27. Blessed is God who creates "the fruit of the tree, the fruit of the ground," Philip Birnbaum, *Daily Prayer Book* (New York: Hebrew Publishing Co., 1977), 778. Blessed is God who creates "unique [distinctive] creatures," Birnbaum, *Daily Prayer Book*, 777; and compare Rabban Gamaliel's response to a beautiful woman: "How manifold are Your works, O Lord, You make them all with great wisdom," BT Avodah Zarah 20A. On seeing the wonders of nature, the tradition prescribes a blessing for God "Who does the work of Creation." On seeing beauties in nature, it prescribes a blessing of God ending in "Who has such [beauties] in God's world," Birnbaum, *Daily Prayer Book*, 775.
28. JT Kiddushin ch. 4, h. 12.
29. Soloveitchik, *Halakhic Man*, 33.

3. Tikkun Olam

1. See Bernhard W. Anderson, *Creation versus Chaos* (Philadelphia: Fortress Press, 1987), 15ff, 115–37.
2. In the High Holy Day liturgy, God is described as the *Melech Chafetz Bachayim*, the Ruler who lusts for life. Philip Birnbaum, *Daily Prayer Book* (New York: Hebrew Publishing Co., 1977), 31, 201, et seq.
3. See in particular the books of Isaiah and minor prophets such as Hosea, Micah, Joel, Zechariah.
4. In early Rabbinic times the "world-to-come" was used to refer to the future Messianic Age, but for the last two millennia it has primarily been used to refer to the spiritual world of immortality after death. This otherworldly interpretation is a retreat from the biblical vision that this mortal world will be fully repaired. See Jacob Neusner, *Theology of the Oral Torah: Revealing the Justice of God* (Montreal: McGill-Queen's University Press, 1999).
5. See for example, Matt Taibbi, *The Divide: American Injustice in the Age of the Wealth Gap* (New York: Spiegel and Grau, 2014).
6. For Isaiah's take on the importance of prosperity, see also Isa. 54:11–12.
7. See Nicholas D. Kristof and Sheryl WuDunn, *Half the Sky: Turning Oppression into Opportunity for Women Worldwide* (Toronto: Alfred A. Knopf, 2009), xii–xvii.

8. Joseph B. Soloveitchik, "The Lonely Man of Faith," *Tradition* 7, no. 2 (Summer 1965): 15.

9. Soloveitchik, "Lonely Man of Faith," 16. Soloveitchik interprets the instruction to Adam in Gen. 1:28, "to fill the earth and conquer it," as a call to fill the world with life and control the environment to increase fruitfulness and expand life. In truth, Soloveitchik often uses the language of control and "domination" loosely; see Soloveitchik, "Lonely Man of Faith," 13. Still, given his own exhortation, "There can be no dignity without responsibility" (14), we can put him on the side of power with limits.

10. Kass fears that the world will end in the kind of tyrannical utopianism portrayed in Aldous Huxley's *Brave New World*. For an excellent statement of his general argument, see Leon R. Kass, "L'chaim and Its Limits: Why Not Immortality?," *First Things*, May 2001.

11. Admittedly, these gains have come within the framework of modern medicine. On the other hand, gains in life extension were also achieved before the deciphering of the genome, the generating of stem cells, and the advent of genetic engineering.

12. BT Kiddushin 30B.

13. See the author's treatment of the High Holy Days, and especially of Yom Kippur, as a conscious attempt to harness the encounter with death into a force for liberating and intensifying life. Irving Greenberg, *The Jewish Way: Living the Holidays* (New York: Summit, 1988), 184–87.

14. See Jon D. Levenson's excellent treatment in *Resurrection and the Restoration of Israel* (New Haven: Yale University Press, 2008).

15. BT Sanhedrin, ch. 11, especially 90A–100A.

16. Mishnah Sanhedrin 10:1; and discussion at BT Sanhedrin 90A. See Maimonides, Commentary on the Mishnah, *loc. cit.*

17. BT Sanhedrin 90B–92B.

18. For example, one could argue that the plain meaning is found in drawing a different parallelism in the verse. "I [God] give death [to some] and I [God] give life [to others]. I wounded [some] and will heal [others]." This parallel actually follows the logical sequence in the words a bit more than the Rabbinically preferred one. But one can argue legitimately for either approach as the plain meaning of the text.

19. See Daniel C. Matt, *Walking Humbly with God: The Life and Writings of Rabbi Hershel Jonah Matt* (New York: Ktav, 1993).

20. See the text of the blessing in Philip Birnbaum, *Daily Prayer Book* (New York: Hebrew Publishing Co., 1977), 83, 161, et seq., and in any traditional

prayer book. One may study the understandable loss of credibility and the triumph of materialist thinking in the liberal Jewish denominations by following the various revisions of the language of the blessing: "who gives life to all" (Reform, Reconstructionist), "who gives eternal life" (Conservative). See Jon D. Levenson's acute, if somewhat unsympathetic, treatment of this process in *Resurrection and the Restoration of Israel* (New Haven CT: Yale University Press, 2008), 7–11.

4. Life against Death

1. A talmudic phrase: literally, the father of all fathers of impurity—that is, the ultimate archetype of impurity. Compare the English formulation, "the mother of all battles."
2. Jacob Milgrom, *Anchor Bible Leviticus 1–16* (New York: Doubleday, 1991), 292ff.
3. The closest relatives are parents, siblings, his own children, and by later implication, his spouse. A priest may not contact impurity by attending burials of cousins, friends, or strangers.
4. Milgrom, *Leviticus 1–16*, 1003. Other ritual laws in Leviticus are part of the same code of life versus death. The prohibition of leavened grain on the sacrificial offerings reflects the fact that leaven is a universal "arch symbol of fermentation, deterioration, and death . . . hence antithetical to the altar of blessing and life" (189). For more on the role of purity-impurity in Leviticus, see Mary Douglas, *Purity and Danger: An Analysis of Concepts of Pollution and Taboo* (New York: Routledge, 2002), 51–71.
5. Lev. 8:10–11, 11:32; Ezek. 44:23. Milgrom, *Leviticus 1–16*, 615ff.
6. For the image of the inner circle and its eventual expansion, the author is indebted to Milgrom, *Leviticus 1–16*, 722–25. For the author's argument that the expansion of the holy people may take the form of the creation of parallel religious and ethical communities, see Irving Greenberg, "Covenantal Pluralism," in *For the Sake of Heaven and Earth* (Philadelphia: Jewish Publication Society, 2004), 185–97 and Greenberg, "Covenants of Redemption," in *For the Sake of Heaven and Earth*, 213–34.
7. Milgrom, *Leviticus 1–16*, 1009–84.
8. Azazel seems to have been a demonic force, living outside of civilization, worshiped by nonmonotheists.
9. See Milgrom, *Leviticus 1–16*, 251ff, 258ff, 261ff.
10. In the case of moral sins, the sacrifice is not efficacious unless the sinner feels remorse, repents, and redresses the evil done to the other person (Lev.

5:20–26). See Milgrom, *Leviticus 1–16*, 345. An extended treatment of these topics is found throughout Milgrom, but especially 256–64.

11. Ezek. 1. This scene has become central to Jewish mysticism as *ma'aseh merkavah* (the work of the chariot), but this focus has diverted Jews from the moral message and core ethics of the Torah.

12. The blood prohibition in Gen. 9:4 is continued with stepped-up intensity in Lev. 17:11 and in the Rabbinically articulated laws of kashrut. For more recent scholarship on the blood prohibition, see Julia Rhyder, *Centralizing the Cult: The Holiness Legislation in Leviticus 17–26* (Tübingen, Ger.: Mohr Siebeck, 2019), 290–359. Another form of the acknowledgment that life is sacred is found in the requirement that the blood of fallen game animals is to be buried (Deut. 5:23) and the blood of animal sacrifices is to be poured onto the altar (Lev. 3:8,17). See also Lev. 7:26–27, 17:1–7.

13. See Milgrom's extensive treatment and citation of the talmudic and legal code sources. Milgrom, *Leviticus 1–16*, 713–17.

14. Mishnah Ḥullin, ch. 3, m. 6.

15. See Milgrom, *Leviticus 1–16*, 722ff.

16. Milgrom, *Leviticus 1–16*, 650–51.

17. Exod. 29:19, 34:26; Deut. 14:21; Milgrom, *Leviticus 1–16*, 740. Milgrom suggests that this same logic applies to the prohibition of slaughtering a father animal and his son on the same day. Lev. 22:28; Jacob Milgrom, *Leviticus 1–16*, 740ff.

18. The author's son J.J., *z"l*, became a vegetarian at a young age (thirteen—the first moment the author and his wife allowed him to decide his own diet). He explained that among the other reasons for this choice (in addition to loving animals) was that he did not want to wait six hours to eat his favorite food, ice cream. Later Kabbalah circles sought to impose a wait time after eating "heavy" (that is, hard cheese) foods, an approach that contradicts the author's interpretation. It also should be noted that German Jews wait only three hours after meat. Dutch Jews wait only one hour.

19. Milgrom, *Leviticus 1–16*, 650–53. Admittedly the repulsion toward pigs was provoked by the Antiochean oppression in Maccabean times that forced pig sacrifices onto religiously faithful Jews.

20. See Milgrom, *Leviticus 1–16*, 682–87.

21. Milgrom, *Leviticus 1–16*, 689.

22. Fourteen days of refraining from sexual intercourse followed by sixty-six days of refraining from entering the sanctuary.

23. See Milgrom, *Leviticus 1–16*, 144, 244, 250.

24. The author's interpretation is strengthened by the language of the Torah that the mother "shall be as unclean as at the time of her menstrual *infirmity*" (Lev. 12:2).

25. His sexual partner is also impure for the day. In his commentary on this passage, Nachmanides suggests that "the individual does not know if the seed [ejaculated sperm] will be wasted or if a child will result," cited by Milgrom, *Leviticus 1–16*, 934. See also Milgrom's explanation of the special degree of ritual impurity stemming from intercourse with a menstruant (941).

26. See Milgrom's decoding of these "icons" in *Leviticus 1–16*, 881.

27. Milgrom points out that the Torah has taken away the magic-exorcism element from the disease aspect of these rites (the exorcism elements dominate in parallel pagan rites). The Torah puts the stress on healing, regrounding in God and vital life energies. Milgrom, *Leviticus 1–16*, 837–38.

28. Milgrom, *Leviticus 1–16*, 889.

29. Milgrom, *Leviticus 1–16*, 693.

30. The midrash points out that the bulk of the Torah's most important elements, *gufei Torah*, are restated here. Sifra (Torat Kohanim) Kedoshim 1:1. Another midrash suggests that the Ten Commandments are (re)stated here.

31. Moses Maimonides, translated by M. Friedlander, *The Guide for the Perplexed* (Skokie IL: Varda Books, 2016), part 1, ch. 42, 146. Maimonides applies the apposition of the words to suggest that good principles lead to life; corrupt principles lead to death. The author is suggesting that good acts lead to life; evil acts lead to death.

32. The author believes that other religious communities, most notably Christianity, are also in covenant with God. See Irving Greenberg, *For the Sake of Heaven and Earth* (Philadelphia: Jewish Publication Society, 2004), esp. 49–102, 162–97.

33. See Milgrom, *Leviticus 1–16*, 616ff.

34. See Num. 35, esp. vv. 33–34.

5. The Commandments

1. JT Nedarim, ch. 9, h. 4.

2. See P'nei Moshe on JT Nedarim, ch. 9, h. 4.

3. JT Nedarim, ch. 9, h. 4.

4. See Deut. 15:7–11; Maimonides, *Mishneh Torah*, Sefer Zeraim, Hilkhot Matnot Aniyim, ch. 10.

5. See Lev. 19:16–17; Maimonides, *Mishneh Torah*, Sefer Mada, Hilkhot De'ot, ch. 7, esp. h. 1.

6. Maimonides, *Mishneh Torah*, Sefer Shoftim, Hilkhot Avel, ch. 14, h. 1.

7. Ben Azzai cites the restatement of this concept in Gen. 5:1–2, "This is the book of the generations of Adam. In the day of the creation of the human by the Lord in the image [likeness] of God, Adam was made. Man and woman were [thus] created. God blessed them and called them Adam [human] on the day they were created." JT Nedarim, ch. 9, h. 4.

8. See the civil laws in the Book of the Covenant, Exod. 20–23, esp. 21–22.

9. Exod. 18:21–22; Deut. 16:18–20, 17:8–13.

10. See the author's treatment of these days in Irving Greenberg, *The Jewish Way: Living the Holidays* (New York: Summit, 1988), 217–82, 373–404.

11. See the author's treatment of these days in Greenberg, *Jewish Way*, 283–304, 314–72.

12. Midrash Tanchuma, Shmini, ch. 7; Bereshit Rabbah, ch. 44, s. 1.

13. The author shall deal with this in future volumes. See a first, partial adumbration of the author's thinking in Sylvia B. Fishman, "Modern Orthodox Responses to Liberalism of Sexual Mores," in *Yitz Greenberg and Modern Orthodoxy: The Road Not Taken*, ed. Adam S. Ferziger, Miri Freud-Kandel, and Steven Bayme (Brookline MA: Academic Studies Press, 2019), 224–53.

14. See BT Berakhot 33B; Vayikra Rabbah 13:3.

15. See God's response that life is good: Gen. 1:12,21,25. God wants more: Gen. 1:11,13,22,28.

16. BT Yevamot 61B–62A. There is a *maḥloket* (disagreement) between the schools of Hillel and Shammai: while the former say that the two must be a boy and a girl, the school of Hillel wins out with its view that any two children suffice.

17. BT Yevamot 62A.

18. The Talmud connects this verse to a story about Rabbi Akiva, who, having seen thousands of his disciples wiped out in the Bar Kochba wars, went back and recruited a new cohort of students—and these became the primary teachers in the Mishnah (BT Yevamot 62B).

19. See for example BT Sanhedrin 19B.

20. Mishnah Bava Metzia, ch. 2, m. 11.

21. The original source is found in BT Makkot 23B. Rav Simlai, who originated the count, says that the 365 negative commandments correspond to the days of the year and the 248 positive commandments correspond to the number of joints and bones in the body—the metaphor being that

the Torah guides all the actions of our body at all times (all the days of the year). Rav Simlai does not give the detailed list of commandments adding up to 613. Many great medieval Jewish scholars compiled such a list of 613 mitzvot. For the record, most compilations differed from each other. The best-known is Maimonides' *Sefer ha-Mitzvot* (Book of Commandments). No detailed total list appears in the Torah itself.

22. BT Sanhedrin 74A.

23. BT Yoma 83A.

24. Haym Soloveitchik, "Religious Law and Change: The Medieval Ashkenazic Example," *AJS Review* 12, no. 2 (Autumn 1987): 207–12.

25. Maimonides, *Mishneh Torah*, Yesodei ha-Torah ch. 5, h. 1–5.

26. This last phrase means that they should understand that they are very important — but they should not arrogate to themselves the absolute power, the right to take life, the other accouterments of pseudodivinity.

27. Jonathan A. Goldstein, *I Book of Maccabees: A New Translation with Introduction and Commentary* (Garden City NY: Anchor Bible, 1976), 1:42, 206.

28. Goldstein, *I Book of Maccabees*, 2:32, 234.

29. Goldstein, *I Book of Maccabees*, 2:33, 234.

30. Goldstein, *I Book of Maccabees*, 2:37, 234.

31. Goldstein, *I Book of Maccabees*, 2:40–41, 234.

32. BT Yoma 85B.

33. At the very same time that the Rabbis were making this ruling, however, the Dead Sea sect at Qumran, possibly the Essenes, were making the opposite judgment on the very same issue. The Qumranians were "purists" in their Jewish faith. Their conception of life in their compound was hierarchical and authoritarian, placing the rules of the group above the life of the individual. Their conception of God was no less authoritarian, demanding obedience, insisting on giving up life to better serve God. In their constitution, the Damascus Covenant, they ruled, "If a person falls in water [on Shabbat, and is drowning] let him not be drawn out by rope, ladder, or hook [for such activity would violate the laws prohibiting labor on Shabbat]." This deeply serious alternative religious approach, by no means to be dismissed as mere formalism, persisted as an underground view into the medieval period — indeed, wherever the emphasis on observance overtook the awareness that love of life is the driving force of Jewish religion.

34. The point of "suspended" is that the work should not be seen as a "violation" of the commandment. The commandment remains valid and communally practiced. Only when a life is in jeopardy is the operation "suspended"

(temporarily) in order to uphold the ultimate goal—the creation and protection of life. Maimonides, *Mishneh Torah*, Sefer Zemanim, Hilkhot Shabbat, ch. 2, h. 1–2.

35. BT Yoma 85B.

36. Maimonides, *Mishneh Torah*, Sefer Zemanim, Hilkhot Shabbat, ch. 2, h. 3.

37. BT Sanhedrin 74A.

38. Such is the title of a book on childhood abuse and incest: Leonard Shengold, *Soul Murder: The Effects of Childhood Abuse and Deprivation* (New York: Ballantine Books, 1991).

39. The author is aware that the concept of *gilui arayot*—sexual perversion—was considerably extended in Rabbinic tradition to cover sexual activity such as premarital sex or showing nudity that in our time would hardly be seen as so evil as to demand sacrificing one's life. The author views these as another example of how in history and society, laws are extended by halo effects to cover wider areas. This blurs the clarity of the principle. In this analysis, the author is trying to restore the core of the principle.

6. The Covenantal Method

1. Printed in Philip Birnbaum, *Daily Prayer Book* (New York: Hebrew Publishing Co., 1977), 155–56. This is the liturgical restatement of the twelfth of Maimonides' Thirteen Principles of the Jewish Faith, set out in his commentary on Mishnah Sanhedrin, ch. 10, m. 1.

2. Maimonides, *Guide for the Perplexed*, part 3, ch. 33.

3. Joseph B. Soloveitchik, *Halakhic Man* (Philadelphia: Jewish Publication Society, 1983), 41. Soloveitchik stresses that the believer appreciates the gift of the world-to-come as a "bonus" for a good life—but the primary religious calling is to act in this world, in this life. Soloveitchik, *Halakhic Man*, 30, 32.

4. For the record: the author feels that the worldview represented in these strands of religions such as Buddhism retains great power. Also, there are trends within those religions that view world improvement more positively.

5. From the morning prayers, Jonathan Sacks, ed., *The Koren Siddur* (Jerusalem: Koren Publishers, 2009), 36.

6. Compare Jer. 12:1; Hab. 1.

7. Isa. 54:9–10; Jer. 33:19–21,25–26. This is not to deny the existence of natural disasters that kill innocent people. Such events challenge faith in God and the natural order. But ultimately covenantal thinking rejects interpreting them as a message or punishment from God.

8. The Jubilee year is also a statement of how the world will look in the final stage of *tikkun*. Slaves will go free. They will be restored to their ancestral lands, lands they can work and so have a source of income, dignity, and freedom (Lev. 25:9–10).

9. BT Kiddushin 20A.

10. See Lev. 25:43; Sifra, ad loc; Maimonides, *Mishneh Torah*, Sefer Kinyan, Hilkhot Avadim, ch. 1, h. 6–9. See also Lev. 25:39–40 and Sifra, ad loc.

11. See the entire treatment of the rebellious son (Deut. 22:18–21) in BT Sanhedrin 70A–71B, esp. 71A.

12. For discussion of Exodus 21:7–11, see Hilary Lipka, "Women, Children, Slaves, and Foreigners," in *The Oxford Handbook of Biblical Law* (New York: Oxford University Press, 2019), 67.

13. See for example the Talmud's further elaboration of better working conditions, better pay, better food and shelter for the Hebrew slaves in BT Kiddushin 21A–22B. Still, the Talmud says that these laws are no longer operative since the people went into exile and the laws of the Jubilee could no longer be practiced (BT Arakhin 29A).

7. Relationship and Choice

1. This idea originates in the thought of Isaac Luria and is repeated throughout kabbalistic tradition; see, for example, *Likutei Moharan* 64:1:2.

2. Isa. 40:26; Ps. 89:3.

3. Maimonides, *Sefer ha-Mitzvot*, Mitzvot Aseh #3; *Mishneh Torah*, Sefer HaMada, Hilkhot Yesodei HaTorah, ch. 2, h. 1.

4. Philip Birnbaum, *Daily Prayer Book* (New York: Hebrew Publishing Co., 1977), 7.

5. See the author's observations in Irving Greenberg, "Voluntary Covenant," CLAL *Perspectives* (October 1982): 35–36.

6. Compare Exod. 19:3–6, 24:3–7.

7. Compare the process of Creation, "He [God] spoke—and so it was" (Ps. 33:9).

8. See Exod. 24:7 for the Book of the Covenant. See all the detail in the Book of the Covenant, Exod. 21–24. The requirement to go up to the House of God three times a year is found in Exod. 23:14–17.

9. See Mishnah Avot, ch. 5, m. 16.

10. Classically, this is ten men. Men were considered to be full citizens of the society, whereas women were restricted and constrained in various ways. In recent times, there has been a push (most successfully, in liberal reli-

gious denominations) to recognize the new equality and full citizenship of women achieved in general society by counting them as full citizens in religious and ritual matters.

11. BT Ta'anit 8A.

12. See Joseph B. Soloveitchik, "The Lonely Man of Faith," *Tradition* 7, no. 2 (Summer 1965): 28.

13. BT Megillah 29B.

14. See, for example, BT Gittin 46A; Sotah 10B, 36B; Shabbat 33A; Bava Kama 113A.

15. See Soloveitchik, "Lonely Man of Faith," 30.

16. Jon D. Levenson, *Sinai and Zion* (San Francisco: Harper and Row, 1985), 50–55.

17. In all this, see Lev. 19:13; Deut. 24:14–15.

18. Anne Frank, *Tales from the Secret Annex* (New York: Bantam, 2004), 87.

19. Joseph B. Soloveitchik, "Shlichut" in *Yemei Zikaron* (Jerusalem: Department of Education and Culture, 1996), 11.

20. Mishnah Avot, ch. 2, m. 4.

21. Maimonides teaches that only human beings are the objects of full Divine Providence. Lower forms of life are attended to as species. He also believes that the covenant of providential attention varies according to an individual's mind development and attainments. See his *Guide for the Perplexed*, part 3, ch. 17.

22. Ps. 23, 27, 30, 31, 56, 86, 91, 107 for starters.

23. Compare the classic song of Rabbi Levi Yitzchak of Berditchev, titled "A Dudu'le": Wherever he looks, wherever he goes, whatever his experience in life, Loving God [Du/You] is there.

24. See Irving Greenberg, *For the Sake of Heaven and Earth* (Philadelphia: Jewish Publication Society, 2004), esp. "Covenantal Partners in a Post-Modern Age," 89–102.

25. Mishnah Avot, ch. 2, m. 16.

8. Covenantal Partnership

1. See Gen. 17:16 in the context of Gen. 12:1. See also Joseph B. Soloveitchik, "The Covenantal Role of Sarah," in *Man of Faith in the Modern World*, vol. 1, ed. A. R. Besdin (New York: Ktav, 1989), 83–91.

2. On justice and righteousness, see especially Gen. 18:19.

3. Jerusalem is meant to be a city of peace.

4. See Lev. 16, 21, 22.

5. See the author's extended exposition of this point in Irving Greenberg, *The*

Jewish Way: Living the Holidays (New York: Summit, 1988), ch. 5, "Shabbat," especially 131–44, 145–53, 157–63.

6. BT Shevuot 39A.

7. Maimonides, *Mishneh Torah*, Sefer Zeraim, Hilkhot Matnot Aniyim, 8:10–18.

8. Yehuda Bauer, *My Brother's Keeper: A History of the American Jewish Joint Distribution Committee, 1929–1939* (Philadelphia: Jewish Publication Society, 1974) is the best treatment but it does not cover the whole history.

9. Gal Beckerman, *When They Come for Us, We'll Be Gone: The Epic Struggle to Save Soviet Jewry* (New York: Houghton Mifflin, 2010). This is a comprehensive treatment of the overall campaign, but it does not do justice to Birnbaum's contribution.

10. Post–Soviet Union scholarship suggests that the secret police fabricated the martyrdom story and the family was framed. See Catriona Kelly, *Comrade Pavlich: The Rise and Fall of a Soviet Boy Hero* (London: Granta Books, 2005), and Yuri Drushnikov, *Informer 001: The Myth of Pavlik Morozov* (Piscataway NJ: Transaction Publishers, 1996).

11. See for example: 1 Kings 18:18–40; Isa. 44:6–20; Jer. 2:4–28, 16:9–21, 19:1–13; Ezek. 20:27–29; Hosea 1–4.

12. See BT Sanhedrin 60A–64B.

13. BT Yevamot 106A.

14. The original text of Rabbeinu Gershom's ruling has been lost to history, but it is referred to in several places in Jewish tradition. See, for example, Ritva on BT Yevamot 44A; Rema on Shulḥan Arukh, Even HaEzer 119:6.

15. See Blu Greenberg, *On Women and Judaism: A View from Tradition* (Philadelphia: Jewish Publication Society, 1981).

16. See for example various resources from the International Beit Din, https://www.internationalbeitdin.org/.

17. See Blu Greenberg, "Feminism, Jewish Orthodoxy, and Human Rights: Strange Bedfellows?" in *Religion and Human Rights: Competing Claims?*, ed. Carrie Gustafson and Peter Juviler (New York: Routledge, 2016), 145–73.

18. Compare Num. 21:21–35 (victory) with Num. 14:26–45 (defeat).

19. See Irving Greenberg, *For the Sake of Heaven and Earth: The New Encounter between Judaism and Christianity* (Philadelphia: Jewish Publication Society, 2004).

20. Michael Wyschogrod, *The Body of Faith: God in the People Israel* (New York: Seabury Press, 1983), 58–70.

21. BT Gittin 56A–B.

22. BT Ketubot 62B–63A.

23. BT Yevamot 62B and BT Berakhot 61B, respectively.

24. See, for example, the ArtScroll series of biblical commentaries (New York: Mesorah Foundation), and in particular Rabbi Nosson Scherman, *The Stone Edition Chumash* (New York: ArtScroll Mesorah Publications, 1993).

25. See Philip Birnbaum, *High Holy Day Prayer Book* (New York: Hebrew Publishing Co., 1979), 653–55 (*Asher Ometz Tehilatekha*, etc., in Shacharit of Yom Kippur) and 787–89 (*Asher Ematekha*, etc., in Musaf of Yom Kippur).

26. There were attempts to coopt the prophets by making them officials of the court. See the story of Micaiah and the other prophets in 1 Kings 22. Most of the prophets, like Zedekiah son of Chenaanah, appear to be on the king's payroll and are little more than yes-men. Micaiah, whom the king does not like, is the only one willing to speak the truth.

27. Again, this was subverted in actual practice by excessive closeness of royalty and priesthood. But the system recognized the danger and strove to correct for it.

28. Compare the close cooperation and joint exercise of authority between Simon ben Shetaḥ and Queen Shlomit Alexandra (for example, BT Berakhot 48A) with the confrontation between Simon and King Alexander Janneus (for example, BT Sanhedrin 19A–B).

9. Covenantal Time

1. Mishnah Avot, ch. 2, m. 21.

2. Compare Exod. 24:7.

3. Jacob Milgrom suggests that touching the Torah scroll with *tzitzit* and kissing the string constitute a symbolic ritual pledge to take on and observe all that is written in the Torah. See Milgrom, *Numbers* (Philadelphia: Jewish Publication Society, 1996), 411.

4. See on all this Jon D. Levenson, *Sinai and Zion* (New York: HarperCollins, 1985), 80–86.

5. Rashi on Deut. 6:6.

6. *Ahavah Rabbah* prayer, in Philip Birnbaum, *Daily Prayer Book* (New York: Hebrew Publishing Co., 1977), 73, 79, 81.

7. Rabbi Shai Held, "Returning to Sinai Every Seventh Year: Equality, Vulnerability, and the Making of Community," in *The Heart of Torah*, vol. 2 (Philadelphia: Jewish Publication Society, 2017), 275; Parashat Nitzavim—Va Yelech 5774, also available at Hadar, https://www.hadar.org/torah-resource/returning-sinai-every-seventh-year#source-1675.

8. Shemot Rabbah 3:1 on Exod. 3:6.

9. See Samuel, Kings, and the canonical prophets.

10. See Exod. 28:15–30; Lev. 24:10–14; Num. 9:1–14, Num. 36.

11. See Judges, Samuel, and Kings, *seriatim*.

12. Richard E. Friedman, *The Disappearance of God: A Divine Mystery* (Boston: Little, Brown, 1995).

13. See, for example, Ezek. 11; Jer. 7.

14. For example, cf. Isa. 40, 42, 49:14–21, 51:17–23, 54:4–10; Jer. 7, 9, 12, 16, 23, 25, 32–33; Hosea 1–3.

15. See Irving Greenberg, *For the Sake of Heaven and Earth: The New Encounter between Judaism and Christianity* (Philadelphia: Jewish Publication Society, 2004), 64–75, 98–102, 124–41, 144–61, 162–84.

16. BT Bava Metzia 59B.

17. BT Bava Batra 12A.

18. BT Shabbat 119B. Cf. Joseph B. Soloveitchik, *Halakhic Man* (Philadelphia: Jewish Publication Society, 1983), 105–6.

19. See Joseph B. Soloveitchik, "The Lonely Man of Faith," *Tradition* 7, no. 2 (Summer 1965): 34–38.

20. BT Hullin 139B.

21. See the interpretation of Esther 6:1 in BT Megillah 15B.

22. See on all this BT Gittin 55B–57B and its treatment in Jeffrey L. Rubenstein, *Rabbinic Stories* (New York: Paulist Press, 2002), 38–49.

23. BT Yoma 9B.

24. Shabbat 88A.

10. Modernity

1. Richard E. Friedman, *The Disappearance of God* (Boston: Little, Brown, 1995).

2. Jonathan Israel, *Enlightenment Contested: Philosophy, Modernity, and the Emancipation of Man, 1670–1752* (New York: Oxford University Press, 2006), 61–222.

3. See for example, Mark C. Taylor, *After God* (Chicago: University of Chicago Press, 2007), 165, 187ff.

4. William D. Nordhaus, "Irving Fisher and the Contribution of Improved Longevity to Living Standards," *American Journal of Economics and Sociology* 64, no. 1 (2005): 367–92.

5. Thomas Pakenham, *The Scramble for Africa: The White Man's Conquest of the Dark Continent from 1876 to 1912* (London: Abacus, 1992); David van Reybrouck, *Congo: The Epic History of a People* (New York: Harper Collins, 2014).

6. See Robert D. Putnam, *Bowling Alone: The Collapse and Revival of American Community* (New York: Simon and Schuster, 2000) for a portrayal of the decline of community, the growth of a poorly balanced individualist culture, and a consequent weakening of cohesion in society.

7. "Declaration of Principles—The Pittsburgh Platform," Central Conference of American Rabbis (November 16–19, 1885), https://www.ccarnet.org /rabbinic-voice/platforms/article-declaration-principles/.

8. "Declaration of Principles," Central Conference of American Rabbis.

9. "Declaration of Principles," Central Conference of American Rabbis.

10. "Declaration of Principles," Central Conference of American Rabbis.

11. Both approaches are stressed in S. R. Hirsch, *Nineteen Letters of Ben Uziel* (Jerusalem: Feldheim, 1995).

12. See for example, Hirsch, "Seventh Letter: Yisroel among the Nations," in *Nineteen Letters of Ben Uziel*, 104–7.

13. How else can one explain the widespread Orthodox rabbinic refusal to unleash all the systemic mechanisms found in halakhah to free *agunot*? For a dramatization of the issue of suppressing the emotion of compassion in order to uphold a law that denies individual love and fulfillment, see David Hartman, *The God Who Hates Lies* (Nashville TN: Jewish Lights, 2010), 111–32. Blu Greenberg, *On Women and Judaism: A View from Tradition* (Philadelphia: Jewish Publication Society, 1981) portrays many areas where the tradition gives women less than equality or justice but has managed not to recognize this.

14. Maimonides, *Mishneh Torah*, Sefer Zemanim, Hilkhot Shabbat, 2:3.

15. Maimonides, *Mishneh Torah*, Sefer Zemanim, Hilkhot Shabbat, 2:3. This is actually a quote and a broadened application of a verse from Ezek. 20:25.

11. The Holocaust

1. Cf. Henry Friedlander, *The Origins of Nazi Genocide: From Euthanasia to the Final Solution* (Chapel Hill: University of North Carolina Press, 1995).

2. See on this Ingo Muller, *Hitler's Justice: The Courts of the Third Reich* (Cambridge MA: Harvard University Press, 1994).

3. Raul Hilberg, *The Destruction of the European Jews*, 3rd edition (New Haven CT: Yale University Press, 2003), vol. 2, 424–33, 434–500, 584–99, 599–702, and vol. 3, 1077ff. See also Christopher Browning, *The Path to Genocide* (Cambridge: Cambridge University Press, 1992), 125–44; Christopher Browning and Jurgen Matthaus, *The Origins of the Final Solution* (Lincoln: University of Nebraska Press, 2014), 398–415; Uwe Adam, *Juden Politik im Dritten Reich* (Dusseldorf: Droste Verlag, 1972); Raul Hilberg, "German Railroads / Jewish

Souls," in *The Nazi Holocaust: Historical Articles on the Destruction of the European Jews*, ed. Michael Marrus (Westport CT: Meckler, 1989).

4. From a speech by Heinrich Himmler before senior SS officers in Poznan, October 4, 1943. See document no. 161 in *Documents on the Holocaust: Selected Sources on the Destruction of the Jews of Germany and Austria, Poland and the Soviet Union* (Jerusalem: Yad Vashem, 1981), 344–45.

5. "Protocol of the Wannsee Conference, January 20, 1942," Yad Vashem, https://www.yadvashem.org/docs/wannsee-conference-protocol.html.

6. See Claudia Koonz, *The Nazi Conscience* (Cambridge MA: Belknap Press, 2003), 7.

7. See on this A. Roy Eckardt, *Elder and Younger Brothers: The Encounter of Jews and Christians* (New York: Schocken Books, 1973).

8. Eric Metaxas, *Bonhoeffer: Pastor, Martyr, Prophet, Spy* (Nashville TN: Thomas Nelson, 2010), 346.

9. The research of Eliezer Schwartz establishes that IG Farben managers made matters even worse. IG Farben constructed a factory complex at Auschwitz (the camp known as "Buna") for the manufacture of synthetic rubber and fuel. The choice of location was significantly influenced by the promise of an endless, cheap supply of Jewish forced laborers from Auschwitz-Birkenau. Egregious failures in the planning and construction inflated costs and delayed completion. To cut machinery and fuel costs, the company had the prisoners do the work of heavy hauling machines. To overcome the delays, IG Farben's managers subjected the forced laborers to brutal treatment and an extra forced pace, which spent their strength rapidly. Then they were quickly dispatched to Birkenau for gassing. Eliezer Schwartz, "The Role of IG Farben-Auschwitz in the Construction of the Birkenau Extermination Camp," *Yad Vashem Studies* 38, no. 2 (2010): 11–45.

10. Fred Taylor, ed., *The Goebbels Diaries, 1939-1941* (New York: G. P. Putnam and Sons, 1983), 23.

11. Kurt Schlesinger, "One Man's Passage," typescript memoir given to the author by Schlesinger's grandson, Mark Rosenbaum, of Portland, Oregon, 20-25. Schlesinger, an established Jewish lawyer with good connections, continued to represent his Jewish clients to the authorities as best he could, but after Kristallnacht, everything broke down (24-25).

12. See Joe O'Connor, "Being Jewish Meant Being Dead," *Martyrdom and Resistance* 40, no. 2 (November/December 2013): 6.

13. Wolfgang Sofsky, *The Order of Terror: The Concentration Camp* (Princeton NJ: Princeton University Press, 1992), 35.

14. Primo Levi, *Survival in Auschwitz* (London: Penguin Books, 1979), 90.

15. Alon Confino, *A World without Jews* (New Haven CT: Yale University Press, 2014).

16. Saul Friedlander, *Nazi Germany and the Jews, Volume 1: The Years of Persecution, 1933–1939* (New York: Harper, 1998), 116.

17. Cited in Saul Friedlander, *Nazi Germany and the Jews, Volume 2: The Years of Extermination, 1939–1945* (New York: Harper, 2007), 83.

18. See the article by Dov Levin, "How the Jewish Police in the Kovno Ghetto Saw Itself," Yad Vashem, https://www.yadvashem.org/yv/en/exhibitions/through-the-lens/images/until-last-jew/dov_levin.pdf. Mark Dworzecki, a doctor in the Vilna ghetto, describes how the Jewish women temporized, delaying their abortions while risking being detected as they clung to some hope that the tide of war would shift or the decree would be lifted. They waited desperately for some word from the Yalta Conference meeting of Roosevelt, Churchill, and Stalin, imagining that the world leaders would demand that the Nazis moderate their assault on the Jews.

19. Avraham Tory, *Surviving the Holocaust: The Kovno Ghetto Diary* (Cambridge MA: Harvard University Press, 1991), 114. See also the Shoah Resource Center, www.yadvashem.org.

20. Jonathan Harrison, "'Pregnant Women Will Be Put to Death': Policies on Childbirth," *Holocaust Controversies* (blog), December 22, 2012, http://holocaustcontroversies.blogspot.com/2012/12/pregnant-women-will-be-put-to-death.html.

21. Rivka Yosselevska's testimony is reprinted in Raul Hilberg, *Documents of Destruction* (Chicago: Quadrangle, 1971), 59–67.

22. See Samuel Kassow, *Who Will Write Our History? Emanuel Ringelblum, the Warsaw Ghetto, and the Oyneg Shabes Archive* (Bloomington: Indiana University Press, 2007). A documentary film based on this book, *Who Will Write Our History*, by Roberta Grossman, produced by Nancy Spielberg, was released in 2018.

23. Myron Winick, ed., *Hunger Disease: Studies by the Jewish Physicians in the Warsaw Ghetto* (New York: Wiley, 1979).

24. See Isaiah Trunk, *Judenrat: The Jewish Councils in Eastern Europe under Nazi Occupation* (Lincoln: University of Nebraska Press, 1946).

25. The following account is primarily based on Menachem Keren-Kratz, *The Satmar Rebbi: Rabbe Yoel Teitelbaum*, a forthcoming biography excerpted in "Hast Thou Escaped and Also Taken Possession? The Responses of the Satmar Rebbe—Rabbi Yoel Teitelbaum—and His Followers to Criticism of His Conduct during and after the Holocaust," in *Dapim: Studies on the Holo-*

caust 28, no. 2 (2014): 97–120, and adapted online in "The Satmar Rebbe and the Destruction of Hungarian Jewry," *Tablet*, part 1, July 16, 2014, https://www.tabletmag.com/sections/arts-letters/articles/satmar-rebbe-1, and part 2, July 17, 2014, https://www.tabletmag.com/sections/arts-letters/articles/satmar-rebbe-2.

26. Yoel Teitelbaum, *Kuntres al HaGeulah v'al HaTemurah* [On redemption and on exchange] (Brooklyn NY: Sender Deutch Printers, 1966).

27. Elchanan Wasserman, "Ikvita d'Meschichah" (New York, 1938) excerpts in Steven T. Katz, Shlomo Biederman, Gershon Greenberg, eds., *Wrestling with God: Jewish Theological Responses During and After the Holocaust* (Oxford: Oxford University Press, 2007), 35–36.

28. Fred Skolnik, ed., *Encyclopedia Judaica*, 2nd edition (Jerusalem: Keter Publishing, 1973), vol. 16, column 362.

29. S. B. Unsdorfer, "Siftei Shlomo, Vayehi" (January 3, 1942), excerpted in Katz et al., *Wrestling with God*, 58.

30. The response is printed in Joseph Kermish, ed., *To Live with Honor and Die with Honor: Documents from the Warsaw Ghetto Underground Archives* (Jerusalem: Yad Vashem, 1986), 795–96.

31. Title transcribed as "Fire of Holiness" by Nehemia Polen in his PhD thesis and his article "Divine Weeping: Rabbi Kalonymos Shapiro's Theology of Catastrophe in the Warsaw Ghetto," *Modern Judaism* 7, no. 3 (October 1987): 253–69. In this chapter the author uses the English translation by J. Hershy Worch, *Sacred Fire: Torah from the Years of Fury 1939–1942* (Northvale NJ: Jason Aronson, 2000).

32. Shapira, *Sacred Fire*, 13–14. The author is indebted to Don Seeman for reporting this extraordinary move in his article, "Ritual Efficacy, Hasidic Mysticism and 'Useless Suffering' in the Warsaw Ghetto," *Harvard Theological Review* 101, nos. 3–4 (2008): 465–505. See esp. 483–87.

33. Shapira, *Sacred Fire*, 255.

34. Shapira, *Sacred Fire*, 187.

35. Shapira, *Sacred Fire*, 288, 210.

36. See Polen, "Divine Weeping," 257.

37. Polen, "Divine Weeping," 236.

38. Yissachar Shlomo Teichtal, *Eim Habanim Semaycha*, reprint (Jerusalem: Urim Publications, 2013).

12. Responses after the Holocaust

1. Jonathan Sacks, ed., *Koren Siddur* (Jerusalem: Koren Publishers, 2009), 136.

2. Rachel Auerbach, "In the Fields of Treblinka," reprinted in *The Death Camp Treblinka: A Documentary*, ed. Alexander Donat (New York: Holocaust Remembrance Library, n.d.), 37.

3. Traditional morning prayer service, author's translation.

4. Quoted in Roger Manvell, *S.S. and Gestapo: Rule by Terror* (New York: Ballantine Books, 1969), 109.

5. "You are my witnesses, says the Lord, and I am God" (Isa. 43:12).

6. Elie Wiesel, "Jewish Values in the Post-Holocaust Future," *Judaism* 16, no. 3 (Summer 1967): 261.

7. See A. Roy Eckardt, "Recantation of the Covenant," in *Confronting the Holocaust: The Impact of Elie Wiesel*, ed. Alvin Rosenfeld and Irving Greenberg (Bloomington: Indiana University Press, 1978), 163ff. See also the author's expanded comments on this paper in Irving Greenberg, *For the Sake of Heaven and Earth: The New Encounter between Judaism and Christianity* (Philadelphia: Jewish Publication Society, 2004), 26–31.

8. See Irving Greenberg, "Cloud of Smoke, Pillar of Fire: Judaism, Christianity and Modernity after the Holocaust," in *Auschwitz: Beginning a New Era?*, ed. Eva Fleischner (New York: Ktav, 1977), 441.

9. Benjamin Lau, "A Farewell to My Father, Naphtali Lau-Lavie," *Times of Israel*, December 15, 2014, https://blogs.timesofisrael.com/a-farewell-to-my-father-naphtali-lau-lavie/.

10. Irving Greenberg, *Voluntary Covenant* (New York: Perspectives, National Jewish Center for Learning and Leadership, 1982), 35.

11. Greenberg, *Voluntary Covenant*, 43n60.

12. Katz also argued that the author's use of the term "paradox" did not solve the credibility problem in employing and affirming contradiction. Steven Katz, "Irving Greenberg and the Voluntary Covenant," in *Historicism, the Holocaust and Zionism* (New York: NYU Press, 1962), 225–50. For the author's argument that the freely accepted *brit* would evoke higher commitment levels, see Greenberg, *Voluntary Covenant*, 39–40, 41–42.

13. Some of the developments can be tracked in the essays published in Irving Greenberg, *For the Sake of Heaven and Earth: The New Encounter between Judaism and Christianity* (Philadelphia: Jewish Publication Society, 2004), 103–234.

14. Evan Burr Bukey, *Jews and Intermarriage in Nazi Austria* (Cambridge: Cambridge University Press, 2010), 80ff.

15. On Bulgaria, see Tzvetan Todorov, *The Fragility of Goodness* (Princeton NJ: Princeton University Press, 2003); and compare Randolph Braham, "The German Allied States and the Holocaust: A Comparative Overview," *Yad*

Vashem Studies 47 (2013): 129–50. In Serbia and Croatia, governments led by aggressive antisemites, most of the Jews were killed. On Denmark, see Bo Lidegard, *Countrymen* (New York: Knopf, 2013). On Albania, see Harvey Sarnar, *Rescue in Albania* (Toronto: Brunswick Press, 1997).

16. Christoph Dieckmann, *Deutsche Besatzungspolitik in Litauen, 1941–1944* [German occupation policies in Lithuania 1941–1944] (Göttingen: Wallstein Verlag, 2016) describes the antisemitic legislation and murders of Jews carried out by an extreme right Lithuanian government installed by the Nazis. Donald Bloxham, *The Final Solution: A Genocide* (Oxford: Oxford University Press, 2009) points out that active local collaboration in the murder of the Lithuanian Jews confirmed the Nazis' feeling that a policy of killing all the Jews was possible and would not be opposed or condemned by the surrounding populations.

17. This observation should be parsed in two ways. First, God is speaking through *tzimtzum* (self-reduction) while being fully present among the suffering. The author admits that even religious leadership mostly failed to hear the Divine message. Second, God speaks through human agents. Here the letters, appeals, applications for visas of millions of people communicated the message but few listened or heard. For example, the failure of the mainstream press to cover the ongoing Holocaust except in marginal ways turned out to be devastating in failing to generate human pleas for help. Laurel Leff, *Buried by the Times: The Holocaust and America's Most Important Newspaper* (Cambridge: Cambridge University Press, 2005); Deborah Lipstadt, *Beyond Belief: The American Press and the Coming of the Holocaust* (New York: Free Press, 1986).

18. For a history of the women's movement, see Ruth Rosen, *The World Split Open: How the Modern Women's Movement Changed America* (New York: Viking, 2000).

19. For a history of the LGBTQ+ liberation movement, see John D'Emilio and Estelle B. Freedman, *Intimate Matters: A History of Sexuality in America* (Chicago: University of Chicago, 1998), 301–60. For a history of the disability rights movement, see Judith Heumann with Kristen Joiner, *Being Heumann: An Unrepentant Memoir of a Disability Rights Activist* (Boston: Beacon, 2020).

20. Yosef Mendelevich's speech at the American Jewish Historical Society event honoring Soviet Jewish activists and marking the creation of an archive of the Soviet Jewry movement at AJHS, November 20, 2013. See his full account in his memoir, Yosef Mendelevich, *Unbroken Spirit: A Heroic Story of Faith, Courage, and Survival* (Jerusalem: Gefen, 2012).

21. See, for example, M. K. Gandhi, "The Jews," *Harijan*, November 28, 1935. Gandhi commented that if ever a war by Britain and France would be justified, it would be to fight Hitler. Still, he insisted that no war is ever right. George Orwell's critique, "Reflections on Gandhi," was first published in *Partisan Review* 16, no. 1 (January 1949): 85–92.

22. Judith M. Brown, in her biography, *Gandhi, Prisoner of Hope* (New Haven CT: Yale University Press, 1989), comes to a conclusion similar to Orwell's.

23. R. J. Rummel, "Democracy, Power, Genocide, and Mass Murder," *Journal of Conflict Resolution* 39, no. 1 (March 1995): 3–26.

24. Irving Greenberg, "Theology after the Shoah: The Transformation of the Core Paradigm," *Modern Judaism* 26, no. 3 (October 2006): 213–39.

25. Leonard Cohen, "Anthem," *The Future*, Columbia Records, 1992.

26. Greenberg, "Theology after the Shoah," 227.

27. See Irving Greenberg, *For the Sake of Heaven and Earth: The New Encounter between Judaism and Christianity* (Philadelphia: Jewish Publication Society, 2004).

28. BT Yevamot 63B.

29. Chayim Yachil, "The Activity of the Palestinian Mission to the She'arit Hapleta, 1945–1949," *Yalkut Moreshet* 30 (1980): 31 [Hebrew].

30. See David Gushee, *The Righteous Gentiles of the Holocaust* (Minneapolis MN: Paragon House, 1994), 91–117; Samuel Oliner and Pearl Oliner, *The Altruistic Personality* (New York: Free Press, 1988), 19–141; Nechama Tec, *When Light Pierced the Darkness* (New York: Oxford University Press, 1986), 113–93.

31. United Nations General Assembly, "The Universal Declaration of Human Rights," December 10, 1948, https://www.un.org/en/about-us/universal-declaration-of-human-rights#.

32. Joseph B. Soloveitchik, *Man of Faith in the Modern World: Reflections of the Rav*, vol. 2, ed. A. R. Besdin (New York: Ktav, 1989), 84–85.

33. Ahron Soloveitchik, *Logic of the Mind, Logic of the Heart: Wisdom and Reflections on Topics of Our Times* (Jerusalem: Genesis Jerusalem Press, 1991), 92–97.

34. See Blu Greenberg, *On Women and Judaism: A View from Tradition* (Philadelphia: Jewish Publication Society, 1981), and many subsequent publications.

35. Compare this with "The land must not be sold permanently, for the land is Mine" (Lev. 25:23).

36. See the treatments in Yair Sheleg, "Ushlaḥ orkha l'rasheha, sareha, v'yo'atzeha," *Ha'aretz*, February 5, 2008; Joseph Taboury, "The Piety of Politics: Jewish Prayers for the State of Israel," in *Liturgy and the Life of the Syn-*

agogue, ed. Ruth Langer and Steve Fine (University Park PA: Eisenbrauns, 2008), 225–46.

37. Irving Greenberg "Toward Jewish Religious Unity: A Symposium," *Judaism* 15, no. 2 (Spring 1966): 135.

38. Many personal conversations between the author and Rabbi David Hartman from 1970 to 2013.

13. The State of Israel

1. See Shlomo Avineri, *Herzl's Vision: Theodor Herzl and the Foundation of the Jewish State* (Katonah NY: Blue Bridge, 2011), esp. 52–82, 114–40.

2. Quoted in Shabtai Teveth, *Ben-Gurion: The Burning Ground, 1886–1948* (Boston: Houghton Mifflin, 1987), 846.

3. Quoted in Martin Gilbert, *Israel: A History* (New York: William Morrow, 1998), 181.

4. Provisional Government of Israel, *Declaration of the Establishment of the State of Israel* (Tel Aviv: *Official Gazette,* no. 1, May 14, 1948). The aspiration for "freedom, justice, and peace" confirmed Isaiah's proclamation that Israel would be "a light unto the nations" (Isa. 42:6).

5. Dan Senor and Saul Singer, *Start-Up Nation: The Story of Israel's Economic Miracle* (New York: Twelve, 2011).

6. Israel was ranked the fourth strongest military power in the world by the *US News & World Report,* "2022 Best Countries," https://www.usnews.com /news/best-countries/israel/. See "Israel Ranks among 10 Most Powerful Countries in Annual List: 4th Strongest Military," *Times of Israel,* January 2, 2023, https://www.timesofisrael.com/israel-among-10-most-powerful -countries-in-the-world-in-annual-list/.

7. "Israel Defense Forces: Ruach Tzahal—Code of Ethics," Jewish Virtual Library, https://www.jewishvirtuallibrary.org/ruach-tzahal-idf-code-of-ethics.

8. Israel Ministry of Foreign Affairs, *The 2014 Gaza Conflict: Factual and Legal Aspects* (June 14, 2015), gov.il/en/Departments/General/operation -protective-edge-full-report.

9. "Report: Israel Paid Ceausescu Cash for Jewish Immigrants," *Associated Press News,* December 30, 1989, https://apnews.com/article /9b8131f4d99dddbd1de1ba8d9e452a0e.

10. "Israel's Fertility Rate Is Far Higher than Rest of OECD," *Times of Israel,* March 14, 2018, https://www.timesofisrael.com/report-finds-israels -fertility-rate-significantly-higher-than-rest-of-oecd/. See also Sergio Del-

laPergola, "Actual, Intended and Appropriate Family Size among Jews in Israel," *Contemporary Jewry* 29, no. 2 (2009): 127–52.

11. See "Israel Independence Day, Remembrance Day: A Hard-Won Miracle," JPost editorial, *Jerusalem Post*, April 25, 2023, https://www.jpost.com/opinion/article-740177.

12. "World Economic Outlook Database," October 2022, Israel, International Monetary Fund, https://www.imf.org/en/Publications/weo/weo-database/2022/October/weo-report?c=436,&s=ngdp_rpch,ngdpd,pppgdp,ngdpdpc,ppppc,pcpipch,lur,ggxwdg_ngdp,&sy=1980&ey=2027&ssm=0&scsm=1&scc=0&ssd=1&ssc=0&sic=0&sort=country&ds=.&br=1.

13. Guttman Israel Institute of Applied Social Research, *Israel—Jews: A Portrait, Beliefs, Observance of Tradition and Values of Jews in Israel, 2000* (Jerusalem: Israel Institute of Democracy, 2002).

14. See Joshua Muravchik, *Making David into Goliath: How the World Turned against Israel* (New York: Encounter Books, 2015).

15. BT Bava Batra 12B.

14. Judaism in the Third Era

1. Letter from Bonhoeffer to Eberhard Bethge, May 29, 1944, in Dietrich Bonhoeffer, *Letters and Papers from Prison* (New York: Simon and Schuster, 1997), 404–7.

2. See Mishnah Avot, ch. 6, m. 2.

3. JT Kiddushin ch. 4, h. 12.

4. Hanoch Ben-Pazi, "Holiness Streams toward the Future: Sexuality in Rav Kook's Thought," *Nashim: A Journal of Jewish Women's Studies and Gender Issues* 21 (Spring 2011): 160–78.

5. "Between them": BT Sotah 17A.

6. Interestingly, the Torah does not address lesbianism. The intensity of its condemnation of males engaged in homosexual activity undoubtedly played a role in the Rabbinic tradition's conclusion that lesbianism was also a prohibited activity. Yet these prohibitions are phrased in far milder language. See Reena Zeidman, "Marginal Discourse: Lesbianism in Jewish Law," in *Women in Judaism: A Multidisciplinary E-Journal* 1 (1997).

7. Compare Jer. 7, where the prophet condemns those who meticulously honor the rules of the Holy Temple and of sacrifice, even as they oppress the workers and the poor. This offends God, who abandons such dens of thievery and oppression and allows them to be destroyed.

8. See Jacob Milgrom, *Leviticus 1–16*, Anchor Yale Bible Commentaries (New

York: Doubleday, 1991), 251–64ff, 1033ff. See also Jacob Milgrom, "Israel's Sanctuary: The Priestly 'Picture of Dorian Gray'," in *Studies in Cultic Theology and Terminology* (Leiden, Neth.: E. J. Brill, 1983), 75–84.

9. See the panel's position paper on their ruling, archived on the Orthodox Union's website, at ou.org/assets/Responses-of-Rabbinic-Panel.pdf.

10. Joseph B. Soloveitchik, "Slavery and Freedom," in *Festival of Freedom* (Jersey City NJ: Ktav, 2006), 35–54.

11. See "Feminist Jewish Ritual: The United States," *Jewish Women's Archive*, updated June 23, 2021, jwa.org/encyclopedia/article/ritual-in-united-states #pid-17101.

12. Mishnah Arakhin, ch. 1, m. 1.

13. For more, see Julia Watts Belser, *Loving Our Own Bones: Disability Wisdom and the Spiritual Subversiveness of Knowing Ourselves Whole* (Boston: Beacon, 2023).

14. JT Nedarim, ch. 9, h. 4.

15. Compare, for example, the Kaufmann manuscript of the Mishnah (Sanhedrin, ch. 4, m. 5) and the Vilna edition of the Babylonian Talmud (Sanhedrin 37A).

16. BT Yevamot 61A.

17. BT Shabbat 31A.

18. See BT Shabbat 88A and Tosafot s.v. *moda'a rabbah l'orayta*; see also Carey A. Moore, "The Additions to Esther," in *Daniel, Esther and Jeremiah: The Additions*, Anchor Yale Bible Commentaries (New York: Doubleday, 1977), 151–252.

19. See Abba Kovner, *Scrolls of Testimony* (Philadelphia: Jewish Publication Society, 2001).

20. For example: seeing God in the miraculous laws of nature described by physics and in the unbelievably rich biological systems and their fine-tuned interaction with each other.

21. Seymour Lachman and Barry Kosmin, *One Nation under God: Religion in Contemporary American Society* (New York: Harmony Books, 1993).

22. Donald Feldstein, "The Jewish Federations: The First Hundred Years," *Journal of Jewish Communal Service* 72, nos. 1–2 (Fall/Winter 1995/96): 5–11.

23. BT Bava Batra 12B—from the time of the destruction of the Temple, prophecy was taken away (and authority given to the *hakhamim* [wise men and Rabbis]).

24. The *baraita* of Rabbi Yishmael, appended to the beginning of the Sifra. These thirteen interpretive principles were placed in the early prayer book to be recited in the sacrifices section. These passages were studied as

Talmud but primarily "reminds us of the indissoluble connection between the Written Law (the Mosaic books) and the Oral Law (Mishna, Midrash and Talmud)," Jonathan Sacks, ed., *Koren Siddur* (Jerusalem: Koren Publishers, 2009), 54.

25. Mishnah Avot, ch. 5, m. 17. The Mishnah holds that disagreements motivated by presumption and falsehood are illegitimate. By contrast, the method of analysis and disagreements used by the schools of Hillel and Shammai is affirmed as legitimate and constructive. Out of such disagreements emerges the [multiple] truth and correct application(s) of the word of God.

26. BT Shabbat 23A.

27. For a comprehensive and detailed exposition see Irving Greenberg, "On the Road to a New Encounter between Judaism and Christianity: A Personal Journey," in *For the Sake of Heaven and Earth: The New Encounter between Judaism and Christianity* (Philadelphia: Jewish Publication Society, 2004), 3–48.

28. See Robert Wistrich, *Antisemitism, the Longest Hatred* (New York: Pantheon, 1992).

Index

Bush administration, 30
bystanders, 242

Cambodia, 105
Camus, Albert, 235
Canaanite slaves, 112
capacities: Divine, 18, 19–20, 27, 42–
    43; human, 27, 38–44, 60, 81, 108,
    135–37, 158, 168–69, 184, 230, 249,
    290, 304
capital punishment, 27–28, 333n2
cardinal sins of Jewish tradition, 91
casualties, civilian, 273, 284
Catholic Church, 158
Central Bureau (Hungary), 226
Chabad, 263–64, 317
chaos, 15–17, 21
checks and balances, 159, 249–50
children, 29–30, 80–86, 126
Children of Israel, 169–70, 173
China, 49, 105, 145–46
choice. See *tikkun olam* (world repair)
choose life, 44, 67, 72, 131–32, 134–37,
    295
chosenness, 194, 293
Christians/Christianity, 3, 97; and cov-
    enantal community, 126; and the
    covenant of redemption, 133; and
    God as the sole redeemer, 98; and
    Jewish-Christian dialogue, 133,
    254, 259–60, 323; and messianism,
    265; and movements, 103–5; and
    Nazi ideology, 218; and pluralism,
    323–24; and Rabbinic Judaism,
    173; and religion-based hatred of
    Jews, 309; and resurrection, 57, 59;
    and role models, 157–58; and the
    world-to-come, 87, 100

Christian Science, 22
Churchill, Winston, 114, 350n18
circumcision, 162–63, 166–67, 333n9
citizenship, 193, 194, 196, 215, 257, 270,
    276, 282, 305, 310, 343–44n10
civil rights, 246–47
Civil War (U.S.), 113
CLAL. *See* The National Jewish Center
    for Learning and Leadership
    (CLAL)
Cleaver, Eldridge, 246–47
coercion, 107–10, 111, 152–53, 178, 290
Cohen, Leonard, 253
commandments, 75–94; and the
    "great principle" as the root of
    mitzvot, 75–80; and increase of
    life, 80–86; and negative com-
    mandments, 340–41n21; and
    pluralism, 319; and positive com-
    mandments, 340n21; and the
    primacy of saving a life, 86–94;
    and ritual commandments, 78–
    80; and suspended Shabbat, 90,
    341n34
commitment, 120–25, 128, 131
communism, 97, 104–5, 189, 208–9,
    217, 275
completion, 23, 132–34, 161, 292
conflict, asymmetrical, 273
Congregation of Israel, 231
Conservative movement, 320
consumerism, 193, 197
continuity, 151, 162–63, 287, 291, 311, 315
conversion, 87, 163, 271
cosmic processes, 15, 21–22, 55, 322
cosmos, 13, 15–18, 140, 188, 268
counterlife, 47
countervoices, 253–54

Crusades, 87
cultural assumptions, 149, 152
cultural Jews, 167
cultural minorities, 247
cultural Zionists, 196

daily life, expanding holiness in, 300–303
Dalai Lama, 102–3
Damascus Covenant, 341n33
day schools, 248, 305, 317
the dead, 56, 57, 63, 71–72, 76, 93
deaf-mutes, 308
death: assault of on Jews and Judaism, 218–24; and biblical struggle of life against death, 62–74; and choosing life, 134–37; and human power, 241–44; and martyrdom, 87–88; and restoring the image of God, 255; and resurrection, 56–61; and revelation, 21; and the rhythms of Creation, 17–18; and the supremacy of life, 75–94; and *tikkun olam*, 53–56; and voluntary covenant, 238–39
decision-making, 128, 203, 205, 250, 318
degradation, 42, 48–49, 59, 93–94, 116, 190, 221, 259, 309–11
dehumanization, 51, 219, 256
Deity, 40, 92, 152, 188, 240, 289
democracy, 114, 196, 206, 208–11, 250, 278–81, 287
demographic growth, 276–77
demonic forces, 71–72, 186, 337n8
Denmark and Danish Jewry, 242–43
dependability, 121–22
derashot (sermons), 229–30

destruction of the Temple, 157, 171–72, 174, 176–77, 315, 357n23
Deuteronomy, 39, 57, 173
devaluation, 310–11
dialectical materialism, 104
Diaspora and diaspora Jewry, 1, 144, 263, 267, 275–76, 277–78, 280, 286–87, 290, 317
dictatorships, 52, 257, 278
dietary rituals, 67–70, 332n11
dignities of human beings. *See* equality; infinite value; uniqueness
dignities of the image of God, 27–34, 76–78, 303–4
dignity, 48–50, 150; of all life, 23–26; of animal life, 295; of the disabled, 247, 308; and equality, 291; women, 51, 306–7; of workers, 302
disability inclusion, 247, 307–8
disagreements, 340n16, 358n25
discrimination, 32, 51–52, 276
dissolution, 277
distinctiveness, 248, 305–6, 311, 312, 316
diverse covenants, 147
diverse religions, 311
diversity, 308
Divine behavior, 20, 149
Divine delegation of power, 303–4, 322
Divine emotion, 119–20
Divine freedom, 20, 43
Divine-human partnership, 39–40, 107, 110–11, 152–59, 160, 169, 175, 187–90, 245, 289–92, 301, 322, 324. *See also* covenantal partnership
Divine image, 79–80, 298
Divine initiative, 173, 183, 324
Divine interventions, 2, 38, 168, 177, 183–85, 188

government regulation and legislation, 303

Great Britain, 244, 278

great eras of Jewish history, three, 327–29

"great principle," 75–80

Greek Empire, 89–90

Greek Orthodox tradition, 87

Greenberg, Blu, 259, 307

Greenberg, Moshe, 29

Gush Emunim (Bloc of the faithful), 263, 282

Haganah (Zionist military force), 269

Hagar, 155–56

hakhel (assembly) ceremony, 167

halakhah/halakhot (Jewish law): of daily life, 267; and the dignity of life, 23–25; and disability inclusion, 308; and halakhic behaviors, 129, 303; and human pace, 149–51; and ideal norms, 112; and increase of life, 84; of kashrut, 294–96; and messianism, 264–65; and modernity, 201–7; and pluralism, 320; and preparing food, 295; and Rabbinic culture, 267–68; releases those who are not free and equal, 306; and religious response, 304; and upgrading the image of God, 259

Halakhic Man (Soloveitchik), 333n3

halutzim (pioneers), 268–69

Haman, 176, 221

Hamas, 273, 280–81, 282–85

hametz (leavened) products, 203

Hanukkah, 79, 88

haredi Jews or *haredim*, 198–99, 201, 205–6, 232–33, 258, 272, 279, 286, 305–6, 320–21, 322

haredi religious parties, 279

harhakot (distancings), 297

Hartman, Rabbi David, 203, 264, 319–20

hashgahah (Divine Providence), 132–33

Hasidism, 198, 226

Hasmonean rulers, 159

Hatam Sofer. *See* Sopher, Rabbi Moses

Hebrew Bible, 217

Hebrew language, 268, 277

Hebrew prophets, 47, 133

Hebrew slaves, 112–13

hegemony, cultural, 251

Held, Rabbi Shai, 167

Hellenism, 172

Herzl, Theodor, 195–96, 268, 278

hester panim (hiddenness of God's face), 230

heter, 205

Heydrich, Reinhard, 222

Hezbollah, 275, 284

hidden God, 175, 178, 184–85, 240–41, 293, 299, 312–13, 314, 317, 319, 325

hiddenness, 176, 184–85, 236, 240–41

Hillel, 131, 310, 317

hillul ha-Shem (desecration of God's name), 127

Himmler, Heinrich, 215, 235

Hinduism, 87, 101–3

Hirsch, Rabbi Samson Raphael, 200–201

historical outcomes, 176–77

Hitler, Adolf, 105, 210, 216, 227, 239, 241–42, 248

hol, 72–73

Intifada, 283
intrinsic dignities, 32–33, 35, 52, 53, 75, 76–77
Iran, 275, 284–85
Isaac, 1, 155–56, 230, 267
Isaiah, 42–43, 46, 50, 52, 54–55, 56, 62, 74, 84, 132, 153–54, 307–8, 311, 355n4
Ishmael, 156
Islam, 87, 97, 98, 100, 126
Israel, Land of: *aliyah* (immigration) to, 199; and the creation of the State of Israel, 266; and idolatry, 148–49, 309; and Jewish sovereignty, 267; and maturation in the covenant, 169–79; and ongoing renewal, 167; and prophets, 46–47; and responses after the Holocaust, 225–36; and rituals, 64–72; and *shemitah* (sabbatical year), 204–5
Israel, State of, 2, 266–88; and American Jewry, 142–43; Basic Laws of, 279; creation of, 262, 266, 271; declaration of independence, 270, 28; in an era of hope but no certainty, 287–88; and an ethic of power, 271–75; and democracy, 278–81; and Diaspora relations, 286–87; and Ethiopian Jewry, 144; and Federations, 316; and growth, 275–78; and human assumption of power, 199; and immersive Jewish experiences, 317; and the Jewish past, 270–71; and Jewish people's contribution in the Third Era, 290; and the Law of Return, 257, 270, 276; and the messianism

of human life and dignity, 262–65; and modernity, 206–7, 209–10; and the Palestinians, 281–85; and religious pluralism, 285–86; and responses after the Holocaust, 235–36; and response to the message of modernity, 267–70; and the responsibility to assume power, 266–67; and restoring the image of God, 257; Supreme Court of, 273, 279, 286
Israel Defense Forces (IDF), 272–75
Israel fatigue, 286–87
Israeli Arabs, 272, 279
Israeli rabbinate, 262, 279
Israelites, people of Israel 6, 13, 15, 46, 112, 119, 123, 125–127, 148, 154, 156, 167, 169–172, 225–226, 309; and the covenantal relationship, 118–20, 123–27; as covenantal role model, 153–154; and the covenantal way of life, 112; and divine love, 42–43; and holiness, 64–70, 72; and human scale, 140
Israel's press, 272–73

Jacob, 58, 156, 267
JDC. *See* American Jewish Joint Distribution Committee (JDC)
Jeremiah, 113, 119
Jerusalem, 65, 157, 167, 226
Jerusalem Talmud, 75
Jew by choice, 312
Jewish agriculture, 204–5
Jewish attitudes toward gentiles, 308–11
Jewish-Christian dialogue, 133, 254, 323

Judaism (*continued*)
 sexuality, 297; and idolatry, 217; and increase of life, 83–84; and message for humanity, 325–26; and messianism, 264; and modern culture, 200; and modernization, 198; and paganism, 309; and pluralism, 286; and the primacy of saving a life, 86–94; and Rabbinic culture, 267–68; and resurrection, 57, 59–61; and retreats and retreat centers, 314; and revelation, 20–22; and state-building, 266; in the Third Era, 289–326; and voluntary covenant, 238–39; women's exclusion from, 258–59; women's status in, 305–6; and the world-to-come, 100. *See also* God; *tikkun olam* (world repair)
Judea, 282
Judenrat, 224
judicial activism, 279
judiciary, 279–80

kabbalistic tradition, 167, 173, 343n1
Kahan Commission, 275
Kant, Immanuel, 138–39
Karo, R. Joseph, 297
kashrut, 68, 79, 136, 202, 294–96, 310, 332n11, 338n12
Kass, Leon, 54, 336n10
Katz, Steven, 238, 352n12
kavanot (intentional reflections), 313
Kemp, Richard, 273
Kersten, Felix, 235
ketubah (marriage contract), 150, 292–93
Khmer Rouge, 97, 105

kiddush ha-Shem (sanctification of God's name), 91, 93, 127
Kingdom of Judah, 157
klal gadol ba-Torah (great principle of the Torah), 75–80
klal yisrael (the totality of Jewry), 116–17, 321
A Kol in der Midbar (A voice in the desert) (newspaper), 225
kol yisrael arevim zeh lazeh (every Jew is responsible for every other one), 142
Kook, Rabbi Abraham Isaac, 204–5, 297–98
Korczak, Janusz, 224
kosher animals, 67–69, 295
kosher food, 25, 175, 221, 223, 271, 310
Kovner, Abba, 313
Kovno ghetto, 222
Kristallnacht, 210, 218

Lau-Lavie, Naphtali, 237
law and bureaucracy, 214–15
Law of Return, 257, 270, 276
laws of prayer, 79–80
laws of Shabbat, 88–94
lay era, 169
legislation, 34–35, 114, 116, 214–15, 303
lesbianism, 356n6
Levi, Primo, 221
Leviticus, 62, 69, 72–73, 90, 93, 337n4
LGBTQ+ liberation movement, 247
LGBTQ+ people, 129, 279, 299–300
liberalism, 196, 208, 211, 217
liberalization, 305
liberal Jews, 259
liberal movements, 320–22
liberation movements, 106, 109, 189, 246–47, 276

Mao Zedong, 145–46
marginalized groups, 246–47
marriage, 121, 125, 150, 192, 271, 292–93, 296–97, 299
Marshall, George C., 269
martyrdom, 87–88, 89, 91, 94, 230, 239
Marxism, 104–5, 189
Marxist-Leninist vision of socio-economic equality, 145
mass movements, 208
material equality, 32
materialism, 197
maturation, 123–24, 168–79, 318, 324–25
meat eating, 33, 67–69
medical insurance, 49
medical labors, 90–91
medieval halakhic codes, 309
medieval Judaism, 22, 87, 100, 142, 165–66, 306
Megillot Ha-Edut (Scrolls of Testimony) (Kovner), 313
meḥayeh hameitim (who revives the dead), 57
melakhah (holy work), 300–301
Mendelevich, Yosef, 247, 353n20
menstruation, 70, 297
Messiah, 98–99, 199, 227–28, 254, 268, 325
Messianic Age, 45, 46, 55, 57, 74, 186, 228, 265, 311, 325, 335n4
messianic impulses, 263, 265, 266
messianic movements, 98
messianic reality, 47, 65, 332n12
messianic standards, 303–11
messianism, 3, 45, 47, 53–54, 216, 262–65, 287–88
mezuzah, 79, 277

Micah, 52
microcosms, 55, 64–65, 138–41, 290, 301, 326
middah k'neged middah (measure for measure) theology, 229–32
Middle Ages, 309
Middle East, 46, 257, 269, 271, 275, 283
mikveh, 63, 70, 79, 163, 221, 223
Milgrom, Jacob, 63, 65, 71, 338n17, 339n27, 346n3
minicosmos, 271, 320
miracles, 21, 60–61, 98–99, 132–33, 171, 176–79, 185, 325; hidden and visible, 176–78
Mishnah, 27, 28, 31, 33–34, 35, 57, 157, 333n2, 333n4, 358n25
Mishneh Torah (Maimonides), 90, 204
mitzvah, 80–94, 162, 301
mitzvot, 21, 62, 63, 75–80, 226, 267
Mizraḥi Jews, 168, 271, 277, 279
modern culture, 199–200, 202, 208, 215, 232, 245, 260, 277, 278
modern industrial farming, 294
modernity, 4, 183–212; and gentiles, 310; and the Holocaust, 225; human agency and power in, 241–55; and humanity as the sole redeemer, 103–5; and humanity without a Divine partner, 187–90; Jewish responses to, 193–96; and messianic breakthrough, 232; and messianic impulses, 262–63; and Modern Orthodoxy, 258; and Nazis/Nazism, 213–16; and a response the message of, 267–70; and the State of Israel, 288; and the survival of Jewry, 207–12; and voluntary covenant, 239–

40; without limits, 190–93; and
women, 305
modernization, 189, 190–91, 194, 198–
200, 209
modernization identity model,
277–78
Modern Orthodoxy, 199–203, 207,
258
modern science, 188, 214
modern society, 213–16
modern values, 196, 210
modesty standards, 205
money, 29–30, 48, 142, 193, 275
monotheism, 3, 99, 324
moral army, 273–74
moral codes, 119, 145, 188, 272, 291
moral heroism, 274
moral obligations to gentiles, 309
moral sins, 337n10
Mordecai, 176
morning prayers, 108–9, 119
Morocco, 285
Morozov, Pavel Trofimovich, 145–46
Moses, 20, 117, 126, 132, 134–35, 156,
162, 169–70, 230
movements, 103–6
moving from nonlife to life, 17–18, 55.
See also death
murder and sexual violation, 91–94,
217
Muselmänner, 221
museums, commemorative, 315
Muslims, 51–52, 59, 283, 309

Nachmanides, 303, 339n25
nakba (catastrophe), 284
Napoleon, 198
nationalism, 195, 209

National Jewish Center for Learning
and Leadership (CLAL), 320
national liberation movements, 246
National Socialism, 104–5, 216–18, 228
natural law, 98, 108, 185, 188, 322
natural order, 108, 188, 289, 342n7
natural phenomena, 15, 185
Nazis and Nazism, 1, 104–5, 208, 210–
11, 213–33, 235, 237, 242–44, 247–
48, 250, 255–57, 291, 316
negative commandments, 75–76, 86,
340n21
Netanyahu, Benjamin, 280–81
Neusner, Jacob, 320
New Deal, 209
new Jews, 268
niddah (menstruation), 79
Night (Wiesel), 313
Noahide covenant, 67, 108, 139, 147,
153, 240
no-Gods, 39, 93–94
non-Jews, 197, 209, 211, 242, 259–60,
309–10, 315. See also Arab Israeli
minority
nonkosher foods, 25, 63, 277
non-Orthodox denominations, 207,
286
nonviolence, 248
North Africa, 143, 257, 275
North American Jews, 189, 194, 317
Norway, 323
number seven, 333n9

oath ritual, 27–28
obedience: to modernity, 198; to God,
88–91, 240
objective truth, 253
Olmert, Ehud, 284

post-Holocaust response, 234–65; and covenantal consciousness, 260–61; and the ethical obligation to hold power, 245–48; and human agency and power in modernity, 241–55; and repairing the world, 255–65; and the State of Israel, 269–70; and voluntary covenant, 236–41

postmodern culture, 312, 313, 322, 323

postmodern global economy, 302–3

postmodernism/postmodernity, 251–52, 288

poverty, 48–50, 132, 146, 291

power: and covenantal consciousness, 260–61; ethic of, 291–92; human assumption of, 184–86, 199–206, 266–67; and humanity as the sole redeemer, 103–6; and human power, 41–42, 241–45; and human scale, 139–40; and messianism, 264; and the Third Era, 325–26

power, Divine delegation of, 303–4

prayers, 79–80, 126–27, 186, 290, 313

prayer services, 166, 175, 196, 321

pregnancy, 222–23

presence of God, 14, 44, 54, 62–64, 66, 72, 79–80, 92, 235, 302

prewar Germany, 221

priests and priesthood, 63–65, 170, 293, 307, 346n27

primary teacher, 86

private property, 145, 167

productivity, 50, 187, 190–91, 219, 271, 277, 291

profit motives, 193, 219, 249, 302

proliferation of life, 80–86

promiscuity, 298

propaganda, 214, 217, 219

property ownership, 33

prophecy and prophets, 170–71, 187, 197, 266, 285, 346n26, 357n23

Proverbs, 25

Provisional Council, 269

p'ru urvu (be fruitful and multiply), 80–86

Psalms and the Psalmist, 21, 37–38, 39, 73, 76, 132–33, 157, 175

public demonstrations, 242

public values, 279

punishment(s), 169–72, 226–28, 261

pure freedom, 20

purgation, 65–66

purification rites, 63, 66, 69, 70–72, 175

Purim, 79, 176–78, 221

qualitative development of life, 18, 21, 23

quantity and quality of life, 294–95, 301–3

quietism, 226–28, 232

Qumran, 341n33

Rabbinic cultures, 194, 267–68

Rabbinic era, 169, 174, 177, 303

Rabbinic Judaism, 62, 173, 179, 184, 266–67

Rabbinic second stage of the covenant, 293, 300–303, 312, 318–19

Rabbinic tradition, 86, 127, 342n39, 356n6

Rabbis, 134, 172–77, 217; and capital punishment, 27; and commandments, 79, 89–90; and covenantal commitment, 166; and Diaspora, 267; and dietary rituals, 68–69;

Rabbis (*continued*)
expanding holiness in work and daily life, 300–303; and gentiles, 309–10; and human limitations, 159; and human pace, 149–50; and Jewish leadership for the secular age, 312–13; and Judaism in the Third Era, 292–93; and love in the covenantal relationship, 119–20; and martyrdom, 91–94; oral tradition, 308; and pluralism, 318–19; and resurrection, 56–60; and *tzimtzum* (Divine contraction), 183–84; and walking in God's ways, 39; and women, 305; and the world-to-come, 47

Rachel, 156

racism, 50–52, 113, 211, 257

radicalization, 105, 287

radical settler movement, 263

raḥamim (compassion or mother love), 19, 37–38, 60, 90, 118–19

Rashi, 28, 166, 230

Rava, 178

reason, 100, 188

Rebecca, 156

reconciliation, 254

redemption(s), 45–46; and American Jewry, 211; and commandments, 79; and commitment in the covenantal relationship, 125; in the Exodus, 175; and generations, 165; and human agency, 241; and humanity as the sole redeemer, 98–106; and human scale, 139–41; and Judaism in the Third Era, 290–91; and the messianism of human life and dignity, 262;

microcosms of, 326; and modernization, 198; and Nazi idolatry, 216–18; and pluralism, 321, 323–25; and Purim, 176; and renewal of the covenant, 237; and theological implications of the Holocaust, 225–33; and voluntary covenant, 238–39; and women, 306; and you are not alone, 132–33

redemptive movements, 133, 145, 150

Reed Sea, 170

Reform Jews and Reform Judaism, 196–98, 201, 207, 210, 320

refuseniks, 247

relativism, 252–54

religion, 21–23, 38, 42, 43, 185, 188, 189–90, 195, 196–97, 235–36, 245

religion-based hatred of Jews, 309

religious authorities, 116, 189

religious behaviors, 86, 268, 304

religious consciousness, 183–84

religious freedom, 286

religious groups, 192–93, 325

religious humanism, 287

religious Jews, 199, 229, 261, 268, 316

religious leadership, 293, 306, 312–13, 321–22

religious pluralism, 285–86

religious response, 304

religious status and roles of women, 305–7

religious traditions, 51, 196, 200, 254–55, 311, 324

religious Zionists, 205–6, 279–80

renewal of the covenant, 119, 132, 165–68, 235, 237, 239–40, 241, 266

repentance, 232, 245

reproduction, 80–86

water as symbol of life, 69. See also
    mikveh
wealth, 48–50, 193
West Bank, 263, 273, 281–84
West Bank separation wall, 273
Western Europe/Western European
    Jews, 186, 187, 191, 196, 199–200
whole Land of Israel (*eretz yisrael
    hashleimah*), 282
Wiesel, Elie, 236, 313
will of God, 22, 114–15, 185
witnesses, 27–28, 305–7
women: and acceptance of the
    covenant, 166; and covenantal
    demands of relational sexual-
    ity, 299; and full citizenship,
    343–44n10; halakhic treatment
    of, 149–50; and the incremental
    as eternal, 115–16; and individ-
    ualism, 192; and Judaism in the
    Third Era, 292–93; and liberation
    movements, 247; and moder-
    nity, 201–3, 205–7; and oppres-
    sion, 51; religious leadership roles
    for, 321–22; and resistance, 242;
    status and roles of, 304–7; and the
    struggle for democracy, 278–80;
    and upgrading the image of God,
    258–60
word of God, 114–16, 203, 318, 358n25
work, expanding holiness in, 300–303
World Health Organization, 29–30
world Jewry, 276, 281, 285, 287
worldly activities, 100, 124
world redemption, 216, 241, 291, 316
world-to-come, 47, 57, 87, 99–101,
    335n4, 342n3

World War II, 269, 316
World Zionist Organization, 278
Written Torah, 57, 167, 174
Wyschogrod, Michael, 154

xenophobia, 211, 257

Yad Vashem, 315
Yalta Conference, 350n18
Yavneh, 157
Yehoshua ben Ḥananiah, Rabbi, 173
yeshivot and *batei midrash* (Torah
    study houses), 223
Yishmael, Rabbi, 357n24
Yishuv (pre-State settlement), 199,
    228, 246, 269–70, 278
Yochanan ben Zakkai, Rabban, 157
Yoel Teitelbaum, Rabbi, 226
Yom ha-Atzmaut, 79
Yom ha-Shoah, 79
Yom Kippur, 65–67, 158, 221, 277
Yom Kippur War, 282
Yosselevska, Rivka, 223
you are not alone, 132–34

Zeitlin, Hillel, 229
Zionism: and covenantal messianism,
    287–88; and democracy, 278–81;
    and human assumption of power,
    199; and modernity, 195–96, 202,
    209–10, 268–69; and nonviolence,
    248; and redemption, 99; and
    state-building, 266; and theologi-
    cal implications of the Holocaust,
    226–28; and *Yishuv* leaders, 246
zone of holiness, expanding, 63–65,
    292–303